CW01497824

MISHKĀT-UL-MĀṢABĪḤ

VOL. I

(KITĀB-UL-ĪMĀN-KITĀB-UL-TAHĀRAH)
(AḤĀDĪTH No. 1-563)

**SHAIKH WALĪ-UD-DĪN MOḤAMMAD BIN
ʿABDULLAH AL-KHAṬĪB AL-ʿUMARĪ AL-TABRIZĪ**

Translated and annotated
by

ʿABDUL ḤAMEED ṢIDDIQUĪ

KITAB BHAVAN
New Delhi - 1100 02

Kitab Bhavan
Publishers, Distributors, Exporters & Importers
1784, Kalan Mahal, Darya Ganj
New Delhi - 1100 02 (India)

Phones	:	(91-11) 23277392/93, 23274686, 30906494
website	:	www.kitabbhavan.com
Email	:	nasri@vsnl.com
Email	:	nusrat@bol.net.in
Fax	:	(91-11) 23263383

First Published in India ... 1980
5th Edition 2009

ISBN : 81-7151- 037-X (Set)
ISBN : 81-7151- 038-X (Vol.I)
Book Code : ZZZ011

Printed & Published in India by :
Nusrat Ali Nasri for Kitab Bhavan
1784, Kalan Mahal, Darya Ganj
New Delhi - 1100 02 [India]

CONTENTS

بِسْمِ اللهِ الرَّحْمٰنِ الرَّحِيْمِ

INTRODUCTION

The Qur'ān and the *Sunnah* are the two foundations upon which is raised the structure of Islam; the one being the Word of God, and the other being its elucidation in the form of *Sunnah* of the Holy Prophet (may peace be upon him). The Qur'ān says:

He it is Who sent His Messenger with guidance and the religion of truth that He may cause it to prevail over all religions. (9 : 34)

This verse clearly shows that the only reliable source through which the *Will* of God has been made known to mankind is Muḥammad (may peace and blessings of Allāh be upon him). He is the final recipient of revelation amongst the Prophets of God, and as such he is Divinely authorised to explain its practical implications with the help of his words and deeds. The Qur'ān says:

And We have revealed to thee the Reminder that thou mayest make clear to men that which has been revealed to them, and that haply they reflect. (16 : 44)

The exposition of the Qur'ānic injunctions is thus one of the main responsibilities of the Holy Prophet (peace and blessings of Allah be upon him) which he had to undertake on the authority of the Lord Who had revealed to him the Holy Qur'ān. This task of exposition and elucidation has a divine sanction behind it as the Holy Prophet does not speak or act of his own accord. Whatever he says and whatever he does emanates from the Lord Himself.

He does not speak of his own desire. (103 : 8)

I follow only that which is revealed to me from my Lord. (7 : 203)

This shows that he speaks only when there is an objective necessity for it and he acts because God commands him to do so. In a number of verses of the Holy Qur'ān, the Muslims are enjoined upon to accept his guidance as final in all spheres of life, since his guidance is Divinely inspired and as such, is as binding on a Muslim as the guidance found in the Qur'ān.

And whatsoever the Messenger gives you, accept; and whatsoever he forbids you, avoid. (59 : 7)

Right from the time of the Companions down to this day there has been consensus of opinion amongst the Muslims that whatever is authentically transmitted to us from the Holy Prophet, be it in the form of the Qur'ānic revelation or his commands, or his explanations and enunciations of the Will of God, is the only reliable source of Islamic *Shari'ah*.

The Qur'ān makes it clear that it is an act of hostility on the part of a person to ignore or cast aside the elucidations made by the Holy Prophet of the commands of God:

And as for him, who opposes the Messenger after guidance has been clearly elucidated, follows a path other than that of the believers— him shall We leave with that which he himself has chosen, and shall cause him to endure Hell and how evil a journey's end. (4 : 115)

There are so many verses of the Qur'ān in which it has been made clear by Allāh that it is not only the Qur'ān which was revealed to the Holy Prophet but 'wisdom' was also vouchsafed to him, *e.g.*, in Sūrah *al-Baqarah*:

And remember Allāh's favour to you and that which He has revealed to you of the Book and Wisdom admonishing you thereby. (2 : 231)

Then, in Sūrah *an-Nisā*', the Qur'ān says :

And Allāh has revealed to thee the Book and the Wisdom and taught thee what thou knewest not, and Allāh's Grace on thee is very great.

(4 : 113)

Here the point to note is that *Wisdom* has been described as something separate from the *Book*. And what else can Wisdom be except the elucidations and enunciations of the Will of Allāh by the Holy Prophet? If the Holy Qur'ān embodies the Will of God, the authentic records of *aḥādīth* embody its practical implications which are called Wisdom and which it was the duty of the Holy Prophet (peace and blessings of Allāh be upon him) to vouchsafe to humanity as was his duty to vouchsafe the Qur'ān to the human race.

Assuredly Allāh conferred a favour on the believers when He raised unto them an Apostle from amongst themselves reciting to them His revelation and purifying them and teaching them the Book and the Wisdom. (3 : 163)

Thus reciting of Lord's revelation, purifying the souls of the people, teaching the Book and explaining the Wisdom contained therein—all these are the different aspects of the prophetic ministry and all of them are the time-less expression of the *Will* of God.

For full twenty-three years, the Holy Prophet (may peace and blessings of Allah be upon him) poured his wisdom along with the reciting of the Qur'ān. Thousands of suits were brought to him for decision and thousands of men came to ask him the questions pertaining to morality and conscience, religion and spiritual and social life and he answered their questions forthwith on the spot without faltering and without hesitation and he is not known ever to have made a mistake. How did he manage it? Through intellect? Certainly not, since intellect is not immune to error. He did it with *Ḥikmat* (Divine wisdom) and that was why his judgements and decisions were free from errors. It is, therefore, the height of folly to discard this source of Divine knowledge which is contained in the *Sunnah*.

Such is the incalculable importance of this 'wisdom' of the Prophet that the Muslims have been ordained not only to recite the Qur'ān but to recite the *wisdom* also.

And remember that which is recited in your houses of the Messages of Allah and the wisdom. (33 : 34)

As the sacred life of Muhammad (may peace of Allāh be upon him) provides the living example of the ideals being transmuted into practical shape. it has been made as model pattern for the Muslims; in fact, for anyone who believes in Allah and the Day of Judgement.

Verily in the Apostle of Allāh you have the best example for anyone who looks forward towards God and the Day of Judgement. (33 : 21)

It should be borne in mind that it is from the authentic records of *aḥādīth* that we can understand some of the verses of the Qur'ān which furnish elaborate background to them. We quote below some of the verses :
So when Zaid dissolved her marriage tie, We gave her to thee as a wife.
(33 : 37)
He frowned and turned away because the blind man came to him.
(80 : 12)
Never set foot in such a place, only a house of worship founded from the very first day upon God-consciousness is worthy of thy setting foot therein—(a house of worship) wherein there are men desirous of growing in purity; for God loves all who purify themselves. (9 : 108)

What can we understand from the above-mentioned verses unless we know their background and the context in which these were revealed? If the records of *aḥādīth* are not available, the meanings and implications of these verses would not be clear to us.

Moreover, many of the religious practices to which the Holy Qur'ān referred later on had been already introduced by Allāh's Prophet (may peace and blessings of Allah be upon him). We give two examples in support of this contention :

The funeral prayer and the congregational prayer of Friday are the two important acts of devotion which have vital social significance in Muslim community. And both these had been introduced by the Holy Prophet before any reference had been made about them in the Qur'ān. The words of the Qur'ān bear ample testimony to this fact:

And never offer prayer for anyone of them (hypocrites) who dies, and never stand by his grave. (9 : 84)

So is the case with the congregational prayer of Friday.
But when the prayer is ended, disperse abroad in the land and seek Allāh's grace and remember Allah much that you may be successful. (62 : 11)

All these facts prove beyond any shadow of doubt that the *Sunnah* of the Holy Prophet (may peace be upon him) is an integral part of Islamic *Sharī'ah* and whatever has been transmitted to us as the *Sunnah* is as binding on the Muslims as the injunctions contained in the Qur'ān. The Muslims have always been fully conscious of it as is evident from the following *ḥadīth* :

It is narrated on the authority of 'Abdullah b. Mas'ūd that he said: Allāh curses those who pluck hair from their faces and who make spaces between their teeth for beauty thus changing that what God has created. Then this news reached a woman of Banū Asad who was called Umm Ya'qū b and she used to recite the Holy Qur'ān. She came to 'Abdullah and said: This news has been brought to me that you curse those who tattoo and those who pluck hair from their faces and those who get them plucked and those who make spaces between their teeth for beauty and thus changing what Allāh has created. Thereupon, 'Abdullah said: Should I not curse those whom Allāh has cursed, and this is what is found in the Book of Allāh. Thereupon, the woman said: I have read the Qur'ān from cover to cover but I did not find anything like it therein: 'Abdullah said: Had you read the Qur'ān, you would have definitely found it, that Allāh, the Exalted and Glorious, said: Take whatsoever Messenger gives you and abstain from whatsoever he forbids you. (*Ṣaḥīḥ Muslim*, Kitāb-ul-Libās wa Zinah, chapter: Taḥrīm Fi'l al-Wasilah, etc.).

This *ḥadīth* which has been narrated on the authority of an eminent companion, 'Abdullah b. Mas'ūd, clearly shows the utmost importance which the early Muslims attached to the commands of the Holy Prophet (peace be upon him). It is stated that when any matter was referred to Ḥadrat Abū Bakr Ṣiddīq for decision, he looked into the Book of Allāh for directive and finding it silent on that particular point, he looked into the *Sunnah* of the Holy Prophet, and in case he found out the proper guidance from that, he gave decision according to it. So did 'Umar, 'Uthmān, 'Alī and other companions of the Holy Prophet (may Allāh be pleased with all of them).[1]

The modern scholar of Islam, Muḥammad Asad, while discussing the importance of *Sunnah* states:

"The *Sunnah* of the Prophet Muhammad is, therefore, next to Qur'ān, the second source of Islamic law of social and personal behaviour. In fact we must regard the *Sunnah* as the only valid explanation of the Qur'ānic teachings and the only means to avoid dissensions concerning their interpretation and adaptation to practical use. Many verses of the Qur'ān have allegorical meaning and could be understood in different ways unless there was some definite system of interpretation. And there are, furthermore, many items of practical importance not explicitly dealt with by the Qur'ān. The spirit prevailing in the Holy Book is, to be sure, uniform throughout; but to deduce from it the practical attitude which we have to adopt is not, in every case, an easy matter. So long as we believe that this Book is the word of God perfect in form and purpose, the only logical conclusion is that it never was intended to be used independently of the personal guidance of the Prophet which is embodied in the system of *Sunnah*."[2]

---

1. For detail see *Qawāid-ul-Taḥdīth* by Sayid Jamāl-ud-Din Qāsimī, pp. 286-296 (Damascus 1353 H).
2. *Islam at the Crossroads*, pp. 117-118.

In view of the basic importance of Allah's Messenger's acts and deeds, his commands, prohibitions and meaningful silence that he observed in certain matters, it is quite conceivable that the Muslims began to record *aḥādīth* during his lifetime. 'Abdullah b. 'Amr al-'Ās recorded thousands of the Prophet's sayings in *Ṣaḥīfa* which goes down in history as *Ṣaḥīfa as-Ṣādiqa*. Another *Ṣaḥīfa* is reported to have been in the possession of Samura b. Jundub. Jabir b. 'Abdullah also had a *Ṣaḥīfa* the contents of which were later on related by Qatāda. Then there is a well-known *Ṣaḥīfa* of Hammam b. Munābbih which contains *aḥādīth* collected by the famous companion of the Holy Prophet, Ḥaḍrat Abū Huraira. 'Abdullah b. 'Abbās also wrote down *aḥādīth* which he learnt from 'Abdullah b. Rafi'.

Evidence is not lacking that the Holy Prophet (peace be upon him) had himself dictated laws with regard to the *Zakāt*, the prayer, the fasts and blood money, etc. The devotion with which the companions of the Holy Prophet preserved *aḥādīth* can be well understood from the following two narrations transmitted on the authority of two eminent companions:

It is reported on the authority of Hadrat Anas: So long as we remained in the company of Allah's Apostle (peace and blessings of Allāh be upon him) we listened attentively to what he uttered and as we departed we repeated them till these were retained in our memories.

It is reported on the authority of Abū Sa'īd Khudrī: We were sitting and writing what we were hearing from Allāh's Messenger (peace and blessings of Allah be upon him) that he turned his attention to us and said: What is this that you are writing? We said: We are writing that what we are hearing from you Whereupon he said: Are you writing another Book alongwith the Book of Allah. Keep the Book of Allāh separate and make its text pure so that there may not be confusion in it.[1]

This explains the background as to why Allāh's Messenger (peace and blessings of Allah be upon him) at one stage prohibited the writing of *aḥādīth*. It should not, however, lead anyone to conclude that he prohibited the recording of *aḥādīth* altogether. What he prohibited was that these should not be recorded alongwith the Book of Allāh.

The famous *Muḥaddith* Imām Khaṭṭābī writes: He (the Holy Prophet) prohibited the writing of the words of the Qur'ān and those of *aḥādīth* together lest there should be any inter-mingling in them and the reader may be confused. The writing of *ḥadīth* (itself) is in no way prohibited.[2]

The practice of recording of *aḥādīth* was thus started in right earnest during the lifetime of the Holy Prophet (may peace and blessings be upon him) and this task was done by his noble companions with a keen sense of devotion.

After the companions, we find a large group of eminent successors (may Allāh have mercy upon them) busy in compiling the records of *aḥādīth*

---

1. *Majma' al-Zawāid*, Vol. IV, p. 152.
2. *Ma'alim Sunan*, Vol. IV, p. 184.

transmitted to them on the authority of the Prophet's companions (may Allāh be pleased with them). The famous amongst them are: Muḥammad Shihāb Zuhrī (124 H), Imām Auzā'ī, Ma'mar b. Rashid, Imām Sufyān b. Thaurī, Hammād b. Salama, Imām 'Abdullah b. Mubārak, Imām Mālik b. Anas.

The compilation of *aḥādīth* is divided into three categories:—

(1) The first one includes *Bukhārī*, *Muslim* and *Muwaṭṭa* of Imām Mālik.

(2) The second one includes, *Jāmi' Tirmidhī*, *Sunan Abū Dāwud*, *Musnad Aḥmad b. Ḥanbal* and *Nasā'ī*.

(3) The third category consists of those *aḥādīth* which include all types of weak traditions. Their chains of transmission have some missing links in them, e.g., *Musnad of 'Uthmān b. Abī Shaiba*, *Musnad of Tayalsī*, *Musnad of 'Abdullah b. Muḥammad b. Abī Shaiba*. Only the learned scholars can derive benefit from them.

It must be remembered in this connection that the authenticity of *ṣaḥīḥ aḥādīth* has been fully established by the scholars of *ḥadīth* as regards the purity of text and the soundness of the chain of transmission. The old scholars have standardized all of them and have performed this work with such precision, objectivity and skill that it is difficult to improve upon it. We can now safely depend upon them for guidance in all important matters of life.

A few words may be said about *al-Mishkāt-ul-Maṣābīḥ*, the translation of which we have the honour to present to the English-knowing lovers of *ḥadīth*.

It was in the early centuries of Islam that a need was felt to prepare a digest of *ḥadīth*. The most important attempt made in this sphere was that of Abū Muḥammad al-Ḥusain b. Mas'ūd b. Muḥammad al-Farra (or ibn-al-Farra) al-Baghāwī (516 H) who selected 4434 *aḥādīth* out of various compilations to be included in his selection known as *Maṣābīḥ as-Sunnāh*. His selection is a representative selection in the sense that he not only culled his material from the principle of *musannaf* works, but he arranged them on the basis of the authenticity of *ḥadīth*. To save space he omitted the chains of transmission, but mentioned the name of the companion of the Holy Prophet through whom each tradition was traced. Each topic was arranged into two sections, the one recording the sound (*saḥīh*) traditions, including those of Bukhārī and Muslim or of both. The other section contained traditions which in technical terms are called good (*ḥasan*), this term being applied by him to *aḥādīth* coming from other sources. It would be interesting to study the observations of the compiler himself in regard to his compilation.

"This is a collection of *aḥādīth* of Allāh's Messenger (peace and blessings of Allāh be upon him). These are lights which shine in the darkness and illuminate the hearts of people. These *aḥādīth* have been transmitted by the eminent *Imams* and I have prepared a collection of the Holy Prophet's traditions so that it may serve as a reliable guide for the servants of Allāh in matters regarding which the Qur'ān is silent and exhort them to obey Allāh and His Prophet (may peace and blessings of Allāh be upon him) with a keen sense of devotion. I have, while making a selection of *aḥadīth*, dropped their chains of transmission, reposing full trust in the authenticity of the *Imāms*. I have, however, mentioned the names of the companions of the Holy Prophet as the first and the foremost links in these chains. Every chapter consists of two sections: containing *saḥīḥ aḥādīth* (*Ṣiḥāḥ*) and the other containing *ḥasan aḥādīth* (*Ḥisān*). By *saḥīḥ ḥadīth* I mean that tradition which is reported either on the authority of Imām Bukhārī or Imām Muslim or that of both. So far as the *ḥasan ḥadīth* I mean that one which is reported by Imām Abū Dāwūd, Imām al-Tirmidhī and others. Quite a large number of *ḥasan aḥādīth* are of the same importance as we find in *Ṣaḥiḥain*. (Quoted by Naṣīr-ud-Dīn al-Bānī).

Since al-Baghāwī did not in his compilation mention the source of each *ḥadīth*, it was difficult for the common man to find out the original Book from which a *ḥadīth* had been taken.

Maṣābiḥ as-Sunnah was no doubt a very valuable contribution to the *ḥadīth* literature and won admiration from a large number of scholars, but it needed improvement for making it a more useful guide for the common man who is not well-versed in the knowledge of *ḥadīth*. This gigantic task was undertaken in the eighth century of Hijra by an eminent scholar, Sheikh Walī-ud-Dīn Muḥammad b. 'Abdullah Tabrizī. He rendered marvellous service in making significant improvement in the compilation of al-Baghāwī. This improvement may be seen in the following spheres:

(a) Walī-ud-Dīn made an addition of 1511 traditions to *Maṣābiḥ-as-Sunnah*, and raised the total from 4434 to 5945.

(b) Al-Baghāwī made some errors of judgement in the categorization of *aḥādīth*. He, in many cases, declared a *ḥadīth* to be *saḥīḥ*, whereas it was *ḥasan*. Walī-ud-Dīn corrected all such errors in his *Mishkāt-ul-Maṣābiḥ*.

(c) He also added at the end of each tradition the name of the source or sources from which it was drawn, and frequently included remarks made about the quality of the tradition in the source from which it was culled. This usually applies to traditions from *Tirmidhī*.

(d) Walī-ud-Dīn also added a third section to the chapters in which he recorded additional traditions from *Bukhārī* and *Muslim* or from other sources connected with the subject of each chapter and thus considerably enhanced its value by making a suitable addition to the existing stock.

So far as the objective behind the compilation of *Mishkāt-ul-Maṣābiḥ* is concerned, one can easily discern it by casting a glance at its topics. The compiler has taken great care to provide *ḥadīth* material to the readers which is indispensable for regulating their practical lives according to the demands of Islam.

It is the practical wisdom of the Holy Prophet (may peace and blessings of Allāh be upon him) with which glistens every word of this compilation and thus no servant of Allāh can afford to ignore it. It has always captivated the minds of all seekers of Truth, whether they are scholars or common Muslims. Serveral commentaries have been written to explain it. The following is a brief list of these:

(1) *Al-Kāshif 'an haqā'iq as-Sunnah* by al-Ḥasan b. Muḥammad at-Tibī (743 H).

(2) *Minhāj al-Mishkāt* by 'Abdul 'Azīz b. Muḥammad b. 'Abd al-'Azīz al-Abharī (895 H).

(3) *Mirqāt al-Mafātih* by 'Alī b. Ṣulṭān al-Qārī, popularly known as Mullah 'Alī Qārī (1014 H).

(4) *Mir'āt al-Mafātih* by 'Abdul Ḥaqq 'Ubaid Ullah b. al-'Allama Muḥammad 'Abdus Salām Mubārakpurī.

(5) *At-Ta'līq-us-Ṣabīḥ 'ala Mishkāt-il-Masābiḥ* by Maulānā Muḥammad Idrīs Kandhalwī.

(6) *Al-Lama'āt* by Sheikh 'Abdul Ḥaqq Dehlvi.

(7) *Mazāhir-i-Ḥaqq* by Maulānā Qutub-ud-Dīn Shahjahanpuri.

A few words may be added in regard to the translation of this marvellous 'digest of *hadīth*'. Translation is in itself a very difficult task, but it becomes still more difficult when the difference in the genius of two languages is immeasurably vast. The Arabic language is rich, colourful, vigorous and is best suited to express thoughts and concepts with more conciseness than any other Aryan language, because of the extraordinary flexibility of its verbs and nouns. English, on the other hand, is the language of understatement. The problem becomes still more difficult when we take into consideration the fact that it is not the matter of translating a book of Arabic into English, but that of translating the words of the Holy Prophet (peace and blessings of Allāh be upon him) who was gifted with a very chaste mode of expression. It is, therefore, too much to expect from any translator of the Book of *hadīth* that his translation would, in any way, be able to produce in the hearts and minds of his readers an effect like the one produced by the Prophet's own utterances. My endeavour has been to convey somehow or the other the meanings of the words of *ahādīth* to the English-knowing readers. Accuracy rather than literary embellishment has been my aim throughout. I have always been careful to avoid giving any slant or flavour of my own making, and have tried to remain as close to the Arabic text as far as it is possible.

It must be stated with sincere humility that the author has no pretentions of having translated *Mishkāt-ul-Maṣābiḥ* with exactness. He has made a very modest attempt in this field. If there is any merit discernible in it, it is absolutely due to the Grace and Mercy of Allāh, and for all acts of omission, the translator alone is to be held responsible.

I am deeply indebted to the veteran scholar Malik Ghulam 'Ali who has been kind enough to revise the translation and make valuable suggestions. I am also grateful to Messers Ashfaq Mirza and Akhlaq Husain, Directors, Islamic Publications Ltd., who have taken keen personal interest in publishing this English translation along with Arabic text in its present form.

Mr. Muhammad Jamil Akhtar and Mr. Muhammad Aslam typed the manuscript with great skill and I am thankful to them for their help and co-operation.

'ABDUL HAMEED SIDDIQI.

SOME TERMS EXPLAINED

(1) Hadith and Sunnah

In the religious literature of Islam these two terms are considered to be synonymous with each other. There is, however, a slight difference in them. The word *Sunnah* means precedent and custom. In the technical sense it implies the doings and practices of the Holy Prophet Muhammad (may peace and belessings of Allah be upon him) only. *Sunnah* is thus a concrete implementation, a tangible form and the actual embodiment of the *Will* of Allah in the form of the Holy Prophet Muhammad's deeds.

Hadith originally means a piece of news, a tale, a story or a report relating to a present or past event. In the technical sense it stands for the report of the words and deeds, approval or disapproval of the Holy Prophet (may peace be upon him). It consists of two parts : the chain of transmission[1] (*Sanad*) and the text (*Matn*).

Classification of Ahadith :

(1) *Sahih* (Sound). This name is given to the utterly faultless *hadith* in which there is no weakness either in regard to the chain of transmission (*isnad*) or in regard to the text (*matn*) and in which there is no tendency to contradict any established belief of Islam.

(2) *Hasan* (Approved). This is like a *Sahih* tradition except for the fact that some of its narrators are found to have a defective memory as compared to narrators of *Sahih hadith*.

(3) *Gharib*. The *hadith* in the chain of transmission of which the number of narrators is reduced to one at any stage is known as *Gharib hadith*.

Imam Tirmidhi has used two special terms in regard to *hasan* and *gharib ahadith* for further categorization of these:

(a) *Hasan sahih*;

(b) *Hasan sahih gharib*.

---

1. It should be clearly noted that the number of *hadith* is counted on the basis of chain of transmission and not on the basis of the text. It is essential to make it clear as the ignorance about this fact has given rise to some serious misgivings under which so many orientalists and westernized Muslims are labouring. When we say that Imam Muslim collected three lakh of *ahadith* and included only 4,000 in his compilation, it does not imply that he rejected the rest of the stock deeming it to be unreliable. What it means is that the words and deeds of the Holy Prophet (may peace be upon him) were transmitted to Imam Muslim through numerous chains of transmission running into lakhs, out of which he selected 4,000 chains as the most authentic, and narrated the texts on their authority. A text (*Matn*) which is transmitted through one hundred *Isnad's* is in *Hadith* literature treated as one hundred traditions, for instance, the text of the first *hadith* in *Bukhari* (The actions are judged on the basis of intention) is counted as a selection of one out of 700 *ahadith* since it has been transmitted through such a large number of *isnads*.

(*i*) *Hasan sahih hadith* is one which according to Imam Tirmidhi stands at a higher level than mere *hasan*, but at a bit lower level than *sahih*.

(*ii*) *Hasan sahih* is at times qualified by the word *gharib* when the link of transmission is joined to another at certain point by one transmitter only. Obviously, it is *hasan* in regard to its soundness and *gharib* in regard to its chain of transmission.

(4) *Mutawatir* (continuous) is a tradition reported by a large number of people in different times, so as to make it impossible for any falsehood to creep into it.

(5) *Mashhur* (well-known) is a tradition which is handed down by at least three different reliable authorities, or, according to another view, a tradition which, although widely disseminated later, was originally transmitted by one person in the first generation.

(6) *Da'if* (weak) tradition is that in which there is some defect either in the chain of transmission, or in proper understanding of the transmitter, or its contents are not in perfect agreement with Islamic beliefs and practices. It is in fact a tradition of weak or less reliable authority.

(7) *Maudu'* (forged) *hadith* is that which a liar fabricates and then attributes it to the Holy Prophet (may peace be upon him).

(8) *Mursal* (forwarded): If the companion of the Holy Prophet is found missing from the chain of transmission and a Tabi'i (successor of the companion) transmits it from Allah's Apostle (peace and blessings of Allah be upon him) such a *hadith* is called '*Mursal*'.

(9) *Marfu'* (traced directly): A *hadith* which can be traced back to the Holy Prophet directly is known as *Marfu'*.

(10) *Mudallas* (deceptive): If a narrator of *hadith* does not mention the name of his teacher and gives the name of one who is one step higher than his teacher using the word '*an i.e. from so and so*, this type is called *Mudallas* and this act of hiding the name of the teacher is called *Tadlis* (deception).

(11) *Shadh* (Isolated): *Shadh* is that *hadith* in which a comparatively less authentic narrator of *hadith* opposes one whose account is more authentic than his.

(12) *Munkar* (disapproved): *Munkar* is a *hadith* in which a weak transmitter of *ahadith* opposes one who is quite authentic and reliable as a narrator of *hadith*.

(13) *Munqati'* (disjoined): *Munqati'* is a type of *hadith* in which either a link in the chain of transmission is found missing or an unknown narrator is found to join the links.

(14) *Muttasil* or *Mausul* (joined) is a tradition which has got successive narrators without any missing link in them, irrespective of the fact whether it can be traced directly to the Holy Prophet (peace be upon him) or to the companion (may Allah have mercy upon them).

(15) *Maqtu'* (broken): A *hadith* whose chain of transmission cannot be traced beyond a successor (*tabi'i*) is called *Maqtu'*.

(16) *Mauquf* (suspended): *Mauquf* is a *hadith* in which the companion does not make this fact explicitly clear that he is narrating something from Allah's Apostle (peace and blessings of Allah be upon him) *e.g.* the narrator says that Haḍrat 'Umar b. Khattab said so and so.

(17) *Hadith Qudsi* (Holy Hadith): *Hadith Qudsi* is one in which the Holy Prophet states something attributing that to Allah in very clear terms. The following *hadith* transmitted on the authority of Abu Dharr Ghifari (may Allah be pleased with him) in which Allah's Apostle (peace and blessings of Allah be upon him) conveys the message of Allah in His very name, is an example of *Hadith Qudsi*:

O My servants! I have made oppression unlawful for Me and have forbidden this oppression for you also. Therefore, don't oppress one another. You all go astray, except one whom I direct to the right path. Hence beg guidance from Me only. (*Muslim*).

BOOKS MAINLY DEPENDED UPON
AND FREQUENTLY QUOTED

(1) *Mirqat al-Mafatih* by 'Ali b. Sultan Muhammad Qari (popularly known as Mulla 'Ali Qari).

(2) *At-Ta'liq-us-Sabih* by Maulana Muhammad Idris Kandhalwi.

(3) *Fath ul-Bari* (Commentary on *Sahih Bukhari*) by Hafiz Ibn Hajar 'Asqalani.

(4) *'Umdat ul-Qari* (Commentary on *Sahih Bukhari*) by Badr al-Din 'Aini.

(5) *Minhaj al-Talibin* by Muhyi al-Din Abu Zakariya Yahya al-Hizami al-Dimashqi al-Nawawi (Commentary on *Sahih Muslim*).

(6) *Fath al-Mulhim* (Commentary on *Sahih Muslim*) by Maulana Shabbir Ahmad 'Uthmani.

(7) *Mir'at al-Mafatih* by Maulana 'Abdul Haqq 'Ubaidullah b. Muhammad 'Abdus Salam Mubarakpuri.

(8) *Al-Lama'at* by Sheikh 'Abdul Haqq Dehlvi.

(9) *Mazahir-i-Haqq* by Maulana Qutub-ud-Din Shahjahanpuri.

(10) *Zad-ul-Ma'ad* by Hafiz ibn Qayyim.

(11) *Nail-ul-'Autar* by Muhammad b. 'Ali b. Muhammad al-Shaukani.

(12) *'Aun-ul-Ma'bud* (Commentary on *Sunan Abi Dawud*) by Abu 'Abd-ir-Rahman Sharaf al-Haqq.

(13) *Tufatul-Ahwadhi* (Commentary on *Tirmidhi*) by Muhammad 'Abd-ur-Rahman Mubarakpuri.

TRANSLITERATION OF ARABIC WORDS AND NAMES

ﺍ { Consonantal sound }	a	ﻁ	....	ṭ
ﺍ long vowel	ā	ﻅ	....	z̤
ﺏ	b	ﻉ	.... '	inverted apostrophe
ﺕ	t	ﻍ	....	gh
ﺙ	th	ﻑ	....	f
ﺝ	j	ﻕ	....	q
ﺡ	ḥ	ﻙ	....	k
ﺥ	kh	ﻝ	....	l
ﺩ	d	ﻡ	....	m
ﺫ	dh	ﻥ	....	n
ﺭ	r	ﻩ	....	h
ﺯ	z	ﻭ Consonant		w
ﺱ	s	ﻭ long vowel		ū
ﺵ	sh	ﻭ diphthong		au
ﺹ	ṣ	ﻯ consonant		y
ﺽ	ḍ	ﻯ long vowel		ī
		ﻯ diphthong		ai

This English translation is based on the text of
Mishkāt-ul-Masābih edited by Muhammad Nasir-ud-Din al-Bani
published in 1380/1961.

كِتَابُ الْإِيمَانِ

Kitab-ul-Iman

(BOOK OF FAITH)

بِسْمِ اللهِ الرَّحْمٰنِ الرَّحِيمِ

١- وَعَنْ عُمَرَ بْنِ الْخَطَّابِ رَضِيَ اللهُ عَنْهُ، قَالَ: قَالَ رَسُولُ اللهِ ﷺ:
"إِنَّمَا الْأَعْمَالُ بِالنِّيَّاتِ، وَإِنَّمَا لِامْرِئٍ مَّا نَوَى؛ فَمَنْ كَانَتْ هِجْرَتُهُ
إِلَى اللهِ وَرَسُولِهِ فَهِجْرَتُهُ إِلَى اللهِ وَرَسُولِهِ، وَمَنْ كَانَتْ هِجْرَتُهُ إِلَى
دُنْيَا يُصِيبُهَا، أَوِ امْرَأَةٍ يَتَزَوَّجُهَا فَهِجْرَتُهُ إِلَى مَا هَاجَرَ إِلَيْهِ". مُتَّفَقٌ عَلَيْهِ.

1 ‘Umar b. Khattab (Allah be pleased with him) reported
Allah's Messenger (peace and blessings of Allah be upon him)
as saying: Verily the deeds are to be judged by intentions
and for every person (there is in store for him) what he aims
at. He whose migration is for the sake of Allah and His
Messenger his migration (is in fact for Allah and His Messenger)
and he whose migration is for the worldly (end) he would
attain that or for a woman with whom he (likes) to marry, his
migration is for that for which he migrated. (*Agreed upon*)

CHAPTER 1

Section I   ٱلْفَصْلُ الْأَوَّلُ

٢- عَنْ عُمَرَ بْنِ الْخَطَّابِ رَضِيَ اللهُ عَنْهُ، قَالَ: بَيْنَا نَحْنُ عِنْدَ رَسُولِ
اللهِ ﷺ ذَاتَ يَوْمٍ إِذْ طَلَعَ عَلَيْنَا رَجُلٌ شَدِيدُ بَيَاضِ الثِّيَابِ،
شَدِيدُ سَوَادِ الشَّعْرِ، لَا يُرَى عَلَيْهِ أَثَرُ السَّفَرِ، وَلَا يَعْرِفُهُ مِنَّا
أَحَدٌ، حَتَّى جَلَسَ إِلَى النَّبِيِّ ﷺ، فَأَسْنَدَ رُكْبَتَيْهِ إِلَى رُكْبَتَيْهِ، وَ
وَضَعَ كَفَّيْهِ عَلَى فَخِذَيْهِ، وَقَالَ: يَا مُحَمَّدُ أَخْبِرْنِي عَنِ الْإِسْلَامِ
قَالَ: "الْإِسْلَامُ أَنْ تَشْهَدَ أَنْ لَّا إِلٰهَ إِلَّا اللهُ وَأَنَّ مُحَمَّدًا رَسُولُ اللهِ،
وَتُقِيمَ الصَّلَاةَ، وَتُؤْتِيَ الزَّكَاةَ، وَتَصُومَ رَمَضَانَ، وَتَحُجَّ الْبَيْتَ إِنِ
اسْتَطَعْتَ إِلَيْهِ سَبِيلًا". قَالَ: صَدَقْتَ. فَعَجِبْنَا لَهُ يَسْأَلُهُ وَيُصَدِّقُهُ.
قَالَ: فَأَخْبِرْنِي عَنِ الْإِيمَانِ. قَالَ: "أَنْ تُؤْمِنَ بِاللهِ، وَمَلَائِكَتِهِ، وَكُتُبِهِ

وَ رُسُلِهِ ، وَالْيَوْمِ الْاخِرِ، وَ تُؤْمِنَ بِالْقَدَرِ خَيْرِهِ وَ شَرِّهِ" قَالَ :

صَدَقْتَ . قَالَ : فَأَخْبِرْنِي عَنِ الْإِحْسَانِ . قَالَ "أَنْ تَعْبُدَ اللهَ كَأَنَّكَ

تَرَاهُ ، فَإِنْ لَّمْ تَكُنْ تَرَاهُ فَإِنَّهُ يَرَاكَ" قَالَ : فَأَخْبِرْنِي عَنِ السَّاعَةِ .

قَالَ "مَا الْمَسْئُولُ عَنْهَا بِأَعْلَمَ مِنَ السَّآئِلِ". قَالَ : فَأَخْبِرْنِي عَنْ

أَمَارَاتِهَا ۚ قَالَ "أَنْ تَلِدَ الْأَمَةُ رَبَّتَهَا ، وَ أَنْ تَرَى الْحُفَاةَ الْعُرَاةَ

الْعَالَةَ رِعَاءَ الشَّاءِ يَتَطَاوَلُونَ فِي الْبُنْيَانِ". قَالَ : ثُمَّ انْطَلَقَ ، فَلَبِثْتُ

مَلِيًّا ، ثُمَّ قَالَ لِي "يَا عُمَرُ! أَتَدْرِيْ مَنِ السَّآئِلُ؟ قُلْتُ : اَللهُ وَ

رَسُولُهُ أَعْلَمُ . قَالَ "فَإِنَّهُ جِبْرَئِيْلُ أَتَاكُمْ يُعَلِّمُكُمْ دِيْنَكُمْ" رَوَاهُ مُسْلِمٌ .

2 'Umar b. Khattab (Allah be pleased with him) said: One day as we were sitting in the company of Allah's Messenger (peace and blessings of Allah be upon him) there appeared before us all of a sudden a man (dressed) in extremely white clothes with extremely black hair. There seemed to be no sign of fatigue because of journey on him and none amongst us ever knew him. At least he sat near the Prophet (peace and blessings of Allah be upon him). He placed his knees upon his knees and placed his palms on his thighs and said: Muhammad, inform me about al-Islam. He (the Holy Prophet) said: *Al-Islam* implies that you testify that there is no god but Allah and that Muhammad is His Messenger and, that you establish prayer and pay *zakat*, observe fast of *Ramadan* and perform pilgrimage to the House (*Ka'ba*) in case you have means (enough to meet the expenses of journey). He said: You have told the truth. It was amazing for us about him that he would ask the question and then he would himself testify it to be true. He said: Inform me about *Iman*. He said: That you affirm your faith in Allah, His Angels, His Books, His Messengers, in the Hereafter, in the Divine Decree to good and evil. He said: You have told the truth. He again said: Inform me about *Al-Ihsan* (performance of good deed). He said: That you worship Allah as if you are seeing Him. And if you are not seeing Him (perceive) that He is

in fact seeing you. He said: Inform me about (the Last)
Hour. He (the Holy Prophet) said: The one who is inquired
of knows no more than the one who is inquiring. He (the
inquirer) said: Tell me some of its indications. He (the
Holy Prophet) said that the slave-girl would give birth to her
mistress,[1] and that you find bare-footed, destitute, shepherds
exulting in buildings. He ('Umar b. Khattab) said: Then he
(the inquirer) made his way. But I stayed with him (the Holy
Prophet) for a long time. He then said to me: 'Umar, do you
know about this inquirer? I said: Allah and His Messenger
know best. He (the Holy Prophet) said: He was Gabriel,
he came to you in order to instruct you in your religion.

(*Muslim*)

1. This *hadith* has been explained in two different ways. We give
below two interpretations:

   (*a*) A time would come when the rulers would not observe the
   sanctity of marriage. They would bring into their household
   women without marrying them. This licentiousness would
   become so common that the majority of the children would be
   born out of illegal wedlock and they would occupy thrones and
   positions of responsibility. This view is held by Imam Nawawi
   and is quoted by Hafiz Ibn Hajar 'Asqalani.

   (*b*) The children would become disobedient, defiant and unruly
   to their parents and especially to their mothers and they would
   treat them not with respect and honour which the mothers
   rightly deserve but would show an insolent behaviour
   towards them and would treat them on the level of maid-
   servants and slave-girls. (Ibn Hajar 'Asqalani, *Fath-ul-Bari*
   Egypt 1378 H. Vol. I, pp. 130-131).

٣ - وَرَوَاهُ أَبُو هُرَيْرَةَ مَعَ اخْتِلَافٍ، وَفِيهِ: "وَإِذَا رَأَيْتَ الْحُفَاةَ الْعُرَاةَ
الصُّمَّ الْبُكْمَ، مُلُوكَ الْأَرْضِ فِي خَمْسٍ لَا يَعْلَمُهُنَّ إِلَّا اللهُ. ثُمَّ
قَرَأَ: ﴿إِنَّ اللهَ عِنْدَهُ عِلْمُ السَّاعَةِ وَيُنَزِّلُ الْغَيْثَ﴾ الْآيَةَ. مُتَّفَقٌ عَلَيْهِ

3 Abu Huraira transmitted it with a difference containing the
following: When you see the bare-footed, destitutes, the deaf,
the dumb as the kings of the earth. Five things which none
knows but Allah. He then recited. Verily it is with Allah
that there is knowledge of the Last Hour and He sends down

the rain.[1] (*Agreed upon*)

> 1. The complete verse is like this: Verily it is with Allah that there
> is knowledge of the Last Hour and He sends down the rain and
> He knows what is in the wombs and none knows what he will
> earn on the morrow and none knows any of the land in which
> he will die. Surely Allah is All-Knowing. (31 : 34).

٤- وَعَنِ ابْنِ عُمَرَ، قَالَ : قَالَ رَسُولُ اللهِ ﷺ "بُنِيَ الْإِسْلَامُ عَلَى خَمْسٍ :
شَهَادَةِ أَنْ لَا إِلٰهَ إِلَّا اللهُ وَأَنَّ مُحَمَّدًا عَبْدُهُ وَرَسُولُهُ ، وَ إِقَامِ
الصَّلَاةِ ، وَإِيتَاءِ الزَّكَاةِ ، وَالْحَجِّ ، وَصَوْمِ رَمَضَانَ." مُتَّفَقٌ عَلَيْهِ.

4 Ibn 'Umar reported, Allah's Messenger (peace and blessings
of Allah be upon him) as saying: The (edifice) of Islam is
constructed on five (things):   Testimony to the fact that there
is no god but Allah that Muhammad is His bondsman and
Messenger, the establishment of prayer, payment of *zakat*, (the
performance of) *Hajj* and the fast of *Ramadan*.   (*Agreed upon*)

٥- وَعَنْ أَبِي هُرَيْرَةَ ، قَالَ : قَالَ رَسُولُ اللهِ ﷺ "الْإِيمَانُ بِضْعٌ
سَبْعُونَ شُعْبَةً ، فَأَفْضَلُهَا : قَوْلُ لَا إِلٰهَ إِلَّا اللهُ ، وَأَدْنَاهَا : إِمَاطَةُ
الْأَذَى عَنِ الطَّرِيقِ ، وَالْحَيَاءُ شُعْبَةٌ مِّنَ الْإِيمَانِ." مُتَّفَقٌ عَلَيْهِ.

5 Abu Huraira reported, Allah's Messenger (peace and blessings
of Allah be upon him) as saying: The faith has more than
seventy branches and the sublimest of these is the statement
that there is no god but Allah, and the lowest of these is to
remove anything harmful from the path and modesty is a
branch of faith. (*Agreed upon*)

٦- وَعَنْ عَبْدِ اللهِ بْنِ عَمْرٍو، قَالَ : قَالَ رَسُولُ اللهِ ﷺ "الْمُسْلِمُ مَنْ
سَلِمَ الْمُسْلِمُونَ مِنْ لِسَانِهِ وَيَدِهِ ، وَالْمُهَاجِرُ مَنْ هَجَرَ مَا نَهَى اللهُ
عَنْهُ" هٰذَا لَفْظُ الْبُخَارِيِّ. وَلِمُسْلِمٍ قَالَ "إِنَّ رَجُلًا سَأَلَ النَّبِيَّ
ﷺ : أَيُّ الْمُسْلِمِينَ خَيْرٌ؟ قَالَ : مَنْ سَلِمَ الْمُسْلِمُونَ مِنْ لِسَانِهِ وَيَدِهِ؟"

6 **'Abdullah b. 'Amr** reported Allah's Messenger (peace and blessings of Allah be upon him) as saying: A Muslim is one from whose tongue and hand the Muslims are safe. And the emigrant is one who abstains from that which Allah has prohibited. These are the words of *Bukhari*: The words contained in *Sahih Muslim* are: A person asked Allah's Messenger (peace and blessings of Allah be upon him) who amongst the Muslims is better. He said: One from whose tongue and hand the Muslims are safe.

٧ـ وَعَنْ أَنَسٍ رَضِيَ اللهُ عَنْهُ ، قَالَ : قَالَ رَسُولُ اللهِ ﷺ "لَا يُؤْمِنُ أَحَدُكُمْ حَتّى أَكُوْنَ أَحَبَّ إِلَيْهِ مِنْ وَالِدِهِ وَوَلَدِهِ وَالنَّاسِ أَجْمَعِيْنَ" مُتَّفَقٌ عَلَيْهِ

7 **Anas** (Allah be pleased with him) reported that Allah's Messenger (peace and blessings of Allah be upon him) said: None of you would be a believer till I am dearer to him than his father, his children and (in fact) the whole of mankind. *(Agreed upon)*

٨ـ وَعَنْهُ ، قَالَ : قَالَ رَسُولُ اللهِ ﷺ "ثَلَاثٌ مَنْ كُنَّ فِيْهِ وَجَدَ بِهِنَّ حَلَاوَةَ الإِيْمَانِ : مَنْ كَانَ اللهُ وَرَسُولُهُ أَحَبَّ إِلَيْهِ مِمَّا سِوَاهُمَا ، وَمَنْ أَحَبَّ عَبْدًا لَا يُحِبُّهُ إِلَّا لِلّهِ ، وَمَنْ يَكْرَهُ أَنْ يَعُوْدَ فِي الكُفْرِ بَعْدَ أَنْ أَنْقَذَهُ اللهُ مِنْهُ كَمَا يَكْرَهُ أَنْ يُلْقَى فِي النَّارِ" مُتَّفَقٌ عَلَيْهِ

8 **He (Anas)** also reported Allah's Messenger (peace and blessings of Allah be upon him) as saying: Three (are the qualities) whosoever possesses them, has tasted the sweetness of the faith: He to whom Allah and His Messenger are the dearest of all else. He who loves a slave (person) and he does not love him but for the sake of Allah and he who abhors relapsing into unbelief from which Allah has redeemed him as he would abhor being cast into fire. *(Agreed upon)*

٩ـ وَعَنِ العَبَّاسِ بْنِ عَبْدِ المُطَّلِبِ ، قَالَ : قَالَ رَسُولُ اللهِ ﷺ : ذَاقَ طَعْمَ الإِيْمَانِ مَنْ رَضِيَ بِاللهِ رَبًّا ، وَبِالإِسْلَامِ دِيْنًا ، وَبِمُحَمَّدٍ رَسُوْلًا" رَوَاهُ مُسْلِمٌ

9 Ibn ʻAbbas b. ʻAbdul Muttalib reported Allah's Messenger (peace and blessings of Allah be upon him) as saying: He in fact tasted the sweetness of faith who is well pleased with Allah as Lord and Islam as the code of life and Muhammad as the Messenger. (*Muslim*)

١- وَعَنْ أَبِى هُرَيْرَةَ، قَالَ: قَالَ رَسُولُ اللهِ ﷺ "وَالَّذِى نَفْسُ مُحَمَّدٍ بِيَدِهِ، لَا يَسْمَعُ بِى أَحَدٌ مِنْ هٰذِهِ الْأُمَّةِ يَهُودِىٌّ وَلَا نَصْرَانِىٌّ، ثُمَّ يَمُوتُ وَلَمْ يُؤْمِنْ بِالَّذِى أُرْسِلْتُ بِهِ؛ إِلَّا كَانَ مِنْ أَصْحَابِ النَّارِ" رَوَاهُ مُسْلِمٌ.

10 Abu Huraira reported Allah's Messenger (peace and blessings of Allah be upon him) as saying: By One in whose hand is the life of Muhammad whosoever from amongst this people, be he a Jew or Christian hears about my advent and then dies without affirming his faith in that with which I have been sent, would be amongst the denizens of Hell. (*Muslim*)

١١- وَعَنْ أَبِى مُوسَى الْأَشْعَرِىِّ، قَالَ: قَالَ رَسُولُ اللهِ ﷺ "ثَلَاثَةٌ لَهُمْ أَجْرَانِ: رَجُلٌ مِنْ أَهْلِ الْكِتَابِ آمَنَ بِنَبِيِّهِ وَ آمَنَ بِمُحَمَّدٍ، وَالْعَبْدُ الْمَمْلُوكُ إِذَا أَدَّى حَقَّ اللهِ وَحَقَّ مَوَالِيهِ، وَرَجُلٌ كَانَتْ عِنْدَهُ أَمَةٌ يَطَؤُهَا فَأَدَّبَهَا فَأَحْسَنَ تَأْدِيبَهَا، وَعَلَّمَهَا فَأَحْسَنَ تَعْلِيمَهَا، ثُمَّ أَعْتَقَهَا فَتَزَوَّجَهَا؛ فَلَهُ أَجْرَانِ" مُتَّفَقٌ عَلَيْهِ.

11 Abu Musa Ashʻari reported Allah's Messenger (peace and blessings of Allah be upon him) as saying: Three (are the persons) for whom there is a double reward. The person from amongst the people of the Book who affirmed his faith in his Prophet and affirmed faith in Muhammad; the slave who does his duty to Allah as well as his duty to his master, the person who having had connection with his female slave, taught her manners and in fact taught her good manners, imparted her knowledge and (in fact) imparted her good

knowledge, then set her free and married her, for him there is
a double reward. (*Agreed upon*)

١٢- وَعَنِ ابْنِ عُمَرَ رَضِيَ اللهُ عَنْهُمَا، قَالَ: قَالَ رَسُوْلُ اللهِ ﷺ "أُمِرْتُ أَنْ
أُقَاتِلَ النَّاسَ حَتَّى يَشْهَدُوا أَنْ لَّا إِلٰهَ إِلَّا اللهُ وَأَنَّ مُحَمَّدًا رَّسُوْلُ
اللهِ، وَيُقِيْمُوا الصَّلَاةَ، وَيُؤْتُوا الزَّكَاةَ. فَإِذَا فَعَلُوا ذٰلِكَ عَصَمُوا مِنِّي
دِمَاءَهُمْ وَأَمْوَالَهُمْ إِلَّا بِحَقِّ الْإِسْلَامِ، وَحِسَابُهُمْ عَلَى اللهِ" مُتَّفَقٌ
عَلَيْهِ. إِلَّا أَنَّ مُسْلِمًا لَمْ يَذْكُرْ: إِلَّا بِحَقِّ الْإِسْلَامِ.

12 Ibn 'Umar reported Allah's Messenger (peace and blessings of
Allah be upon him) as saying: I have been commanded that
I should fight with people till they bear testimony to the fact
that there is no god but Allah and Muhammad is His Messenger and they establish prayer, pay *zakat* and in case they do it
then their blood and their riches are safe from me except for
what is due to Islam and their reckoning will be at Allah's
hand.[1] (*Agreed upon*) (Imam) Muslim did not mention:
Except for what is due to Islam.

> 1 For the correct implication of this *hadith* it is essential to keep in
> mind the contents of verse 9 of *sura Tauba*: "Fight those who believe
> not in Allah, nor in the Last Day, nor forbid that which Allah and
> His Messenger have forbidden, nor follow the religion of Truth, out
> of those who have been given the Book, until they pay *Jizyah*, (a tax
> in acknowledgment of superiority) and they are in a state of
> subjection.
>
> *Sura Tauba* was revealed in the ninth year of *Hijra* and it
> contains the final and the most comprehensive commands in regard
> to *Jihad* and fighting against the non-Muslims. The majority of the
> scholars of the Quran and *hadith* is of the view that this *hadith* (12)
> applies to the polytheists and apostates of Arabia and not all the non-
> Muslims who can live under the Islamic state as *Dhimmis* or on the
> basis of treaty with the Islamic State.

١٣- وَعَنْ أَنَسٍ، أَنَّهُ قَالَ: قَالَ رَسُوْلُ اللهِ ﷺ: "مَنْ صَلَّى صَلَاتَنَا، وَ
اسْتَقْبَلَ قِبْلَتَنَا، وَأَكَلَ ذَبِيْحَتَنَا؛ ذٰلِكَ الْمُسْلِمُ الَّذِى لَهُ ذِمَّةُ اللهِ
وَذِمَّةُ رَسُوْلِهِ، فَلَا تُخْفِرُوا اللهَ فِى ذِمَّتِهِ" رَوَاهُ الْبُخَارِىُّ.

13 Anas reported Allah's Messenger (peace and blessings of Allah be upon him) as saying: He who observes our prayer, faces our Qibla and eats the animal slaughtered by us (according to *Shari'ah*) he is a Muslim, one for whom there is guarantee (of the safety of his life and property) from Allah and the guarantee from His Messenger and therefore break not the covenant of Allah with regard to his protection. (*Bukhari*)

١٤- وَعَنْ أَبِى هُرَيْرَةَ ، قَالَ: أَتَى أَعْرَابِىٌ إِلَى النَّبِىّ ﷺ ، فَقَالَ: دُلَّنِى عَلَى عَمَلٍ
إِذَا عَمِلْتُهُ دَخَلْتُ الْجَنَّةَ . قَالَ " تَعْبُدُ اللهَ وَلاَ تُشْرِكُ بِهِ شَيْئًا ، وَ
تُقِيمُ الصَّلَاةَ الْمَكْتُوبَةَ ، وَ تُؤَدِّى الزَّكَاةَ الْمَفْرُوضَةَ ، وَتَصُومُ رَمَضَانَ "
قَالَ: وَالَّذِى نَفْسِى بِيَدِهِ لَا أَزِيدُ عَلَى هٰذَا شَيْئًا وَلَا أَنْقُصُ مِنْهُ
فَلَمَّا وَلَّى، قَالَ النَّبِىُّ ﷺ " مَنْ سَرَّهُ أَنْ يَنْظُرَ إِلَى رَجُلٍ مِنْ أَهْلِ
الْجَنَّةِ فَلْيَنْظُرْ إِلَى هٰذَا" مُتَّفَقٌ عَلَيْهِ .

14 Abu Huraira reported that a desert Arab came to Allah's Messenger (peace and blessings of Allah be upon him) and said: Direct me to an act by the performance of which I may enter Paradise. He said: Worship Allah and associate not anything with Him, establish obligatory prayer, pay the prescribed *zakat*, observe (the fasts) of Ramaḍan. He said: By Him in Whose hand is my life I would not increase anything in it nor make any decrease in it. As he returned Allah's Apostle (peace and blessings of Allah be upon him) said: He who desires that he should see a person from the inmates of Paradise he should look at him. (*Agreed upon*)

١٥- وَعَنْ سُفْيَانَ بْنِ عَبْدِ اللهِ الثَّقَفِىّ ، قَالَ : قُلْتُ : يَا رَسُولَ اللهِ ! قُلْ
لِى فِى الْإِسْلَامِ قَوْلاً لَّا أَسْأَلُ عَنْهُ أَحَدًا بَعْدَكَ ——— وَ فِى رِوَايَةٍ:
غَيْرَكَ ——— قَالَ:" قُلْ" آمَنْتُ بِاللهِ ، ثُمَّ اسْتَقِمْ" رَوَاهُ مُسْلِمٌ؛

15 Sufyan b. 'Abdullah al-Thaqafi reported: I said: Allah's Messenger, tell me about Islam something (so comprehensive which may dispense me with the need) of asking anything about it after you. In another narration (the words) are: Anyone else. He said: Say: I affirm my faith in Allah and then abide by it (permanently). (*Muslim*)

١٦- وَعَنْ طَلْحَةَ بْنِ عُبَيْدِ اللهِ، قَالَ : جَاءَ رَجُلٌ إِلَى رَسُولِ اللهِ ﷺ : مِنْ أَهْلِ نَجْدٍ، ثَائِرُ الرَّأْسِ، نَسْمَعُ دَوِيَّ صَوْتِهِ وَلَا نَفْقَهُ مَا يَقُولُ، حَتَّى دَنَا مِنْ رَسُولِ اللهِ ﷺ ، فَإِذَا هُوَ يَسْأَلُ عَنِ الْإِسْلَامِ. فَقَالَ رَسُولُ اللهِ ﷺ "خَمْسُ صَلَوَاتٍ فِي الْيَوْمِ وَاللَّيْلَةِ"، فَقَالَ : هَلْ عَلَيَّ غَيْرُهُنَّ ؟ فَقَالَ "لَا، إِلَّا أَنْ تَطَوَّعَ. قَالَ رَسُولُ اللهِ ﷺ "وَصِيَامُ شَهْرِ رَمَضَانَ". قَالَ : هَلْ عَلَيَّ غَيْرُهُ ؟ قَالَ "لَا، إِلَّا أَنْ تَطَوَّعَ". قَالَ : وَذَكَرَ لَهُ رَسُولُ اللهِ ﷺ الزَّكَاةَ، فَقَالَ، هَلْ عَلَيَّ غَيْرُهَا، فَقَالَ "لَا، إِلَّا أَنْ تَطَوَّعَ" قَالَ : فَأَدْبَرَ الرَّجُلُ وَهُوَ يَقُولُ : وَاللهِ لَا أَزِيدُ عَلَى هٰذَا وَلَا أَنْقُصُ مِنْهُ. فَقَالَ رَسُولُ اللهِ ﷺ "أَفْلَحَ الرَّجُلُ إِنْ صَدَقَ" مُتَّفَقٌ عَلَيْهِ.

16 Talha b. 'Ubaid Allah reported: A person with dishevelled hair, from amongst the inhabitants of Najd, came to Allah's Messenger (peace and blessings of Allah be upon him). We could hear the humming of his voice but could not make out what he had been saying till he came nigh to Allah's Messenger (peace and blessings of Allah be upon him). (We perceived) that he had been asking about Islam, whereupon Allah's Messenger (peace and blessings of Allah be upon him) said: Five prayers (are obligatory) during the day and night. He said: Is there upon me (any other obligation) in regard to prayer besides these? Whereupon he (the Holy Prophet) said: No, but what you do voluntarily. The Messenger of Allah (peace and blessings of Allah be upon him) said: And the fast of Ramaḍan. And he said: Is there (any other obligation upon me in regard to fasting) besides these. He (the Holy Prophet) said: No, but what you do voluntarily. And then Allah's Messenger (peace and blessings of Allah be upon him) made a mention of *zakat*. He said: Is there upon me (any other obligation) in regard to the payment of *zakat*, besides

this. He said: No but that you do voluntarily. The **man**
returned saying: By Allah, I will make no addition to it nor
will I decrease anything out of it.   Thereupon Allah's Messenger (peace and blessings of Allah be upon him) remarked: He
is successful if he is true to (what he affirms). (*Agreed upon*)

١٤ـ وَعَنِ ابْنِ عَبَّاسٍ رَضِيَ اللهُ عَنْهُمَا ، قَالَ : إِنَّ وَفْدَ عَبْدِ الْقَيْسِ لَمَّا أَتَوُا
النَّبِيَّ ﷺ ، قَالَ رَسُولُ اللهِ ﷺ : "مَنِ الْقَوْمُ ؟ ـــ أَوْ : مَنِ الْوَفْدُ ؟ ــ"
قَالُوْا : رَبِيْعَةُ . قَالَ : "مَرْحَبًا بِالْقَوْمِ ـــ أَوْ : بِالْوَفْدِ ـــ غَيْرَ خَزَايَا وَ
لَا نَدَامَى" قَالُوْا : يَا رَسُوْلَ اللهِ ، إِنَّا لَا نَسْتَطِيْعُ أَنْ نَأْتِيَكَ إِلَّا فِي الشَّهْرِ
الْحَرَامِ ، وَ بَيْنَنَا وَ بَيْنَكَ هٰذَا الْحَيُّ مِنْ كُفَّارِ مُضَرَ ؛ فَمُرْنَا بِأَمْرٍ فَصْلٍ
نُخْبِرُ بِهِ مَنْ وَرَاءَنَا وَ نَدْخُلُ بِهِ الْجَنَّةَ ، وَ سَأَلُوْهُ عَنِ الْأَشْرِبَةِ .
فَأَمَرَهُمْ بِأَرْبَعٍ ، وَنَهَاهُمْ عَنْ أَرْبَعٍ .

أَمَرَهُمْ بِالْإِيْمَانِ بِاللهِ وَحْدَهُ ، قَالَ : "أَتَدْرُوْنَ مَا الْإِيْمَانُ بِاللهِ
وَحْدَهُ ؟ قَالُوْا : اللهُ وَرَسُوْلُهُ أَعْلَمُ . قَالَ : "شَهَادَةُ أَنْ لَا إِلٰهَ إِلَّا اللهُ
وَأَنَّ مُحَمَّدًا رَسُوْلُ اللهِ ، وَإِقَامُ الصَّلَاةِ ، وَإِيْتَاءُ الزَّكَاةِ ، وَ صِيَامُ
رَمَضَانَ ، وَأَنْ تُعْطُوْا مِنَ الْمَغْنَمِ الْخُمُسَ"

وَنَهَاهُمْ عَنْ أَرْبَعٍ : عَنِ الْحَنْتَمِ ، وَالدُّبَّاءِ ، وَالنَّقِيْرِ ، وَالْمُزَفَّتِ .
وَقَالَ : "احْفَظُوْهُنَّ وَ أَخْبِرُوْا بِهِنَّ مَنْ وَرَآءَكُمْ" مُتَّفَقٌ عَلَيْهِ . وَ
لَفْظُهُ لِلْبُخَارِيِّ .

17 Ibn 'Abbas (Allah be pleased with him) reported that a
deputation of the tribe of Abdul Qais[1] came to Allah's Messen-
ger (peace and blessings of Allah be upon him). Allah's
Messenger (peace and blessings of Allah be upon him) said:
Who are the people or of whom the deputation (is constituted).
They said: (The deputation of) Rabi'a. He (the Holy
Prophet) said: Welcome to the people or the **deputation that**

you have come to us without feeling any shame or sense of disgrace. They said: Allah's Messenger, we do not find possible for ourselves to come to you but in the sacred months²—(for) between us and you there is a tribe of unbelievers called Muḍar. Give us a decisive command which we may tell to those behind us and which may entitle us to get into Paradise. And they also asked him about drinks. He commanded them to observe four things and prohibited them (from four things). He commanded them to affirm faith in Allah, the One. He said: Do you know what faith in Allah (the One implies)? They said: Allah and Messenger know best. He said: It implies the bearing of testimony to the fact that there is no god but Allah and that Muhammad is the Messenger of Allah and the establishing of prayer, paying of *zakat*, observing of the fast of Ramaḍan and that you should give the one-fifth of the spoils of war. And he prohibited them (the use of) receptacles smeared with pitch, gourds, hollowed stumps and the varnished jars³ and he said to them: Keep (these things) in your mind and inform about them those behind you.

(Agreed upon, but the wording is that of Bukhari)

1. This tribe is a branch of a large tribe known as the tribe of Rabi'a.
2. These are four months Rajab, Dhi Qa'da, Dhul Hijjāh, and Muharram. Fighting is prohibited in these months.
3. These utensils were initially prohibited, as they were used for preparing, storing and drinking wine but later on when the Muslims had completely given up the use of wine, the orders against the use of these vessels were rescinded.

١٨ـ وَعَنْ عُبَادَةَ بْنِ الصَّامِتِ، قَالَ: قَالَ رَسُوْلُ اللهِ ﷺ، وَحَوْلَهُ عِصَابَةٌ
مِنْ أَصْحَابِهِ: "بَايِعُوْنِيْ عَلَى أَنْ لَّا تُشْرِكُوْا بِاللهِ شَيْئًا، وَلَا تَسْرِقُوْا، وَلَا
تَزْنُوْا، وَلَا تَقْتُلُوْا أَوْلَادَكُمْ، وَلَا تَأْتُوْا بِبُهْتَانٍ تَفْتَرُوْنَهُ بَيْنَ أَيْدِيْكُمْ
وَأَرْجُلِكُمْ، وَلَا تَعْصُوْا فِيْ مَعْرُوْفٍ. فَمَنْ وَفَى مِنْكُمْ فَأَجْرُهُ عَلَى اللهِ،
وَمَنْ أَصَابَ مِنْ ذٰلِكَ شَيْئًا فَعُوْقِبَ بِهِ فِي الدُّنْيَا؛ فَهُوَ كَفَّارَةٌ لَّهُ، وَ
مَنْ أَصَابَ مِنْ ذٰلِكَ شَيْئًا ثُمَّ سَتَرَهُ اللهُ عَلَيْهِ فِي الدُّنْيَا؛ فَهُوَ إِلَى اللهِ:
إِنْ شَاءَ عَفَا عَنْهُ، وَإِنْ شَاءَ عَاقَبَهُ" فَبَايَعْنَاهُ عَلٰى ذٰلِكَ. مُتَّفَقٌ عَلَيْهِ.

18 **'Ubada b. Samit** reported that Allah's Messenger (peace and blessings of Allah be upon him) said in the company of some of his companions: Swear allegiance to me that you would not associate with Allah anything, that you would not steal, that you would not commit fornication, that you would not kill your children, that you would not bring slander which you yourself fabricated, that you would not deviate from what is good and he who amongst you filfilled it (pledge) his reward is with Allah and if anyone commits anything (out of them) and is punished in the world that would be an expiation for him and he who committed anything out of it and Allah kept him unexposed (his case) rests with Allah, for He would forgive him if He would so like and would punish him if He would so like. And we swore allegiance to him on it. (*Agreed upon*)

١٩ - وَعَنْ أَبِي سَعِيدٍ الْخُدْرِيِّ ، قَالَ : خَرَجَ رَسُولُ اللهِ ﷺ فِي أَضْحًى أَوْ
فِطْرٍ إِلَى الْمُصَلَّى ، فَمَرَّ عَلَى النِّسَاءِ ، فَقَالَ " يَا مَعْشَرَ النِّسَاءِ ! تَصَدَّقْنَ ،
فَإِنِّي أُرِيتُكُنَّ أَكْثَرَ أَهْلِ النَّارِ " فَقُلْنَ : وَبِمَ يَا رَسُولَ اللهِ ؟ قَالَ " تُكْثِرْنَ
اللَّعْنَ ، وَتَكْفُرْنَ الْعَشِيرَ ، مَا رَأَيْتُ مِنْ نَاقِصَاتِ عَقْلٍ وَدِينٍ أَذْهَبَ
لِلُبِّ الرَّجُلِ الْحَازِمِ مِنْ إِحْدَاكُنَّ " قُلْنَ وَمَا نُقْصَانُ دِينِنَا وَعَقْلِنَا ؟
يَا رَسُولَ اللهِ ! قَالَ " أَلَيْسَ شَهَادَةُ الْمَرْأَةِ مِثْلَ نِصْفِ شَهَادَةِ الرَّجُلِ ؟ "
قُلْنَ : بَلَى قَالَ " فَذَلِكَ مِنْ نُقْصَانِ عَقْلِهَا . قَالَ : أَلَيْسَ إِذَا حَاضَتْ لَمْ
تُصَلِّ وَلَمْ تَصُمْ ؟ قُلْنَ : بَلَى . قَالَ " فَذَلِكَ مِنْ نُقْصَانِ دِينِهَا " مُتَّفَقٌ عَلَيْهِ .

19 **Abu Sa'id Khudri** reported: Allah's Messenger (peace and blessings of Allah be upon him) went out to the place of worship (outside the city) on the day of *'Id-ul Adha* or *Fitr* and he passed by the women and said to them: O Women, give charity for I have been shown the majority amongst you as the inmates of Hell. They said : Allah's Messenger, wherefore? He said: It is because (of the fact) that you curse one another very much and show ungratefulness to your husbands and I have seen that you in spite of being deficient in wisdom and religion, rob even a wise man of his senses. They said: Allah's Messenger, where lies our deficiency of reason and faith? He said: Is not the evidence of a woman equal to half the evidence of a man. They said: Yes. He said: This is because of the deficiency in their reason. He said: Is it not a fact that when they enter the period of menses they neither observe prayer nor observe fast. They said: Yes. Whereupon he said: This is the deficiency in their faith. (*Agreed upon*)

٢٠- وَعَنْ أَبِى هُرَيْرَةَ ، قَالَ : قَالَ رَسُوْلُ اللهِ ﷺ : «قَالَ اللهُ تَعَالَى : كَذَّبَنِى ابْنُ
اٰدَمَ وَلَمْ يَكُنْ لَهُ ذٰلِكَ ، وَشَتَمَنِى وَلَمْ يَكُنْ لَهُ ذٰلِكَ ؛ فَأَمَّا تَكْذِيْبُهُ
إِيَّايَ فَقَوْلُهُ : لَنْ يُعِيْدَنِى كَمَا بَدَأَنِى ، وَلَيْسَ أَوَّلُ الْخَلْقِ بِأَهْوَنَ عَلَىَّ مِنْ
إِعَادَتِهِ . وَأَمَّا شَتْمُهُ إِيَّايَ ، فَقَوْلُهُ : إِتَّخَذَ اللهُ وَلَدًا ، وَأَنَا الْأَحَدُ
الصَّمَدُ الَّذِىْ لَمْ أَلِدْ وَلَمْ أُوْلَدْ ، وَلَمْ يَكُنْ لِّىْ كُفُوًا أَحَدٌ»

20 Abu Huraira reported Allah's Messenger (peace and blessings of Allah be upon him) as saying: Allah, the Exalted, said: The son of Adam has told a lie about Me and it was not proper for him to do so. He has reviled Me and it was not proper for him to do so. His telling of lie about Allah is his statement: That He will not bring me back to life as He created me in the beginning and the first act of creation is no easier for Me than to bring him back to life; and his reviling Me is his statement: Allah has taken a son whereas I am One independent Who is neither begotten nor has been begotten and Who has no family of His.

٢- وَفِىْ رِوَايَةٍ عَنِ ابْنِ عَبَّاسٍ : «وَأَمَّا شَتْمُهُ إِيَّايَ فَقَوْلُهُ : لِىْ وَلَدٌ ، وَ
سُبْحَانِىْ أَنْ أَتَّخِذَ صَاحِبَةً أَوْ وَلَدًا» رَوَاهُ الْبُخَارِىُّ .

21 Ibn 'Abbas reported that his reviling is his statement that I have a son, far be it from Me that I should have a consort or a son. (*Bukhari*)

٢٢- وَعَنْ أَبِي هُرَيْرَةَ، قَالَ: قَالَ رَسُولُ اللهِ ﷺ: "قَالَ اللهُ تَعَالَى: يُؤْذِينِي ابْنُ آدَمَ يَسُبُّ الدَّهْرَ، وَأَنَا الدَّهْرُ، بِيَدِيَ الأَمْرُ، أُقَلِّبُ اللَّيْلَ وَ النَّهَارَ." مُتَّفَقٌ عَلَيْهِ.

22 **Abu Huraira** reported Allah's Messenger (peace and blessings of Allah be upon him) as saying: The son of Adam has vexed Me a pain as he abuses time whereas I am **Time.**[1] Authority is in My hand. I alternate day and night. (*Agreed upon*)

> 1. What this means is that all that happens in the Universe is the outcome of a Planning Will.

٢٣- وَعَنْ أَبِي مُوسَى الأَشْعَرِيِّ، قَالَ: قَالَ رَسُولُ اللهِ ﷺ: "مَا أَحَدٌ أَصْبَرُ عَلَى أَذًى يَسْمَعُهُ مِنَ اللهِ، يَدْعُونَ لَهُ الْوَلَدَ، ثُمَّ يُعَافِيهِمْ وَيَرْزُقُهُمْ." مُتَّفَقٌ عَلَيْهِ.

23 **Abu Musa Ash'ari** reported Allah's Messenger (peace and blessings of Allah be upon him) having said: None shows more forbearance than Allah on the blasphemies which He hears: they ascribe to Him a son; still He protects them and provides them sustenance. (*Agreed upon*)

٢٤- وَعَنْ مُعَاذٍ، قَالَ: كُنْتُ رِدْفَ رَسُولِ اللهِ ﷺ عَلَى حِمَارٍ، لَيْسَ بَيْنِي وَبَيْنَهُ إِلَّا مُؤَخِّرَةُ الرَّحْلِ، فَقَالَ: "يَا مُعَاذُ! هَلْ تَدْرِي مَا حَقُّ اللهِ عَلَى عِبَادِهِ؟ وَمَا حَقُّ الْعِبَادِ عَلَى اللهِ؟ قُلْتُ: اللهُ وَرَسُولُهُ أَعْلَمُ. قَالَ: "فَإِنَّ حَقَّ اللهِ عَلَى الْعِبَادِ أَنْ يَعْبُدُوهُ وَلَا يُشْرِكُوا بِهِ شَيْئًا، وَحَقُّ الْعِبَادِ عَلَى اللهِ أَنْ لَا يُعَذِّبَ مَنْ لَا يُشْرِكُ بِهِ شَيْئًا." فَقُلْتُ: يَا رَسُولَ اللهِ! أَفَلَا أُبَشِّرُ بِهِ النَّاسَ؟ قَالَ: "لَا تُبَشِّرْهُمْ فَيَتَّكِلُوا." مُتَّفَقٌ عَلَيْهِ.

24 **Mu'adh** reported that I was riding behind Allah's Messenger (peace and blessings of Allah be upon him) on a pony and there was nothing between him and me but the rear part of the saddle that he said : Mu'adh, do you know what is the right of Allah upon His servants and what is right of the servants upon Allah. I said: Allah and His Messenger know best; whereupon he said: The right of Allah upon His servants is that they worship Him and associate not anything with Him and the right of servants upon Allah is that He would not punish one who does not associate anything with Him. I said: Allah's Messenger, should I not give this tiding to the people. He said: Don't give this tiding to them for they would completely rely upon it. (*Agreed upon*)

٢٥ـ وَعَنْ أَنَسٍ ،أَنَّ النَّبِيَّ ﷺ ، وَمُعَاذٌ رَدِيفُهُ عَلَى الرَّحْلِ قَالَ :يَا مُعَاذُ؟ قَالَ لَبَّيْكَ يَا رَسُولَ اللهِ وَسَعْدَيْكَ . قَالَ :يَا مُعَاذُ؟ قَالَ : لَبَّيْكَ يَا رَسُولَ اللهِ وَسَعْدَيْكَ قَالَ :يَا مُعَاذُ؟ قَالَ : لَبَّيْكَ يَا رَسُولَ اللهِ وَ سَعْدَيْكَ ،ـ ثَلَاثًا ـ قَالَ :مَا مِنْ أَحَدٍ يَشْهَدُ أَنْ لَا إِلَهَ إِلَّا اللهُ وَأَنَّ مُحَمَّدًا رَسُولُ اللهِ ، صِدْقًا مِنْ قَلْبِهِ إِلَّا حَرَّمَهُ اللهُ عَلَى النَّارِ قَالَ : يَا رَسُولَ اللهِ !أَفَلَا أُخْبِرُ بِهِ النَّاسَ فَيَسْتَبْشِرُوا؟ قَالَ :إِذًا يَتَّكِلُوا ؛ فَأَخْبَرَ بِهَا مُعَاذٌ عِنْدَ مَوْتِهِ تَأَثُّمًا . مُتَّفَقٌ عَلَيْهِ

25 Anas reported that Mu'adh was riding behind Allah's Apostle (peace and blessings of Allah be upon him) that he said: Mu'adh. He said: Allah's Messenger, here I am at thy service and at thy pleasure. He (the Holy Prophet) again said: Mu'adh and he said: Allah's Messenger, here I am at thy service and at thy pleasure. He said this thrice. Then he (the Holy Prophet) said: He who bears testimony to the fact that there is no god but Allah and Muhammad is His Messenger sincerely from (the depth) of his heart, Allah would make him immune from Hell-Fire. He said: Allah's Messenger, should I not inform people about this and give them this glad tiding; whereupon he said: Then they would rely upon it (exclusively). Mu'adh informed (people) about it at the time of his death to avoid sinning.[1] (*Agreed upon*)

1. It is sin not to transmit the words of the Holy Prophet to the other Muslims because what he did or said was Divinely inspired and as such the people should know it is an integral part of his ministry of prophethood.

٢٦ـ وَعَنْ أَبِى ذَرٍّ قَالَ : أَتَيْتُ النَّبِىَّ ۞ ، وَعَلَيْهِ ثَوْبٌ أَبْيَضُ ، وَهُوَ

نَآئِمٌ ، ثُمَّ أَتَيْتُهُ وَقَدِ اسْتَيْقَظَ ، فَقَالَ : ‟مَا مِنْ عَبْدٍ قَالَ : لَآ إِلهَ إِلَّا

اللهُ ، ثُمَّ مَاتَ عَلَى ذَلِكَ ، إِلَّا دَخَلَ الْجَنَّةَ ˮ قُلْتُ : وَإِنْ زَنَى وَإِنْ سَرَقَ؟

قَالَ : وَإِنْ زَنَى وَإِنْ سَرَقَ ، قُلْتُ : وَإِنْ زَنَى وَإِنْ سَرَقَ؟ قَالَ : وَإِنْ

زَنَى وَإِنْ سَرَقَ ، قُلْتُ : وَإِنْ زَنَى وَإِنْ سَرَقَ ؟! قَالَ : ‟وَإِنْ زَنَى وَإِنْ

سَرَقَ عَلَى رَغْمِ أَنْفِ أَبِى ذَرٍّ ˮ ، وَكَانَ أَبُو ذَرٍّ إِذَا حَدَّثَ بِهذَا قَالَ : وَ

إِنْ رَغِمَ أَنْفُ أَبِى ذَرٍّ . مُتَّفَقٌ عَلَيْهِ .

26 Abu Dharr reported: I came to Allah's Apostle (peace and blessings of Allah be upon him) and found him sleeping under a white sheet. I again came and he was awake. He said: There is none amongst the servants who said: There is no god but Allah, and died with this belief, but would be admitted into Paradise. I said: Even if he commits fornication and even if he commits theft. He said: Even if he commits fornication and even if he commits theft. I (again) said: Even if he commits fornication and even if he commits theft. He said: Even if he commits fornication and he commits theft and in spite of Abu Dharr's dislike.[1] And when Abu Dharr narrated this he remarked 'in spite of Abu Dharr's dislike.' (*Agreed upon*)

1. *Raghima anfuhu* is a phrase meaning 'May his nose cleave to the earth or dust'. In idiomatic sense it means may he be abased, humbled or render submissive against his will. In this *hadith* the meanings of the phrase are quite clear. A pious man like Abu Dharr could hardly believe that an adulterer or a thief could ever be admitted to Paradise. The Holy Prophet was giving a verdict against his views. It was at this juncture that the Holy Prophet said: It is so, despite Abu Dharr's dislike.

٢٧ـ وَعَنْ عُبَادَةَ بْنِ الصَّامِتِ ، قَالَ : قَالَ رَسُولُ اللهِ ۞ : ‟مَنْ شَهِدَ أَنْ

لَآ إِلهَ إِلَّا اللهُ وَحْدَهُ لَا شَرِيكَ لَهُ وَأَنَّ مُحَمَّدًا عَبْدُهُ وَرَسُولُهُ ، وَأَنَّ

عِيسَى عَبْدُ اللهِ وَرَسُولُهُ وَابْنُ أَمَتِهِ وَكَلِمَتُهُ أَلْقَاهَا إِلَى مَرْيَمَ ، وَ

رُوحٌ مِنْهُ ، وَالْجَنَّةُ وَالنَّارُ حَقٌّ ، أَدْخَلَهُ اللهُ الْجَنَّةَ عَلَى مَا كَانَ مِنَ

الْعَمَلِ ˮ مُتَّفَقٌ عَلَيْهِ .

27 **'Ubada b. Samit** reported: He who bears a testimony to the fact that there is no god but Allah, the One having no partner with Him and Muhammad is His servant and His Messenger and Isa (Jesus Christ) is the bondsman of Allah and His Messenger and the son of His slave girl and His word breathed into Mary and His spirit[1] and that Paradise and Hell is a fact, Allah will admit him to Paradise whatever his act may be. (*Agreed upon*)

> 1. Jesus has been called a 'word' which Allah communicated to Mary signifying the fact that he was brought into existence by the command of Allah without the ordinary instrumentality of a father. (Baiḍawi) If the whole universe could be emerged into being by a single word of Allah and Adam could be created without the instrumentality of both father and mother it is quite conceivable that a command of Allah can easily bring into being a man without the instrumentality of fathe.r
>
> The word 'spirit' used for Jesus does not carry him a step beyond the limits of mortality as for Adam also it has been said: I breathed My spirit into him. In fact according to the Holy Qurān the spirit of God is breathed into every man.
>
> "Then He made him complete and breathed into him of His spirit and gave you hearing and sight and hearts". (**32 : 9**)
>
> The epithet *ruh-um-minhu* (a spirit from Him) does not imply that the soul of Allah has incarnated in Jesus; it only signifies the eminence of Christ, as it has been explained by the famous commentators of the Holy Quran, Ibn 'Abbas, Ibn Jarir, Ibn Kathir.

٢٨ ـ وَعَنْ عَمْرِو بْنِ الْعَاصِ، قَالَ : أَتَيْتُ النَّبِيَّ ﷺ فَقُلْتُ : أَبْسُطْ يَمِينَكَ فَلِأُبَايِعْكَ، فَبَسَطَ يَمِينَهُ ، فَقَبَضْتُ يَدَى ، فَقَالَ : "مَالَكَ يَا عَمْرُو ؟ قُلْتُ : أَرَدْتُ أَنْ أَشْتَرِطَ فَقَالَ : "تَشْتَرِطُ مَاذَا ؟ قُلْتُ : أَنْ يُغْفَرَلِى. قَالَ : "أَمَا عَلِمْتَ يَا عَمْرُو ! إِنَّ الْإِسْلَامَ يَهْدِمُ مَا كَانَ قَبْلَهُ ، وَ إِنَّ الْهِجْرَةَ تَهْدِمُ مَا كَانَ قَبْلَهَا ، وَ إِنَّ الْحَجَّ يَهْدِمُ مَا كَانَ قَبْلَهُ ؟! رَوَاهُ مُسْلِمٌ.

وَ الْحَدِيثَانِ الْمَرْوِيَانِ عَنْ أَبِي هُرَيْرَةَ ، قَالَ : "قَالَ اللّٰهُ تَعَالَى أَنَا أَغْنَى الشُّرَكَآءِ عَنِ الشِّرَاكِ" وَ الْأَخَرُ : "أَلْكِبْرِيَآءُ رِدَآئِى" سَنَذْكُرُهُمَا فِي بَابِ الرِّيَآءِ وَ الْكِبْرِ إِنْ شَآءَ اللّٰهُ تَعَالَى .

28 'Amr b. al-'As reported: I came to Allah's Apostle (peace and blessings of Allah be upon him) and said: (Kindly) **stretch** your hand so that I should swear allegiance to you. He stretched his hand but I clenched my hand. He said: 'Amr, what is the matter with you? I said: I wish to lay down a condition: He (the Holy Prophet) said: What is the condition that you intend to lay down? I said (the condition is) that I should be assured of forgiveness. He said: 'Amr, do you know that Islam obliterates what has preceded it and the emigration obliterates that has preceded it and the *Hajj* obliterates what has preceded it.. (*Muslim*)

Both the *ahadith* have been transmitted on the authority of Abu Huraira the first is that he (the Holy Prophet) said: Allah, the Exalted, declared: I am the One Who is most able to dispense with any partnership and the second one is that exaltedness is My cloak. We would make a mention of them in the chapter of "showing off and vanity" if Allah, the most High, so wills.

Section II الْفَصْلُ الثَّانِى

٢٩ ـ عَنْ مُعَاذٍ، قَالَ : قُلْتُ يَا رَسُوْلَ اللهِ ! أَخْبِرْنِى بِعَمَلٍ يُدْخِلُنِى الْجَنَّةَ وَيُبَاعِدُنِى مِنَ النَّارِ. قَالَ "لَقَدْ سَأَلْتَ عَنْ أَمْرٍ عَظِيْمٍ، وَ إِنَّهُ لَيَسِيْرٌ عَلَى مَنْ يَسَّرَهُ اللهُ تَعَالَى عَلَيْهِ : تَعْبُدُ اللهَ وَلَا تُشْرِكُ بِهِ شَيْئًا، وَ تُقِيْمُ الصَّلَاةَ، وَ تُؤْتِى الزَّكَاةَ، وَ تَصُوْمُ رَمَضَانَ، وَ تَحُجُّ الْبَيْتَ" ثُمَّ قَالَ "أَلَا أَدُلُّكَ عَلَى أَبْوَابِ الْخَيْرِ؟ أَلصَّوْمُ جُنَّةٌ، وَ الصَّدَقَةُ تُطْفِئُ الْخَطِيْئَةَ كَمَا يُطْفِئُ الْمَآءُ النَّارَ، وَ صَلَاةُ الرَّجُلِ فِى جَوْفِ اللَّيْلِ" ثُمَّ تَلَا : (تَتَجَافَى جُنُوْبُهُمْ عَنِ الْمَضَاجِعِ...) حَتَّى بَلَغَ (يَعْمَلُوْنَ) ثُمَّ قَالَ "أَلَا أَدُلُّكَ بِرَأْسِ الْأَمْرِ وَ عَمُوْدِهِ وَ ذِرْوَةِ سَنَامِهِ؟ قُلْتُ بَلَى يَا رَسُوْلَ اللهِ! قَالَ "رَأْسُ الْأَمْرِ الْإِسْلَامُ، وَ عَمُوْدُهُ الصَّلَاةُ، وَذِرْوَةُ سَنَامِهِ الْجِهَادُ" ثُمَّ قَالَ "أَلَا أُخْبِرُكَ بِمِلَاكِ ذَلِكَ كُلِّهِ؟ قُلْتُ بَلَى

يَانَبِيَّ اللّٰهِ ! فَأَخَذَ بِلِسَانِهِ فَقَالَ :"كُفَّ عَلَيْكَ هٰذَا" فَقُلْتُ : يَانَبِيَّ اللّٰهِ!
وَ إِنَّا لَمُؤَاخَذُوْنَ بِمَا نَتَكَلَّمُ بِهِ ؛ قَالَ :"ثَكِلَتْكَ أُمُّكَ يَامُعَاذُ! وَ هَلْ
يُكَبُّ النَّاسُ فِى النَّارِ عَلٰى وُجُوْهِهِمْ ،أَوْعَلٰى مَنَاخِرِهِمْ ،إِلاَّ حَصَآئِدُ
أَلْسِنَتِهِمْ" رَوَاهُ أَحْمَدُ ،وَالتِّرْمِذِيّ ،وَ ابْنُ مَاجَةَ.

29 Mu'adh reported: I said to Allah's Messenger (peace and blessings of Allah be upon him) to inform me about an act which would entitle me to get into Paradise, and remove me away from Hell-Fire. He (the Holy Prophet) said: You have asked me about a matter (which ostensibly appears to be) difficult but it is easy to him for whom Allah, the Exalted, has made things easy. Worship Allah and do not associate anything with him, establish prayer, pay *Zakat*, observe fast of Ramadan and perform *Hajj* of the (sacred) House (Ka'ba). He again said: Should I not direct you to the gateways of good? listen to me: The fasting is a shield against evil and the charity extinguishes (the fire of sin) just as water extinguishes fire and the prayer of a person during mid-night and then he recited: Who forsake their beds up to . . . . . they used to do.[1] Then he said : Should I not direct you to the highest level of this matter, to the pillar on which (it rests) and its top. I said: Allah's Messenger yes, (do tell me). He said: The upper-most level of the matter is *Al-Islam*. Its pillar is the prayer and its top is *Jihad*. He then said: Should I not inform you of the sheet anchor of all this. I said: Allah's Apostle, (of course do it). He took hold of his tongue and said: Exercise restraint on it. I said: The Apostle of Allah, would we be held responsible for what we talk with it? Thereupon he said: Mu'adh, May your mother be bereaved. Will anything else besides the (irresponsible) talk cause the people to be thrown into the Hell-Fire upon their faces or on their nostrils. (*Ahmad, Trimidhi, Ibn Maja*)

1. The complete verse is this: Who forsake their beds to call upon their Lord in fear and hope and spend of that what We have bestowed on them. No soul knoweth what is kept hid for them of joy, as a reward for what they used to do. (**32** : 16, 17).

٣٠ـ وَعَنْ أَبِى أُمَامَةَ، قَالَ قَالَ رَسُوْلُ اللهِ ﷺ "مَنْ أَحَبَّ بِلهِ، وَأَبْغَضَ
بِلهِ، وَ أَعْطَى بِلهِ، وَمَنَعَ لِلهِ؛ فَقَدِ اسْتَكْمَلَ الْإِيْمَانَ " رَوَاهُ أَبُوْ دَاوُدَ.

30 **Abu Umama** reported that Allah's Messenger (peace and
blessings of Allah be upon him) said: He who loved for
Allah's sake and hated for Allah's sake and donated for Allah's
sake and withheld for Allah's sake, he in fact caused perfec-
tion of the faith.   (*Abu Dawud*)

٣١ـ وَرَوَاهُ التِّرْمِذِيُّ عَنْ مُعَاذِ ابْنِ أَنَسٍ مَعَ تَقْدِيْمٍ وَّ تَأْخِيْرٍ، وَ فِيْهِ
" فَقَدِ اسْتَكْمَلَ إِيْمَانَهُ "؛

31 This *hadith* has been recorded on the authority of Mu'adh b.
Anas with a transposition of phrase : 'He in fact perfected his
faith.'

٣١ـ وَعَنْ أَبِى ذَرٍّ، قَالَ: قَالَ رَسُوْلُ اللهِ ﷺ "أَفْضَلُ الْأَعْمَالِ أَلْحُبُّ فِى
اللهِ وَالْبُغْضُ فِى اللهِ" رَوَاهُ أَبُوْ دَاوُدَ.

32 **Abu Dharr** reported Allah's Messenger (peace and blessings of
Allah be upon him) as saying: The best of the deed is the love
for the sake of Allah and hatred for the sake of Allah.
                  (*Abu Dawud*)

٣٣ـ وَعَنْ أَبِى هُرَيْرَةَ، قَالَ: قَالَ رَسُوْلُ اللهِ ﷺ "أَلْمُسْلِمُ مَنْ سَلِمَ
الْمُسْلِمُوْنَ مِنْ لِسَانِهِ وَ يَدِهِ، وَالْمُؤْمِنُ مَنْ أَمِنَهُ النَّاسُ عَلَى دِمَآئِهِمْ
وَ أَمْوَالِهِمْ"؛ رَوَاهُ التِّرْمِذِيُّ، وَ النَّسَائِيُّ.

33 **Abu Huraira** reported Allah's Messenger (peace and blessings
of Allah be upon him) as saying: A Muslim is one from whose
tongue and hand the Muslims are safe and a believer is one in
whom people repose trust in regard to their life and wealth.
              (*Trimidhi and Nasa'i*)

٣٤ـ وَزَادَ الْبَيْهَقِيُّ فِى "شُعَبِ الْإِيْمَانِ" بِرِوَايَةٍ فَضَالَةَ: وَالْمُجَاهِدُ مَنْ
جَاهَدَ نَفْسَهُ فِى طَاعَةِ اللهِ، وَ الْمُهَاجِرُ مَنْ هَجَرَ الْخَطَايَا وَالذُّنُوْبَ:

34 **Baihaqi** added in *Shu'ab ul-Iman* on the report of **Faḍala**: And the *mujahid* is one who strives with his self as regards obedience to Allah and the *Muhajir* (emigrant) is one who abandons crimes and sins.

٣٥ - وَعَنْ أَنَسٍ رَضِيَ اللهُ عنه .قَالَ : قَلَّمَا خَطَبَنَا رَسُولُ اللهِ ﷺ إِلَّا

قَالَ : " لَا إِيمَانَ لِمَنْ لَّا أَمَانَةَ لَهُ وَلَا دِينَ لِمَنْ لَّاعَهْدَ لَهُ " رَوَاهُ

الْبَيْهَقِيُّ فِي " شُعَبِ الْإِيمَانِ "

35 **Anas** (Allah be pleased with him) reported: Seldom did the Messenger of Allah (peace and blessings of Allah be upon him) address us when he did not say: There is no faith in him who is not trustworthy and there is no religion in him who does not respect his covenant. (*Baihaqi in Shu'ab ul-Iman*)

Section III الْفَصْلُ الثَّالِثُ

٣٦ - عَنْ عُبَادَةَ بْنِ الصَّامِتِ رَضِيَ اللهُ عَنْهُ ، قَالَ سَمِعْتُ رَسُولَ اللهِ

ﷺ يَقُولُ : " مَنْ شَهِدَ أَنْ لَّا إِلَهَ إِلَّا اللهُ وَ أَنَّ مُحَمَّدًا رَسُولُ اللهِ ،

حَرَّمَ اللهُ عَلَيْهِ النَّارَ "

36 **'Ubada b. Samit** (Allah be pleased with him) reported: I heard Allah's Messenger (peace and blessings of Allah be upon him) as saying: He who bears testimony to the fact that there is no god but Allah and that Muhammad is the Messenger of Allah, Allah makes him immune from Hell-Fire.

٣٧ - وَعَنْ عُثْمَانَ رَضِيَ اللهُ عَنْهُ ، قَالَ : قَالَ رَسُولُ اللهِ ﷺ " مَنْ مَاتَ

وَ هُوَ يَعْلَمُ أَنَّهُ لَا إِلَهَ إِلَّا اللهُ دَخَلَ الْجَنَّةَ " رَوَاهُ مُسْلِمٌ

37 **'Uthman** (Allah be pleased with him) reported Allah's Messenger (peace and blessings of Allah be upon him) as saying: He who died knowing (and acknowledging it) that there is no god but Allah, he is in fact entitled to get into Paradise. (*Muslim*)

٣٨ ـ وَعَنْ جَابِرٍ رَضِيَ اللهُ عَنْهُ، قَالَ: قَالَ رَسُوْلُ اللهِ ﷺ "ثِنْتَانِ
مُوْجِبَتَانِ" قَالَ رَجُلٌ: يَا رَسُوْلَ اللهِ! مَا الْمُوْجِبَتَانِ؟ قَالَ "مَنْ مَاتَ
يُشْرِكُ بِاللهِ شَيْئًا دَخَلَ النَّارَ، وَ مَنْ مَاتَ لَا يُشْرِكُ بِاللهِ شَيْئًا
دَخَلَ الْجَنَّةَ" رَوَاهُ مُسْلِمٌ.

38 Jabir (Allah be pleased with him) reported : Allah's Messenger (peace and blessings of Allah be upon him) said : Two things yield inevitable results. A person said : Allah's Messenger, what these two things are? He said : He who died associating anything with Allah would definitely enter into Hell-Fire and he who died without associating anything with Allah he in fact entitled himself to get into Paradise. (*Muslim*)

٣٩ ـ وَعَنْ أَبِيْ هُرَيْرَةَ رَضِيَ اللهُ عَنْهُ، قَالَ: كُنَّا قُعُوْدًا حَوْلَ رَسُوْلِ
اللهِ ﷺ وَ مَعَنَا أَبُوْبَكْرٍ وَ عُمَرُ رَضِيَ اللهُ عَنْهُمَا فِيْ نَفَرٍ، فَقَامَ رَسُوْلُ
اللهِ ﷺ مِنْ بَيْنِ أَظْهُرِنَا، فَأَبْطَأَ عَلَيْنَا، وَ خَشِيْنَا أَنْ يُقْتَطَعَ دُوْنَنَا،
وَ فَزِعْنَا فَقُمْنَا، فَكُنْتُ أَوَّلَ مَنْ فَزِعَ، فَخَرَجْتُ أَبْتَغِيْ رَسُوْلَ اللهِ
ﷺ، حَتَّى أَتَيْتُ حَائِطًا لِلْأَنْصَارِ لِبَنِيْ النَّجَّارِ، فَسَاوَرْتُ بِهِ، هَلْ
أَجِدُ لَهُ بَابًا؟ فَلَمْ أَجِدْ، فَإِذَا رَبِيْعٌ يَدْخُلُ فِيْ جَوْفِ حَائِطٍ مِنْ بِئْرٍ
خَارِجَةٍ ـ وَ الرَّبِيْعُ الْجَدْوَلُ ـ قَالَ: فَاحْتَفَزْتُ فَدَخَلْتُ عَلَى رَسُوْلِ
اللهِ ﷺ. فَقَالَ "أَبُوْ هُرَيْرَةَ" فَقُلْتُ: نَعَمْ يَا رَسُوْلَ اللهِ! قَالَ "مَا
شَأْنُكَ؟" قُلْتُ: كُنْتَ بَيْنَ أَظْهُرِنَا نَقَمْتَ فَأَبْطَأْتَ عَلَيْنَا، فَخَشِيْنَا
أَنْ تُقْتَطَعَ دُوْنَنَا، فَفَزِعْنَا، فَكُنْتُ أَوَّلَ مَنْ فَزِعَ، فَأَتَيْتُ هٰذَا الْحَائِطَ،
فَاحْتَفَزْتُ كَمَا يَحْتَفِزُ الثَّعْلَبُ، وَ هٰؤُلَاءِ النَّاسُ وَرَائِيْ. فَقَالَ "يَا
أَبَا هُرَيْرَةَ!" وَ أَعْطَانِيْ نَعْلَيْهِ. فَقَالَ "إِذْهَبْ بِنَعْلَيَّ هَاتَيْنِ فَمَنْ لَقِيْتَ

مِنْ وَرَآءِ هٰذَا الْحَائِطِ يَشْهَدُ أَنْ لَّا إِلٰهَ إِلَّا اللهُ مُسْتَيْقِنًا بِهَا قَلْبُهُ؛
فَبَشِّرْهُ بِالْجَنَّةِ ۞ فَكَانَ أَوَّلَ مَنْ لَقِيْتُ عُمَرُ فَقَالَ، مَا هَاتَانِ الشَّعْلَانِ
يَآ أَبَا هُرَيْرَةَ؟ قُلْتُ، هَاتَانِ نَعْلَا رَسُوْلِ اللهِ صَلَّى اللهُ عَلَيْهِ وَسَلَّمَ
بَعَثَنِي بِهِمَا، مَنْ لَقِيْتُ يَشْهَدُ أَنْ لَّا إِلٰهَ إِلَّا اللهُ مُسْتَيْقِنًا بِهَا قَلْبُهُ
بَشَّرْتُهُ بِالْجَنَّةِ، فَضَرَبَ عُمَرُ بَيْنَ ثَدْيَيَّ، فَخَرَرْتُ لِاِسْتِي. فَقَالَ،
اِرْجِعْ يَآ أَبَا هُرَيْرَةَ! فَرَجَعْتُ إِلَى رَسُوْلِ اللهِ ۞ فَأَجْهَشْتُ بِالْبُكَاءِ
وَرَكِبَنِي عُمَرُ، وَ إِذَا هُوَ عَلَى أَثَرِي. فَقَالَ رَسُوْلُ اللهِ ۞ "مَالَكَ
يَآ أَبَا هُرَيْرَةَ؟" فَقُلْتُ، لَقِيْتُ عُمَرَ فَأَخْبَرْتُهُ بِالَّذِيْ بَعَثْتَنِي بِهِ، فَضَرَبَ
بَيْنَ ثَدْيَيَّ ضَرْبَةً خَرَرْتُ لِاِسْتِي. فَقَالَ، اِرْجِعْ. فَقَالَ رَسُوْلُ اللهِ
۞ "يَا عُمَرُ! مَا حَمَلَكَ عَلَى مَا فَعَلْتَ؟" قَالَ، يَا رَسُوْلَ اللهِ! بِأَبِيْ
أَنْتَ وَ أُمِّي، أَبَعَثْتَ أَبَا هُرَيْرَةَ بِنَعْلَيْكَ، مَنْ لَقِيَ يَشْهَدُ أَنْ لَّا
إِلٰهَ إِلَّا اللهُ مُسْتَيْقِنًا بِهَا قَلْبُهُ بَشَّرَهُ بِالْجَنَّةِ؟ قَالَ، "نَعَمْ" قَالَ،
فَلَا تَفْعَلْ، فَإِنِّيْ أَخْشَى أَنْ يَّتَّكِلَ النَّاسُ عَلَيْهَا، فَخَلِّهِمْ يَعْمَلُوْنَ.
فَقَالَ رَسُوْلُ اللهِ ۞ "فَخَلِّهِمْ" رَوَاهُ مُسْلِمٌ.

39 Abu Huraira (Allah be pleased with him) reported: We were sitting around Allah's Messenger (peace and blessings of Allah be upon him) and theer were with us Abu Bakr and 'Umar (may Allah be pleased with both of them) amongst the group of (audience). It was during that time that Messenger of Allah (peace and blessings of Allah be upon him) got up and (left the place). He delayed in coming back to us which caused consternation that he might be attacked by some enemy while we would not be with him. So being alarmed, we got up. I was the first to be alarmed. I went out to look for the Messenger of Allah (peace and blessings of Allah be upon him) and came to a garden belonging to Banu An-Najjar. I went around it looking for a gate but failed to find one. Seeing a Rabi' (a streamlet) flowing into the garden from the well outside, I drew myself to go like a fox and slinked into the (place) where God's Messenger (peace and blessings of Allah be upon him) had been. He (the Holy Prophet) said: Is it Abu Huraira. I said: Yes, Messenger of Allah, it is so. He said: What is the matter with you? I said: You were amongst us but you got up and went away and delayed for the time, so fearing that you might be attacked by some enemy when we would not be with you, we became alarmed. I was the first to be alarmed so I came to this garden and I drew myself to go as a fox goes and these people are following me. Thereupon he said : O, Abu Huraira, and he gave me his sandals saying : Take away these sandals of mine and when you meet anyone outside this garden who testifies that there is no god but Allah believing in it from his heart gladden him by announcing that he shall go to Paradise. Now the first one whom I met was 'Umar. He said: Abu Huraira, what are these sandals. I said: These are the sandals of Allah's Messenger (peace and blessings of Allah be upon him) with which he has sent me to gladden anyone I meet who bears testimony to the fact there is no god but Allah and having implicit faith of it in his heart, with the announcement that he would go to Paradise. Thereupon, 'Umar struck me on the breast and I fell on my back. So I returned to Allah's Messenger (peace and blessings of Allah be upon him) and I began to weep loudly. 'Umar followed close after. Allah's Messenger (peace and blessings of Allah be upon him) said: Abu Huraira, what is the matter with you? I said to him: I met 'Umar and informed him of that which you sent me but he struck me in my chest that I fell upon my back and he also asked me to go away. Thereupon Allah's Messenger (peace and blessings of Allah be upon him) said to 'Umar: What prompted you to do this? He (Haḍrat 'Umar) said: Allah's Messenger (may my father and mother be taken ransom for you); did you send Abu Huraira with your sandals to gladden anyone he met and who testified that there is no god but Allah bearing witness from his heart with the tidings that he would go to Paradise. He said: **Yes.** 'Umar said: **Please** don't do that for I fear that people will rely upon it **alone**; let them go on doing good deeds. The Messenger of **Allah** (peace and blessings of Allah be upon him) said: Well, let them do.[1] (*Muslim*)

> 1. The question is often raised about this *hadith* as to what right 'Umar had got to interfere with the commands of the Holy Prophet. A little bit of thinking would make the point clear that 'Umar (may Allah be pleased with him) was not doubting the fact told to Abu Huraira by the Holy Prophet. His only objection was that if it were given on unrestricted circulation, it might cool down the zeal of the people in carrying out the commands of Allah and His Prophet. There were not a few people who were new converts to Islam, they had not yet fully imbibed the true spirit of the faith and the great revolution which it aimed at bringing about in the individuals and social life of the human beings. It required hard work and unceasing labour. Mere lip service to Allah was not enough. What 'Umar apprehended was that if this message was conveyed to all the Muslims, the raw minds who had not yet fully attuned themselves to the teachings of Islam might rely on this and regard it as a mere passport to Paradise. Affirmation in the oneness of God without associating anything with Him is certainly the golden rule to enter into Paradise but it entails heavy responsibility which the new converts could not fully appreciate and understand at that stage. That is why 'Umar objected to it. What he did was perfectly in accordance with the wishes of the Holy Prophet as is clear from the fact that he accepted the proposal of Hadrat 'Umar and did not deem it advisable to give a wide publicity to this glad tidings at that stage. If he had held a different view from that of Hadrat 'Umar he could not have accepted his view as the view of the Holy Prophet is inspired by Allah, and, therefore, it must dominate and prevail upon all other views.

٤٠ ـ وَعَنْ مُعَاذِ بْنِ جَبَلٍ، قَالَ: قَالَ لِيْ رَسُوْلُ اللهِ ﷺ: "مَفَاتِيْحُ الْجَنَّةِ شَهَادَةُ أَنْ لَا إِلٰهَ إِلَّا اللهُ" رَوَاهُ أَحْمَدُ.

40 Mu'adh b. Jabal reported Allah's Messenger (peace and blessings of Allah be upon him) having said to him: The key to Paradise is the testimony to the fact that there is no god but Allah. (*Ahmad*)

٤١ـ وَعَنْ عُثْمَانَ، رَضِىَ اللهُ عَنْهُ، قَالَ: إِنَّ رِجَالاً مِنْ أَصْحَابِ النَّبِيِّ
ﷺ حِينَ تُوُفِّىَ حَزِنُوا عَلَيْهِ، حَتَّى كَادَ بَعْضُهُمْ يُوَسْوِسُ قَالَ عُثْمَانُ:
وَكُنْتُ مِنْهُمْ، فَبَيْنَا أَنَا جَالِسٌ مَرَّ عَلَىَّ عُمَرُ، وَسَلَّمَ فَلَمْ أَشْعُرْ بِهِ،
فَاشْتَكَى عُمَرُ إِلَى أَبِى بَكْرٍ رَضِىَ اللهُ عَنْهُمَا، ثُمَّ أَقْبَلَا حَتَّى سَلَّمَا عَلَىَّ
جَمِيعًا، فَقَالَ أَبُوبَكْرٍ: مَا حَمَلَكَ عَلَى أَنْ لَا تَرُدَّ عَلَى أَخِيكَ عُمَرَ
سَلَامَهُ؟ قُلْتُ: مَا فَعَلْتُ. فَقَالَ عُمَرُ: بَلَى، وَاللهِ لَقَدْ فَعَلْتَ. قَالَ، قُلْتُ:
وَاللهِ مَا شَعُرْتُ أَتَّكَ مَرَرْتَ وَلَاسَلَّمْتَ قَالَ أَبُوبَكْرٍ: صَدَقَ عُثْمَانُ.
قَدْ شَغَلَكَ عَنْ ذَلِكَ أَمْرٌ. فَقُلْتُ: أَجَلْ قَالَ: مَا هُوَ؟ قُلْتُ: تَوَفَّى اللهُ
تَعَالَى نَبِيَّهُ ﷺ قَبْلَ أَنْ تَسْأَلَهُ عَنْ نَجَاةِ هَذَا الْأَمْرِ. قَالَ أَبُوبَكْرٍ
قَدْ سَأَلْتُهُ عَنْ ذَلِكَ. فَقُمْتُ إِلَيْهِ وَقُلْتُ لَهُ: بِأَبِى أَنْتَ وَأُمِّى أَنْتَ
أَحَقُّ بِهَا. قَالَ أَبُوبَكْرٍ: قُلْتُ يَا رَسُولَ اللهِ مَا نَجَاةُ هَذَا الْأَمْرِ؟ فَقَالَ
رَسُولُ اللهِ ﷺ "مَنْ قَبِلَ مِنِّى الْكَلِمَةَ الَّتِى عَرَضْتُ عَلَى عَمِّى فَرَدَّهَا،
فَهِىَ لَهُ نَجَاةٌ" رَوَاهُ أَحْمَدُ.

41 'Uthman (Allah be pleased with him) reported that when the Holy Prophet (peace and blessings of Allah be upon him) died, some of his companions were so much aggrieved (at his death) that they were disposed to doubts. 'Uthman said : I was one amongst them. While I was sitting there happened to pass by me 'Umar and he offered me salutation which I did not take notice of. 'Umar (may Allah be pleased with him) made a complaint of that to Abu Bakr (may Allah be pleased with him). Then both of them came and offered me salutation and Abu Bakr said: What prompted you that you did not respond the salutation of your brother, 'Umar. I said: I never did that. 'Umar said: By Allah, you of course did that. I said: By Allah I did not perceive that you passed by me and paid salutation. Abu Bakr said: 'Uthman is speaking the truth and something must have absorbed your mind (that you did not take notice of this matter). I said: Yes it is so. He said: What is that? He said: Allah has taken away His Prophet (peace and blessings of Allah be upon him) before we asked him how we could free ourselves from the snares of the world and the devil. Abu Bakr said: I did ask about that. So I got near to him and said to him: May my father and mother be taken as ransom for you and you were the worthiest to ask. Thereupon Abu Bakr said: I said to Allah's Messenger (peace and blessings of Allah be upon him), how one could free oneself from the snares of the world and devil. Thereupon Allah's Messenger (peace and blessings of Allah be upon him) said: He who accepted from me the word that I presented to my uncle and he rejected it for him is the freedom (from them) (Affirmation of the Oneness of Allah and the Apostlehood of Muhammad). (*Ahmad*)

٤٢ - وَعَنِ الْمِقْدَادِ، أَنَّهُ سَمِعَ رَسُولَ اللهِ ﷺ يَقُولُ: "لَا يَبْقَى عَلَى ظَهْرِ
الْأَرْضِ بَيْتُ مَدَرٍ وَّ لَا وَبَرٍ إِلَّا أَدْخَلَهُ اللهُ كَلِمَةَ الْإِسْلَامِ، بِعِزِّ عَزِيزٍ
وَّذُلِّ ذَلِيلٍ، إِمَّا يُعِزُّهُمُ اللهُ فَيَجْعَلُهُمْ مِنْ أَهْلِهَا، أَوْ يُـذِلُّـهُـمْ
فَيَدِينُونَ لَهَا". قُلْتُ: فَيَكُونُ الدِّينُ كُلُّهُ لِلّهِ. رَوَاهُ أَحْمَدُ.

42 Miqdad (Allah be pleased with him) reported that he heard Allah's Messenger (peace and blessings of Allah be upon him) as saying: There will not remain upon the surface of the earth a mud brick-house or a camel's hair tent but Allah will penetrate in that the word of Islam bringing both mighty honour and abject humiliation. Allah will either honour them by making them worthy of it and those whom He humiliates, shall have to render submission to it. I said: The religion will then be entirely for Allah. (*Ahmad*)

٤٣ - وَعَنْ وَهْبِ بْنِ مُنَبِّهٍ، قِيلَ لَهُ: أَلَيْسَ لَآ إِلٰهَ إِلَّا اللهُ مِفْتَاحُ الْجَنَّةِ؟
قَالَ: بَلَى، وَلَيْسَ مِفْتَاحٌ إِلَّا وَلَهُ أَسْنَانٌ، فَإِنْ جِئْتَ بِمِفْتَاحٍ لَهُ
أَسْنَانٌ فُتِحَ لَكَ، وَإِلَّا لَمْ يُفْتَحْ لَكَ. رَوَاهُ الْبُخَارِيُّ فِي تَرْجَمَةِ بَابٍ

43 Wahb b. Munabbih reported that it was said to him: Is this a fact that the (*Kalima*): There is no god but Allah is the key to Paradise. He said: Yes, but there is no key which has no wards. If you bring a key with wards (adjusting to the inner structure of the lock) it will open for you otherwise it will not. (*Bukhari transmitted it in a chapter heading*)

٤٤ ـ وَعَنْ أَبِى هُرَيْرَةَ (رَضِىَ اللهُ عَنْهُ ، قَالَ : قَالَ رَسُولُ اللهِ ﷺ " إِذَا أَحْسَنَ أَحَدُكُمْ إِسْلَامَهُ ، فَكُلُّ حَسَنَةٍ يَعْمَلُهَا تُكْتَبُ لَهُ بِعَشْرِ أَمْثَالِهَا إِلَى سَبْعِ مِائَةِ ضِعْفٍ ، وَكُلُّ سَيِّئَةٍ يَعْمَلُهَا تُكْتَبُ بِمِثْلِهَا حَتَّى لَقِىَ اللهَ : مُتَّفَقٌ عَلَيْهِ

44 Abu Huraira (Allah be pleased with him) reported Allah's Messenger (peace and blessings of Allah be upon him) as saying: If one amongst you is good in Islam all the good deeds which he would do would be recorded for him ten to seven hundred times and evil that he will commit would be recorded as it is till he meets Allah. (*Agreed upon*)

٤٥ ـ وَعَنْ أَبِى أُمَامَةَ (رَضِىَ اللهُ عَنْهُ) ، أَنَّ رَجُلاً سَأَلَ رَسُولَ اللهِ ﷺ مَا الإِيمَانُ ؟ قَالَ : إِذَا سَرَّتْكَ حَسَنَتُكَ ، وَسَاءَتْكَ سَيِّئَتُكَ ؛ فَأَنْتَ مُؤْمِنٌ ؛ قَالَ : يَا رَسُولَ اللهِ ! فَمَا الإِثْمُ ؟ قَالَ " إِذَا حَاكَ فِى نَفْسِكَ شَىْءٌ فَدَعْهُ " . رَوَاهُ أَحْمَدُ .

45 Abu Umama reported that a person asked Allah's Messenger (peace and blessings of Allah be upon him): What is faith? He said: When good deed becomes a source of pleasure for you and evil deed becomes a source of disgust for you then you are a believer. He again said Allah's Messenger: What is a sin? Whereupon he said: When something pricks thy conscience, give it up. (*Ahmad*)

٤٦ - وَعَنْ عَمْرِو بْنِ عَبَسَةَ رَضِىَ اللهُ عَنْهُ، قَالَ : أَتَيْتُ رَسُوْلَ اللهِ
ﷺ فَقُلْتُ : يَا رَسُوْلَ اللهِ! مَنْ مَعَكَ عَلَى هٰذَا الْأَمْرِ؟ قَالَ: "حُرٌّ وَعَبْدٌ"
قُلْتُ : مَا الْإِسْلَامُ؟ قَالَ: "طِيْبُ الْكَلَامِ، وَ إِطْعَامُ الطَّعَامِ" قُلْتُ : مَا
الْإِيْمَانُ؟ قَالَ: "أَلصَّبْرُ وَالسَّمَاحَةُ" قَالَ : قُلْتُ : أَىُّ الْإِسْلَامِ أَفْضَلُ؟
قَالَ: "مَنْ سَلِمَ الْمُسْلِمُوْنَ مِنْ لِّسَانِهِ وَ يَدِهِ" قَالَ : قُلْتُ : أَىُّ الْإِيْمَانِ
أَفْضَلُ؟ قَالَ: "خُلُقٌ حَسَنٌ" قَالَ : قُلْتُ : أَىُّ الصَّلَاةِ أَفْضَلُ؟ قَالَ: "طُوْلُ
الْقُنُوْتِ" قَالَ : قُلْتُ : أَىُّ الْهِجْرَةِ أَفْضَلُ؟ قَالَ : أَنْ تَهْجُرَ مَا كَرِهَ رَبُّكَ"
قَالَ : فَقُلْتُ فَأَىُّ الْجِهَادِ أَفْضَلُ؟ قَالَ: "مَنْ عُقِرَ جَوَادُهُ وَأُهْرِيْقَ دَمُهُ"
قَالَ : قُلْتُ : أَىُّ السَّاعَاتِ أَفْضَلُ؟ قَالَ جَوْفُ اللَّيْلِ الْاٰخِرُ" رَوَاهُ أَحْمَدُ

46 'Amr b. 'Abasa (may Allah be pleased with him) reported: I came to Allah's Messenger (peace and blessings of Allah be upon him) and said to him: Allah's Messenger, who are with you in this (sacred) mission? He said: A freeman and slave.[1] I said: What is Islam? He said: Pleasant talk and serving of food. I said: What is *Iman*? He said: Endurance and benevolence. I said: Which Islam is excellent? He said: One who safeguards a Muslim against (aggression) of his tongue, and hand. I said: Which faith is excellent? He said: Amiable disposition. I said: Which prayer is excellent? He said: Standing for a long time in humility (and devotion). I said: Which migration is excellent? He said: One by which you abandon which your Lord dislikes. I said: Which *jihad* (fighting in the way of Allah) is excellent? He said: (In which) one gets one's steed wounded and his blood is shed. I said: Which hour is most excellent? He said: The fag end of the darkest part of night. (*Ahmad*)

1. Freeman implies Ḥaḍrat Abu Bakr Siddiq and the slave implies Ḥaḍrat Bilal (may Allah be pleased with them).

٤٧- وَعَنْ مُعَاذِ بْنِ جَبَلٍ ، رَضِيَ اللهُ عَنْهُ ، قَالَ : سَمِعْتُ رَسُوْلَ اللهِ ۝
يَقُوْلُ : مَنْ لَقِيَ اللهَ لَا يُشْرِكُ بِهِ شَيْئًا ، وَيُصَلِّي الْخَمْسَ ، وَيَصُوْمُ رَمَضَانَ ؟
غُفِرَلَهُ ، قُلْتُ : أَفَلَا أُبَشِّرُهُمْ يَا رَسُوْلَ اللهِ ؟ قَالَ : دَعْهُمْ يَعْمَلُوْا ، رَوَاهُ أَحْمَدُ

47 Mu'adh b. Jabal (Allah be pleased with him) reported: I heard Allah's Messenger (peace and blessings of Allah be upon him) as saying: He who would meet Allah (in the state) that he has not associated anything with Him and he has offered five (daily prayers) and observed the fast of Ramaḍan he would be pardoned. I said: Allah's Messenger, should I not convey this happy news to them (to the Muslims). He said: Let them go on doing good deeds. *(Ahmad)*

٤٨- وَعَنْهُ أَنَّهُ سَأَلَ النَّبِيَّ ۝ عَنْ أَفْضَلِ الْإِيْمَانِ ؛ قَالَ : أَنْ تُحِبَّ لِلّهِ ، وَ
تُبْغِضَ لِلّهِ ، وَ تُعْمِلَ لِسَانَكَ فِيْ ذِكْرِ اللهِ ؛ قَالَ : وَمَاذَا يَا رَسُوْلَ اللهِ ؟ قَالَ :
وَأَنْ تُحِبَّ لِلنَّاسِ مَا تُحِبُّ لِنَفْسِكَ ، وَتَكْرَهَ لَهُمْ مَا تَكْرَهُ لِنَفْسِكَ ، رَوَاهُ أَحْمَدُ

48 It is reported on the same authority that he (Mu'adh b. Jabal) asked Allah's Messenger (peace and blessings of Allah be upon him) as to which faith is excellent. He said: That you love (any person or thing) for the sake of Allah and hate for the sake of Allah that you keep your tongue busy in the remembrance of Allah. He said: Allah's Messenger, is there any thing besides this? He said: You like for the people what you like for yourself, and you dislike for them what you dislike for yourself. *(Ahmad)*

———————◄●►———————

CHAPTER 2
PERTAINING TO MAJOR SINS AND THE CHARACTERISTICS OF HYPOCRISY[1]

Section I   اَلْفَصْلُ الْأَوَّلُ

1. The word *Nifaq* which we have translated as hypocrisy is derived from *nafaqa* and the word *an-nafaq* means a tunnel which has its both sides open. It is mentioned in the Quran:
Then seek out if you can build a tunnel or a passway into the earth. (6 : 35).
In the religious terminology *nifaq* means to profess a thing and act contrary to that. *Nifaq* is of two types: (1) *Nifaq fil-i'tiqad* and (2) *Nifaq fil-'amal*. *Nifaq fil-i'tiqad* is that one makes a declaration of one's *Iman* in public but does not believe it from the heart. *Nifaq fil-'amal* implies that whatever man professes he does not put it into practice. In the words of Hasan Basari *Nifaq fil-'amal* is the name of dissemblance between inner and the outer life of a man, *i.e.*, in his beliefs and his practices.

٢٩ ـ عَنْ عَبْدِ اللهِ بْنِ مَسْعُودٍ ، رَضِيَ اللهُ عَنْهُ ، قَالَ : قَالَ رَجُلٌ : يَا
رَسُولَ اللهِ ! أَىُّ الذَّنْبِ أَكْبَرُ عِنْدَ اللهِ ؟ قَالَ : أَنْ تَدْعُوَ لِلهِ نِدًّا
وَهُوَ خَلَقَكَ : قَالَ : ثُمَّ أَىُّ ؟ قَالَ : أَنْ تَقْتُلَ وَلَدَكَ خَشْيَةَ أَنْ
يَطْعَمَ مَعَكَ : قَالَ : ثُمَّ أَىُّ ؟ قَالَ : أَنْ تَزْنِىَ حَلِيلَةَ جَارِكَ : فَأَنْزَلَ
اللهُ تَعَالَى ، تَصْدِيقَهَا : وَالَّذِينَ لَا يَدْعُونَ مَعَ اللهِ إِلَهًا أَخَرَ ، وَلَا
يَقْتُلُونَ النَّفْسَ الَّتِى حَرَّمَ اللهُ إِلَّا بِالْحَقِّ وَلَا يَزْنُونَ ، الْآيَةَ . مُتَّفَقٌ عَلَيْهِ،

49 **'Abdullah b. Mas'ud** (may Allah be pleased with him) reported that a person said: Allah's Messenger, which sin is most grievous in the eye of Allah. He said that you hold anyone as compeer with Allah (despite of the fact that He has created you). He said: Then what ? He (the Holy Prophet) said: That you kill your child fearing that he would share food with you. He said: Then what ? He said that you commit adultery with the wife of your neighbour.[1] Then Allah, the Exalted testifies it with this verse:
"Those who call not another god along with Allah and slay not any soul which Allah has forbidden except in the case

of justice nor commit fornication and he who does this shall commit a requital of sin." (**25**: 68). (*Agreed upon*)

1. Adultery is in itself is a very grave offence, but it is mortally grave when it is committed with the wife of a neighbour. A person can justly expect goodness and sense of security from his neighbour; what an enormous crime it is that a neighbour who has to serve as the protector of the honour of the other neighbour lays his hand on his wife.

٥٠ ـ وَعَنْ عَبْدِ اللهِ بْنِ عَمْرٍو، قَالَ: قَالَ رَسُولُ اللهِ ﷺ: "اَلْكَبَائِرُ: اَلْإِشْرَاكُ بِاللهِ، وَعُقُوقُ الْوَالِدَيْنِ، وَقَتْلُ النَّفْسِ، وَالْيَمِينُ الْغَمُوسُ" رَوَاهُ الْبُخَارِيُّ.

50 'Abdullah b. 'Amr reported: Allah's Messenger (peace and blessings of Allah be upon him) having said: Amongst the grievous sins are associating anything with Allah, disobedience to parents, killing a person and deliberate perjury.

(*Bukhari*)

٥١ ـ وَفِي رِوَايَةٍ لِأَنَسٍ: "وَشَهَادَةُ الزُّورِ" بَدَلَ: "الْيَمِينُ الْغَمُوسُ" مُتَّفَقٌ عَلَيْهِ.

51 Anas in another version has reported: Bearing false witness (*shahadat al-zur*) instead of 'deliberate perjury'. (*Agreed upon*)

٥٢ ـ وَعَنْ أَبِي هُرَيْرَةَ، قَالَ: قَالَ رَسُولُ اللهِ ﷺ: "إِجْتَنِبُوا السَّبْعَ الْمُوبِقَاتِ" قَالُوا: يَا رَسُولَ اللهِ وَمَا هُنَّ؟ قَالَ: "اَلشِّرْكُ بِاللهِ، وَالسِّحْرُ، وَقَتْلُ النَّفْسِ الَّتِي حَرَّمَ اللهُ إِلَّا بِالْحَقِّ، وَأَكْلُ الرِّبَا، وَأَكْلُ مَالِ الْيَتِيمِ، وَالتَّوَلِّي يَوْمَ الزَّحْفِ، وَقَذْفُ الْمُحْصَنَاتِ الْمُؤْمِنَاتِ الْغَافِلَاتِ" مُتَّفَقٌ عَلَيْهِ.

52 Abu Huraira reported: Allah's Messenger (peace and blessings of Allah be upon him) having said: Shun seven mortally grave sins. They (the Companions) said: Allah's Messenger, what are those? He said: Associating anything with Allah, practising of magic, killing of a person, whom Allah has declared inviolate without just cause, consuming of interest and misappropriating the property of an orphan, turning back (upon one's heel) when the army advances and slandering chaste believing women who are unwary.[1] (*Agreed upon*)

1. The term *al-mohsanatul mominatul-ghafelat* means that they know nothing about the indecent and obscene acts. They are much absorbed in their own work that are unware of the mud-slinging of the mischief-mongers.

٥٣ـ وَعَنْهُ، قَالَ: قَالَ رَسُولُ اللهِ ﷺ: "لَا يَزْنِي الزَّانِي حِينَ يَزْنِي وَ هُوَ مُؤْمِنٌ، وَلَا يَسْرِقُ السَّارِقُ حِينَ يَسْرِقُ وَ هُوَ مُؤْمِنٌ، وَلَا يَشْرَبُ الْخَمْرَ حِينَ يَشْرَبُهَا وَ هُوَ مُؤْمِنٌ، وَلَا يَنْتَهِبُ نُهْبَةً يَرْفَعُ النَّاسُ إِلَيْهِ فِيهَا أَبْصَارَهُمْ حِينَ يَنْتَهِبُهَا وَهُوَ مُؤْمِنٌ، وَلَا يَغُلُّ أَحَدُكُمْ حِينَ يَغُلُّ وَ هُوَ مُؤْمِنٌ؛ فَإِيَّاكُمْ إِيَّاكُمْ". مُتَّفَقٌ عَلَيْهِ.

53 Abu Huraira reported Allah's Messenger (peace and blessings of Allah be upon him) as saying: No fornicator commits fornication in the state of being a believer so long as he is busy in committing it. No thief commits theft in the state of being a believer so long as he commits this (sin). No drunkard drinks in the state of being a believer so long as he is busy in drinking. No plunderer plunders something which can attract the eyes of the people, is a believer as long he is busy in the act of plundering and none of you defrauds in the state of being a believer so long as you are busy in defrauding, so shun them. (*Agreed upon*)

٥٤ـ وَفِي رِوَايَةِ ابْنِ عَبَّاسٍ: "وَلَا يَقْتُلُ حِينَ يَقْتُلُ وَهُوَ مُؤْمِنٌ". قَالَ عِكْرِمَةُ: قُلْتُ لِابْنِ عَبَّاسٍ: كَيْفَ يُنْزَعُ الْإِيمَانُ مِنْهُ، قَالَ هَكَذَا، وَ شَبَّكَ بَيْنَ أَصَابِعِهِ ثُمَّ أَخْرَجَهَا، فَإِنْ تَابَ عَادَ إِلَيْهِ هَكَذَا، وَشَبَّكَ بَيْنَ أَصَابِعِهِ. وَقَالَ أَبُو عَبْدِ اللهِ: لَا يَكُونُ هَذَا مُؤْمِنًا تَامًّا، وَلَا يَكُونُ لَهُ نُورُ الْإِيمَانِ. هَذَا لَفْظُ الْبُخَارِيِّ.

54 In the narration transmitted on the authority of Ibn 'Abbas (the words) are: And anyone who kills is not a believer as long as he is busy in killing. 'Ikrima reported (I asked Ibn

'Abbas): How the faith can be snatched away from him. He said: Thus, and he interlaced his fingers and then separated them and added: If he repents it would return to him like this and he then interlaced his fingers. Abu 'Abdullah (the Kunaya) of Imam Bukhari said: Such a one is not a perfect believer and there is not the light of faith in him. (*Bukhari*)

٥٥ ـ وَعَنْ أَبِى هُرَيْرَةَ ، قَالَ ، قَالَ رَسُولُ اللهِ ﷺ : "آيَةُ الْمُنَافِقِ ثَلَاثٌ ،
زَادَ مُسْلِمٌ ، وَ إِنْ صَامَ وَصَلَّى وَ زَعَمَ أَنَّهُ مُسْلِمٌ ، ثُمَّ اتَّفَقَا "إِذَا حَدَّثَ
كَذَبَ ، وَ إِذَا وَعَدَ أَخْلَفَ ، وَ إِذَا اؤْتُمِنَ خَانَ ،"

55 Abu Huraira reported Allah's Messenger (peace and blessings of Allah be upon him) as saying: Three are the distinguishing marks of a hypocrite. *Muslim* added: Even if he fasts and prays and makes a claim of being a Muslim. Thereafter both *Bukhari* and *Muslim* said: Whenever he would speak he would tell a lie, whenever he makes a promise he would break it and whenever he is trusted he betrays a trust.

٥٦ ـ وَعَنْ عَبْدِ اللهِ بْنِ عَمْرٍو ، قَالَ : قَالَ رَسُولُ اللهِ ﷺ : "أَرْبَعٌ مَّنْ كُنَّ
فِيـهِ كَانَ مُنَافِقًا خَالِصًا ، وَ مَنْ كَانَتْ فِيهِ خَصْلَةٌ مِنْهُنَّ كَانَتْ فِيْهِ
خَصْلَةٌ مِّنَ النِّفَاقِ حَتَّى يَدَعَهَا : إِذَا اؤْتُمِنَ خَانَ ، وَ إِذَا حَدَّثَ كَذَبَ ،
وَ إِذَا عَاهَدَ غَدَرَ ، وَ إِذَا خَاصَمَ فَجَرَ" مُتَّفَقٌ عَلَيْهِ .

56 'Abdullah b. 'Amr reported Allah's Messenger (peace and blessings of Allah be upon him) having said: Four are the characteristics which if found in one would make him a sheer hypocrite and one who possesses one of them possesses a characteristic of hypocrisy, till he abandons it. When he is trusted, he betrays trust; when he speaks, he lies and when he makes a covenant, he acts treacherously and when he falls out he deviates from the path of truth.[1] (*Agreed upon*)

> 1. Fajara is generally translated as he used abusive language but Imam Nawawi has translated it as *Mala 'Anil Haq*. He deviated from the truth.

٥٤ـ وَعَنِ ابْنِ عُمَرَ، قَالَ: قَالَ رَسُولُ اللهِ ﷺ: مَثَلُ الْمُنَافِقِ كَالشَّاةِ الْعَائِرَةِ بَيْنَ الْغَنَمَيْنِ تَعِيرُ إِلَى هٰذِهِ مَرَّةً وَ إِلَى هٰذِهِ مَرَّةً. رَوَاهُ مُسْلِمٌ.

57 Ibn 'Umar reported Allah's Messenger (peace and blessings of Allah be upon him) having said: The example of a hypocrite is that of a roaring ewe between two flocks. It turns at one time to one and at another time to the other. (*Muslim*)

Section II   أَلْفَصْلُ الثَّانِى

٥٨ـ عَنْ صَفْوَانَ بْنِ عَسَّالٍ، قَالَ: قَالَ يَهُودِىٌّ لِصَاحِبِهِ: إِذْهَبْ بِنَا إِلَى هٰذَا النَّبِىِّ ﷺ. فَقَالَ لَهُ صَاحِبُهُ: لَا تَقُلْ: نَبِىٌّ، إِنَّهُ لَوْ سَمِعَكَ كَانَ لَهُ أَرْبَعُ أَعْيُنٍ. فَأَتَيَا رَسُولَ اللهِ ﷺ، فَسَأَلَاهُ عَنْ تِسْعِ آيَاتٍ بَيِّنَاتٍ، فَقَالَ رَسُولُ اللهِ ﷺ: لَا تُشْرِكُوا بِاللهِ شَيْئًا، وَلَا تَسْرِقُوا، وَلَا تَزْنُوا، وَلَا تَقْتُلُوا النَّفْسَ الَّتِى حَرَّمَ اللهُ إِلَّا بِالْحَقِّ، وَلَا تَمْشُوا بِبَرِىءٍ إِلَى ذِى سُلْطَانٍ لِيَقْتُلَهُ، وَلَا تَسْحَرُوا، وَلَا تَأْكُلُوا الرِّبَا، وَلَا تَقْذِفُوا مُحْصَنَةً، وَلَا تُوَلُّوا لِلْفِرَارِ يَوْمَ الزَّحْفِ، وَعَلَيْكُمْ خَاصَّةً ـ الْيَهُودُ ـ أَنْ لَا تَعْتَدُوا فِى السَّبْتِ. قَالَ: فَقَبَّلَا يَدَيْهِ وَ رِجْلَيْهِ، وَقَالَا: نَشْهَدُ أَنَّكَ نَبِىٌّ. قَالَ: فَمَا يَمْنَعُكُمْ أَنْ تَتَّبِعُونِى؟ قَالَا: إِنَّ دَاوُدَ عَلَيْهِ السَّلَامُ دَعَا رَبَّهُ أَنْ لَا يَزَالَ مِنْ ذُرِّيَّتِهِ نَبِىٌّ، وَ إِنَّا نَخَافُ إِنْ تَبِعْنَاكَ أَنْ تَقْتُلَنَا الْيَهُودُ. رَوَاهُ التِّرْمِذِىُّ، وَ أَبُودَاوُدَ، وَ النَّسَائِىُّ.

58 Safwan b. 'Assal reported that a Jew said to his friend: Let us go to this Prophet (peace and blessings of Allah be upon him); but his friend said to him: Don't call him Prophet for if he would hear you (saying this) he would feel delighted. So they however came to Allah's Messenger (peace and blessings of Allah be upon him) and asked him about nine clear commandments revealed to Moses. Allah's Messenger (peace and blessings of Allah be upon him) said : Associate not anything

with Allah, don't steal, don't commit fornication, and don't kill
the soul whom Allah has declared inviolate but with just cause
and don't take an innocent person before the man of authority
(to a tyrant ruler) so that he may kill him. Don't practise
magic, don't take interest and do not slander the chaste
women and do not flee in the battle-field and this is particularly
for you, the Jews, that you don't transgress the Sabbath. They
kissed his hands and feet and said: We bear testimony to the
fact that you are a Prophet. Thereupon he (the Holy
Prophet) said: What prevents you from following me. They
said: David (peace be upon him) prayed to His Lord that the
Prophets might never cease to arise but from his posterity and
we fear that if we follow you the Jews may kill us.

(*Tirmidhi, Abu Dawud and Nasa'i*)

٥٩ - وَعَنْ أَنَسٍ، قَالَ، قَالَ رَسُولُ اللهِ ﷺ "ثَلَاثٌ مِنْ أَصْلِ الْإِيمَانِ :
أَلْكَفُّ عَمَّنْ قَالَ : لَآ إِلٰهَ إِلَّا اللهُ، لَا تُكَفِّرْهُ بِذَنْبٍ، وَلَا تُخْرِجُهُ مِنَ
الْإِسْلَامِ بِعَمَلٍ. وَالْجِهَادُ مَاضٍ مُنْذُ بَعَثَنِيَ اللهُ إِلَى أَنْ يُقَاتِلَ اٰخِرُ هٰذِهِ
الْأُمَّةِ الدَّجَّالَ، لَا يُبْطِلُهُ جَوْرُ جَائِرٍ، وَلَا عَدْلُ عَادِلٍ. وَ الْإِيمَانُ
بِالْأَقْدَارِ" رَوَاهُ أَبُوْدَاوُدَ.

59 **Anas** reported that Allah's Messenger (peace and blessings of
Allah be upon him) said: Three are the things pertaining to
the basis of faith and these are: Abstaining from laying one's
hand on one who says there is no god but Allah; not labelling
one as a disbeliever because of a sinful act (committed by
him) and not turning out one from the fold of Islam because
of his deeds. *Jihad* (striving in the way of Allah) must continue for ever since Allah sent me till the last (man) of this
Ummah would fight against Dajjal. It would not be annulled
by the tyranny of a tyrant nor the justice of a just one and
belief in the Divine Decree. (*Abu Dawud*)

٦٠ - وَعَنْ أَبِيْ هُرَيْرَةَ، قَالَ، قَالَ رَسُولُ اللهِ ﷺ "إِذَا زَنَى الْعَبْدُ خَرَجَ
مِنْهُ الْإِيمَانُ، فَكَانَ فَوْقَ رَأْسِهِ كَالظُّلَّةِ، فَإِذَا خَرَجَ مِنْ ذٰلِكَ الْعَمَلِ
رَجَعَ إِلَيْهِ الْإِيمَانُ" رَوَاهُ التِّرْمِذِيُّ، وَأَبُوْدَاوُدَ.

60 Abu Huraira reported : When a person commits fornication there goes out of him the faith and hovers like an awning over his head and when he quits this act the faith reverts to him again. (*Tirmidhi and Abu Dawud*)

Section III اَلْفَصْلُ الثَّالِثُ

٦١ ـ عَنْ مُعَاذٍ، قَالَ: أَوْصَانِى رَسُولُ اللهِ ﷺ بِعَشْرِ كَلِمَاتٍ، قَالَ: "لَا تُشْرِكْ بِاللهِ شَيْئًا وَ إِنْ قُتِلْتَ وَ حُرِّقْتَ، وَلَا تَعُقَّنَّ وَالِدَيْكَ وَ إِنْ أَمَرَاكَ أَنْ تَخْرُجَ مِنْ أَهْلِكَ وَ مَالِكَ، وَلَا تَتْرُكَنَّ صَلَاةً مَكْتُوبَةً مُتَعَمِّدًا؛ فَإِنَّ مَنْ تَرَكَ صَلَاةً مَكْتُوبَةً مُتَعَمِّدًا فَقَدْ بَرِئَتْ مِنْهُ ذِمَّةُ اللهِ. وَلَا تَشْرَبَنَّ خَمْرًا فَإِنَّهُ رَأْسُ كُلِّ فَاحِشَةٍ، وَ إِيَّاكَ وَ الْمَعْصِيَةَ؛ فَإِنَّ بِالْمَعْصِيَةِ حَلَّ سَخَطُ اللهِ، وَ إِيَّاكَ وَ الْفِرَارَ مِنَ الزَّحْفِ وَ إِنْ هَلَكَ النَّاسُ، وَ إِذَا أَصَابَ النَّاسَ مَوْتٌ وَ أَنْتَ فِيهِمْ، فَاثْبُتْ، وَ أَنْفِقْ عَلَى عَيَالِكَ مِنْ طَوْلِكَ، وَ لَا تَرْفَعْ عَنْهُمْ عَصَاكَ أَدَبًا وَ أَخِفْهُمْ فِي اللهِ". رَوَاهُ أَحْمَدُ.

61 Mu'adh reported: Allah's Messenger (peace and blessings of Allah be upon him) instructed me to do ten things saying: Do not associate anything with Allah even if you are killed and burnt on that account. Don't be disobedient to your parents even if they command you to abandon your family and your property, and do not deliberately neglect to observe a prescribed prayer for he who neglects the prescribed prayer deliberately he will get out from the protection of Allah. Do not drink wine for it is the height of every obscenity and shun evil for with evil there descends the wrath of Allah. Beware of running away from the battle-field even if the people perish and the death overtakes them and you are one amongst them. Show steadfastness and spend on your children according to your means and do not refrain from using pressure with a view to training them and inculcating in them the fear of Allah. (*Ahmad*)

٦٢ - وَعَنْ حُذَيْفَةَ ، قَالَ : إِنَّمَا النِّفَاقُ كَانَ عَلَى عَهْدِ رَسُولِ اللهِ ﷺ ،

فَأَمَّا الْيَوْمَ ، فَإِنَّمَا هُوَ الْكُفْرُ ، أَوِ الْإِيمَانُ ، رَوَاهُ الْبُخَارِيُّ .

62 Hudhaifa reported: Hypocrisy was there during the life-time of Allah's Messenger (peace and blessings of Allah be upon him) whereas today there is only unbelief of faith. (*Bukhari*)

CHAPTER 3
PERTAINING TO EVIL SUGGESTIONS OR PROMPTINGS

Section I ٱلْفَصْلُ ٱلْأَوَّلُ

٦١ - عَنْ أَبِي هُرَيْرَةَ ، قَالَ : قَالَ رَسُولُ اللهِ ﷺ : "إِنَّ اللهَ ، تَعَالَى ، تَجَاوَزَ
عَنْ أُمَّتِي مَا وَسْوَسَتْ بِهِ صُدُورُهَا ، مَا لَمْ تَعْمَلْ بِهِ أَوْ تَتَكَلَّمْ"
مُتَّفَقٌ عَلَيْهِ .

63 Abu Huraira reported Allah's Messenger (peace and blessings of Allah be upon him) as saying: Verily Allah, the Exalted, would forgive my people the evil promptings which spring up in their hearts unless they act upon them or give utterance to them. (*Agreed upon*)

٦٢ - وَعَنْهُ ، قَالَ : جَاءَ نَاسٌ مِنْ أَصْحَابِ رَسُولِ اللهِ ﷺ إِلَى النَّبِيِّ ﷺ
فَسَأَلُوهُ : إِنَّا نَجِدُ فِي أَنْفُسِنَا مَا يَتَعَاظَمُ أَحَدُنَا أَنْ يَتَكَلَّمَ بِهِ ! قَالَ "أَوَ
قَدْ وَجَدْتُمُوهُ ؟" قَالُوا : نَعَمْ . قَالَ : "ذَاكَ صَرِيحُ الْإِيمَانِ" رَوَاهُ مُسْلِمٌ .

64 Abu Huraira reported that there came to Allah's Apostle (peace and blessings of Allah be upon him) (some people) from amongst the companions of Allah's Messenger (peace and blessings of Allah be upon him) and said: We perceived in our minds that which every one of us considers it too grave to be expressed. He (the Holy Prophet) said: Do you really perceive it. They said: Yes. Upon this he remarked: This is the faith manifest.[1] (*Muslim*)

1. The rankling of the evil thought indicates the birth of moral-self, the real basis of *Iman*.

٦٥ - وَعَنْهُ ، قَالَ : قَالَ رَسُولُ اللهِ ﷺ : "يَأْتِي الشَّيْطَانُ أَحَدَكُمْ ، فَيَقُولُ :
مَنْ خَلَقَ كَذَا ؛ مَنْ خَلَقَ كَذَا ؛ حَتَّى يَقُولَ : مَنْ خَلَقَ رَبَّكَ ؛ فَإِذَا بَلَغَهُ :
فَلْيَسْتَعِذْ بِاللهِ وَلْيَنْتَهِ" مُتَّفَقٌ عَلَيْهِ .

65 **Abu Huraira** reported Allah's Messenger (peace and blessings of Allah be upon him) as saying: (Sometimes) the Satan would come to one of you and would say: Who created that who created that, till he would say who created your Lord. When he comes to that one should seek réfuge with Allah and keep away from it. (*Agreed upon*)

٦٥ ـ وَعَنْهُ ، قَالَ : قَالَ رَسُولُ اللهِ ﷺ : " لَا يَزَالُ النَّاسُ يَتَسَاءَلُونَ حَتَّى
يُقَالَ : هَذَا خَلَقَ اللهُ الْخَلْقَ، فَمَنْ خَلَقَ اللهَ ؟ فَمَنْ وَجَدَ مِنْ ذَلِكَ شَيْئًا :
فَلْيَقُلْ : آمَنْتُ بِاللهِ وَرُسُلِهِ " مُتَّفَقٌ عَلَيْهِ .

66 **Abu Huraira** reported Allah's Messenger (peace and blessings of Allah be upon him) as saying: The people will continue to question one another till it would be said: Allah created all things but who created Allah. He who finds himself confronted with such a situation he should say: I affirm my faith in Allah and His Messenger. (*Agreed upon*)

٦٧ ـ وَعَنِ ابْنِ مَسْعُودٍ ، قَالَ : قَالَ رَسُولُ اللهِ ﷺ : " مَا مِنْكُمْ مِنْ أَحَدٍ
إِلَّا وَقَدْ وُكِّلَ بِهِ قَرِينُهُ مِنَ الْجِنِّ وَقَرِينُهُ مِنَ الْمَلَائِكَةِ " قَالُوا :
وَإِيَّاكَ يَا رَسُولَ اللهِ ؟ قَالَ ؛ وَإِيَّايَ ، وَلَكِنَّ اللهَ أَعَانَنِي عَلَيْهِ فَأَسْلَمَ فَلَا
يَأْمُرُنِي إِلَّا بِخَيْرٍ " رَوَاهُ مُسْلِمٌ .

67 **Ibn Mas'ud** reported: Allah's Messenger (peace and blessings of Allah be upon him) as saying: There is none amongst you who does not have his associate amongst the jinns and angels. They (the companions of the Holy Prophet) said: Allah's Messenger, for you, too He said: Yes for me also but Allah helped me against him and he accepted Islam so he does not command me but to do good. (*Muslim*)

٦٨ ـ وَعَنْ أَنَسٍ ، قَالَ : قَالَ رَسُولُ اللهِ ﷺ : " إِنَّ الشَّيْطَانَ يَجْرِى مِنَ
الْإِنْسَانِ مَجْرَى الدَّمِ " مُتَّفَقٌ عَلَيْهِ .

68 **Anas** reported Allah's Messenger (peace and blessings of Allah be upon him) as saying: Verily the Satan circulates in the body of a man like the circulation of blood. (*Agreed upon*)

٦٩ - وَعَنْ أَبِى هُرَيْرَةَ ، قَالَ : قَالَ رَسُولُ اللهِ ﷺ "مَا مِنْ بَنِى آدَمَ مَوْلُودٌ
إِلاَّ يَمَسُّهُ الشَّيْطَانُ حِينَ يُولَدُ ، فَيَسْتَهِلُّ صَارِخًا مِنْ مَسِّ الشَّيْطَانِ ،
غَيْرَ مَرْيَمَ وَابْنِهَا " مُتَّفَقٌ عَلَيْهِ .

69 Abu Huraira reported Allah's Messenger (peace and blessings
of Allah be upon him) as saying: There is none amongst the
sons of Adam who is born but not touched by the Satan at the
time of his birth. So he cries loudly because of Satan's touch.
But this is not the case with Mary and her son. (*Agreed upon*)

٧٠ - وَعَنْهُ ، قَالَ : قَالَ رَسُولُ اللهِ ﷺ "صِيَاحُ الْمَوْلُودِ حِينَ يَقَعُ نَزْغَةٌ
مِنَ الشَّيْطَانِ " مُتَّفَقٌ عَلَيْهِ .

70 Abu Huraira reported Allah's Messenger (peace and blessings
of Allah be upon him) as saying: The cry of an infant at the
moment of birth is due to the prick of the Satan. (*Agreed upon*)

٧١ - وَعَنْ جَابِرٍ ، قَالَ : قَالَ رَسُولُ اللهِ ﷺ "إِنَّ إِبْلِيسَ يَضَعُ عَرْشَهُ
عَلَى الْمَاءِ ، ثُمَّ يَبْعَثُ سَرَايَاهُ يَفْتِنُونَ النَّاسَ ، فَأَدْنَاهُمْ مِنْهُ مَنْزِلَةً
أَعْظَمُهُمْ فِتْنَةً . يَجِىءُ أَحَدُهُمْ فَيَقُولُ : فَعَلْتُ كَذَا وَكَذَا . فَيَقُولُ :
مَا صَنَعْتَ شَيْئًا . قَالَ : ثُمَّ يَجِىءُ أَحَدُهُمْ فَيَقُولُ : مَا تَرَكْتُهُ حَتَّى
فَرَّقْتُ بَيْنَهُ وَبَيْنَ امْرَأَتِهِ . قَالَ : فَيُدْنِيهِ مِنْهُ ، وَيَقُولُ : نِعْمَ أَنْتَ
قَالَ الْأَعْمَشُ : أُرَاهُ قَالَ "فَيَلْتَزِمُهُ " رَوَاهُ مُسْلِمٌ .

71 Jabir reported Allah's Messenger (peace and blessings of
Allah be upon him) as saying: Satan places his throne on the
water, then sends detachments (to different corners) with a
view to putting people to trial and the nearer to him in status
is one who is most expert in creating mischief. One would
come (amongst the followers of Satan) and say: I have done
so and so and he (Satan) would say: You have done nothing;
then another one amongst them would come and say: I did
not abandon my effort (in leading people astray) till I brought

about separation between him and his wife: and he would say:
Bring him near to himself saying : What a fine fellow you
are! A'mash said : I think that he said: He then embraces
him. (*Muslim*)

٧٢ - وَعَنْهُ ـ قَالَ : قَالَ رَسُولُ اللهِ ﷺ : "إِنَّ الشَّيْطَانَ قَدْ أَيِسَ مِنْ أَنْ يَعْبُدَهُ
الْمُصَلُّونَ فِي جَزِيرَةِ الْعَرَبِ، وَلَكِنْ فِي التَّحْرِيشِ بَيْنَهُمْ" رَوَاهُ مُسْلِمٌ.

72 He also reported Allah's Messenger (peace and blessings of
Allah be upon him) as saying: Verily the Satan is completely
disappointed that he would ever be worshipped in the land of
Arabia. But (he is hopeful) that he would be able to sow the
seed of dissension amongst them. (*Muslim*)

Section II　　　اَلْفَصْلُ الثَّانِى

٧٣ - عَنِ ابْنِ عَبَّاسٍ : أَنَّ النَّبِيَّ ﷺ جَاءَهُ رَجُلٌ ، فَقَالَ : إِنِّي أُحَدِّثُ
نَفْسِي بِالشَّيْءِ لَأَنْ أَكُونَ حُمَمَةً أَحَبُّ إِلَيَّ مِنْ أَنْ أَتَكَلَّمَ بِهِ . قَالَ :
"اَلْحَمْدُ للهِ الَّذِي رَدَّ أَمْرَهُ إِلَى الْوَسْوَسَةِ" رَوَاهُ أَبُو دَاوُدَ .

73 **Ibn 'Abbas** reported that a person came to Allah's Apostle
(peace and blessings of Allah be upon him) and said: There
occurs to my mind something that I prefer to be reduced to a
charcoal rather than express it. Thereupon he said: Allah be
praised Who turned this affair of his (that is the affair of a
Satan) to a mere evil suggestion. (*Abu Dawud*)

٧٤ - وَعَنِ ابْنِ مَسْعُودٍ ـ قَالَ : قَالَ رَسُولُ اللهِ ﷺ : "إِنَّ لِلشَّيْطَانِ لَمَّةً بِابْنِ
آدَمَ ، وَلِلْمَلَكِ لَمَّةً : فَأَمَّا لَمَّةُ الشَّيْطَانِ فَإِيعَادٌ بِالشَّرِّ ، وَتَكْذِيبٌ بِالْحَقِّ ،
وَأَمَّا لَمَّةُ الْمَلَكِ فَإِيعَادٌ بِالْخَيْرِ وَتَصْدِيقٌ بِالْحَقِّ . فَمَنْ وَجَدَ ذَلِكَ ؛
فَلْيَعْلَمْ أَنَّهُ مِنَ اللهِ ، فَلْيَحْمَدِ اللهَ وَمَنْ وَجَدَ الْأُخْرَى ؛ فَلْيَتَعَوَّذْ بِاللهِ مِنَ
الشَّيْطَانِ الرَّجِيمِ" ثُمَّ قَرَأَ :﴿الشَّيْطَانُ يَعِدُكُمُ الْفَقْرَ وَيَأْمُرُكُمْ
بِالْفَحْشَاءِ﴾ رَوَاهُ التِّرْمِذِيُّ ، وَقَالَ ، هَذَا حَدِيثٌ غَرِيبٌ .

74 Ibn Mas'ud reported: Allah's Messenger (peace and blessings of Allah be upon him) as saying: Satan exercises his influence upon the son of Adam and so does the angel exercise his influence (upon him). The influence of Satan is that he holds the promise of evil and denial of truth. And the influence of the angel is that he holds the promise of good and the affirmation of truth. He who perceives this (that is the promise of good and the affirmation of truth), he should understand that it is from God. He should praise Allah and he who finds contrary to it he should seek refuge with Allah from the Satan, the accursed. He then recited this verse:

"Satan threatens you with the prospect of poverty and bids you to be indecent" (**2 : 268**)

(*Trimidhi said : This is a gharib hadith*)

٧٥ ـ وَعَنْ أَبِي هُرَيْرَةَ، عَنْ رَسُولِ اللهِ ﷺ قَالَ : "لَا يَزَالُ النَّاسُ يَتَسَاءَلُونَ حَتَّى يُقَالَ : هٰذَا خَلَقَ اللهُ الْخَلْقَ، فَمَنْ خَلَقَ اللهَ؟ فَإِذَا قَالُوا ذَالِكَ فَقُولُوا : اللهُ أَحَدٌ، اللهُ الصَّمَدُ، لَمْ يَلِدْ وَلَمْ يُولَدْ، وَلَمْ يَكُنْ لَهُ كُفُواً أَحَدٌ، ثُمَّ لِيَنْفُلْ عَنْ يَسَارِهِ ثَلَاثًا، وَلْيَسْتَعِذْ بِاللهِ مِنَ الشَّيْطَانِ الرَّجِيمِ" رَوَاهُ أَبُو دَاوُدَ. وَسَنَذْكُرُ حَدِيثَ عَمْرِو بْنِ الْأَحْوَصِ فِي بَابِ خُطْبَةِ يَوْمِ النَّحْرِ إِنْ شَاءَ اللهُ تَعَالَى.

75 Abu Huraira reported Allah's Messenger (peace and blessings of Allah be upon him) as saying: People would never cease asking one another till they Would come to propound : It is Allah Who created the creation but Who created Allah and when they say this then you should say: Allah is One, Allah is Independent. He neither begot anyone and nor was begotten by anyone and none is like him. Then you should spit on the left side thrice and seek refuge with Allah from Satan, the accursed. (*Abu Dawud*)

We would, if Allah so wills, make a mention of the *hadith* transmitted on the authority of 'Amr b. al-Aḥwas in the chapter of the *sermon on the day of sacrifice.*

Section III   اَلْفَصْلُ الثَّالِثُ

٧٦ ـ عَنْ أَنَسٍ، قَالَ: قَالَ رَسُوْلُ اللهِ ﷺ: "لَنْ يَبْرَحَ النَّاسُ يَتَسَاءَلُوْنَ
حَتّى يَقُوْلُوْا: هذَا اللهُ خَلَقَ كُلَّ شَيْءٍ، فَمَنْ خَلَقَ اللهَ عَزَّ وَجَلَّ؟"
رَوَاهُ الْبُخَارِيُّ وَلِمُسْلِمٍ، قَالَ: قَالَ اللهُ عَزَّ وَجَلَّ: إِنَّ أُمَّتَكَ لَا
يَزَالُوْنَ يَقُوْلُوْنَ: مَاكَذَا؟ مَاكَذَا؟ حَتّى يَقُوْلُوْا: هذَا اللهُ خَلَقَ
الْخَلْقَ، فَمَنْ خَلَقَ اللهَ عَزَّ وَجَلَّ؟"

76 Anas reported: Allah's Messenger (peace and blessings of
Allah be upon him) as saying: People would continue asking
one another till they would come to say: It is Allah who
created everything but who created Allah, the Exalted and
Glorious, (Reported by *Bukhari* and the words in the *Muslim*
are): Allah the Glorious and Exalted said: Verily your *Ummah*
would never cease saying: What is this, what is this till they
would come to say: It is Allah Who created the creation but
who created Allah, the Exalted, and Glorious.

٧٧ ـ وَعَنْ عُثْمَانَ بْنِ أَبِي الْعَاصِ، قَالَ: قُلْتُ: يَا رَسُوْلَ اللهِ إِنَّ الشَّيْطَانَ
قَدْ حَالَ بَيْنِي وَبَيْنَ صَلَاتِي وَبَيْنَ قِرَآءَتِي يَلْبِسُهَا عَلَيَّ، فَقَالَ رَسُوْلُ
اللهِ ﷺ: "ذَاكَ شَيْطَانٌ يُقَالُ لَهُ خِنْزَبٌ، فَإِذَا أَحْسَسْتَهُ فَتَعَوَّذْ بِاللهِ
مِنْهُ، وَاتْفُلْ عَلَى يَسَارِكَ ثَلَاثًا" فَفَعَلْتُ ذلِكَ فَأَذْهَبَهُ اللهُ عَنِّي
رَوَاهُ مُسْلِمٌ.

77 'Uthman b. Abu al-'As reported: I said: Allah's Messenger,
Verily the Satan intervenes between me and my prayer and
my recitation and it confounds me. Thereupon Allah's
Messenger (peace and blessings of Allah be upon him) said:
That is Satan who is called as Khinzab so when you perceive
him (his presence) then seek refuge with Allah from him and
spit on your left side thrice. I did this myself and Allah
removed him from me. (*Muslim*)

٧٨ ـ وَعَنِ الْقَاسِمِ بِنِ مُحَمَّدٍ : أَنَّ رَجُلًا سَأَلَهُ فَقَالَ : إِنِّي أَهِمُّ فِي صَلَاتِي
تَيَكْثُرُ ذَلِكَ عَلَيَّ ، فَقَالَ لَهُ : إِمْضِ فِي صَلَاتِكَ ، فَإِنَّهُ لَنْ يَذْهَبَ ذَلِكَ
عَنْكَ حَتَّى تَنْصَرِفَ وَ أَنْتَ تَقُولُ : مَا أَتْمَمْتُ صَلَاتِي ۖ رَوَاهُ مَالِكٌ ·

78 Qasim b. Muhammad reported that a person asked him (the
Holy Prophet) saying: I am much troubled with doubt during
prayer and this thing hangs heavy upon me; thereupon he
(the Holy Prophet) said to him: You should remain busy with
your prayer for it would never remove from you till you have
finished your prayer and you have uttered these words: I
have not performed my prayer perfectly. (*Malik*)

بَابُ الإِيمَانِ بِالقَدَرِ

Kitab-ul-Qadr
(BOOK OF DESTINY)

CHAPTER 4

FAITH IN THE DIVINE DECREE

Before reading the *ahadith* recorded under Faith in the Divine Decree it is essential to study this introductory note in order to make the problem of *Taqdir* clear.

Whether the fate of man is predestined or he himself is the architect of it, is a question which has been very often discussed by the scholars of all times. This problem is significantly important as no sensible man, not even the man in the street, can afford to ignore it. Faith in *Taqdir* (destiny) has a very deep impact upon our lives and we always find our lives oscillating between determinism and freewill. As a man looks round himself and looks to his ownself and within himself, he finds that there are hundred and one things in the shaping and re-shaping of which he has no hand, e.g. in determining the climate of land in which he lives, in canalizing the courses of rivers which flow therein and in determining the nature of the soil he finds himself absolutely powerless. As he looks to himself he finds that there are so many things in him which are beyond his control viz., the measure of intellect he has been endowed with, the shape and form of his physical structure with which he has been sent in this world, and the inclinations and so many other qualities of head and heart which are embedded in his very nature. In all these aspects of life he finds himself helpless before the Great and Mighty Power that created him.

On the other hand there are so many things in which man finds himself quite powerful. As he looks to the marvellous achievements of man despite all odds he finds it difficult to believe that he is a mere puppet in the mighty hand of nature. This problem of predestination and freewill in which man finds his life hanging, has been adequately solved by the Qur'an and *Sunnah*. We give below a brief summary of their elucidations :

(1) The first principle which Islam lays down in regard to *Taqdir* is that man is neither completely the master of his own fate nor is he bound to the blind law of pre-destination. So far as the Sovereignty of Allah is concerned it is all pervading and nothing falls outside its orbit. Not even a leaf therefore

stirs without His Will.   It is His Will that prevails everywhere.

"To God belongs the sovereignty of Heavens and the Earth. He created what He pleaseth. Giving to whom He pleaseth females and to whom He pleaseth males or conjoining them males and females and He maketh whom He pleaseth barren; verily He hath knowledge and power."   (**42** : 48).

Men are, therefore, completely subordinate to the overruling power of God, they cannot do anything unless God wills so.

"Whom God guideth he is the rightly guided. Whom He sendeth stray thou wilt not find a patron to set him right."
(**18** : 16).

His Mighty grasp is, therefore, over everything. The Almighty Lord Who has created everything and has determined its nature and course, has in His infinite wisdom and mercy, conferred upon man a limited autonomy according to which a man is free to do or not to do a certain thing. It is because of this autonomy enjoyed by man that he is held accountable for his deeds. The concept of human responsibility and that of his answerability for his deeds and misdeeds, becomes meaningless if he is deprived of this autonomy. There are large number of verses in the Holy Qur'an which make a pointed reference to the autonomy conferred upon man.

"Man shall have nothing but that what he strives for."
(**53** : 39).

"Allah does not change the condition of the people until they change it themselves."   (**8** : 53).

"Those who strive in His path are guided in the right path while those who persist in the denial and sinful living have their hearts sealed against faith."   (**117**: 26; **4**: 155; **6**: 102).

"Allah does not compel belief and leaves the people free to believe or disbelieve."   (**4** : 35, 150; **16** : 9).

"Whoever has done an atom weight of good shall meet with its reward and whoever has done an atom weight of evil shall meet its consequences."   (**99** : 7, 8).

It should be borne in mind in this connection that the word *Taqdir* used in the Qur'an does not always signify something pre-destined. It at times implies a measure or the latent potentiality or possibilities with which Allah created man and all things of nature. For example:

"He created everything for its destiny (or its Measure)"

(**25** : **2**).

In Sura **54** verse 9 (the words are):

"We created everything according to a measure or destiny".

In both these verses destiny implies the inward reach of things, their latent potentialities or possibilities.

The idea of destiny, as we find in the *hadith* that God wrote down the decrees regarding the created world fifty thousand years before He created the Heavens and the Earth, does not in any way mean that God created a block Universe, finished off and complete, bound to the iron formulae of nature. Here the idea behind *Taqdir* is that the creation of this Universe is not accidental but something pre-planned and pre-conceived and it was shaped according to the grand Design of the Greatest Designer. There is no element of chance in creation of this Universe. Everything is well set and well planned.

The idea that Allah has a fore knowledge of everything that He created and the events unfold themselves exactly according to it, does not imply that the human-beings have been deprived of the freedom to choose an act. The fore knowledge of God is an acknowledged fact but it should not be interpreted in the sense of pre-destination for if we do so we shall have to conceive of eternity as a store-house of ready made events, from which they drop one by one like particles of sand in a glass hour. If we take the fore knowledge to be a reflecting mirror we shall have to deprive the Creator and the Controller of Universe of His Creative activity. Iqbal has shed a good deal of light over this problem. He says :

"Divine knowledge must be conceived as a living creative activity to which all objects that appear to exist in their own right are organically related. By conceiving God's knowledge as a kind of reflecting mirror, we no doubt, save His fore knowledge of future events, but it is obvious that we do so at the expense of His freedom. The future certainly pre-exists in the organic whole of God's creative life, but it pre-exists as an open possibility, not as a fixed order of events with definite outline." (*The Recons-truction of Religious Thought in Islam*).

We should bear in mind that the idea of past, present and future is something relative and is conceived by the finite mind of man, it is however a great 'now' in the eye of All-Seeing God. The whole expanse of eternity lies before Him in the shape of 'now'. Knowledge, therefore, is an act of creative activity and mere reflection of it. When He decrees a thing it happens and He knows it before it happens. God in Islam is not, therefore, a prisoner of necessity. He is a free Creator.

The concept of pre-destination in Islam, therefore, does not, in any way, mean helpless abandonment of oneself to otherwise unwelcome fate. It means rather cooperation with God, studying His Will and bringing oneself into unison with His Planning Will.

Destiny as conceived by Islam is, thus by no stretch of imagination, fatal to the freedom of conduct and unfoldment of one's inherent possibilities; it is a source of inspiration and encouragement and opens up vast fields of human activity. It is not a message of despondency and despair, but a source of solace, comfort and inspiration and a powerful means of evoking a sense of piety and humility and self-surrender to the Will of God. It does not inculcate in mind frustration and pessimism, making his life dark and dreary devoid of hope and promise for the future, but it teaches him to put his heart and soul in the sublime work as assigned to him by his Master.

Section I الْفَصْلُ الْأَوَّلُ

٧٩ ـ عَنْ عَبْدِ اللهِ بْنِ عَمْرٍو، قَالَ: قَالَ رَسُولُ اللهِ ﷺ كَتَبَ اللهُ مَقَادِيْرَ الْخَلَائِقِ قَبْلَ أَنْ يَخْلُقَ السَّمٰوَاتِ وَالْأَرْضَ بِخَمْسِيْنَ أَلْفَ سَنَةٍ" قَالَ: "وَكَانَ عَرْشُهُ عَلَى الْمَاءِ" رَوَاهُ مُسْلِمٌ.

79 **'Abdullah b. 'Amr** reported Allah's Messenger (peace and blessings of Allah be upon him) having said this: Allah pre-scribed the Decrees of all creatures 50,000 years before He created the heavens and the earth and he (further) said : His throne was on water. (*Muslim*)

٨٠ ـ وَعَنِ ابْنِ عُمَرَ، قَالَ: قَالَ رَسُولُ اللهِ ﷺ: "كُلُّ شَىْءٍ بِقَدَرٍ حَتَّى الْعَجْزِ وَالْكَيْسِ"، رَوَاهُ مُسْلِمٌ.

80 Ibn 'Umar reported Allah's Messenger (peace and blessings of
Allah be upon him) as saying : Everything has been decreed
even the imprudence and the shrewdness. (*Muslim*)

٨١ ـ وَعَنْ أَبِى هُرَيْرَةَ، قَالَ: قَالَ رَسُولُ اللهِ ﷺ: "إِحْتَجَّ آدَمُ وَمُوسَى
عِنْدَ رَبِّهِمَا، فَحَجَّ آدَمُ مُوسَى: قَالَ مُوسَى: أَنْتَ آدَمُ الَّذِى خَلَقَكَ
اللهُ بِيَدِهِ؛ وَنَفَخَ فِيكَ مِنْ رُوحِهِ، وَأَسْجَدَ لَكَ مَلَائِكَتَهُ، وَأَسْكَنَكَ
فِى جَنَّتِهِ، ثُمَّ أَهْبَطْتَ النَّاسَ بِخَطِيئَتِكَ إِلَى الْأَرْضِ؟ قَالَ آدَمُ: أَنْتَ
مُوسَى الَّذِى اصْطَفَاكَ اللهُ بِرِسَالَتِهِ وَبِكَلَامِهِ، وَأَعْطَاكَ الْأَلْوَاحَ فِيهَا
تِبْيَانُ كُلِّ شَىْءٍ، وَقَرَّبْتَ نَجِيًّا، فَبِكَمْ وَجَدْتَ اللهَ كَتَبَ التَّوْرَاةَ
قَبْلَ أَنْ أُخْلَقَ؟ قَالَ مُوسَى: بِأَرْبَعِينَ عَامًا قَالَ آدَمُ: فَهَلْ وَجَدْتَ فِيهَا
﴿وَعَصَى آدَمُ رَبَّهُ فَغَوَى﴾؟ قَالَ: نَعَمْ. قَالَ: أَفَتَلُومُنِى عَلَى أَنْ عَمِلْتُ
عَمَلًا كَتَبَهُ اللهُ عَلَىَّ أَنْ أَعْمَلَهُ قَبْلَ أَنْ يَخْلُقَنِى بِأَرْبَعِينَ سَنَةً؟ قَالَ
رَسُولُ اللهِ ﷺ: "فَحَجَّ آدَمُ مُوسَى"، رَوَاهُ مُسْلِمٌ.

81 Abu Huraira reported Allah's Messenger (peace and blessings
of Allah be upon him) as saying: Adam and Moses debated
before Allah and they exchanged arguments. Moses said:
You are Adam whom Allah created with His own Hand and
He breathed the spirit in you from His Spirit and He asked
His Angels to prostrate before you and provide you abode in
the Paradise. Then you, because of your failing, made the
people come down upon the earth. Adam said: You are Moses
whom Allah chose for His messengership and for His conversation, and He conferred upon you the Tablets on which
everything was clearly defined, and He brought you honour
for an intimate talk. What is your opinion as to how long
Allah would have written the Torah before He created me?

Moses said: Forty years. Adam said: Did you find in that: 'And Adam disobeyed his Lord and committed error.'[1] He said: Yes. Adam said: Do you then blame me for doing a deed which Allah had decreed forty years before He created me? Thereupon Allah's Messenger said: So Adam got better of Moses. (*Muslim*)

1. Al-Qur'ān, 20: 121.

٨٢ - وَعَنِ ابْنِ مَسْعُودٍ، قَالَ حَدَّثَنَا رَسُولُ اللهِ ﷺ وَهُوَ الصَّادِقُ الْمَصْدُوقُ
إِنَّ خَلْقَ أَحَدِكُمْ يُجْمَعُ فِي بَطْنِ أُمِّهِ أَرْبَعِينَ يَوْمًا نُطْفَةً، ثُمَّ يَكُونُ
عَلَقَةً مِثْلَ ذَلِكَ، ثُمَّ يَكُونُ مُضْغَةً مِثْلَ ذَلِكَ، ثُمَّ يَبْعَثُ اللهُ إِلَيْهِ
مَلَكًا بِأَرْبَعِ كَلِمَاتٍ، فَيَكْتُبُ عَمَلَهُ، وَأَجَلَهُ وَرِزْقَهُ، وَشَقِيٌّ أَوْ
سَعِيدٌ، ثُمَّ يُنْفَخُ فِيهِ الرُّوحُ، فَوَالَّذِي لَا إِلهَ غَيْرَهُ إِنَّ أَحَدَكُمْ
لَيَعْمَلُ بِعَمَلِ أَهْلِ الْجَنَّةِ حَتَّى مَا يَكُونُ بَيْنَهُ وَبَيْنَهَا إِلَّا ذِرَاعٌ
فَيَسْبِقُ عَلَيْهِ الْكِتَابُ، فَيَعْمَلُ بِعَمَلِ أَهْلِ النَّارِ فَيَدْخُلُهَا، وَإِنَّ
أَحَدَكُمْ لَيَعْمَلُ بِعَمَلِ أَهْلِ النَّارِ حَتَّى مَا يَكُونُ بَيْنَهُ وَبَيْنَهَا إِلَّا
ذِرَاعٌ، فَيَسْبِقُ عَلَيْهِ الْكِتَابُ، فَيَعْمَلُ بِعَمَلِ أَهْلِ الْجَنَّةِ فَيَدْخُلُهَا
مُتَّفَقٌ عَلَيْهِ

82 Ibn Mas'ud reported that Allah's Messenger (peace and blessings of Allah be upon him) who is truthful and who has been attested as Truthful said: Verily He created every one amongst you by keeping in the form of a life-germ in the womb of his mother for forty days. Then it becomes a clot within a similar period. Then it becomes a lump of flesh for a similar period. Then Allah sends towards it an Angel with four words who records his deeds, the span of life, his means of sustenance, his misfortune or fortune, he then breathes spirit in him. By Him other than Whom is no god, every one of you will act in accordance with the acts befitting the inmates of Paradise till there would be no distance between him and that (Paradise), but only of a span. Then the Decree would supersede him and he would do the deed of the denizens of Hell and that would make him enter that and verily anyone of you would do the deed of the denizens of Hell till there would be left only a small span between him and that (the Hell) and the Decree supersedes him and he would do the deeds of the inmates of Paradise and that would make him enter that. (*Agreed upon*)

٨٣ - وَعَنْ سَهْلِ بْنِ سَعْدٍ ، قَالَ : قَالَ رَسُولُ اللهِ ﷺ "إِنَّ الْعَبْدَ لَيَعْمَلُ عَمَلَ أَهْلِ النَّارِ وَ إِنَّهُ مِنْ أَهْلِ الْجَنَّةِ ، وَ يَعْمَلُ عَمَلَ أَهْلِ الْجَنَّةِ وَ إِنَّهُ مِنْ أَهْلِ النَّارِ ، وَ إِنَّمَا الْأَعْمَالُ بِالْخَوَاتِيمِ" مُتَّفَقٌ عَلَيْهِ

83 Sahl b. Sa'd reported Allah's Messenger (peace and blessings of Allah be upon him) as saying: Verily the servant does the deed of the denizens of Hell whereas he is amongst the inmates of Paradise and he does the deeds of the inmates of Paradise whereas he is amongst the denizens of Hell and (the nature) of the deeds is determined how they finally end. (*Agreed upon*)

٨٤ - وَعَنْ عَائِشَةَ ، رَضِيَ اللهُ عَنْهَا ، قَالَتْ دُعِيَ رَسُولُ اللهِ ﷺ إِلَى جَنَازَةِ صَبِيٍّ مِنَ الْأَنْصَارِ ، فَقُلْتُ : يَا رَسُولَ اللهِ طُوبَى لِهَذَا ، عُصْفُورٌ مِنْ عَصَافِيرِ الْجَنَّةِ ، لَمْ يَعْمَلِ السُّوءَ وَ لَمْ يُدْرِكْهُ . فَقَالَ : أَوَ غَيْرَ ذَلِكَ يَا عَائِشَةُ ! إِنَّ اللهَ خَلَقَ لِلْجَنَّةِ أَهْلًا ، خَلَقَهُمْ لَهَا وَ هُمْ فِي أَصْلَابِ آبَائِهِمْ ، وَ خَلَقَ لِلنَّارِ أَهْلًا ، خَلَقَهُمْ لَهَا وَ هُمْ فِي أَصْلَابِ آبَائِهِمْ . رَوَاهُ مُسْلِمٌ .

84 'Aisha (Allah be pleased with her) reported that Allah's Messenger (peace and blessings of Allah be upon him) was called to the funeral procession of a child of *Ansar*. She said: Allah's Messenger, this one is a blessed sparrow amongst the sparrows of Paradise. He committed no evil and he did not attain the age in which one can commit evil. Upon this he (the Holy Prophet) remarked: 'Aisha, it may be otherwise, verily Allah created some persons for Paradise doing so, when they were in the loins of their parents, and

He created some persons for Hell and doing so, when they were still in their fathers' loins. (*Muslim*)

٨٥ - وَعَنْ عَلِيٍّ ، رَضِيَ اللهُ عَنْهُ ، قَالَ : قَالَ رَسُوْلُ اللهِ ﷺ : "مَا مِنْكُمْ مِنْ
أَحَدٍ إِلَّا وَقَدْ كُتِبَ مَقْعَدُهُ مِنَ النَّارِ وَ مَقْعَدُهُ مِنَ الْجَنَّةِ ؛ قَالُوْا :
يَارَسُوْلَ اللهِ ! أَفَلَا نَتَّكِلُ عَلَى كِتَابِنَا وَ نَدَعُ الْعَمَلَ ؛ قَالَ : "إِعْمَلُوْا
فَكُلٌّ مُّيَسَّرٌ لِمَا خُلِقَ لَهُ ؛ أَمَّا مَنْ كَانَ مِنْ أَهْلِ السَّعَادَةِ فَسَيُيَسَّرُ
لِعَمَلِ السَّعَادَةِ ، وَ أَمَّا مَنْ كَانَ مِنْ أَهْلِ الشَّقَاوَةِ فَسَيُيَسَّرُ لِعَمَلِ
الشَّقَاوَةِ ، ثُمَّ قَرَأَ : رفَأَمَّا مَنْ أَعْطَى وَ اتَّقَى وَصَدَّقَ بِالْحُسْنَى) الْآيَةَ."
مُتَّفَقٌ عَلَيْهِ .

85 'Ali (Allah be pleased with him) reported Allah's Messenger (peace and blessings of Allah be upon him) having said: There is none amongst you for whom his place in the Hell and his place in the Paradise is not determined. They said: Allah's Messenger, would we then not rely upon that what has been decreed for us and abandon the doing of (good) deeds. Whereupon he said: Perform (good) deeds for everyone things have been made easy for which he has been created; for one who is amongst the blessed, the doing of good deeds has been made easy for him and he who is amongst the unfortunate it would be easy for him to perform evil deeds. He then recited: As for him who donates, fears Allah and testifies what is best to be true.[1] (*Agreed upon*)

    1. The complete verses are like this: We facilitate for him (the way to ease). And as for him who is niggardly and considers himself self-sufficient and rejects what is good—we facilitate for him (the way which is rough). (92: 5, 10).

٨٦ - وَعَنْ أَبِيْ هُرَيْرَةَ ، قَالَ : قَالَ رَسُوْلُ اللهِ ﷺ : "إِنَّ اللهَ كَتَبَ عَلَى ابْنِ
اٰدَمَ حَظَّهُ مِنَ الزِّنَا ، أَدْرَكَ ذٰلِكَ لَا مَحَالَةَ ، فَزِنَا الْعَيْنِ النَّظَرُ ،
وَ زِنَا اللِّسَانِ الْمَنْطِقُ وَ النَّفْسُ تَمَنَّى وَ تَشْتَهِى ، وَ الْفَرْجُ يُصَدِّقُ
ذٰلِكَ وَ يُكَذِّبُهُ ." مُتَّفَقٌ عَلَيْهِ .

وَفِىْ رِوَايَةٍ لِّمُسْلِمٍ قَالَ : "كُتِبَ عَلَى ابْنِ اٰدَمَ نَصِيبُهُ مِنَ الزِّنَا مُدْرِكٌ
ذٰلِكَ لَا مَحَالَةَ ، الْعَيْنَانِ زِنَاهُمَا النَّظَرُ ، وَ الْاُذُنَانِ زِنَاهُمَا الْاِسْتِمَاعُ ،
وَ اللِّسَانُ زِنَاهُ الْكَلَامُ ، وَ الْيَدُ زِنَاهَا الْبَطْشُ ، وَ الرِّجْلُ زِنَاهَا الْخُطَا ،
وَ الْقَلْبُ يَهْوٰى وَ يَتَمَنّٰى ، وَ يُصَدِّقُ ذٰلِكَ الْفَرْجُ وَ يُكَذِّبُهُ":

86 **Abu Huraira** reported Allah's Messenger (peace and blessings
of Allah be upon him) as saying: Allah has decreed for the
son of Adam a portion of fornication which he will inevitably
commit, fornication of the eye is (the evil) glance; the fornication of the tongue is (the obscene) talk; the soul longs and
desires and his private part does according (to his soul's
desire) or it does contrary to that.   In the narration recorded
in *Muslim* the words are: There has been decreed for the son
of Adam portion of fornication, he would inevitably commit
it.   The fornication of the two eyes is (the evil) glance, the
fornication of the two ears is the hearing, (obscene) talk is the
fornication of the tongue and the fornication of the hand is
(evil) touch and grasp, and the fornication of the foot is the
steps (taken by him for committing evil); the heart desires and
longs and the private part either accords with it or does
contrary to it (his desire[1]).   (*Agreed upon*)

1. Most of the persons have committed grave error in the proper understanding of this *hadith*.   They argue that if a share of adultery that
one of necessity has to commit, then why an extremely severe punishment has been prescribed by Islam for his offence.   This argument
exposes the lack of understanding on their part.   The simple and
straight meaning of this *hadith* is that just as each person is created
as a separate entity having distinct inborn qualities—physical, intel-
lectual—of his own, in spite of his being the member of human race,
in the same way each person is endowed with a sexual lust of a
certain measure, according to which he has his sexual yearnings from
which he cannot find escape.

   The second portion of *hadith* is highly meaningful and solves all
the difficulties which one faces in the matter of *Taqdir*.   What the
Holy Prophet (may peace be upon him) wanted to instil in the minds
of the people is that different are the channels of the expression of
sexual yearnings in man: lustful look, licentious speech, listening to
the voluptuous songs and talk or even actually committing the act of
adultery.   But it, however, depends upon the will of a person
whether he avoids this sin in all its forms or yields to his sexual lust
and commits this evil.   In other words Allah has endowed him with

a certain measure of sexual instinct for the preservation of human race, building up of a family unit and for the preservation of the moral health of society. Then the choice lies with him whether he commits adultery by misusing this power, or he employs it to the same ends for which it has been embedded in his nature.

٨٧ـ وَعَنْ عِمْرَانَ بْنِ حُصَيْنٍ : أَنَّ رَجُلَيْنِ مِنْ مُّزَيْنَةَ قَالَا : يَا رَسُوْلَ اللّٰهِ ! أَرَأَيْتَ مَا يَعْمَلُ النَّاسُ الْيَوْمَ وَيَكْدَحُوْنَ فِيْهِ ؟ أَشَيْءٌ قُضِىَ عَلَيْهِمْ وَمَضَى فِيْهِمْ مِّنْ قَدَرٍ سَبَقَ ، أَوْ فِيْمَا يَسْتَقْبِلُوْنَ بِهِ مِمَّا أَتَاهُمْ بِهٖ نَبِيُّهُمْ وَثَبَّتَتِ الْحُجَّةُ عَلَيْهِمْ ؟ فَقَالَ : لَا ، بَلْ شَيْءٌ قُضِىَ عَلَيْهِمْ وَمَضَى فِيْهِمْ ، وَتَصْدِيْقُ ذٰلِكَ فِىْ كِتَابِ اللّٰهِ عَزَّ وَجَلَّ : (وَ نَفْسٍ وَّمَا سَوَّاهَا فَأَلْهَمَهَا فُجُوْرَهَا وَتَقْوٰىهَا)ؕ رَوَاهُ مُسْلِمٌ ۰

87 '**Imran b. Husain** reported that two persons from amongst the tribe of Muzaina said: Allah's Messenger, what is your opinion (about this): What the people do today or undergo hardship is it decreed for them or is it something which their Prophet brought for them and made signs manifest for them? Whereupon he (the Holy Prophet) said: No but it is something which has been destined for them and previously determined for them and the testification of this is found in the Book of Allah, the Exalted and Glorious:

"And by the soul and Him who perfected it, and inspired it (with conscience of) what is wrong for it and what is right for it."[1] (**91**: 7). (*Muslim*)

1. This verse explains the nature of destiny in Islam. The concept of destiny in Islam is not that what we find in so many other religions that man is cast in an iron-mould and nothing has been left to his will and discrimination; he is a mere puppet in the hand of destiny. Such a view of Divine Decree is alien to the spirit of Islam. The conception of Divine Decree in Islam is that Allah being the sole Master of the Universe has created both evil and good and that too with a measure. This is what is called *Decree* (*Qadr*) but He has at the same time conferred upon man a sort of limited autonomy in which is afforded opportunities to choose a certain path and avoid the other one. It is upon this power of man to choose an act and reject the other one, that the accountability in this life and the Hereafter depends. If man is devoid of freedom of action and considered as a will-less automaton in the hand of nature the whole pheno-

menon of the institution of prophethood, persuasion and the accountability become meaningless. If we believe that man is dictated from
above and he has no will of his own, and no power of discrimination
between piety and wickedness then the whole process of religious
training appears to be a farce. Various statements and teachings of
the Holy Qur'an and *Hadith* pertaining to pre-destination and free
will should be read together in order to find the true nature and
limitations as regards human freedom of will and action.

٨٨ - وَعَنْ أَبِى هُرَيْرَةَ ، قَالَ: قُلْتُ: يَا رَسُوْلَ اللهِ! إِنِّى رَجُلٌ شَابٌّ
وَأَنَا أَخَافُ عَلَى نَفْسِى الْعَنَتَ ، وَلَا أَجِدُ مَا أَتَزَوَّجُ بِهِ النِّسَاءَ، كَأَنَّهُ
يَسْتَأْذِنُهُ فِى الْاِخْتِصَاءِ، قَالَ: فَسَكَتَ عَنِّى ، ثُمَّ قُلْتُ مِثْلَ ذَلِكَ، فَسَكَتَ
عَنِّى ، ثُمَّ قُلْتُ مِثْلَ ذَلِكَ، فَسَكَتَ عَنِّى ، ثُمَّ قُلْتُ مِثْلَ ذَلِكَ، فَقَالَ
النَّبِىُّ ﷺ : يَا أَبَا هُرَيْرَةَ! جَفَّ الْقَلَمُ بِمَا أَنْتَ لَاقٍ، فَاخْتَصِ عَلَى
ذَلِكَ أَوْ ذَرْ " رَوَاهُ الْبُخَارِىُّ

88 Abu Huraira reported that he said: Allah's Messenger, I am
a young man and I am afraid that I may commit fornication
but at the same time I do not find means to marry a woman.
(He uttered these words before the Holy Prophet in a way)
as if he was seeking permission for castration. He (Abu
Huraira) further said: He (the Holy Prophet) observed silence
(and gave me no reply). I again said to him that but he
gave me no reply. I again said to him like that. Thereupon
Allah's Messenger (peace and blessings of Allah be upon him)
said: Abu Huraira, the Pen has written what is destined for
you. You may then castrate[1] or leave things as they are.

(*Bukhari*)

1. These words do not imply any sanction for castration but its forbid-
dance. *Mirqat*, Vol. I, p. 159.

٨٩ - وَعَنْ عَبْدِ اللهِ بْنِ عَمْرٍو ، قَالَ: قَالَ رَسُوْلُ اللهِ ﷺ : إِنَّ قُلُوْبَ بَنِى
اٰدَمَ كُلَّهَا بَيْنَ إِصْبَعَيْنِ مِنْ أَصَابِعِ الرَّحْمَنِ كَقَلْبٍ وَّاحِدٍ، يُصَرِّفُهُ كَيْفَ
يَشَاءُ " ثُمَّ قَالَ رَسُوْلُ اللهِ ﷺ " أَللّٰهُمَّ مُصَرِّفَ الْقُلُوْبِ صَرِّفْ قُلُوْبَنَا
عَلَى طَاعَتِكَ " رَوَاهُ مُسْلِمٌ.

89 'Abdullah b. 'Amr reported Allah's Messenger (peace and blessings of Allah be upon him) as saying: Verily the hearts of sons of Adam are between the two of the Fingers of the Compassionate Lord like one heart. He turns them as He likes and then Allah's Messenger (peace und blessings of Allah be upon him) said: O Allah, the Turner of hearts turn our hearts to your obedience. (*Muslim*)

$$ ٩٠ - وَعَنْ أَبِي هُرَيْرَةَ، قَالَ : قَالَ رَسُولُ اللهِ ﷺ : "مَا مِنْ مَوْلُودٍ إِلَّا يُولَدُ $$
$$ عَلَى الْفِطْرَةِ ، فَأَبَوَاهُ يُهَوِّدَانِهِ أَوْ يُنَصِّرَانِهِ أَوْ يُمَجِّسَانِهِ ، كَمَا تُنْتَجُ $$
$$ الْبَهِيمَةُ بَهِيمَةً جَمْعَاءَ ، هَلْ تُحِسُّونَ فِيهَا مِنْ جَدْعَاءَ ، ثُمَّ يَقُولُ : $$
$$ (فِطْرَةَ اللهِ الَّتِي فَطَرَ النَّاسَ عَلَيْهَا لَا تَبْدِيلَ لِخَلْقِ اللهِ ذَلِكَ الدِّينُ $$
$$ الْقَيِّمُ) مُتَّفَقٌ عَلَيْهِ $$

90 Abu Huraira reported Allah's Messenger (peace and blessings of Allah be upon him) as saying: There is no new born child who is not born on *fitra* (the natural disposition). It is his parents who make him a Jew or Christian or Magian just as beast is born entire in all limbs (or without a defect). Do you find amongst them maimed. He then recited the (verse): "*Fitra* of Allah is that upon which He created mankind. There is no change in the Divine Dispensation and that is a firm religion." (**30**: 30). (*Agreed upon*)

$$ ٩١ - وَعَنْ أَبِي مُوسَى، قَالَ : قَامَ فِينَا رَسُولُ اللهِ ﷺ بِخَمْسِ كَلِمَاتٍ فَقَالَ : $$
$$ "إِنَّ اللهَ لَا يَنَامُ ، وَلَا يَنْبَغِي لَهُ أَنْ يَنَامَ ، يَخْفِضُ الْقِسْطَ وَيَرْفَعُهُ ، $$
$$ يُرْفَعُ إِلَيْهِ عَمَلُ اللَّيْلِ قَبْلَ عَمَلِ النَّهَارِ ، وَعَمَلُ النَّهَارِ قَبْلَ عَمَلِ اللَّيْلِ، $$
$$ حِجَابُهُ النُّورُ ، لَوْ كَشَفَهُ لَأَحْرَقَتْ سُبُحَاتُ وَجْهِهِ مَا انْتَهَى إِلَيْهِ بَصَرُهُ $$
$$ مِنْ خَلْقِهِ ". رَوَاهُ مُسْلِمٌ. $$

91 Abu Musa reported that Allah's Messenger (peace and blessings of Allah be upon him) stood amongst us and uttered five sentences: Allah does not sleep and it is not meet for Him to sleep. He lowers the scale and raises it. The deeds done during the night are presented to Him before the deeds of the day (begin) and so the deeds of day (are presented to him) before the deeds of the night (begin). His veil is light. If He were to remove it, the illumination of His face would burn all His creation as far as His glance would reach. (*Muslim*)

٩٢ - وَعَنْ أَبِى هُرَيْرَةَ، قَالَ: قَالَ رَسُولُ اللهِ ﷺ: "يَدُ اللهِ مَلْأَى لَا تَغِيضُهَا نَفَقَةٌ، سَحَّاءُ اللَّيْلَ وَ النَّهَارَ، أَرَأَيْتُمْ مَا أَنْفَقَ مُنْ خَلَقَ السَّمَاءَ وَ الأَرْضَ؟ فَإِنَّهُ لَمْ يَغِضْ مَا فِى يَدِهِ، وَ كَانَ عَرْشُهُ عَلَى الْمَاءِ، وَبِيَدِهِ الْمِيزَانُ يَخْفِضُ وَ يَرْفَعُ". مُتَّفَقٌ عَلَيْهِ.

وَ فِى رِوَايَةٍ لِمُسْلِمٍ: "يَمِينُ اللهِ مَلْأَى" —قَالَ ابْنُ نُمَيْرٍ مَلْأَنَ— سَحَّاءُ لَا يَغِيضُهَا شَيْءُ اللَّيْلَ وَ النَّهَارَ".

92 Abu Huraira reported Allah's Messenger (peace and blessings of Allah be upon him) as saying: Allah's Hand is always full and no spending causes any decrease in It. Full of Bounties during the night and day. Do you know what He spent since the creation of the heaven and the earth but there is no decrease in that what He has in His Hand, and His Throne was upon the water and in His Hand is the scale of sustenance) which he lowers and raises. In a version by Muslim (the words) are: Allah's right Hand is full. Ibn Numair said: Both the Hands are full. Bountiful and pouring out blessings night and day without decrease of anything. (*Agreed upon*)

٩٣ - وَعَنْهُ، قَالَ: سُئِلَ رَسُولُ اللهِ ﷺ عَنْ ذَرَارِى الْمُشْرِكِينَ، قَالَ: "اَللهُ أَعْلَمُ بِمَا كَانُوا عَامِلِينَ". مُتَّفَقٌ عَلَيْهِ.

93 He also reported that Allah's Messenger (peace and blessings of Allah be upon him) was asked about the offspring of the polytheists. Whereupon he said: Allah knows best what they had been doing. (*Agreed upon*)

Section II   اَلْفَصْلُ الثَّانِیْ

٩٤ - عَنْ عُبَادَةَ بْنِ الصَّامِتِ، رَضِیَ اللهُ عَنْهُ، قَالَ: قَالَ رَسُوْلُ اللهِ ﷺ:
"إِنَّ أَوَّلَ مَا خَلَقَ اللهُ الْقَلَمَ، فَقَالَ لَهُ: أُكْتُبْ. فَقَالَ: مَا أَكْتُبُ؟ قَالَ:
أُكْتُبِ الْقَدَرَ. فَكَتَبَ مَا كَانَ وَمَا هُوَ كَائِنٌ إِلَى الْأَبَدِ". رَوَاهُ التِّرْمِذِيُّ،
وَقَالَ هٰذَا حَدِيْثٌ غَرِیْبٌ إِسْنَادًا.

94 'Ubada b. Samit (Allah be pleased with him) reported Allah's Messenger (peace and blessings of Allah be upon him) as saying: The first thing which Allah created was Pen. He commanded that to write. But It said: What should I write. He said: Write the Decree, so It wrote what had happened and what was going to happen up to eternity. (Tirmidhi said that the *Isnad* of this *hadith* is *gharib*.)

٩٥ - وَعَنْ مُسْلِمِ بْنِ يَسَارٍ، قَالَ: سُئِلَ عُمَرُ بْنُ الْخَطَّابِ (رَضِیَ اللهُ عَنْهُ)
عَنْ هٰذِهِ الْآیَةِ: وَإِذْ أَخَذَ رَبُّكَ مِنْ بَنِیْ اٰدَمَ مِنْ ظُهُوْرِهِمْ ذُرِّیَّتَهُمْ،
الْآیَةَ. قَالَ عُمَرُ: سَمِعْتُ رَسُوْلَ اللهِ ﷺ یُسْأَلُ عَنْهَا فَقَالَ: "إِنَّ اللهَ
خَلَقَ اٰدَمَ، ثُمَّ مَسَحَ ظَهْرَهُ بِیَمِیْنِهِ، فَاسْتَخْرَجَ مِنْهُ ذُرِّیَّةً، فَقَالَ:
خَلَقْتُ هٰؤُلَاءِ لِلْجَنَّةِ، وَبِعَمَلِ أَهْلِ الْجَنَّةِ یَعْمَلُوْنَ، ثُمَّ مَسَحَ ظَهْرَهُ
فَاسْتَخْرَجَ مِنْهُ ذُرِّیَّةً، فَقَالَ: خَلَقْتُ هٰؤُلَاءِ لِلنَّارِ، وَبِعَمَلِ أَهْلِ النَّارِ
یَعْمَلُوْنَ. فَقَالَ رَجُلٌ: فَفِیْمَ الْعَمَلُ؟ یَا رَسُوْلَ اللهِ! فَقَالَ رَسُوْلُ اللهِ
ﷺ: "إِنَّ اللهَ إِذَا خَلَقَ الْعَبْدَ لِلْجَنَّةِ، اسْتَعْمَلَهُ بِعَمَلِ أَهْلِ الْجَنَّةِ حَتَّى یَمُوْتَ عَلٰى
عَمَلٍ مِّنْ أَعْمَالِ أَهْلِ الْجَنَّةِ فَیُدْخِلَهُ بِهِ الْجَنَّةَ، وَإِذَا خَلَقَ الْعَبْدَ
لِلنَّارِ، اسْتَعْمَلَهُ بِعَمَلِ أَهْلِ النَّارِ حَتَّى یَمُوْتَ عَلٰى عَمَلٍ مِّنْ أَعْمَالِ
أَهْلِ النَّارِ فَیُدْخِلَهُ بِهِ النَّارَ". رَوَاهُ مَالِكٌ، وَالتِّرْمِذِيُّ، وَأَبُوْدَاوٗدَ.

95 **Muslim b. Yasar** reported that 'Umar b. Khattab (may Allah be pleased with him) was asked about this verse: And when thy Lord brought forth their offspring from the loins of the children of Adam,[1] 'Umar said: I heard Allah's Messenger (peace and blessings of Allah be upon him) being asked about it and he said: Allah created Adam then touched his back with His right hand and brought forth from it his offspring and then said: I have created for you this Paradise, and they would perform the deeds befitting the inmates of Paradise. He then touched his back and brought forth offspring and said: I have created these for Hell-Fire and they would commit deeds like the denizens of Hell. A person said: Allah's Messenger, then where lies any sense in doing a deed? Thereupon Allah's Messenger (peace and blessings of Allah be upon him) said: When Allah creates a servant for the Paradise, He employs him to do the deeds of the inmates of Paradise till he dies doing the deeds of the inmates of the Paradise and He then makes him enter the Paradise and when He creates the servant for the Hell-Fire He employs him for doing the deeds of the denizens of Hell till he dies on the deeds which the people of the Hell do and He makes him enter the Hell-Fire.

(*Malik, Tirmidhi and Abu Dawud*)

1. The complete verse is this: And when thy Lord brought forth their offspring from the loins of the children of Adam, He (thus) called them to bear witness about themselves, "Am I not your Lord"—(to which) they answered: "Yes, we do bear witness thereto." (7: 172).

٩٦ - وَعَنْ عَبْدِ اللهِ بْنِ عَمْرِو، قَالَ خَرَجَ رَسُولُ اللهِ ﷺ ، وَفِي يَدَيْهِ كِتَابَانِ،

فَقَالَ:« أَتَدْرُونَ مَا هٰذَانِ الْكِتَابَانِ؟ قُلْنَا : لَا ، يَا رَسُولَ اللهِ! إِلَّا أَنْ

تُخْبِرَنَا . فَقَالَ لِلَّذِي فِي يَدِهِ الْيُمْنَى:« هٰذَا كِتَابٌ مِنْ رَبِّ الْعَالَمِينَ ،

فِيهِ أَسْمَاءُ أَهْلِ الْجَنَّةِ ، وَ أَسْمَاءُ آبَائِهِمْ وَ قَبَائِلِهِمْ ، ثُمَّ أُجْمِلَ عَلَى

آخِرِهِمْ ، فَلَا يُزَادُ فِيهِمْ وَ لَا يُنْقَصُ مِنْهُمْ أَبَدًا ۚ ثُمَّ قَالَ لِلَّذِي فِي

شِمَالِهِ :« هٰذَا كِتَابٌ مِنْ رَبِّ الْعَالَمِينَ فِيهِ أَسْمَاءُ أَهْلِ النَّارِ ، وَ

أَسْمَاءُ أَبَائِهِمْ وَ قَبَائِلِهِمْ ، ثُمَّ أُجْمِلَ عَلَى أَحِرِهِمْ ؛ فَلَا يُزَادُ فِيهِمْ
وَ لَا يُنْقَصُ مِنْهُمْ أَبَدًا "، فَقَالَ أَصْحَابُهُ : فَفِيمَ الْعَمَلُ يَارَسُولَ
اللهِ إِنْ كَانَ أَمْرٌ قَدْ فُرِغَ مِنْهُ ؛ فَقَالَ "سَدِّدُوْا وَ قَارِبُوْا ؛ فَإِنَّ صَاحِبَ
الْجَنَّةِ يُخْتَمُ لَهُ بِعَمَلِ أَهْلِ الْجَنَّةِ وَ إِنْ عَمِلَ أَىَّ عَمَلٍ . وَ إِنَّ صَاحِبَ
النَّارِ يُخْتَمُ لَهُ بِعَمَلِ أَهْلِ النَّارِ وَإِنْ عَمِلَ أَىَّ عَمَلٍ؛ ثُمَّ قَالَ
رَسُولُ اللهِ ﷺ بِيَدَيْهِ فَنَبَذَهُمَا، ثُمَّ قَالَ "فَرَغَ رَبُّكُمْ مِنَ الْعِبَادِ
فَرِيْقٌ فِى الْجَنَّةِ وَ فَرِيْقٌ فِى السَّعِيرِ" رَوَاهُ التِّرْمِذِىُّ .

96 'Abdullah b. 'Amr reported that Allah's Messenger (peace and blessings of Allah be upon him) went out and he had in his hand two books. He said: Do you know what these two books are? We said: Allah's Messenger, we do not know but only that you inform us. Thereupon he said: This one which my right hand possesses is a Book from the Lord of the worlds. It contains the names of the inmates of Paradise and the names of their forefathers and those of their tribes. It is most exhaustive and nothing would be added to it nor anything eliminated from it up to eternity. He then said: This one in my left hand is a Book from the Lord of the worlds. It contains the names of the denizens of Hell and the names of their forefathers and their tribes. It is also exhaustive to the end and nothing would be added to it nor anything would be eliminated from it. The Companions said: Allah's Messenger, (if this is the case) then where lies the use of doing a deed if the affair is already decided. Thereupon he said: Stick to the right course and remain as close to it as possible for one who is to be inmate of Paradise would end his life by an act befitting the inmates of Paradise, no matter what he may have done and for one who is the denizen of Hell, his deed would end on that which is a deed of the denizens of Hell, no matter what he may have done (before). Allah's Messenger (peace and blessings of Allah be upon him) then threw the books and by making a gesture with his hand said: Allah has made a decision about his servants (a section will be in Paradise and a section in the blaze). (*Tirmidhi*)

٩٧ - وَعَنْ أَبِي خِزَامَةَ عَنْ أَبِيهِ ، قَالَ : قُلْتُ : يَا رَسُوْلَ اللهِ! أَدَأَيْتَ رُقًى
نَسْتَرْقِيْهَا ، وَ دَوَاءٌ نَتَدَاوَى بِهِ ، وَ تُقَاةً نَتَّقِيْهَا ، هَلْ تَرُدُّ مِنْ
قَدَرِ اللهِ شَيْئًا؟ قَالَ : "هِيَ مِنْ قَدَرِ اللهِ" رَوَاهُ أَحْمَدُ، وَالتِّرْمِذِيُّ،
وَ ابْنُ مَاجَةَ.

97 **Ibn Khizama** reported on the authority of his father that he said: Allah's Messenger, whether the incantation that we invoke, and the medicine that we apply, and the prevention that we observe avert in any way the Decree of Allah. He said that is also a part of the Decree of Allah.

(Ahmad, Tirmidhi and Ibn Majah)

٩٨ - وَعَنْ أَبِي هُرَيْرَةَ. قَالَ : خَرَجَ عَلَيْنَا رَسُوْلُ اللهِ ﷺ وَنَحْنُ نَتَنَازَعُ
فِي الْقَدَرِ، فَغَضِبَ حَتَّى احْمَرَّ وَجْهُهُ، حَتَّى كَأَنَّمَا فُقِيءَ فِي وَجْنَتَيْهِ
حَبُّ الرُّمَّانِ، فَقَالَ "أَبِهَذَا أُمِرْتُمْ؟ أَمْ بِهَذَا أُرْسِلْتُ إِلَيْكُمْ؟ إِنَّمَا
هَلَكَ مَنْ كَانَ قَبْلَكُمْ حِيْنَ تَنَازَعُوْا فِي هَذَا الْأَمْرِ، عَزَمْتُ عَلَيْكُمْ،
عَزَمْتُ عَلَيْكُمْ أَلَّا تَنَازَعُوْا فِيْهِ" رَوَاهُ التِّرْمِذِيُّ.

98 **Abu Huraira** reported Allah's Messenger (peace and blessings of Allah be upon him) came to us as we had been arguing with each other about the Divine Decree. He has annoyed till his face became as red as if there have been squeezed upon on his cheeks the kernel of pomegranates and he said: Is this that you have been commanded to do, and is this with which I have been sent to you? Those who had gone before you were destroyed as they disputed about it. I adjure you, I adjure you not to fall into argumentation in regard to it.

(Tirmidhi)

٩٩ - وَ رَوَى ابْنُ مَاجَةَ نَحْوَهُ عَنْ عَمْرِو بْنِ شُعَيْبٍ، عَنْ أَبِيهِ،
عَنْ جَدِّهِ.

99 This *hadith* had been transmitted on the authority of 'Amr b. Shuaib who narrated it on the authority of his father.

(Ibn Majah)

١٠٠ـ وَعَنْ أَبِى مُوْسٰى، قَالَ سَمِعْتُ رَسُوْلَ اللهِ ﷺ يَقُوْلُ: إِنَّ اللهَ خَلَقَ
اٰدَمَ مِنْ قَبْضَةٍ قَبَضَهَا مِنْ جَمِيْعِ الْأَرْضِ، فَجَاءَ بَنُوْ اٰدَمَ عَلٰى قَدْرِ
الْأَرْضِ، مِنْهُمُ الْأَحْمَرُ وَ الْأَبْيَضُ وَ الْأَسْوَدُ وَبَيْنَ ذٰلِكَ، وَ السَّهْلُ وَ
الْحَزْنُ، وَ الْخَبِيْثُ وَ الطَّيِّبُ، رَوَاهُ أَحْمَدُ وَالتِّرْمِذِيَّ وَ أَبُوْدَاؤدَ.

100 Abu Musa reported: I heard Allah's Messenger (peace and
blessings of Allah be upon him) as saying: Verily Allah created
Adam from a handful which He took up from all parts of
the world. So He made Adam in accordance (with the
different qualities of earth) and amongst them are the red
and the white and the black and in between them also (*i.e.,*
having the different shades of these colours) and the grief and
joy, the evil and the good. (*Ahmad, Tirmidhi and Abu Dawud*)

١٠١ـ وَعَنْ عَبْدِ اللهِ بْنِ عَمْرٍو، قَالَ: سَمِعْتُ رَسُوْلَ اللهِ ﷺ يَقُوْلُ إِنَّ
اللهَ خَلَقَ خَلْقَهُ فِىْ ظُلْمَةٍ، فَأَلْقٰى عَلَيْهِمْ مِنْ نُوْرِهِ، فَمَنْ أَصَابَهُ مِنْ
ذٰلِكَ النُّوْرِ اهْتَدٰى، وَمَنْ أَخْطَأَهُ ضَلَّ فَلِذٰلِكَ أَقُوْلُ: جَفَّ الْقَلَمُ
عَلٰى عِلْمِ اللهِ، رَوَاهُ أَحْمَدُ وَ التِّرْمِذِيَّ.

101 'Abdullah b. 'Amr reported: I heard Allah's Messenger
(peace and blessings of Allah be upon him) as saying: Verily
Allah created the elements of man in darkness and then He
infused in them His light and he who got this light (and then
made use of it) got the right guidance and he who erred was
led astray, and that is why I say that the Pen has no more to
write about God's knowledge. (*Ahmad and Tirmidhi*)

١٠٢ـ وَعَنْ أَنَسٍ، قَالَ: كَانَ رَسُوْلُ اللهِ ﷺ يُكْثِرُ أَنْ يَقُوْلَ: يَا مُقَلِّبَ
الْقُلُوْبِ! ثَبِّتْ قَلْبِىْ عَلٰى دِيْنِكَ، فَقُلْتُ: يَا نَبِىَّ اللهِ! اٰمَنَّا بِكَ وَبِمَا جِئْتَ
بِهِ، فَهَلْ تَخَافُ عَلَيْنَا؟ قَالَ: نَعَمْ! إِنَّ الْقُلُوْبَ بَيْنَ إِصْبِعَيْنِ مِنْ
أَصَابِعِ اللهِ، يُقَلِّبُهَا كَيْفَ يَشَاءُ، رَوَاهُ التِّرْمِذِيَّ وَ ابْنُ مَاجَهْ.

102 Anas reported that Allah's Messenger (peace and blessings of
Allah be upon him) used to say it quite frequently: O, Turner

of the heart, keep me steadfast on your religion. I said: Allah's Apostle, We do affirm faith in you and in that what you have been sent with (despite this) you entertain fear about us; whereupon he said: yes. Verily the hearts are between two Fingers from the Fingers of Allah and He turns them as He likes. (*Tirmidhi and Ibn Majah*)

١٠٣ـ وَعَنْ أَبِى مُوسَى، قَالَ: قَالَ رَسُولُ اللهِ ﷺ: "مَثَلُ الْقَلْبِ كَرِيشَةٍ بِأَرْضِ فَلَاةٍ يُقَلِّبُهَا الرِّيَاحُ ظَهْرًا لِبَطْنٍ" رَوَاهُ أَحْمَدُ.

103 Abu Musa reported Allah's Messenger (peace and blessings of Allah be upon him) as saying: The similitude of heart is that of a feather in a desert. The wind turns it upside down.
(*Ahmad transmitted it*)

١٠٤ـ وَعَنْ عَلِىٍّ، قَالَ: قَالَ رَسُولُ اللهِ ﷺ: "لَا يُؤْمِنُ عَبْدٌ حَتَّى يُؤْمِنَ بِأَرْبَعٍ يَشْهَدُ أَنْ لَا إِلٰهَ إِلَّا اللهُ وَأَنِّى رَسُولُ اللهِ بَعَثَنِى بِالْحَقِّ، وَيُؤْمِنُ بِالْمَوْتِ، وَالْبَعْثِ بَعْدَ الْمَوْتِ، وَيُؤْمِنُ بِالْقَدَرِ". رَوَاهُ التِّرْمِذِىُّ، وَابْنُ مَاجَةَ.

104 'Ali reported Allah's Messenger (peace and blessings of Allah be upon him) as saying : No servant would be a believer (in the true sense of the term) till he affirms his faith in four: He bears witness to the fact that there is no god but Allah and I am His Messenger whom He has sent with Truth and he should affirm his faith in death and in the life after death and he should affirm his faith in the Divine Decree.
(*Tirmidhi and Ibn Majah*)

١٠٥ـ وَعَنِ ابْنِ عَبَّاسٍ، قَالَ: قَالَ رَسُولُ اللهِ ﷺ: "صِنْفَانِ مِنْ أُمَّتِى لَيْسَ لَهُمَا فِى الْإِسْلَامِ نَصِيبٌ: الْمُرْجِئَةُ وَالْقَدَرِيَّةُ". رَوَاهُ التِّرْمِذِىُّ

105 Ibn 'Abbas reported Allah's Messenger (peace and blessings Allah be upon him) as saying: Two are the sections of my *ummah* those who belong to them would have no share of Islam: *Murji'a*[1] and the *Qadariya*.[2]
(*Tirmidhi and he declared it to be a Hasan Sahih gharib hadith*)

1. It is the name of an early sect of Islam, the extreme opponents of the Khawarij. 'Abd al-Kadir Baghdadi mentions three groups of *Murji'a*. Those who taught *irja'* regarding faith and compulsion.

Those who gave faith pre-eminence over works belonged neither to the adherents of the doctrine of free will nor to those of predetermination. So far as the doctrine of free will and predetermination is concerned the *Murji'a* are *jabari* and they oppose the attributing of an act of man to his own person, just as it is wrong to attribute the movement of stone to its ownself.

2. The *Qadariya* believe that man is the master of his own destiny and Allah has nothing to do with the deeds of man.

١٠٦ - وَعَنِ ابْنِ عُمَرَ، قَالَ: سَمِعْتُ رَسُولَ اللهِ ﷺ يَقُولُ: "يَكُونُ فِي أُمَّتِي خَسْفٌ وَّمَسْخٌ، وَذٰلِكَ فِي الْمُكَذِّبِينَ بِالْقَدْرِ". رَوَاهُ أَبُوْدَاوُدَ وَرَوَى التِّرْمِذِيُّ نَحْوَهُ.

106 Ibn 'Umar reported: I heard Allah's Messenger (peace and blessings of Allah be upon him) as saying: There is destined for my *ummah* the sinking in the earth and metamorphosing and that is for those who belie the Divine Decree.

(*Abu Dawud and Tirmidhi*)

١٠٧ - وَعَنْهُ، قَالَ، قَالَ رَسُولُ اللهِ ﷺ: "اَلْقَدَرِيَّةُ مَجُوسُ هٰذِهِ الْأُمَّةِ إِنْ مَرِضُوا فَلَا تَعُودُوهُمْ، وَإِنْ مَاتُوا فَلَا تَشْهَدُوهُمْ". رَوَاهُ أَحْمَدُ وَأَبُوْدَاوُدَ.

107 It is reported on the same authority that Allah's Messenger (peace and blessings of Allah be upon him) said: *Al-Qadariya* are the Magians of my *ummah* if they fall ill don't visit them to enquire after their health, and if they die don't attend their funeral prayer.[1] (*Ahmad and Abu Dawud*)

1. This means that the *Qadariya* hold a view similar to Magians (Zhroastrians and Dualists) making man as the *khaliq al-af'al* (creator of actions) which amounts to dual god-hood.

١٠٨ - وَعَنْ عُمَرَ، قَالَ: قَالَ رَسُولُ اللهِ ﷺ: "لَا تُجَالِسُوا أَهْلَ الْقَدَرِ وَلَا تُفَاتِحُوهُمْ". رَوَاهُ أَبُوْدَاوُدَ.

108 Ibn 'Umar reported Allah's Messenger (peace and blessings of Allah be upon him) as saying: Don't sit with the *Qadariya* and do not offer them salutations first. (*Abu Dawud*)

١٠٩ - وَعَنْ عَائِشَةَ رَضِيَ اللهُ عَنْهَا، قَالَتْ، قَالَ رَسُولُ اللهِ ﷺ: "سِتَّةٌ
لَعَنْتُهُمْ وَ لَعَنَهُمُ اللهُ وَكُلُّ نَبِيٍّ يُجَابُ؛ أَلزَّائِدُ فِي كِتَابِ اللهِ وَالْمُكَذِّبُ
بِقَدَرِ اللهِ، وَالْمُتَسَلِّطُ بِالْجَبَرُوتِ لِيُعِزَّ مَنْ أَذَلَّهُ اللهُ وَ يُذِلَّ مَنْ
أَعَزَّهُ اللهُ، وَ الْمُسْتَحِلُّ لِحَرَمِ اللهِ، وَ الْمُسْتَحِلُّ مِنْ عِتْرَتِي مَا حَرَّمَ
اللهُ، وَ التَّارِكُ لِسُنَّتِي" رَوَاهُ الْبَيْهَقِيُّ فِي "الْمَدْخَلِ" وَ رَزِينٌ فِي
كِتَابِهِ.

109 'Aisha (Allah be pleased with her) reported that Allah's Messenger (peace and blessings of Allah be upon him) said: Six are the types of persons whom I have cursed and Allah has also cursed them and the prayer of every prophet is granted (and the types) are: Who make addition in the Book of Allah, who belie the Decree of Allah; who rule with highhandedness and exalt one whom Allah humiliated and humiliate one whom Allah exalted; who profanes Haram (Ka'ba) of Allah. He who makes violable (the respect of my family) which He has made inviolable and he who abandons my *sunnah*.

(Baihaqi transmitted it in the introduction and Razin in his book)

١١٠ - وَعَنْ مَطَرِ بْنِ عُكَامِسٍ، قَالَ: قَالَ رَسُولُ اللهِ ﷺ: "إِذَا قَضَى اللهُ
لِعَبْدٍ أَنْ يَمُوتَ بِأَرْضٍ جَعَلَ لَهُ إِلَيْهَا حَاجَةً" رَوَاهُ أَحْمَدُ وَ التِّرْمِذِيُّ.

110 Matar b. Ukamis reported Allah's Messenger (peace and blessings of Allah be upon him) having said: When Allah decrees about a person that he has to die in a certain land he creates need for him to go there. *(Ahmad transmitted it)*

١١١ - وَعَنْ عَائِشَةَ، رَضِيَ اللهُ عَنْهَا، قَالَتْ، قُلْتُ: يَا رَسُولَ اللهِ! ذَرَارِيُّ
الْمُؤْمِنِينَ؟ قَالَ: "مِنْ آبَائِهِمْ" فَقُلْتُ: يَا رَسُولَ اللهِ بِلَا عَمَلٍ؟ قَالَ:
"اللهُ أَعْلَمُ بِمَا كَانُوا عَامِلِينَ" قُلْتُ: فَذَرَارِيُّ الْمُشْرِكِينَ؟ قَالَ:
"مِنْ آبَائِهِمْ" قُلْتُ: بِلَا عَمَلٍ؟ قَالَ: "اللهُ أَعْلَمُ بِمَا كَانُوا عَامِلِينَ"
رَوَاهُ أَبُو دَاوُدَ

111 'Aisha (may Allah be pleased with her) reported: I said:

Allah's Messenger, what about (the fate of) the offspring
of the believers. Whereupon he said: They are joined to their
parents. I said: Allah's Messenger, even without (performing)
good deeds. He said: Allah knows best what they had been
doing. I said: What about offspring of the polytheists? He
said: They would be made to join their parents. I said even
without doing anything; whereupon he said: Allah knows
best what they have been doing.   (*Abu Dawud transmitted it*)

١١٢ - وَعَنِ ابْنِ مَسْعُودٍ، رَضِيَ اللهُ عَنْهُ، قَالَ: قَالَ رَسُولُ اللهِ ﷺ: "أَلْوَائِدَةُ

وَالْمَوْؤُدَةُ فِي النَّارِ". رَوَاهُ أَبُودَاوَدَ.

112 Abn Mas'ud (Allah be pleased with him) reported Allah's
Messenger (peace and blessings of Allah be upon him) having
said this: The one who buries his daughter alive and the one
who is buried alive[1] go to Hell.   (*Abu Dawud transmitted it*)

   1. Children of nonbelievers who are buried or die young, if they enter
   hell they are not themselves tormented, but they are used as instru-
   ment of torture for nonbelievers. Some scholars opine that such
   minors will go to Heaven as servants and this view also may be
   inferred from some *Ahadith* and verses of the Holy Qur'an.

Section III   اَلْفَصْلُ الثَّالِثُ

١١٣ - عَنْ أَبِي الدَّرْدَاءِ، قَالَ: قَالَ رَسُولُ اللهِ ﷺ: "إِنَّ اللهَ عَزَّ وَجَلَّ فَرَغَ

إِلَى كُلِّ عَبْدٍ مِنْ خَلْقِهِ مِنْ خَمْسٍ: مِنْ أَجَلِهِ، وَعَمَلِهِ، وَمَضْجَعِهِ،

وَأَثَرِهِ، وَرِزْقِهِ". رَوَاهُ أَحْمَدُ.

113 Abu al-Darda reported Allah's Messenger (peace and blessings of Allah be upon him) as saying: Allah the Exalted and
Glorious, has ordained for every servant amongst his creation
five things: His death, his action, his abode, his place of
moving about and his means of sustenance.   (*Ahmad*)

١١٤ - وَعَنْ عَائِشَةَ، رَضِيَ اللهُ عَنْهَا، قَالَتْ: سَمِعْتُ رَسُولَ اللهِ ﷺ يَقُولُ:

مَنْ تَكَلَّمَ فِي شَيْءٍ مِنَ الْقَدَرِ سُئِلَ عَنْهُ يَوْمَ الْقِيَامَةِ، وَ مَنْ لَّمْ

يَتَكَلَّمْ فِيهِ لَمْ يُسْأَلْ عَنْهُ". رَوَاهُ ابْنُ مَاجَهَ.

114 'Aisha reported: I heard Allah's Messenger (peace and blessings of Allah be upon him) as saying: He who discusses about the Divine Decree would be answerable for it on the Day of Resurrection, and he who would observe silence over it, he would not be answerable for it. *(Ibn Majah)*

١١٥- وَعَنِ ابْنِ الدَّيْلَمِيِّ، قَالَ: أَتَيْتُ أُبَيَّ بْنَ كَعْبٍ، فَقُلْتُ لَهُ: قَدْ وَقَعَ فِي نَفْسِي شَيْءٌ مِنَ الْقَدَرِ، فَحَدِّثْنِي لَعَلَّ اللهَ أَنْ يُذْهِبَهُ مِنْ قَلْبِي. فَقَالَ: لَوْ أَنَّ اللهَ عَزَّ وَجَلَّ عَذَّبَ أَهْلَ سَمَاوَاتِهِ وَأَهْلَ أَرْضِهِ ؛ عَذَّبَهُمْ وَهُوَ غَيْرُ ظَالِمٍ لَهُمْ، وَلَوْ رَحِمَهُمْ كَانَتْ رَحْمَتُهُ خَيْرًا لَهُمْ مِنْ أَعْمَالِهِمْ، وَلَوْ أَنْفَقْتَ مِثْلَ أُحُدٍ ذَهَبًا فِي سَبِيلِ اللهِ مَا قَبِلَهُ اللهُ مِنْكَ حَتَّى تُؤْمِنَ بِالْقَدَرِ، وَتَعْلَمَ أَنَّ مَا أَصَابَكَ لَمْ يَكُنْ لِيُخْطِئَكَ، وَإِنَّ مَا أَخْطَأَكَ لَمْ يَكُنْ لِيُصِيبَكَ. وَلَوْ مُتَّ عَلَى غَيْرِ هٰذَا لَدَخَلْتَ النَّارَ. قَالَ: ثُمَّ أَتَيْتُ عَبْدَ اللهِ بْنَ مَسْعُودٍ. فَقَالَ مِثْلَ ذٰلِكَ قَالَ: ثُمَّ أَتَيْتُ حُذَيْفَةَ بْنَ الْيَمَانِ، فَقَالَ مِثْلَ ذٰلِكَ. ثُمَّ أَتَيْتُ زَيْدَ بْنَ ثَابِتٍ فَحَدَّثَنِي عَنِ النَّبِيِّ ﷺ مِثْلَ ذٰلِكَ. رَوَاهُ أَحْمَدُ وَأَبُو دَاوُدَ

115 Ibn al-Dailmi reported: I came to Ibn Ka'b and said to him: There has been some prompting in my heart about the Divine Decree, so narrate anything to me so that Allah may obliterate it from my heart, whereupon he said: If Allah, the Exalted and Glorious, were to punish (the creatures) of his Heavens and the Earth he would be able to punish them without being tyrant towards them in any way and if He were to show mercy to them, His mercy would be much better than their deeds and if you were to spend (in charity) gold equal to the bulk of Uhud in the way of Allah, He would never accept it from you till you affirm your faith in Divine Decree, and bear in mind, what is in store for you, you would not miss it and what is not in store for you, you will never be able to get it, and if you were to die (without affirming your faith in the Divine Decree) you will go to the Hell. He said: I then came to 'Abdullah b. Mas'ud and he also said like this, and I came to Zaid b. Thabit and he narrated this to me from Allah's Apostle (peace and blessings of Allah be upon him). (*Ahmad, Abu Dawud and Ibn Majah*)

١١٦- وَعَنْ نَافِعٍ، أَنَّ رَجُلًا أَتَى ابْنَ عُمَرَ فَقَالَ: إِنَّ فُلَانًا يُقْرِئُكَ عَلَيْكَ السَّلَامَ فَقَالَ: إِنَّهُ بَلَغَنِي أَنَّهُ قَدْ أَحْدَثَ، فَإِنْ كَانَ قَدْ أَحْدَثَ فَلَا تُقْرِئْهُ مِنِّى السَّلَامَ؛ فَإِنِّى سَمِعْتُ رَسُولَ اللهِ ﷺ يَقُولُ: يَكُونُ فِى أُمَّتِى - أَوْ فِى هٰذِهِ الْأُمَّةِ - خَسْفٌ، أَوْ مَسْخٌ، أَوْ قَذْفٌ فِى أَهْلِ الْقَدَرِ. رَوَاهُ التِّرْمِذِىُّ، وَأَبُو دَاوُدَ، وَابْنُ مَاجَةَ. وَقَالَ التِّرْمِذِىُّ: هٰذَا حَدِيثٌ حَسَنٌ صَحِيحٌ غَرِيبٌ.

116 Nafi' reported that a person came to Ibn 'Umar and said: Such and such (person) sends you greetings. He said: It has reached me that he makes innovation, and if he were to make innovation then don't convey my greeting to him for I heard Allah's Messenger (peace and blessings of Allah be upon him) as saying: There would be in my *ummah* the sinking of evil doers in the earth or metamorphoses or pelting of those who believe in the free will. (*Transmitted by Trimidhi, Abu Dawud, Ibn Majha and Tirmidhi said: This is Hasan Sahih gharib hadith*)

١١٧- وَعَنْ عَلِيٍّ، رَضِيَ اللهُ عَنْهُ، قَالَ: سَأَلَتْ خَدِيجَةُ النَّبِيَّ ﷺ عَنْ وَلَدَيْنِ مَاتَا لَهَا فِى الْجَاهِلِيَّةِ. فَقَالَ رَسُولُ اللهِ ﷺ هُمَا فِى النَّارِ. قَالَ: فَلَمَّا رَأَى الْكَرَاهَةَ فِى وَجْهِهَا قَالَ: لَوْ رَأَيْتِ مَكَانَهُمَا لَأَبْغَضْتِهِمَا. قَالَتْ: يَا رَسُولَ اللهِ! فَوَلَدِى مِنْكَ؟ قَالَ: فِى الْجَنَّةِ. ثُمَّ قَالَ رَسُولُ اللهِ ﷺ إِنَّ الْمُؤْمِنِينَ وَأَوْلَادَهُمْ فِى الْجَنَّةِ، وَإِنَّ الْمُشْرِكِينَ وَأَوْلَادَهُمْ فِى النَّارِ. ثُمَّ قَرَأَ رَسُولُ اللهِ ﷺ: ﴿وَالَّذِينَ آمَنُوا وَاتَّبَعَتْهُمْ ذُرِّيَّتُهُمْ بِإِيمَانٍ أَلْحَقْنَا بِهِمْ ذُرِّيَّتَهُمْ﴾، رَوَاهُ أَحْمَدُ.

117 'Ali (Allah be pleased with him) reported: Khadijah asked Allah's Apostle (peace and blessings of Allah be upon him) about her children who had died in the days of ignorance. Thereupon Allah's Messenger (peace and blessings of Allah be upon him) said: They are in Hell Fire and when he saw the sign of disgust on her face he said if you were to see their station you would hate them. She said: Allah's Messenger, what about my child that was born of your loins? He said: It is in Paradise. Then Allah's Messenger (peace and blessings of Allah be upon him) said: Verily the believers and their children would be in Paradise and the polytheists and their children in the Hell Fire. Allah's Messenger (peace and blessings of Allah be upon him) then recited this verse: And those who believe and whose offspring follow them in faith We unite with them their offspring and I shall deprive them of naught on their work.[1] (*Ahmad*)

1. The small children who have not attained the age of maturity are sent to Paradise, whereas those offsprings who have reached the stage of discrimination between good and evil would meet their polytheist parents in the Hell.

١١٨ـ وَعَنْ أَبِى هُرَيْرَةَ ، قَالَ : قَالَ رَسُولُ اللهِ ﷺ "لَمَّا خَلَقَ اللهُ اٰدَمَ مَسَحَ ظَهْرَهُ فَسَقَطَ عَنْ ظَهْرِهِ كُلُّ نَسَمَةٍ هُوَ خَالِقُهَا مِنْ ذُرِّيَّتِهِ إِلٰى يَوْمِ الْقِيَامَةِ ، وَجَعَلَ بَيْنَ عَيْنَىْ كُلِّ إِنْسَانٍ مِنْهُمْ وَبِيصًا مِنْ نُورٍ ، ثُمَّ عَرَضَهُمْ عَلٰى اٰدَمَ نَقَالَ : أَىْ رَبِّ ! مَنْ هٰؤُلَاءِ ؟ قَالَ ذُرِّيَّتُكَ. فَرَاٰى رَجُلًا مِنْهُمْ فَأَعْجَبَهُ وَبِيصُ مَا بَيْنَ عَيْنَيْهِ ، قَالَ : أَىْ رَبِّ ! مَنْ هٰذَا ؟ قَالَ : دَاوُدُ. فَقَالَ : رَبِّ ! كَمْ جَعَلْتَ عُمُرَهُ ؟ قَالَ : سِتِّيْنَ سَنَةً. قَالَ رَبِّ زِدْهُ مِنْ عُمُرِى أَرْبَعِيْنَ سَنَةً ، قَالَ رَسُولُ اللهِ ﷺ "فَلَمَّا انْقَضٰى عُمُرُ اٰدَمَ إِلَّا أَرْبَعِيْنَ جَاءَهُ مَلَكُ الْمَوْتِ ، فَقَالَ اٰدَمُ : أَوَ لَمْ يَبْقَ مِنْ عُمُرِى أَرْبَعُوْنَ سَنَةً ؟ قَالَ أَوَ لَمْ تُعْطِهَا ابْنَكَ دَاوُدَ ؟ فَجَحَدَ اٰدَمُ ، فَجَحَدَتْ ذُرِّيَّتُهُ ، وَ نَسِىَ اٰدَمُ فَأَكَلَ مِنَ الشَّجَرَةِ ، فَنَسِيَتْ ذُرِّيَّتُهُ ، وَخَطِئَ وَ خَطِئَتْ ذُرِّيَّتُهُ" رَوَاهُ التِّرْمِذِىُّ.

118 Abu Huraira reported Allah's Messenger (may peace be upon him) as saying: When Allah created Adam, He touched his back and there fell from his back every soul that He would create from his offspring till the Day of Resurrection and He created between the two eyes of every person a gleam of light. Then He presented them to Adam and he said : My Lord who are they? He (the Lord) said: They are your off-spring. He (Adam) saw a person from amongst them and he felt attracted towards him and the sparkle of light between his two eyes. He said: My Lord, who is he? (The Lord) said: It is David. He (Adam) said: My Lord, how much span of life have you allotted to him. He replied: Sixty years. He said: My Lord, enhance his age from my age (to the extent of forty years). Allah's Messenger (may peace be upon him) said: Then Adam completed his age but only forty years were left that there came to him the angel of death. Thereupon Adam said: Are not forty years left from my age? The angel said : Did you not confer to your son (forty years). Adam denied it and so did his offspring deny. Adam forgot and ate (the fruit) of the tree and so his off-spring also forgot and he (Adam) committed an error and so did his offspring commit an error. (*Tirmidhi*)

١١٩- وَعَنْ أَبِى الدَّرْدَاءِ، عَنِ النَّبِيِّ ﷺ قَالَ : ﴿خَلَقَ اللهُ أَدَمَ حِيْنَ خَلَقَهُ فَضَرَبَ كَتِفَهُ الْيُمْنَى، فَأَخْرَجَ ذُرِّيَّةً بَيْضَاءَ كَأَنَّهُمُ الذَّرُّ، وَ ضَرَبَ كَتِفَهُ الْيُسْرَى فَأَخْرَجَ ذُرِّيَّةً سَوْدَآءَ كَأَنَّهُمُ الْحُمَمُ فَقَالَ لِلَّذِى فِى يَمِيْنِهِ : إِلَى الْجَنَّةِ وَ لَا أُبَالِىْ، وَقَالَ لِلَّذِى فِى كَتِفِهِ الْيُسْرَى : إِلَى النَّارِ وَلَا أُبَالِىْ﴾ رَوَاهُ أَحْمَدُ ٠

119 Abu Al-Darda reported Allah's Messenger (may peace be upon him) as saying : Allah created Adam when He had to create him and He struck his right shoulder and there emitted from it white offspring as if it were white ants. He struck his left shoulder and there emitted from it the black offspring as if it were charcoals. He then said (to those who had been emitted) from right (shoulder) : For Paradise and I do not mind and then He said to those (who had been emitted) from his left shoulder: They are for Hell and I do not mind.

(Ahmad)

١٢٠- وَعَنْ أَبِى نَضْرَةَ، أَنَّ رَجُلاً مِنْ أَصْحَابِ النَّبِيِّ ﷺ . يُقَالُ لَهُ:
أَبُو عَبْدِ اللهِ ـ دَخَلَ عَلَيْهِ أَصْحَابُهُ يَعُوْدُوْنَهُ وَ هُوَ يَبْكِى، فَقَالُوا لَهُ
مَا يُبْكِيكَ ؟ أَلَمْ يَقُلْ لَّكَ رَسُوْلُ اللهِ ﷺ خُذْ مِنْ شَارِبِكَ ثُمَّ أَقِرَّهُ
حَتَّى تَلْقَانِى ؟ قَالَ : بَلَى ، وَلٰكِنْ سَمِعْتُ رَسُوْلَ اللهِ ﷺ يَقُوْلُ : "إِنَّ
اللهَ عَزَّ وَ جَلَّ قَبَضَ بِيَمِيْنِهِ قَبْضَةً وَّ أُخْرَى بِالْيَدِ الْأُخْرَى وَقَالَ
هٰذِهِ لِهٰذِهِ ، وَ هٰذِهِ لِهٰذِهِ ، وَ لَا أُبَالِى ، وَ لَا أَدْرِى فِى أَيِّ الْقَبْضَتَيْنِ
أَنَا . رَوَاهُ أَحْمَدُ .

120 Abu Nadra reported that a person from amongst the companions of Allah's Apostle (peace and blessings of Allah be upon him) who was called 'Abdullah, was visited by the companions of the Holy Prophet who had come to enquire after his health (and they found him weeping). They said to him: What makes you weep? Did Allah's Messenger (peace and blessings of Allah be upon him) not say to you: Clip your moustache[1] and then keep it like that till you meet me (at) Houd Kauthar. He said: Yes but I have also heard Allah's Messenger (peace of Allah be upon him) as saying: Verily Allah, the Exalted and Glorious, took a handful in His right hand and the (other handful) in His left hand. This is for this and this is for that and I do not mind. I do not know in which handful I would be (and that makes me weep). *(Ahmad)*

1. This is a symbolic expression of the fact that the yoke of Allah is easy and light and one has not to undergo unbearable hardship for attaining salvation in the Hereafter. The companion of the Holy Prophet was consoled, no doubt, but he had the fear in his mind that it is Allah Who is the Judge of the actions of man. Mere piety and good deeds do not entitle any one to get into Paradise. This hadith explains another hadith in which it has been stated that one should look to the mercy of the Merciful Lord and try to adhere to the path of righteousness but he should at the same time bear this in mind that his success in the Hereafter lies in the hand of God and the virtuous deeds alone do not guarantee his salvation.

١٢١ - وَعَنِ ابْنِ عَبَّاسٍ، رَضِيَ اللهُ عَنْهُ، عَنِ النَّبِيِّ ﷺ قَالَ: أَخَذَ
اللهُ الْمِيْثَاقَ مِنْ ظَهْرِ آدَمَ بِنَعْمَانَ - يَعْنِي عَرَفَةَ - فَأَخْرَجَ مِنْ
صُلْبِهِ كُلَّ ذُرِّيَّةٍ ذَرَأَهَا، فَنَثَرَهُمْ بَيْنَ يَدَيْهِ كَالذَّرِّ، ثُمَّ كَلَّمَهُمْ
قَبِلًا قَالَ: أَلَسْتُ بِرَبِّكُمْ، قَالُوا: بَلَى! شَهِدْنَا أَنْ تَقُوْلُوْا يَوْمَ الْقِيَامَةِ
إِنَّا كُنَّا عَنْ هٰذَا غَافِلِيْنَ - أَوْ تَقُوْلُوْا إِنَّمَا أَشْرَكَ آبَاؤُنَا مِنْ قَبْلُ وَ
كُنَّا ذُرِّيَّةً مِنْ بَعْدِهِمْ أَفَتُهْلِكُنَا بِمَا فَعَلَ الْمُبْطِلُوْنَ ۚ رَوَاهُ أَحْمَدُ

121 Ibn 'Abbas (may Allah be pleased with him) reported Allah's Apostle (peace and blessings of Allah be upon him) as saying: That when Allah made covenant[1] (with the whole of mankind) while creating it from Adam's back in Na'man i.e. 'Arafa and emitting from his loins all his offspring and that He created and scattered them before Him like ant. He then spoke to them in their presence and said : Am I not your Lord (to which) they answered : Yes, we do bear witness thereto (of this We remind you) lest you say on the Day of Resurrection : Verily, we were unaware of this. Or lest you say : Verily, these were our forefathers in times gone by, who began to ascribe divinity to other things besides God and we were but their late offspring. Wilt Thou then destroy us for doings of those inventors of falsehood. (7: 172, 173) (*Ahmad*)

> 1. Adam's seed carries on the existence of Adam and succeeds to his spiritual heritage ; humanity as such has a corporate aspect. According to the Qurān and Sunnah the ability to perceive the existence of the Supreme Power is inborn in human nature (Fitra) and it is this instinctive cognition which may or may not be subsequently blurred by self-indulgence or adverse environmental influences—that makes every sane human being bear witness about himself before God. The man in its uncorrupted state has natural tendency to acknowledge truth and if he deviates from it that is due to aberrations.

١٢٢ - وَعَنْ أُبَيِّ بْنِ كَعْبٍ فِي قَوْلِ اللهِ عَزَّ وَجَلَّ : (وَإِذْ أَخَذَ رَبُّكَ مِنْ
بَنِيْ آدَمَ مِنْ ظُهُوْرِهِمْ ذُرِّيَّتَهُمْ)، قَالَ جَمَعَهُمْ فَجَعَلَهُمْ أَزْوَاجًا، ثُمَّ

صَوَّرَهُمْ فَاسْتَنْطَقَهُمْ ، فَتَكَلَّمُوا ، ثُمَّ أَخَذَ عَلَيْهِمُ الْعَهْدَ وَ الْمِيثَاقَ ،
(وَ أَشْهَدَ هُمْ عَلَى أَنْفُسِهِمْ أَلَسْتُ بِرَبِّكُمْ) ، قَالُوا : بَلَى . قَالَ : فَإِنِّى أُشْهِدُ
عَلَيْكُمُ السَّمٰوٰتِ السَّبْعَ وَ الْأَرَضِينَ السَّبْعَ ، وَ أُشْهِدُ عَلَيْكُمْ آبَاكُمْ
آدَمَ أَنْ تَقُولُوا يَوْمَ الْقِيَامَةِ : لَمْ نَعْلَمْ بِهٰذَا . إِعْلَمُوا أَنَّهُ لَا إِلٰهَ
غَيْرِى ، وَ لَا رَبَّ غَيْرِى ، وَ لَا تُشْرِكُوا بِى شَيْئًا ، إِنِّى سَأُرْسِلُ إِلَيْكُمْ
رُسُلِى يُذَكِّرُونَكُمْ عَهْدِى وَ مِيثَاقِى ، وَ أُنْزِلُ عَلَيْكُمْ كُتُبِى . قَالُوا
شَهِدْنَا بِأَنَّكَ رَبُّنَا وَ إِلٰهُنَا . لَا رَبَّ لَنَا غَيْرُكَ ، وَ لَا إِلٰهَ لَنَا غَيْرُكَ
فَأَقَرُّوا بِذٰلِكَ ، وَ رُفِعَ عَلَيْهِمْ آدَمُ عَلَيْهِ السَّلَامُ يَنْظُرُ إِلَيْهِمْ فَرَأَى الْغَنِىَّ
وَ الْفَقِيرَ ، وَ حَسَنَ الصُّورَةِ وَ دُونَ ذٰلِكَ . فَقَالَ : رَبِّ لَوْ لَا سَوَّيْتَ بَيْنَ
عِبَادِكَ ! قَالَ : إِنِّى أَحْبَبْتُ أَنْ أُشْكَرَ وَ رَأَى الْأَنْبِيَاءَ . فِيهِمْ مِثْلَ
السُّرُجِ عَلَيْهِمُ النُّورُ ، خُصُّوا بِمِيثَاقٍ آخَرَ فِى الرِّسَالَةِ وَ النُّبُوَّةِ وَهُوَ
قَوْلُهُ تَبَارَكَ وَتَعَالَى : (وَ إِذْ أَخَذْنَا مِنَ النَّبِيِّينَ مِيثَاقَهُمْ) إِلَى قَوْلِهِ :
(عِيسَى بْنِ مَرْيَمَ) ، كَانَ فِى تِلْكَ الْأَرْوَاحِ ، فَأَرْسَلَهُ إِلَى مَرْيَمَ عَلَيْهِمَا
السَّلَامُ نَحَدَّثَ عَنْ أُبَىِّ : أَنَّهُ دَخَلَ مِنْ فِيهَا . رَوَاهُ أَحْمَدُ .

122 **Ubayy b. Ka'ab** said in regard to the words of Allah, the Exalted and Glorious, "Your Lord brought forth their off-spring from the loins of the children of Adam". (7: 172)

He (Ubayy) said : He gathered them and made them pairs then fashioned them and endowed them with the power of speech and they began to speak. He then made an agreement and covenant with them calling them : He made them bear witness about their selves (saying) Am I not your Lord. They said: Yes. He said : I call to witness seven heavens and seven earths regarding you and I call witness your father Adam regarding you lest you should say on the Day of Resurrection: We do not know this. Bear this in mind that there is no god besides Me and there is no Lord

besides Me and do not associate anything with Me. It is I
Who should be sending to you My messengers in order to
remind you My agreement and My covenant and it is I Who
would send you My Books. They said : We bear witness to
the fact that Thou art our Lord, Thou art our Object of
worship. There is no Lord besides Thee and there is
no object of worship besides Thee. They confirmed this
(pledge). Adam was raised above them so that he should see
them and he saw the rich and the poor and those having
handsome faces and even those inferior to them and he said :
My Lord, why is it that Thou hast made not Thine servants
alike? He said: I wish that I should be thanked.[1] And he also
saw the Prophets, some amongst them like lamps with light in
them, distinguished with another covenant regarding messengership and prophethood, *viz.* the words of the Blessed and
the High : And when We made covenant with the Prophets
—upto His words: Jesus son of Mary (33: 7). He was among
those spirits and He sent him to Mary (peace be upon both of
them). And it is narrated by Ubayy that he entered by her
mouth. (*Ahmad*)

1. God has not created all the individuals of human race alike because
   it is with this difference of status, tastes and tendency that there
   emerges the idea of social life with dependences of one upon the
   other. Fidelity of a man for the Lord is tested in varying
   circumstances for example if a man is poor, God will see whether
   the man is contented in his poverty or not, and if the man is rich,
   God will see whether he spends his riches according to the will of
   the Lord.

١٢٣- وَعَنْ أَبِى الدَّرْدَآءِ ، قَالَ : بَيْنَمَا نَحْنُ عِنْدَ رَسُوْلِ اللهِ ﷺ نَتَذَاكَرُ
مَا يَكُوْنُ ، إذْ قَالَ رَسُوْلُ اللهِ ﷺ "إذَا سَمِعْتُمْ بِجَبَلٍ زَالَ عَنْ
مَكَانِهِ فَصَدِّقْ قَوْهُ ، وَإِذَا سَمِعْتُمْ بِرَجُلٍ تَغَيَّرَ عَنْ خُلُقِهِ فَلَا تُصَدِّقُوْا
بِهِ ، فَإِنَّهُ يَصِيْرُ إِلَى مَا جُبِلَ عَلَيْهِ" رَوَاهُ أَحْمَدُ .

123 Abu Darda reported : While we were with the Messenger of
Allah (peace and blessings of Allah be upon him) and discussing what would come to pass that Allah's Messenger
(peace and blessings of Allah be upon him) remarked: If you

hear that the mountain has deviated from its place you may confirm it but if you hear of a person that his inborn disposition has changed, don't attest it. For a man always adheres to his inborn disposition. (*Ahmad*)

١٢٤ - وَعَنْ أُمِّ سَلَمَةَ قَالَتْ: يَا رَسُولَ اللهِ! لَا يَزَالُ يُصِيبُكَ فِى كُلِّ عَامٍ وَجَعٌ مِنَ الشَّاةِ الْمَسْمُومَةِ الَّتِى أَكَلْتَ قَالَ "مَا أَصَابَنِى شَىْءٌ مِنْهَا إِلَّا وَهُوَ مَكْتُوبٌ عَلَىَّ وَ آدَمُ فِى طِينَتِهِ" رَوَاهُ ابْنُ مَاجَةَ.

124 **Umm Salama** reported that she said: Allah's Messenger, you necessarily develop trouble every year because of the eating of the poisoned (meat) of sheep.[1] He said : Nothing befalls me but only that which is destined for me while Adam was still a lump of clay. (*Ibn Majah*)

1. A Jewish woman of Khaibar had invited the Holy Prophet (may peace and blessings of Allah be upon him) to a feast and prepared such meat. He only took a morsel of it when Allah informed him and he stopped eating.

CHAPTER 5
PERTAINING TO THE CONFIRMATION OF
THE TORMENT IN THE GRAVE

Section I ﺍﻟﻔﺼﻞُ ﺍﻟْﺄَﻭّﻝُ

١٢٥ـ ﻋَﻦِ ﺍﻟْﺒَﺮَﺍﺀِ ﺑْﻦِ ﻋَﺎﺯِﺏٍ، ﻋَﻦِ ﺍﻟﻨّﺒِﻲِّ ﷺ، ﻗَﺎﻝَ: "ﺍَﻟْﻤُﺴْﻠِﻢُ ﺇِﺫَﺍ ﺳُﺌِﻞَ ﻓِﻲ
ﺍﻟْﻘَﺒْﺮِ؛ ﻳَﺸْﻬَﺪُ ﺃَﻥْ ﻟَﺎ ﺇِﻟٰﻪَ ﺇِﻻَّ ﺍﻟﻠﻪُ ﻭَﺃَﻥَّ ﻣُﺤَﻤّﺪًﺍ ﺭَّﺳُﻮﻝُ ﺍﻟﻠﻪِ، ﻓَﺬٰﻟِﻚَ
ﻗَﻮْﻟُﻪُ: ﴿ ﻳُﺜَﺒِّﺖُ ﺍﻟﻠﻪُ ﺍﻟّﺬِﻳﻦَ ﺁﻣَﻨُﻮﺍ ﺑِﺎﻟْﻘَﻮْﻝِ ﺍﻟﺜَّﺎﺑِﺖِ ﻓِﻲ ﺍﻟْﺤَﻴٰﻮﺓِ ﺍﻟﺪُّﻧْﻴَﺎ
ﻭَﻓِﻲ ﺍﻟْﺂﺧِﺮَﺓِ ﴾".

ﻭَﻓِﻲ ﺭِﻭَﺍﻳَﺔٍ ﻋَﻦِ ﺍﻟﻨّﺒِﻲِّ ﷺ، ﻗَﺎﻝَ: "﴿ ﻳُﺜَﺒِّﺖُ ﺍﻟﻠﻪُ ﺍﻟّﺬِﻳﻦَ ﺁﻣَﻨُﻮﺍ ﺑِﺎﻟْﻘَﻮْﻝِ
ﺍﻟﺜَّﺎﺑِﺖِ ﴾، ﻧَﺰَﻟَﺖْ ﻓِﻲ ﻋَﺬَﺍﺏِ ﺍﻟْﻘَﺒْﺮِ، ﻳُﻘَﺎﻝُ ﻟَﻪُ: ﻣَﻦْ ﺭَّﺑُّﻚَ؛ ﻓَﻴَﻘُﻮﻝُ: ﺭَﺑِّﻲَ ﺍﻟﻠﻪُ
ﻭَﻧَﺒِﻴِّﻲ ﻣُﺤَﻤّﺪٌ": ﻣُﺘّﻔَﻖٌ ﻋَﻠَﻴْﻪِ.

125 Bara b. 'Azib reported Allah's Messenger (peace and blessings
of Allah be upon him) as saying: When the Muslim is questioned in the grave he testifies that there is no god but Allah,
that Muhammad is the Messenger of Allah. That is verified
by His words: Allah confirms those who believe with the sure
words in this world's life and in the Hereafter. (14: 27)

In another version Allah's Apostle (peace and blessings of
Allah be upon him) is reported to have said that he said:
Allah confirms those who believe with the sure word revealed
in regard to the torment of the grave. It would be said to
him: Who is thy Lord? And he would say: Allah is my
Lord and Muhammad is my Apostle. (*Agreed upon*)

١٢٦ـ ﻭَﻋَﻦْ ﺃَﻧَﺲٍ، ﻗَﺎﻝَ ﻗَﺎﻝَ ﺭَﺳُﻮﻝُ ﺍﻟﻠﻪِ ﷺ: "ﺇِﻥَّ ﺍﻟْﻌَﺒْﺪَ ﺇِﺫَﺍ ﻭُﺿِﻊَ ﻓِﻲ ﻗَﺒْﺮِﻩِ، ﻭَ
ﺗَﻮَﻟّﻰٰ ﻋَﻨْﻪُ ﺃَﺻْﺤَﺎﺑُﻪُ ﴿ﻭَ﴾، ﺇِﻧّﻪُ ﻟَﻴَﺴْﻤَﻊُ ﻗَﺮْﻉَ ﻧِﻌَﺎﻟِﻬِﻢْ ﺃَﺗَﺎﻩُ ﻣَﻠَﻜَﺎﻥِ ﻓَﻴُﻘْﻌِﺪَﺍﻧِﻪِ
ﻓَﻴَﻘُﻮﻻَﻥِ: ﻣَﺎ ﻛُﻨْﺖَ ﺗَﻘُﻮﻝُ ﻓِﻲ ﻫٰﺬَﺍ ﺍﻟﺮّﺟُﻞِ؛ ﻟِﻤُﺤَﻤّﺪٍ ﺻَﻠّﻰ ﺍﻟﻠﻪُ ﻋَﻠَﻴْﻪِ ﻭَﺗَﺴَﻠّﻢ﴾

فَأَمَّا الْمُؤْمِنُ فَيَقُولُ: أَشْهَدُ أَنَّهُ عَبْدُ اللهِ وَرَسُولُهُ، فَيُقَالُ لَهُ:
انْظُرْ إِلَى مَقْعَدِكَ مِنَ النَّارِ، قَدْ أَبْدَلَكَ اللهُ بِهِ مَقْعَدًا مِنَ الْجَنَّةِ،
فَيَرَاهُمَا جَمِيعًا. وَأَمَّا الْمُنَافِقُ وَالْكَافِرُ فَيُقَالُ لَهُ: مَا كُنْتَ تَقُولُ فِي
هَذَا الرَّجُلِ، فَيَقُولُ: لَا أَدْرِى! كُنْتُ أَقُولُ مَا يَقُولُ النَّاسُ! فَيُقَالُ:
لَا دَرَيْتَ وَلَا تَلَيْتَ، وَيُضْرَبُ بِمَطَارِقَ مِنْ حَدِيدٍ ضَرْبَةً، فَيَصِيحُ
صَيْحَةً يَسْمَعُهَا مَنْ يَلِيهِ غَيْرَ الثَّقَلَيْنِ" مُتَّفَقٌ عَلَيْهِ، وَلَفْظُهُ لِلْبُخَارِى.

126 Anas reported Allah's Messenger (peace and blesings of Allah
be upon him) as saying: When the servant is placed in a
grave and his friends abandon him he hears the noise of their
shoes. There come two angels and make him sit and say:
What you have to say about this person Muhammad (peace
and blessings of Allah be upon him). The believer would
say: I bear witness to the fact that he is the servant of Allah
and His Messenger. It would be said to him: Look to your
seat in the Hell Fire. Verily Allah has changed it for your
seat in the Paradise, and he sees them both and it would be
said to the hypocrite and unbeliever: What did you say about
this person (Allah's Apostle) and he would say: I do not
know. I used to say the same what other people used to
say and it would be said: You neither did know nor follow
those who have been saved from Hell Fire (believers) and he
would be beaten with the iron hammers and thus utter a shout
which would be heard by all near him excepting man and
jinn.[1]   *(Agreed upon and Bukhari's words)*

1. The voice is not audible to the men and the jinns because if it were
   audible the belief in the torment of the grave would cease to be an
   unseen reality.

١٢٧- وَعَنْ عَبْدِ اللهِ بِنِ عُمَرَ، قَالَ: قَالَ رَسُولُ اللهِ ﷺ: "إِنَّ أَحَدَكُمْ إِذَا
مَاتَ عُرِضَ عَلَيْهِ مَقْعَدُهُ بِالْغَدَاةِ وَالْعَشِيِّ، إِنْ كَانَ مِنْ أَهْلِ الْجَنَّةِ،
فَمِنْ أَهْلِ الْجَنَّةِ، وَإِنْ كَانَ مِنْ أَهْلِ النَّارِ فَمِنْ أَهْلِ النَّارِ، فَيُقَالُ: هَذَا
مَقْعَدُكَ حَتَّى يَبْعَثَكَ اللهُ إِلَيْهِ يَوْمَ الْقِيَامَةِ" مُتَّفَقٌ عَلَيْهِ.

127 **'Abdullah b. 'Umar** reported Allah's Messenger (peace and blessings of Allah be upon him) as saying: When one of you dies there is presented before him his seat morning and evening. If he is amongst dwellers of Paradise (the seat) of the dwellers of Paradise (would be shown to him) and if he is from the dwellers of Hell Fire (the seat) of the dwellers of Hell Fire would be shown to him and it would be said: This is your seat till Allah will finally raise you on the Day of Resurrection. (*Agreed upon*)

١٢٨ ـ وَعَنْ عَائِشَةَ، رَضِيَ اللهُ عَنْهَا، أَنَّ يَهُودِيَّةً دَخَلَتْ عَلَيْهَا، فَذَكَرَتْ
عَذَابَ الْقَبْرِ، فَقَالَتْ لَهَا، أَعَاذَكِ اللهُ مِنْ عَذَابِ الْقَبْرِ، فَسَأَلَتْ
عَائِشَةُ رَسُولَ اللهِ ﷺ عَنْ عَذَابِ الْقَبْرِ. فَقَالَ "نَعَمْ، عَذَابُ الْقَبْرِ
حَقٌّ" قَالَتْ عَائِشَةُ: فَمَا رَأَيْتُ رَسُولَ اللهِ ﷺ بَعْدُ صَلَّى صَلَاةً إِلَّا
تَعَوَّذَ بِاللهِ مِنْ عَذَابِ الْقَبْرِ. مُتَّفَقٌ عَلَيْهِ .

128 **'A'isha** (may Allah be pleased with her) reported that a Jewess came to her and made a mention of the torment of the grave. She said to her: May Allah save you from the torment of the grave. 'A'isha asked Allah's Messenger (may peace and blessings of Allah be upon him) about the torment of the grave. Whereupon he said: The torment of the grave is a fact. 'A'isha said: Never did I see henceforth Allah's Messenger (peace and blessings of Allah be upon him) observe his prayer and not seek refuge with Allah from the torment of the grave. (*Agreed upon*)

١٢٩ ـ وَعَنْ زَيْدِ بْنِ ثَابِتٍ، قَالَ: بَيْنَا رَسُولُ اللهِ ﷺ فِي حَائِطٍ لِبَنِي النَّجَّارِ
عَلَى بَغْلَةٍ لَهُ وَنَحْنُ مَعَهُ، إِذْ حَادَتْ بِهِ وَكَادَتْ تُلْقِيهِ. وَإِذَا أَقْبُرٌ
سِتَّةٌ أَوْ خَمْسَةٌ، فَقَالَ "مَنْ يَعْرِفُ أَصْحَابَ هَذِهِ الْأَقْبُرِ؟" قَالَ رَجُلٌ:
أَنَا. قَالَ "فَمَتَى مَاتُوا؟" قَالَ: فِي الشِّرْكِ. فَقَالَ "إِنَّ هَذِهِ الْأُمَّةَ تُبْتَلَى
فِي قُبُورِهَا. فَلَوْ لَا أَنْ لَا تَدَافَنُوا لَدَعَوْتُ اللهَ أَنْ يُسْمِعَكُمْ مِنْ عَذَابِ

الْقَبْرِ الَّذِى أَسْمَعُ مِنْهُ ؛ ثُمَّ أَقْبَلَ عَلَيْنَا بِوَجْهِهِ ، فَقَالَ ، تَعَوَّذُوا بِاللهِ

مِنْ عَذَابِ النَّارِ. قَالُوا : نَعُوذُ بِاللهِ مِنْ عَذَابِ النَّارِ؛ قَالَ : تَعَوَّذُوا

بِاللهِ مِنْ عَـذَابِ الْقَبْرِ؛ قَالُوا : نَعُوذُ بِاللهِ مِنْ عَذَابِ الْقَبْرِ.

قَالَ : تَعَوَّذُوا بِاللهِ مِنَ الْفِتَنِ مَا ظَهَرَ مِنْهَا وَ مَا بَطَنَ؛ قَالُوا : نَعُوذُ

بِاللهِ مِنَ الْفِـتَنِ مَا ظَهَرَ مِنْهَا وَ مَا بَطَنَ . قَالَ : تَعَوَّذُوا بِاللهِ

مِنْ فِتْنَةِ الدَّجَّالِ؛ قَالُوا : نَعُوذُ بِاللهِ مِنْ فِتْنَةِ الدَّجَّالِ

رَوَاهُ مُسْلِمٌ.

129 Zaid b. Thabit reported: We were with the Messenger of Allah (peace and blessings of Allah be upon him) as he was riding his mule in a garden of Bani Najjar that the mule shied and was about to throw him (that there appeared before him) five or six graves. He said: Who knows about those buried in these graves? A person said: It is I. He said: In which period they died. He said: They died in polytheism (pre-Islamic days). Whereupon he said: These people are undergoing the torment in their graves and if it were not that you would cease to bury, I would have requested Allah that He would have made you hear the torment of the graves which I am hearing. He then turned his face towards us and said: Seek refuge with Allah from the torment of the Hell Fire. They said: We seek refuge with Allah from the torment of Hell Fire. He said: Seek refuge with Allah from the torment of the grave. They said: We seek refuge with Allah from the torment of the grave. He said: Seek refuge with Allah from the turmoil open and secret. They said: We seek refuge with Allah from the turmoil which is open and secret. He said: Seek refuge with Allah from the trial of Dajjal (Anti-Christ) They said: We seek refuge with Allah from the trial of Dajjal. (*Muslim*)

Section II اَلْفَصْلُ الثَّانِي

١٣٠- عَنْ أَبِى هُرَيْرَةَ، قَالَ: قَالَ رَسُوْلُ اللهِ ﷺ: "إِذَا أُقْبِرَ الْمَيِّتُ أَتَاهُ مَلَكَانِ أَسْوَدَانِ أَزْرَقَانِ يُقَالُ لِأَحَدِهِمَا: الْمُنْكَرُ، وَلِلْآخَرِ: النَّكِيْرُ. فَيَقُوْلَانِ: مَاكُنْتَ تَقُوْلُ فِى هٰذَا الرَّجُلِ؟ فَيَقُوْلُ: هُوَعَبْدُ اللهِ وَرَسُوْلُهُ، أَشْهَدُ أَنْ لَّا إِلٰهَ إِلَّا اللهُ وَأَنَّ مُحَمَّدًا عَبْدُهُ وَرَسُوْلُهُ. فَيَقُوْلَانِ: قَدْ كُنَّا نَعْلَمُ أَنَّكَ تَقُوْلُ هٰذَا، ثُمَّ يُفْسَحُ لَهُ فِى قَبْرِهِ سَبْعُوْنَ ذِرَاعًا فِى سَبْعِيْنَ، ثُمَّ يُنَوَّرُ لَهُ فِيْهِ، ثُمَّ يُقَالُ لَهُ: نَمْ. فَيَقُوْلُ: أَرْجِعُ إِلٰى أَهْلِى فَأُخْبِرُهُمْ. فَيَقُوْلَانِ: نَمْ كَنَوْمَةِ الْعَرُوْسِ الَّذِى لَا يُوْقِظُهُ إِلَّا أَحَبُّ أَهْلِهِ إِلَيْهِ حَتّٰى يَبْعَثَهُ اللهُ مِنْ مَضْجَعِهِ ذٰلِكَ. وَإِنْ كَانَ مُنَافِقًا قَالَ: سَمِعْتُ النَّاسَ يَقُوْلُوْنَ قَوْلًا فَقُلْتُ مِثْلَهُ، لَا أَدْرِى. فَيَقُوْلَانِ قَدْ كُنَّا نَعْلَمُ أَنَّكَ تَقُوْلُ ذٰلِكَ، فَيُقَالُ لِلْأَرْضِ: إِلْتَئِمِى عَلَيْهِ، فَتَلْتَئِمُ عَلَيْهِ فَتَخْتَلِفُ أَضْلَاعُهُ، فَلَا يَزَالُ فِيْهَا مُعَذَّبًا حَتّٰى يَبْعَثَهُ اللهُ مِنْ مَضْجَعِهِ ذٰلِكَ." رَوَاهُ التِّرْمِذِىُّ.

130 Abu Huraira reported Allah's Messenger (peace and blessings of Allah be upon him) as saying: When the dead body is buried in the grave there appear before him two Angels, both having black faces and blue eyes. One is called *Munker* and the other is called *Nakir* and they say: Say what you have to say about this person and he would say: He is the servant of Allah and His Messenger. I bear testimony to the fact that there is no god but Allah and that Muhammad is His servant and His Messenger and they both would say: We already knew that you would say this. Then his grave would be expanded to the extent of 4900 square cubic feet and it would be illuminated, then it would be said to him: Go to sleep and he would say: I intend to go to my family in order to inform them and they would say: Go to sleep like

the sleep of a newly wedded bride whom no one awakens
but one who is dearest to her amongst his family members,
only God would resurrect him from his resting place and
if he were a hypocrite he would say : I heard people make
a statement (pertaining to the oneness of God and the
apostlehood of Muhammad) and I said the same but I
do not know. And they would say : We already knew
that you have to say this and it would be said to the earth to
press him and it would press him till his ribs are clasped
together and he would not be relieved of the torment till Allah
would resurrect him from his resting place. (*Tirmidhi*)

١٣١- وَعَنِ الْبَرَاءِ بْنِ عَازِبٍ، عَنْ رَسُولِ اللهِ ﷺ، قَالَ : يَأْتِيهِ مَلَكَانِ
فَيُجْلِسَانِهِ، فَيَقُولَانِ لَهُ : مَنْ رَبُّكَ ؟ فَيَقُولُ : رَبِّيَ اللهُ. فَيَقُولَانِ لَهُ :
مَا دِينُكَ ؟ فَيَقُولُ : دِينِيَ الْإِسْلَامُ. فَيَقُولَانِ : مَا هٰذَا الرَّجُلُ الَّذِىْ
بُعِثَ فِيكُمْ ؟ فَيَقُولُ : هُوَ رَسُولُ اللهِ. فَيَقُولَانِ لَهُ : وَ مَا يُدْرِيْكَ ؟
فَيَقُولُ : قَرَأْتُ كِتَابَ اللهِ فَآمَنْتُ بِهِ وَ صَدَّقْتُ ، فَذٰلِكَ قَوْلُهُ :﴿يُثَبِّتُ
اللهُ الَّذِيْنَ آمَنُوْا بِالْقَوْلِ الثَّابِتِ﴾، الْآيَةَ. قَالَ : فَيُنَادِىْ مُنَادٍ مِّنَ السَّمَاءِ :
أَنْ صَدَقَ عَبْدِىْ فَأَفْرِشُوهُ مِنَ الْجَنَّةِ ، وَ أَلْبِسُوهُ مِنَ الْجَنَّةِ ، وَ افْتَحُوا
لَهُ بَابًا إِلَى الْجَنَّةِ ، وَ يُفْتَحُ. قَالَ : فَيَأْتِيهِ مِنْ رَّوْحِهَا وَطِيبِهَا ، وَ يُفْسَحُ
لَهُ فِيهَا مَدَّ بَصَرِهِ وَ أَمَّا الْكَافِرُ فَذَكَرَ مَوْتَهُ ، قَالَ : وَ يُعَادُ رُوحُهُ فِىْ
جَسَدِهِ ، وَ يَأْتِيهِ مَلَكَانِ ، فَيُجْلِسَانِهِ فَيَقُولَانِ : مَنْ رَبُّكَ ؟ فَيَقُولُ :
هَاهْ هَاهْ ، لَا أَدْرِىْ ! فَيَقُولَانِ لَهُ : مَا دِينُكَ ؟ فَيَقُولُ : هَاهْ هَاهْ ، لَا
أَدْرِىْ ! فَيَقُولَانِ : مَا هٰذَا الرَّجُلُ الَّذِىْ بُعِثَ فِيكُمْ؟ فَيَقُولُ : هَاهْ هَاهْ
لَا أَدْرِىْ ! فَيُنَادِىْ مُنَادٍ مِنَ السَّمَاءِ : أَنْ كَذَبَ فَأَفْرِشُوهُ مِنَ النَّارِ، وَ
أَلْبِسُوهُ مِنَ النَّارِ، وَ افْتَحُوا لَهُ بَابًا إِلَى النَّارِ. قَالَ : فَيَأْتِيهِ مِنْ حَرِّهَا
وَ سَمُومِهَا. قَالَ : وَيَضِيقُ عَلَيْهِ قَبْرُهُ حَتَّى يَخْتَلِفَ فِيهِ أَضْلَاعُهُ ، ثُمَّ

يُقَيِّضُ لَهُ أَعْمَى أَصَمَّ مَعَهُ مِرْزَبَّةٌ مِنْ حَدِيدٍ لَوْ ضُرِبَ بِهَا جَبَلٌ لَصَارَ
تُرَابًا ، فَيَضِرِبُهُ بِهَا ضَرْبَةً يَسْمَعُهَا مَا بَيْنَ الْمَشْرِقِ وَالْمَغْرِبِ إِلَّا الثَّقَلَيْنِ ،
فَيَصِيرُ تُرَابًا ، ثُمَّ يُعَادُ فِيهِ الرُّوحُ " . رَوَاهُ أَحْمَدُ ، وَأَبُوْدَاوُدَ .

131 Bara b. 'Azib reported Allah's Messenger (may peace and
blessings of Allah be upon him) as saying: Two Angels would
come and they would make him sit and say to him: Who is
thy Lord? And he would say: Allah is my Lord and they
would say to him: What is your religion? He would say:
Islam is my religion and they would say: Who is this person
who was sent to you. He would say: He is the Messenger
of Allah and they would say to him: What made you know
of him? And he would say: I read the Book of Allah,
affirmed my faith in it and testified like His words: Allah
confirms those who believe with the sure word. He said: An
announcer from the Heaven would make an announcement:
Verily my servant has testified, so make a bed for him in
Paradise and clothe him (with the cloths of Paradise) and
open for him door leading to Paradise and it would open and
he would perceive its odour and fragrance and there would
be expanded for him the space so far as his eyes would be able
to see and mention was made about the death of a non-believer
and he said: His soul would be restored to his body and two
Angels would come as they would make him sit and say:
Who is thy Lord and he would say: Alas, alas, I do not
know and they would say to him: What is your religion?
And he would say: Alas, alas I do not know and they would
say: Who is this man who was sent to you and he would
say: Alas, alas, I do not know. Then an announcer from
the Heaven would make an announcement: Verily he has
belied. prepare a bed of the Hell Fire for him and clothe him
(with the cloths of Hell Fire) and they would open for him a
door leading to Hell Fire and he said: And there would
come to him its heat and poisonous (wind) and he said:
There would straiten for him his grave till his ribs would be
compressed. Then he would be delivered to the charge of
one who is blind and dumb, having such a sledge hammer

that if the mountain were to be struck with it, it would become
dust and when he would be beaten with it (he would) utter a
shout which would be heard by everything (existing between
the east and the west) except the men and jinns and he will
become dust, then the spirit would be restored to him.

(Ahmad, Abu Dawud)

١٣٢ - وَعَنْ عُثْمَانَ رَضِيَ اللهُ عَنْهُ، أَنَّهُ كَانَ إِذَا وَقَفَ عَلَى قَبْرٍ بَكَى حَتَّى يَبُلَّ
لِحْيَتَهُ، فَقِيلَ لَهُ تَذْكُرُ الْجَنَّةَ وَالنَّارَ فَلَا تَبْكِى، وَتَبْكِى مِنْ هٰذَا؟! فَقَالَ: إِنَّ رَسُولَ
اللهِ ﷺ قَالَ: إِنَّ الْقَبْرَ أَوَّلُ مَنْزِلٍ مِنْ مَنَازِلِ الْآخِرَةِ فَإِنْ نَجَا مِنْهُ فَمَا بَعْدَهُ
أَيْسَرُ مِنْهُ، وَإِنْ لَمْ يَنْجُ مِنْهُ فَمَا بَعْدَهُ أَشَدُّ مِنْهُ؛ قَالَ: وَقَالَ رَسُولُ اللهِ
ﷺ: مَا رَأَيْتُ مَنْظَرًا قَطُّ إِلَّا وَالْقَبْرُ أَفْظَعُ مِنْهُ. رَوَاهُ التِّرْمِذِيُّ، وَابْنُ
مَاجَةَ. وَقَالَ التِّرْمِذِيُّ: هٰذَا حَدِيثٌ غَرِيبٌ.

132 'Uthman (may Allah be pleased with him) reported that
when he stood by the side of grave, he wept and he wept so
bitterly that his beard became wet with tears. It was said
to him: You do not weep over the discussion of the Paradise
and the Hell, but you weep over it (grave); where upon he said
that Allah's Messenger (peace and blessings of Allah be upon
him) had said: Verily grave is the first step from the stages
of the Hereafter and if he finds salvation (at this stage) the
succeeding (stages) become easy for him and if he does not
find salvation in it what follows this stage is very hard upon
him. Allah's Messenger (peace and blessings of Allah be
upon him) also said: I have never seen a site more horrible
than that of the grave. (*Transmitted by Tirmidhi, Ibn Majah and
Tirmidhi said this is a gharib hadith*)

١٣٣ - وَعَنْهُ، قَالَ: كَانَ النَّبِيُّ ﷺ إِذَا فَرَغَ مِنْ دَفْنِ الْمَيِّتِ وَقَفَ عَلَيْهِ،
فَقَالَ: اسْتَغْفِرُوا لِأَخِيكُمْ، ثُمَّ سَلُوا لَهُ بِالتَّثْبِيتِ، فَإِنَّهُ الْآنَ يُسْأَلُ.
رَوَاهُ أَبُو دَاوُدَ.

133 It is reported on the same authority that when Allah's Apostle
(peace and blessings of Allah be upon him) had finished the

burial of a dead person he stood by it and said: Ask forgiveness for your brother; then (he said): Ask (from Allah) to grant him steadfastness (in this hour of trial) for now he is being questioned. (*Abu Dawud*)

١٣٤ - وَعَنْ أَبِي سَعِيدٍ، قَالَ: قَالَ رَسُولُ اللهِ ﷺ: لَيُسَلَّطُ عَلَى الْكَافِرِ فِي قَبْرِهِ تِسْعَةٌ وَتِسْعُونَ تِنِّينًا. تَنْهَسُهُ وَتَلْدَغُهُ حَتَّى تَقُومَ السَّاعَةُ. لَوْ أَنَّ تِنِّينًا مِنْهَا نَفَخَ فِي الْأَرْضِ مَا أَنْبَتَتْ خَضِرًا" رَوَاهُ الدَّارِمِيُّ وَرَوَى التِّرْمِذِيُّ، نَحْوَهُ. وَقَالَ: "سَبْعُونَ" بَدَلَ "تِسْعَةٌ وَّتِسْعُونَ"

134 Abu Sa'id reported Allah's Messenger (peace and blessings of Allah be upon him) as saying: There dominate ninety-nine dragons over the unbeliever in the grave. They (constantly) bite him and sting him till there comes the hour (of resurrection). (These dragons are so poisonous) that if one of them exhales in the earth, no verdure would ever grow upon it. (*Reported by Darimi, Tirmidhi transmitted something similar but he said seventy instead of ninety-nine*)

Section III   اَلْفَصْلُ الثَّالِثُ

١٣٥ - عَنْ جَابِرٍ، قَالَ: خَرَجْنَا مَعَ رَسُولِ اللهِ ﷺ إِلَى سَعْدِ بْنِ مُعَاذٍ حِينَ تُوُفِّيَ، فَلَمَّا صَلَّى عَلَيْهِ رَسُولُ اللهِ ﷺ وَوُضِعَ فِي قَبْرِهِ وَسُوِّيَ عَلَيْهِ، سَبَّحَ رَسُولُ اللهِ ﷺ، فَسَبَّحْنَا طَوِيلاً، ثُمَّ كَبَّرَ، فَكَبَّرْنَا، فَقِيلَ: يَا رَسُولَ اللهِ! لِمَ سَبَّحْتَ ثُمَّ كَبَّرْتَ؟ قَالَ: "لَقَدْ تَضَايَقَ عَلَى هَذَا الْعَبْدِ الصَّالِحِ قَبْرُهُ حَتَّى فَرَّجَهُ اللهُ عَنْهُ" رَوَاهُ أَحْمَدُ.

135 Jabir reported: We went along with Allah's Messenger (peace and blessings of Allah be upon him) to the house of Sa'd b. Mu'adh when he died. When Allah's Messenger (peace and blessings of Allah be upon him) had offered (funeral) prayer over him, he had been placed in his grave and it had been filled with earth, Allah's Messenger (peace and blessings of Allah be upon him) extolled Allah (by saying Subhan Allah) and we also extolled for a (fairly) long duration. He then glorified His greatness (by saying Allah-ho-Akbar) and we also did it. He was asked: Allah's Messenger: Why did you (first) extol (Allah) and then glorified Him. He said: The grave had become narrow for this pious servant (of Allah) and Allah expanded it (because of the extolling of Allah and glorifying Him). (*Ahmad*)

١٣٦ - وَعَنِ ابْنِ عُمَرَ، قَالَ : قَالَ رَسُولُ اللهِ ﷺ : هٰذَا الَّذِى تَحَرَّكَ لَهُ الْعَرْشُ، وَفُتِحَتْ لَهُ أَبْوَابُ السَّمَاءِ، وَشَهِدَهُ سَبْعُونَ أَلْفًا مِّنَ الْمَلَائِكَةِ، لَقَدْ ضُمَّ ضَمَّةً ثُمَّ فُرِّجَ عَنْهُ. رَوَاهُ النَّسَائِيُّ.

136 Ibn 'Umar reported Allah's Messenger (peace and blessings of Allah be upon him) having said this: He (Sa'd) is one for whom Throne (of Allah) was stirred and there were opened for him the doors of the heaven and seventy angels participated (in his funeral prayer), then (his grave) was compressed and later on it was expanded for him. (*Nisai*)

١٣٧ - وَعَنْ أَسْمَاءَ بِنْتِ أَبِي بَكْرٍ، قَالَتْ : قَامَ رَسُولُ اللهِ ﷺ خَطِيبًا، فَذَكَرَ فِتْنَةَ الْقَبْرِ الَّتِي يُفْتَنُ فِيهَا الْمَرْءُ، فَلَمَّا ذَكَرَ ذٰلِكَ، ضَجَّ الْمُسْلِمُونَ ضَجَّةً. رَوَاهُ الْبُخَارِيُّ هٰكَذَا، وَزَادَ النَّسَائِيُّ : حَالَتْ بَيْنِي وَبَيْنَ أَنْ أَفْهَمَ كَلَامَ رَسُولِ اللهِ ﷺ فَلَمَّا سَكَنَتْ ضَجَّتُهُمْ قُلْتُ لِرَجُلٍ قَرِيبٍ مِّنِّي : أَيْ بَارَكَ اللهُ فِيكَ، مَاذَا قَالَ رَسُولُ اللهِ ﷺ فِي آخِرِ قَوْلِهِ؟ قَالَ : قَدْ أُوحِيَ إِلَيَّ أَتَّكُمْ تُفْتَنُونَ فِي الْقُبُورِ قَرِيبًا مِّنْ فِتْنَةِ الدَّجَّالِ.

137 'Asma bint Abu Bakr reported that Allah's Messenger (peace and blessings of Allah be upon him) stood up for delivering a sermon and made mention of the trial of the grave to which a person would be put. And when he made mention of that, the Muslims raised the voices in lamentation. This is transmitted by *Bukhari* and addition is made in this by *Nisai*: This lamentation prevented me from understanding the words of Allah's Messenger (peace and blessings of Allah be upon him) and when the voice of lamentation was calmed, **I** said to the person who was nearby me: May Allah bless you what did Allah's Messenger say at the end of his speech. Whereupon he said (that the Holy Prophet had said): It has been revealed to me that you would be put to trial in the grave similar to the trial of Dajjal. (*Bukhari and Nisai*)

١٣٨ـ وَعَنْ جَابِرٍ، عَنِ النَّبِيِّ ﷺ قَالَ :"إِذَا أُدْخِلَ المَيِّتُ القَبْرَ مُثِّلَتْ لَهُ الشَّمْسُ عِنْدَ غُرُوبِهَا، فَيَجْلِسُ يَمْسَحُ عَيْنَيْهِ، وَيَقُولُ : دَعُونِي أُصَلِّي. رَوَاهُ ابْنُ مَاجَهْ.

138 **Jabir** reported Allah's Messenger (peace and blessings of Allah be upon him) as saying: When the dead body is buried in the grave there is presented before him (the scene of the setting sun). He then sits down and rubs his eyes (to ascertain whether he is not seeing dream) and he says: Leave me so that I should observe my prayer. (*Ibn Majah*)

١٣٩ـ وَعَنْ أَبِي هُرَيْرَةَ عَنِ النَّبِيِّ ﷺ :قَالَ :"إِنَّ المَيِّتَ يَصِيرُ إِلَى القَبْرِ، فَيَجْلِسُ الرَّجُلُ فِي قَبْرِهِ مِنْ غَيْرِ فَزِعٍ وَلاَ مَشْعُوبٍ، ثُمَّ يُقَالُ :فِيمَ كُنْتَ؟ فَيَقُولُ :كُنْتُ فِي الإِسْلاَمِ. فَيُقَالُ :مَا هَذَا الرَّجُلُ؟ فَيَقُولُ :مُحَمَّدٌ رَسُولُ اللهِ جَاءَنَا بِالبَيِّنَاتِ مِنْ عِنْدِ اللهِ، فَصَدَّقْنَاهُ. فَيُقَالُ لَهُ : هَلْ رَأَيْتَ اللهَ؟ فَيَقُولُ :مَا يَنْبَغِي لِأَحَدٍ أَنْ يَرَى اللهَ، فَيُعْرَجُ لَهُ فُرْجَةً قِبَلَ النَّارِ، فَيَنْظُرُ إِلَيْهِ يَحْطِمُ بَعْضُهَا بَعْضًا، فَيُقَالُ لَهُ : أُنْظُرْ إِلَى مَا وَقَاكَ اللهُ، ثُمَّ يُعْرَجُ لَهُ فُرْجَةً قِبَلَ الجَنَّةِ فَيَنْظُرُ إِلَى زَهْرَتِهَا وَمَا فِيهَا، فَيُقَالُ لَهُ : هَذَا مَقْعَدُكَ عَلَى اليَقِينِ كُنْتَ، وَعَلَيْهِ مِتَّ، وَعَلَيْهِ تُبْعَثُ إِنْ شَاءَ اللهُ تَعَالَى. وَيَجْلِسُ الرَّجُلُ السَّوْءُ فِي قَبْرِهِ فَزِعًا مَشْعُوبًا، فَيُقَالُ :فِيمَ كُنْتَ؛ فَيَقُولُ :لاَ أَدْرِي فَيُقَالُ لَهُ : مَا هَذَا الرَّجُلُ؟ فَيَقُولُ :سَمِعْتُ النَّاسَ يَقُولُونَ قَوْلاً فَقُلْتُهُ، فَيُفْتَحُ لَهُ قِبَلَ الجَنَّةِ، فَيَنْظُرُ إِلَى زَهْرَتِهَا وَمَا فِيهَا، فَيُقَالُ لَهُ : أُنْظُرْ إِلَى

مَا صَرَفَ اللهُ عَنْكَ ، ثُمَّ يُفْتَحُ لَهُ فُرْجَةٌ إِلَى النَّارِ ، فَيَنْظُرُ إِلَيْهَا يَحْطِمُ

بَعْضُهَا بَعْضًا ، فَيُقَالُ : هٰذَا مَقْعَدُكَ ، عَلَى الشَّكِّ كُنْتَ ، وَعَلَيْهِ مِتَّ ، وَعَلَيْهِ

تُبْعَثُ إِنْ شَاءَ اللهُ تَعَالَى". رَوَاهُ ابْنُ مَاجَهَ .

139 Abu Huraira reported Allah's Messenger (peace and blessings
of Allah be upon him) as saying: When the dead body is
buried in the grave the person is made to sit in his grave without entertaining any fear or agitation in his mind then it is
said (to him): Which (religion) did you profess. He would
say: I had been (the follower) of Islam. It would be said to
him: Who is this man? He would say: He is Muhammad
(Messenger of Allah) who came to us with clear signs from
Allah. We testified him. It would be said to him: Have
you seen Allah. He would say: It is not (within the reach of
men) to see Allah. Then an opening would be made for him
towards the Hell Fire and he would see it consuming some
part of it the other one. It would be said to him. Look
towards that from which Allah saved you. Then the (opening
would be made for him) towards the Paradise and he would
cast a glance at its freshness and what it contains and it
would be said to him. This is your abode, because of your
firm faith which you had and on which you died and he
would be resurrected (in the same condition) if Allah so wills.
Then the evil person would be made to sit in the grave in fear
and anxiety. It would be said to him: What was your
religion? And he would say: I do not know. It would be
said to him: Who is this person? He would say: I heard
people saying something which I said. Then opening would
be made for him towards Paradise and he would see its
freshness and what it contains and it would be said to him:
Cast a glance at that which Allah has withheld from thee.
Then an opening would be made towards the Hell Fire and he
would see towards it (and find) some parts of it consuming the
other. It would be said to him: That is your abode, because of
your scepticism which you had and on which you died and if
Allah, Exalted, so wills you will be resurrected on it. (*Ibn Majah*)

CHAPTER 6

ADHERING STRICTLY TO THE HOLY BOOK AND THE SUNNAH

Section I الْفَصْلُ الْأَوَّلُ

١٤٠ - عَنْ عَائِشَةَ، قَالَتْ: قَالَ رَسُولُ اللهِ ﷺ: "مَنْ أَحْدَثَ فِي أَمْرِنَا هٰذَا
مَا لَيْسَ مِنْهُ فَهُوَ رَدٌّ" مُتَّفَقٌ عَلَيْهِ.

140 **'A'isha** reported Allah's Messenger (peace and blessings of Allah be upon him) having said: Whosoever introduces any thing new into our affairs[1] whereas it does not form part of it, is to be rejected. (*Agreed upon*)

> 1. This act of fabrication of doctrines and practices which are not sanctioned by the word of Allah or by the practice of His Apostle (may Allah be pleased with him) is called *bid'at*, in Shari'ah. Literally, it means innovation, but in religious terminology it implies a kind of innovation which has no sanction behind it from the Qurān and the Sunnah and is opposed to both of them in letter and spirit. Mere newness does not come under the head of innovation.

١٤١ - وَعَنْ جَابِرٍ، قَالَ: قَالَ رَسُولُ اللهِ ﷺ: "أَمَّا بَعْدُ فَإِنَّ خَيْرَ الْحَدِيثِ كِتَابُ
اللهِ، وَخَيْرَ الْهَدْيِ هَدْيُ مُحَمَّدٍ، وَشَرَّ الْأُمُورِ مُحْدَثَاتُهَا، وَكُلُّ بِدْعَةٍ
ضَلَالَةٌ" رَوَاهُ مُسْلِمٌ.

141 **Jabir** reported Allah's Messenger (peace and blessings of Allah be upon him) having said : To proceed: The best discourse is the Book of Allah and the best guidance is the guidance given by Muhammad. The worst of affairs (in religion) is their innovations and every innovation is straying from the right path. (*Muslim*)

١٤٢ - وَعَنِ ابْنِ عَبَّاسٍ، قَالَ: قَالَ رَسُولُ اللهِ ﷺ: "أَبْغَضُ النَّاسِ إِلَى اللهِ
ثَلَاثَةٌ: مُلْحِدٌ فِي الْحَرَمِ، وَمُبْتَغٍ فِي الْإِسْلَامِ سُنَّةَ الْجَاهِلِيَّةِ، وَمُطَّلِبُ
دَمِ امْرِئٍ بِغَيْرِ حَقٍّ لِيُهْرِيقَ دَمَهُ" رَوَاهُ الْبُخَارِيُّ.

142 Ibn 'Abbas reported Allah's Messenger (peace and blessings of Allah be upon him) as saying : Three are the persons who are most hateful in the sight of Allah. The non-believer in the sacred territory.[1] One who wishes to introduce the practices of pre-Islamic days in Islam and the one who claims the blood of a man without just cause in order that he may shed his blood. (*Bukhari*)

> 1. Haram means sanctuary and applies here to the sacred territory of Mecca, in which blood-shed of every description including the killing of the wild game is forbidden. The third person condemned here is one who brings a false charge of murder against an innocent man in a court of justice with a view to bringing him to gallows.

١٤٣ـ وَعَنْ أَبِي هُرَيْرَةَ، قَالَ: قَالَ رَسُولُ اللهِ ﷺ : كُلُّ أُمَّتِي يَدْخُلُونَ الْجَنَّةَ إِلَّا مَنْ أَبَى: قِيلَ : وَمَنْ أَبَى؟ قَالَ: "مَنْ أَطَاعَنِي دَخَلَ الْجَنَّةَ، وَمَنْ عَصَانِي فَقَدْ أَبَى" رَوَاهُ الْبُخَارِيُّ .

143 Abu Huraira reported Allah's Messenger (peace and blessings of Allah be upon him) as saying : All my followers would get into Paradise but one who refuses (to get into Paradise). It was said : Who is one who refuses (to get into Paradise). He said : He who would obey me would get into Paradise and who would disobey me would in fact refuse (to get into Paradise). (*Bukhari*)

١٤٤ـ وَعَنْ جَابِرٍ، قَالَ: جَاءَتْ مَلَائِكَةٌ إِلَى النَّبِيِّ ﷺ وَهُوَ نَائِمٌ، فَقَالُوا: إِنَّ لِصَاحِبِكُمْ هٰذَا مَثَلًا، فَاضْرِبُوا لَهُ مَثَلًا. قَالَ بَعْضُهُمْ: إِنَّهُ نَائِمٌ، وَ قَالَ بَعْضُهُمْ: إِنَّ الْعَيْنَ نَائِمَةٌ وَ الْقَلْبَ يَقْظَانُ. فَقَالُوا : مَثَلُهُ كَمَثَلِ رَجُلٍ بَنَى دَارًا وَجَعَلَ فِيهَا مَأْدُبَةً وَبَعَثَ دَاعِيًا، فَمَنْ أَجَابَ الدَّاعِيَ دَخَلَ الدَّارَ وَ أَكَلَ مِنَ الْمَأْدُبَةِ، وَمَنْ لَمْ يُجِبِ الدَّاعِيَ لَمْ يَدْخُلِ الدَّارَ وَلَمْ يَأْكُلْ مِنَ الْمَأْدُبَةِ. فَقَالُوا: أَوِّلُوهَا لَهُ يَفْقَهُهَا. قَالَ بَعْضُهُمْ: إِنَّهُ نَائِمٌ، وَقَالَ بَعْضُهُمْ إِنَّ الْعَيْنَ نَائِمَةٌ وَ الْقَلْبَ يَقْظَانُ. فَقَالُوا: الدَّارُ الْجَنَّةُ، وَ الدَّاعِي مُحَمَّدٌ، فَمَنْ أَطَاعَ مُحَمَّدًا فَقَدْ أَطَاعَ اللهَ، وَ

مَنْ عَصَى مُحَمَّدًا فَقَدْ عَصَى اللهَ، وَ مُحَمَّدٌ فَرَّقَ بَيْنَ النَّاسِ. رَوَاهُ
الْبُخَارِيُّ.

144 **Jabir** reported that there came angels to Allah's Apostle (peace and blessings of Allah be upon him) while he was asleep and they said (to one another): There is for this friend of yours a parable. So relate it. Some of them said: He is asleep whereas others said: His eyes sleep but his heart remains awake. They said: The parable of him is like the parable of a person who built a house and arranged feast in it and then he sent a caller to extend invitation. He who responded to his invitation, he entered the house and partook of the feast and he who did not respond he did not enter the house and did not partake of the feast. They said: Elucidate it so that he may understand it. Some of them said : He is asleep whereas others said: His eyes sleep but his heart is awake. They said: The house implies the Paradise and the host is Muhammad. And he who obeyed Muhammad in fact obeyed Allah and he who disobeyed Muhammad he in fact disobeyed Allah and Muhammad is in fact the criterion[1] (by which a distinction can be made between the persons). (*Bukhari*)

1. It is the belief in Muhammad (peace and blessings of Allah be upon him) as the final dispenser of the will of God that the distinction can be drawn between believers and non-believers in mankind. Those who believe in him as the last Messenger of Allah and who hold his message as the final message delivered by God and who hold his personality as the mercy of the worlds and fountain head of right guidance are Muslims and as such are entitled to get into Paradise and those who do not hold these beliefs about Muhammad are non-believers and are the denizens of Hell.

١٤٥- وَعَنْ أَنَسٍ. قَالَ، جَاءَ ثَلَاثَةُ رَهْطٍ إِلَى أَزْوَاجِ النَّبِيِّ ﷺ يَسْأَلُونَ
عَنْ عِبَادَةِ النَّبِيِّ ﷺ. فَلَمَّا أُخْبِرُوا بِهَا كَأَنَّهُمْ تَقَالُّوهَا، فَقَالُوا: أَيْنَ نَحْنُ
مِنَ النَّبِيِّ ﷺ وَقَدْ غَفَرَ اللهُ لَهُ مَا تَقَدَّمَ مِنْ ذَنْبِهِ وَمَا تَأَخَّرَ، فَقَالَ
أَحَدُهُمْ: أَمَّا أَنَا فَأُصَلِّي اللَّيْلَ أَبَدًا، وَقَالَ الْآخَرُ: أَنَا أَصُومُ النَّهَارَ أَبَدًا،
وَلَا أُفْطِرُ. وَقَالَ الْآخَرُ: أَنَا أَعْتَزِلُ النِّسَاءَ فَلَا أَتَزَوَّجُ أَبَدًا، فَجَاءَ النَّبِيُّ

۞ إِلَيْهِمْ فَقَالَ: أَنْتُمُ الَّذِينَ قُلْتُمْ كَذَا وَكَذَا ؟؟ أَمَا وَ اللهِ إِنِّي لَأَخْشَاكُمْ

لِلّٰهِ، وَأَتْقَاكُمْ لَهُ، لٰكِنِّي أَصُومُ وَأُفْطِرُ، وَأُصَلِّي وَأَرْقُدُ وَأَتَزَوَّجُ النِّسَاءَ

فَمَنْ رَغِبَ عَنْ سُنَّتِي فَلَيْسَ مِنِّي؟ مُتَّفَقٌ عَلَيْهِ .

145 Anas reported: There came a group of three persons to the wives of Holy Prophet (peace and blessings of Allah be upon him) and asked about the manner of worship of Allah's Apostle (peace and blessings of Allah be upon him): When they were told about that (their reaction showed) that they thought it to be somewhat insufficient. They said: Where do we stand in comparison to Allah's Apostle (peace and blessings of Allah be upon him) for Allah has forgiven his earlier and later sins? One of them said: As for me, I will observe prayer during the whole night for ever. The other one said: I will observe fast during the day for ever, and I would not break it. While the still other said: I will keep away from the women and would never marry. (As they were talking about this) Allah's Apostle (peace and blessings of Allah be upon him) came to them and said: Is it you who said such and such thing. As for me, by Allah I fear Allah most amongst you and I am most conscious of my duties amongst you; but I fast and eat also; I observe my prayer and sleep also, and I marry, and he who turns away from my way is not of me.

(*Agreed upon*)

١٤٦- وَ عَنْ عَائِشَةَ رَضِيَ اللهُ عَنْهَا. قَالَتْ : صَنَعَ رَسُولُ اللهِ ۞ شَيْئًا،

فَرَخَّصَ فِيهِ، فَتَنَزَّهَ عَنْهُ قَوْمٌ، فَبَلَغَ ذٰلِكَ رَسُولَ اللهِ ۞ فَخَطَبَ

فَحَمِدَ اللهَ، ثُمَّ قَالَ :"مَا بَالُ أَقْوَامٍ يَتَنَزَّهُونَ عَنِ الشَّيْءِ أَصْنَعُهُ؟؟

فَوَ اللهِ إِنِّي لَأَعْلَمُهُمْ بِاللهِ، وَ أَشَدُّهُمْ لَهُ خَشْيَةً : مُتَّفَقٌ عَلَيْهِ .

146 'A'isha (may Allah be pleased with her) reported that Allah's Messenger (peace and blessings of Allah be upon him) performed an act and gave the permission (to his followers) to do it, but some people kept themselves aloof from it. This news reached Allah's Messenger (peace and blessings of Allah be upon him) and he delivered sermon in which he extolled

Allah and then said: What is the matter with the people who avoid doing a thing which I do. By Allah I have the best knowledge of Allah amongst them and I fear Him most amongst them. (*Agreed upon*)

١٤٧ـ وَعَنْ رَافِعِ بْنِ خَدِيجٍ ، قَالَ : قَدِمَ نَبِيُّ اللهِ ﷺ الْمَدِينَةَ وَهُمْ يُؤَبِّرُونَ النَّخْلَ فَقَالَ : مَا تَصْنَعُونَ ؟ قَالُوا كُنَّا نَصْنَعُهُ . قَالَ : لَعَلَّكُمْ لَوْ لَمْ تَفْعَلُوا كَانَ خَيْرًا : نَتَرَكُوهُ : فَنَقَصَتْ قَالَ فَذَكَرُوا ذٰلِكَ لَهُ . فَقَالَ : إِنَّمَا أَنَا بَشَرٌ ؛ إِذَا أَمَرْتُكُمْ بِشَىْءٍ مِنْ أَمْرِ دِينِكُمْ فَخُذُوا بِهِ ؛ وَإِذَا أَمَرْتُكُمْ بِشَىْءٍ مِنْ رَأْيِي ، فَإِنَّمَا أَنَا بَشَرٌ : رَوَاهُ مُسْلِمٌ.

147 Rafi' b. Khadij reported that Allah's Messenger (peace and blessings of Allah be upon him) came to Medina (and he found) the people of Medina fecundating the date palm trees. He said: What are you doing? They said: We are doing this (fecundating the palm trees), whereupon he said: If you were not do it, it would be perhaps better for you. So they abandoned this practice and their yield dwindled. He (the reporter) said: They made a mention of that to him whereupon he said: I am a human being, so if I command you about anything which pertains to your religion, accept it and if I command you about a thing from my own discretion (bear in mind) that I am a human being.[1] (*Muslim*)

1. Note with what noble frankness the Holy Prophet (peace and blessings of Allah be upon him) circumscribes the extent of his ministry of prophethood. He was a voice of God, the unerring Guidance in all those matters of life which came under the purview of religion and as such involve moral and spiritual responsibilities. The technical know-how does not fall within the orbit of religion and as such it is outside the ministry of prophethood.

١٤٨ـ وَعَنْ أَبِي مُوسَى ، قَالَ : قَالَ رَسُولُ اللهِ ﷺ : إِنَّمَا مَثَلِي وَمَثَلُ مَا بَعَثَنِي اللهُ بِهِ كَمَثَلِ رَجُلٍ أَتَى قَوْمًا ، فَقَالَ : يَا قَوْمِ إِنِّي رَأَيْتُ الْجَيْشَ بِعَيْنَيَّ ، وَإِنِّي أَنَا النَّذِيرُ الْعُرْيَانُ ؛ فَالنَّجَاءَ النَّجَاءَ . فَأَطَاعَهُ طَائِفَةٌ مِنْ قَوْمِهِ فَأَدْلَجُوا فَانْطَلَقُوا عَلَى مَهَلِهِمْ ، فَنَجَوْا ، وَكَذَّبَتْ طَائِفَةٌ مِنْهُمْ فَأَصْبَحُوا مَكَانَهُمْ

فَصَبَّحَهُمُ الْجَيْشُ فَأَهْلَكَهُمْ وَاجْتَاحَهُمْ . فَذَلِكَ مَثَلُ مَنْ أَطَاعَنِي فَاتَّبَعَ
مَاجِئْتُ بِهِ ، وَمَثَلُ مَنْ عَصَانِي وَكَذَّبَ مَاجِئْتُ بِهِ مِنَ الْحَقِّ : مُتَّفَقٌ عَلَيْهِ .

148 Abu Musa reported Allah's Messenger (peace and blessings of Allah be upon him) as saying: The parable of mine and the parable of that with which Allah sent me is like this that a person came to the people and said: O people I have seen an army with my own eyes and I am a plain warner, so flee, flee. A section of the people obeyed him and decamped by night and went away well in time and thus escaped. The other section from amongst them belied him and the morning found them at their own places. The army fell upon them, it destroyed and killed them and that is the parable of those who obeyed me and followed that with which I have been sent and of those who disobeyed and belied the truth with which I have been sent. (*Agreed upon*)

١٤٩ ـ وَعَنْ أَبِي هُرَيْرَةَ ، قَالَ : قَالَ رَسُولُ اللهِ ﷺ "مَثَلِي كَمَثَلِ رَجُلٍ
اسْتَوْقَدَ نَارًا ، فَلَمَّا أَضَاءَتْ مَا حَوْلَهَا ، جَعَلَ الْفَرَاشُ وَهَذِهِ الدَّوَابُّ
الَّتِي تَقَعُ فِي النَّارِ يَقَعْنَ فِيهَا ، وَجَعَلَ يَحْجُزُهُنَّ وَيَغْلِبْنَهُ فَيَتَقَحَّمْنَ
فِيهَا . فَأَنَا آخِذٌ بِحُجَزِكُمْ عَنِ النَّارِ ، وَأَنْتُمْ تَقَحَّمُونَ فِيهَا : هَذِهِ رِوَايَةُ
الْبُخَارِيِّ ، وَلِمُسْلِمٍ نَحْوُهَا ، وَقَالَ فِي آخِرِهَا : قَالَ "فَذَلِكَ مَثَلِي وَمَثَلُكُمْ
أَنَا آخِذٌ بِحُجَزِكُمْ عَنِ النَّارِ : هَلُمَّ عَنِ النَّارِ ، هَلُمَّ عَنِ النَّارِ ! فَتَغْلِبُونِي
تَقَحَّمُونَ فِيهَا" مُتَّفَقٌ عَلَيْهِ .

149 Abu Huraira reported Allah's Messenger (peace and blessings of Allah be upon him) as saying: The parable of mine is that of a person who kindled fire and when all round it is all ablaze, the moths and insects that fall into fire begin to fall in it, and though he tries hard to keep them away from it, they thwart him and fall into it. Thus I do, I strive to hold you back from fire, but you are jumping into that. This is transmitted by Bukhari and the Muslim has the similar report but he said that at the end of it he (The Prophet) said: The same is the case with you and me. I am the one to prevent you from falling into the fire. (I ask you to) save yourself from fire, save yourself from fire. But you are thwarting me to fall headlong into the fire. (*Agreed upon*)

١٥٠ـ وَعَنْ اَبِىْ مُوْسَى، قَالَ: قَالَ رَسُوْلُ اللهِ ﷺ: مَثَلُ مَا بَعَثَنِىَ اللهُ بِهِ مِنَ الْهُدَى وَ الْعِلْمِ كَمَثَلِ الْغَيْثِ الْكَثِيْرِ اَصَابَ اَرْضًا، فَكَانَتْ مِنْهَا طَائِفَةٌ طَيِّبَةٌ قَبِلَتِ الْمَاءَ، فَاَنْبَتَتِ الْكَلَاَ وَ الْعُشْبَ الْكَثِيْرَ، وَ كَانَتْ مِنْهَا اَجَادِبُ اَمْسَكَتِ الْمَاءَ، فَنَفَعَ اللهُ بِهَا النَّاسَ، فَشَرِبُوْا وَ سَقَوْا وَ زَرَعُوْا، وَ اَصَابَ مِنْهَا طَائِفَةً اُخْرَى، اِنَّمَا هِىَ قِيْعَانٌ لَا تُمْسِكُ مَاءً وَلَا تُنْبِتُ كَلَاَ، فَذَلِكَ مَثَلُ مَنْ فَقُهَ فِىْ دِيْنِ اللهِ وَنَفَعَهُ مَا بَعَثَنِىَ اللهُ بِهِ فَعَلِمَ وَ عَلَّمَ، وَ مَثَلُ مَنْ لَمْ يَرْفَعْ بِذَلِكَ رَأْسًا، وَلَمْ يَقْبَلْ هُدَى اللهِ الَّذِىْ اُرْسِلْتُ بِهِ: مُتَّفَقٌ عَلَيْهِ.

150 Abu Musa reported Allah's Messenger (peace and blessings of Allah be upon him) as saying: The similitude of that with which Allah has sent me with guidance and knowledge is like that of down-pour of rain upon the earth. There is a piece of good land in it. It receives water with which grow much green grass and hay. There is also patch of hard and barren land which retains the water and the people derive benefit from it. They drink it, make their animals drink and irrigate their lands and cultivate them. But some of it fell on another piece of land; it retains no water and nothing grow thereby. This is the similitude of one who tries to comprehend the religion of Allah and derives benefit from that with which Allah has sent me; he then learns it, teaches it to other and the similitude of one who shows no regard to it is like that of a person who neither (cares) to raise his head (to see) nor accepts the guidance of Allah with which I have been sent. (*Agreed upon*)

١٥١ـ وَعَنْ عَائِشَةَ، قَالَتْ: تَلَا رَسُوْلُ اللهِ ﷺ: (هُوَ الَّذِىْ اَنْزَلَ عَلَيْكَ الْكِتَبَ مِنْهُ اَيَاتٌ مُحْكَمَتٌ)، وَ قَرَاَ اِلَى: (وَمَا يَذَّكَّرُ اِلَّا اُولُوا الْاَلْبَابِ)، قَالَتْ:

قَالَ رَسُولُ اللهِ ﷺ : "فَإِذَا رَأَيْتَ - وَعِنْدَ مُسْلِمٍ رَأَيْتُمُ - الَّذِينَ يَتَّبِعُونَ
مَا تَشَابَهَ مِنْهُ ، فَأُولَئِكَ الَّذِينَ سَمَّاهُمُ اللهُ ، فَاحْذَرُوهُمْ" مُتَّفَقٌ عَلَيْهِ :

151 **'A'isha** reported that Allah's Messenger (peace and blessings
of Allah be upon him) recited: He it is who sent upon you
the Book in which there are clear and decisive verses and he
recited upto: And reflect not except men of understanding[1].
She said that Allah's Messenger (peace and blessings of Allah
be upon him) observed: So when you see—and in the Muslim
it is a plural form—those who follow what is allegorical in it
those are they whom Allah named, so be on your guard
against them. (*Agreed upon*)

1. The complete verse is this: He it is Who has revealed the Book to
thee; some of its verses are decisive—they are the basis of the Book—
and others are allegorical. Then those in whose hearts is perversity,
follow the part of it which is allegorical seeking to mislead, and
seeking to give it (their own) interpretation. And none knows its
interpretation save Allah, and those firmly rooted in knowledge,
they say: We believe in it, it is all from our Lord. And none mind
except men of understanding.

١٥٢ - وَعَنْ عَبْدِ اللهِ بْنِ عَمْرٍو ، قَالَ : هَجَّرْتُ إِلَى رَسُولِ اللهِ ﷺ يَوْمًا
قَالَ : فَسَمِعَ أَصْوَاتَ رَجُلَيْنِ إِخْتَلَفَا فِي آيَةٍ ، فَخَرَجَ عَلَيْنَا رَسُولُ اللهِ ﷺ
يُعْرَفُ فِي وَجْهِهِ الْغَضَبُ ، فَقَالَ : "إِنَّمَا هَلَكَ مَنْ كَانَ قَبْلَكُمْ بِاخْتِلَافِهِمْ
فِي الْكِتَابِ" رَوَاهُ مُسْلِمٌ :

152 **'Abdullah b. 'Amr** reported: I went to Allah's Messenger
(peace and blessings of Allah be upon him) at noon. He (the
Holy Prophet) listened to the voices of two persons disputing
about a verse (of the Qurān). Allah's Messenger (peace and
blessings of Allah be upon him) came to us and there was
sign of anger on his face and he said: Those before you were
destroyed because of their disputations in the Book. (*Muslim*)

١٥٣ - وَعَنْ سَعْدِ بْنِ أَبِي وَقَّاصٍ ، قَالَ : قَالَ رَسُولُ اللهِ ﷺ : "إِنَّ أَعْظَمَ
الْمُسْلِمِينَ فِي الْمُسْلِمِينَ جُرْمًا مَنْ سَأَلَ عَنْ شَيْءٍ لَمْ يُحَرَّمْ عَلَى النَّاسِ
فَحُرِّمَ مِنْ أَجْلِ مَسْأَلَتِهِ" مُتَّفَقٌ عَلَيْهِ :

153 Sa'd b. Abi Waqqas reported: The gravest offender amongst the Muslims is he who questioned about a thing which had not been prohibited to the people, and it was then prohibited because of his (constant) questioning[1]. (*Agreed upon*)

> 1. This has a reference to the verses 101, 102 of Sura al-Ma'idah of the Holy Quran:
>
> O you who believe! Do not ask about matters which, if they were to be made manifest to you (in terms of law) might cause you harm; for, if you should ask about them while the Qurān is being revealed, they might (indeed) be made manifest to you (as laws). God has absolved (you from any obligation) in this respect. For God is much-forgiving, forbearing. People before your times have indeed asked such questions and in consequence thereof have come to deny the truth.
>
> In these verses the reference is to the Jews whose excessive devotion to juristic formalism gave birth to pharisaism which has become synonymous with hypocrisy. Too much legalism tends to externalize religion altogether and thereby impoverishes the inner piety. This dry formalism saps spiritual freedom which is an essential aspect of religion.

١٥٤- وَعَنْ أَبِى هُرَيْرَةَ ، قَالَ: قَالَ رَسُولُ اللهِ ﷺ : يَكُونُ فِى آخِرِ الزَّمَانِ
دَجَّالُونَ كَذَّابُونَ يَأْتُونَكُمْ مِنَ الْأَحَادِيثِ بِمَا لَمْ تَسْمَعُوا أَنْتُمْ وَلَا آبَاؤُكُمْ
فَإِيَّاكُمْ وَإِيَّاهُمْ ، لَا يُضِلُّونَكُمْ وَلَا يَفْتِنُونَكُمْ" رَوَاهُ مُسْلِمٌ

154 Abu Huraira reported Allah's Messenger (peace and blessings of Allah be upon him) as saying: At the end of the age there would appear the Dajjals, the liars, who would relate you a hadith which neither you heard nor did your forefathers hear. So be on your guard against them and they should be kept away from you so that they may not lead you astray or put you to trial. (*Muslim*)

١٥٥- وَعَنْهُ ، قَالَ كَانَ أَهْلُ الْكِتَابِ يَقْرَؤُونَ التَّوْرَاةَ بِالْعِبْرَانِيَّةِ ، وَيُفَسِّرُونَهَا
بِالْعَرَبِيَّةِ لِأَهْلِ الْإِسْلَامِ. فَقَالَ رَسُولُ اللهِ ﷺ "لَا تُصَدِّقُوا أَهْلَ الْكِتَابِ
وَلَا تُكَذِّبُوهُمْ وَقُولُوا : آمَنَّا بِاللهِ وَمَا أُنْزِلَ إِلَيْنَا" الْآيَةَ. رَوَاهُ الْبُخَارِيُّ.

155. It is reported on the same authority that some people of the Book used to recite the Torah in Hebrew and then explained it in Arabic for the Muslims. Thereupon Allah's Messenger (peace and blessings of Allah be upon him) said: Neither testify the people of the Book nor do belie them but simply say: We affirm faith in Allah and what has been revealed to us. (*Bukhari*)

١٥٦- وَعَنْهُ، قَالَ: قَالَ رَسُولُ اللهِ ﷺ: كَفَى بِالْمَرْءِ كَذِبًا بِأَنْ يُحَدِّثَ بِكُلِّ مَا سَمِعَ " رَوَاهُ مُسْلِمٌ.

156 It is reported on the same authority that Allah's Messenger (peace and blessings of Allah be upon him) said: It is enough to render a man a liar that he relates everything he hears.[1] (*Muslim*)

1. Without verifying its authenticity.

١٥٧- وَعَنِ ابْنِ مَسْعُودٍ، قَالَ: قَالَ رَسُولُ اللهِ ﷺ: مَا مِنْ نَبِيٍّ بَعَثَهُ اللهُ فِي أُمَّتِهِ قَبْلِي إِلَّا كَانَ لَهُ فِي أُمَّتِهِ حَوَارِيُّونَ وَأَصْحَابٌ يَأْخُذُونَ بِسُنَّتِهِ، وَيَقْتَدُونَ بِأَمْرِهِ، ثُمَّ إِنَّهَا تَخْلُفُ مِنْ بَعْدِهِمْ خُلُوفٌ يَقُولُونَ مَا لَا يَفْعَلُونَ، وَيَفْعَلُونَ مَا لَا يُؤْمَرُونَ، فَمَنْ جَاهَدَهُمْ بِيَدِهِ فَهُوَ مُؤْمِنٌ، وَمَنْ جَاهَدَهُمْ بِلِسَانِهِ فَهُوَ مُؤْمِنٌ، وَمَنْ جَاهَدَهُمْ بِقَلْبِهِ فَهُوَ مُؤْمِنٌ، وَلَيْسَ وَرَاءَ ذَلِكَ مِنَ الْإِيمَانِ حَبَّةُ خَرْدَلٍ. رَوَاهُ مُسْلِمٌ.

157 Ibn Mas'ud reported Allah's Messenger (peace and blessings of Allah be upon him) as saying: There was never a prophet whom Allah raised in his people before me but he had in his Ummah his disciples and his companions who held fast to his Sunnah and followed his command. Then they were succeeded by people who professed what they did not act upon and acted upon what they were not commanded to do and he who strove hard against them with his hand is a believer and he who strove hard with his tongue is a believer and he who strove hard with his heart is a believer but beyond that there is not even the mustard seed of faith. (*Muslim*)

١٥٨- وَعَنْ أَبِي هُرَيْرَةَ، قَالَ: قَالَ رَسُولُ اللهِ ﷺ: مَنْ دَعَا إِلَى هُدًى كَانَ لَهُ مِنَ الْأَجْرِ مِثْلُ أُجُورِ مَنْ تَبِعَهُ، لَا يَنْقُصُ ذَلِكَ مِنْ أُجُورِهِمْ شَيْئًا.

وَ مَنْ دَعَا إِلَى ضَلَالَةٍ ، كَانَ عَلَيْهِ مِنَ الْإِثْمِ مِثْلُ أَنَامِ مَنْ تَبِعَهُ ، لَا يَنْقُصُ ذٰلِكَ مِنْ أَنَامِهِمْ شَيْئًا ؛ رَوَاهُ مُسْلِمٌ.

158 **Abu Huraira** reported Allah's Messenger (peace and blessings of Allah be upon him) as saying : He who called (people) to right guidance has a reward like the rewards of those who followed him without their reward being lessened thereby in the least bit and he who calls others to the path of error will be guilty of a sin equal to the sins of those who follow his direction without their sins being lightened in the least bit. (*Muslim*)

١٥٩- وَعَنْهُ ، قَالَ : قَالَ رَسُولُ اللهِ ﷺ "بَدَأَ الْإِسْلَامُ غَرِيبًا ، وَ سَيَعُودُ كَمَا بَدَأَ ، فَطُوبَى لِلْغُرَبَاءِ " رَوَاهُ مُسْلِمٌ.

159 It is reported on the same authority that Allah's Messenger (peace and blessings of Allah be upon him) said: That Islam initiated as something strange and it would revert to its (old position) of being strange so let there be tidings for the strangers.[1] (*Muslim*)

> 1. This hadith is generally translated thus: Islam started from the "poor" but it is not correct. What this hadith implies is that although the teachings of Islam are very akin to the nature of man yet when these were preached the people shunned them as strange and unfamiliar things. Secondly, the preaching of Islam was started by Mecca, the birth place of the Holy Prophet, but the atmosphere did not prove congenial to its growth and the Meccans treated the Holy Prophet as a stranger. He had to find a new abode in Medina—a place where he and Islam were both strangers, but it proved to be congenial for it and made an amazing progress. The Holy Prophet became the central figure of the Arabs, and won a large number of adherents.

١٦٠- وَعَنْهُ ، قَالَ : قَالَ رَسُولُ اللهِ ﷺ "إِنَّ الْإِيمَانَ لَيَأْرِزُ إِلَى الْمَدِينَةِ كَمَا تَأْرِزُ الْحَيَّةُ إِلَى جُحْرِهَا ؛ مُتَّفَقٌ عَلَيْهِ .

وَ سَنَذْكُرُ حَدِيثَ أَبِي هُرَيْرَةَ "ذَرُونِي مَا تَرَكْتُكُمْ "فِي كِتَابِ الْمَنَاسِكِ وَ حَدِيثَيْ مُعَاوِيَةَ وَ جَابِرٍ "لَا يَزَالُ مِنْ أُمَّتِي "وَ (الْآخَرُ) "لَا يَزَالُ طَائِفَةٌ مِنْ أُمَّتِي "فِي بَابِ : ثَوَابِ هٰذِهِ الْأُمَّةِ . إِنْ شَاءَ اللهُ تَعَالَى .

160 It is transmitted on the same authority that the Messenger of Allah (peace and blessings of Allah be upon him) said: Verily the faith would recede to Medina just as the serpent crawls back into its hole. (*Agreed upon*)

We shall mention the hadith from Abu Huraira "Leave me as long as I have said nothing to you" in the Book On the Rites of Pilgrimage and the Traditions of Mu'awiya and Jabir "A Section of this people will continue . . . . . In the Chapter 'Reward of this Ummah' if God so wills.

Section II الْفَصْلُ الثَّانِي

١٦١ ـ عَنْ رَبِيعَةَ الْجُرَشِيِّ ، قَالَ : أُتِيَ نَبِيُّ اللهِ ﷺ ، فَقِيلَ لَهُ : لِتَنَمْ عَيْنُكَ ، وَلْتَسْمَعْ أُذُنُكَ ، وَلْيَعْقِلْ قَلْبُكَ . قَالَ "فَنَامَتْ عَيْنِي ، وَسَمِعَتْ أُذُنَايَ ، وَعَقَلَ قَلْبِي" قَالَ "فَقِيلَ لِي : سَيِّدٌ بَنَى دَارًا ، قَصَنَعَ فِيهَا مَأْدُبَةً وَأَرْسَلَ دَاعِيًا : فَمَنْ أَجَابَ الدَّاعِيَ ، دَخَلَ الدَّارَ ، وَأَكَلَ مِنَ الْمَأْدُبَةِ ، وَرَضِيَ عَنْهُ السَّيِّدُ ، وَمَنْ لَمْ يُجِبِ الدَّاعِيَ ، لَمْ يَدْخُلِ الدَّارَ ، وَلَمْ يَأْكُلْ مِنَ الْمَأْدُبَةِ ، وَسَخِطَ عَلَيْهِ السَّيِّدُ . قَالَ "فَاللهُ السَّيِّدُ ، وَمُحَمَّدٌ الدَّاعِي ، وَالدَّارُ الْإِسْلَامُ ، وَالْمَأْدُبَةُ الْجَنَّةُ . رَوَاهُ الدَّارِمِيُّ .

161 Rabi'a-al-Jurashi said: The Prophet of Allah (peace and blessings of Allah be upon him) was shown a heavenly visitant (in a dream) and it was said to him : Let your eyes sleep and your ears hear and your heart perceive. He (the Holy Prophet) said: My eyes slept, my ears heard and my heart perceived. He (the Holy Prophet) said: It was said to me: The master built a house and arranged feast and sent one to issue invitations. He who responded to the host entered the house, ate the feast and the master was well-pleased with him and he who did not respond to the host he did not enter the house and did not eat the feast and the master was annoyed with him. He said: Allah is the Master; Muhammad is one who extends invitation. The house is al-Islam and the feast is the Paradise. (*Darimi*)

١٦٢ـ وَعَنْ أَبِي رَافِعٍ، قَالَ: قَالَ رَسُولُ اللهِ ﷺ: لَا أُلْفِيَنَّ أَحَدَكُمْ مُتَّكِئًا عَلَى
أَرِيكَتِهِ، يَأْتِيهِ الْأَمْرُ مِنْ أَمْرِي مِمَّا أَمَرْتُ بِهِ أَوْ نَهَيْتُ عَنْهُ، فَيَقُولُ:
لَا أَدْرِي، مَا وَجَدْنَا فِي كِتَابِ اللهِ اتَّبَعْنَاهُ. رَوَاهُ أَحْمَدُ، وَأَبُو دَاوُدَ، وَ
التِّرْمِذِيُّ، وَابْنُ مَاجَةَ. وَالْبَيْهَقِيُّ فِي "دَلَائِلِ النُّبُوَّةِ".

162 Abu Rafi' reported Allah's Messenger (peace and blessings of
Allah be upon him) having said: Never do (I wish) to see
anyone of you reclining on his couch and a command out of
my commands in the form of dos and dont's coming to him and
he making this remark on that: I have no knowledge of it.
We only follow what we find in the Book of Allah. (*Transmitted by Ahmad, Abu Dawud, Tirmidhi, Ibn Majah, Al-Baihaqi
in his Dala'il un-Nubuwwa*)

١٦٣ـ وَعَنِ الْمِقْدَامِ بْنِ مَعْدِي كَرِبَ، قَالَ: قَالَ رَسُولُ اللهِ ﷺ: أَلَا إِنِّي
أُوتِيتُ الْقُرْآنَ وَمِثْلَهُ مَعَهُ، أَلَا يُوشِكُ رَجُلٌ شَبْعَانُ عَلَى أَرِيكَتِهِ
يَقُولُ: عَلَيْكُمْ بِهٰذَا الْقُرْآنِ، فَمَا وَجَدْتُمْ فِيهِ مِنْ حَلَالٍ فَأَحِلُّوهُ، وَ
مَا وَجَدْتُمْ فِيهِ مِنْ حَرَامٍ فَحَرِّمُوهُ، وَإِنَّ مَا حَرَّمَ رَسُولُ اللهِ ﷺ
كَمَا حَرَّمَ اللهُ! أَلَا لَا يَحِلُّ لَكُمُ الْحِمَارُ الْأَهْلِيُّ، وَلَا كُلُّ ذِي نَابٍ
مِنَ السِّبَاعِ، وَلَا لُقَطَةُ مُعَاهِدٍ إِلَّا أَنْ يَسْتَغْنِيَ عَنْهَا صَاحِبُهَا، وَمَنْ
نَزَلَ بِقَوْمٍ، فَعَلَيْهِمْ أَنْ يَقْرُوهُ، فَإِنْ لَمْ يَقْرُوهُ، فَلَهُ أَنْ يُعْقِبَهُمْ بِمِثْلِ
قِرَاهُ. رَوَاهُ أَبُو دَاوُدَ. وَرَوَى الدَّارِمِيُّ نَحْوَهُ، وَكَذَا ابْنُ مَاجَةَ إِلَى قَوْلِهِ:
كَمَا حَرَّمَ اللهُ.

163 Miqdam b. Ma'dikarib reported Allah's Messenger (peace and
blessings of Allah be upon him) as saying: Know for certain
that I have been given the Qurān and with it that which is
like unto it. Behold, the time is near that a person having
eaten to its heart's content may be lying on the couch and
saying: It is obligatory for you (to follow) this Qurān and
what you find therein in the form of Halal (permissible) take

it as permissible and what you find in the form of Haram (prohibited) take it as prohibited. And verily what Allah's Messenger (peace and blessings of Allah be upon him) has declared forbidden is like what Allah has prohibted. Behold, don't take permissible for you (eating of) the domestic ass, beasts of prey with fangs, nor the lost thing of a non-Muslim with whom you hold covenant except when its owner renounces its claim (because of its being valueless for him) and he who comes to the people as a guest it is their duty to serve him and if they do not serve him he has a right to receive penalty from them equal to the amount of his entertainment.[1] (*Abu Dawud and Darimi transmitted similar report. Ibn Majah transmitted the same up to 'like what Allah has prohibited'*)

1. The entertainment of a guest has a very great virtue in Islam and those people who do not entertain the guest with a cheerful heart are not liked in Islam. But the imposing of penalty upon the one who does not entertain the guest is not the operative clause of the legal system of Islam. This penalty relates to the early period of Islam when the detachments of the Muslim army had to halt at different habitants and when they were denied cooperation and hospitality by the inhabitants of those villages, it proved to be a source of great trouble for the Muslims. But with the passage of time when the payment of the poor due was made obligatory for the Muslims and the payment of *jizia* for the non-Muslims the clause of imposing penalty was waived and now entertainment of guest has become an act of great virtue and piety. It has, however, ceased to be a cognizable offence.

١٧٤ـ وَعَنِ الْعِرْبَاضِ بْنِ سَارِيَةَ قَالَ: قَامَ رَسُولُ اللهِ ﷺ فَقَالَ: "أَيَحْسِبُ أَحَدُكُمْ مُتَّكِئًا عَلَى أَرِيكَتِهِ يَظُنُّ أَنَّ اللهَ لَمْ يُحَرِّمْ شَيْئًا إِلَّا مَا فِي هٰذَا الْقُرْآنِ ؟! أَلَا وَإِنِّي وَاللهِ قَدْ أَمَرْتُ وَوَعَظْتُ وَنَهَيْتُ عَنْ أَشْيَاءَ إِنَّهَا لَمِثْلُ الْقُرْآنِ أَوْ أَكْثَرُ، وَإِنَّ اللهَ لَمْ يُحِلَّ لَكُمْ أَنْ تَدْخُلُوا بُيُوتَ أَهْلِ الْكِتَابِ إِلَّا بِإِذْنٍ، وَلَا ضَرْبَ نِسَائِهِمْ، وَلَا أَكْلَ ثِمَارِهِمْ إِذَا أَعْطَوْكُمُ الَّذِي عَلَيْهِمْ" رَوَاهُ أَبُو دَاوُدَ وَفِي إِسْنَادِهِ: أَشْعَثُ بْنُ شُعْبَةَ الْمِصِّيصِيُّ، قَدْ تُكُلِّمَ فِيهِ .

164 It is reported on the authority of Al-'Irbad b. Sāriya that Allah's Messenger (peace and blessings of Allah be upon him) got up and said: Does anyone of you reclining upon his couch imagine that Allah has not prohibited anything but only that contained in the Qurān.[1] Behold, by Allah I have commanded and I have exhorted and I have prohibited things like found in the Qurān or even more. Verily Allah did not make it permissible for you that you should get into the houses of the people of the Book but with their permission, or that you beat their women and eat their fruits, when they have paid you what is due from them. (*Abu Dawud. One of his reporters is Ash'ath b. Shu'ubata whose veracity has been qustioned*)

1. This hadith shows that the commands given by the Holy Prophet are as binding for the Muslims as those contained in the Qurān, because the Holy Prophet is divinely authorised to explain the real meaning and practical significance of the teachings of the Qurān. In the above mentioned hadith three examples are given of those injunctions which are not found in the Qurān but they are binding for the Muslims.

١٦٥ـ وَعَنْهُ، قَالَ : صَلّى بِنَا رَسُوْلُ اللهِ ﷺ ذَاتَ يَوْمٍ، ثُمَّ أَقْبَلَ عَلَيْنَا بِوَجْهِهِ فَوَعَظَنَا مَوْعِظَةً بَلِيْغَةً ، ذَرَفَتْ مِنْهَا الْعُيُوْنُ ، وَوَجِلَتْ مِنْهَا الْقُلُوْبُ . فَقَالَ رَجُلٌ : يَا رَسُوْلَ اللهِ ! كَأَنَّ هٰذِهِ مَوْعِظَةُ مُوَدِّعٍ فَأَوْصِنَا، فَقَالَ : "أُوْصِيْكُمْ بِتَقْوَى اللهِ، وَالسَّمْعِ وَالطَّاعَةِ، وَإِنْ كَانَ عَبْدًا حَبَشِيًّا، فَإِنَّهُ مَنْ يَعِشْ مِنْكُمْ بَعْدِىْ فَسَيَرَى اخْتِلَافًا كَثِيْرًا ؛ فَعَلَيْكُمْ بِسُنَّتِىْ وَسُنَّةِ الْخُلَفَاءِ الرَّاشِدِيْنَ الْمَهْدِيِّيْنَ ، تَمَسَّكُوْا بِهَا وَعَضُّوْا عَلَيْهَا بِالنَّوَاجِذِ ، وَإِيَّاكُمْ وَمُحْدَثَاتِ الْأُمُوْرِ ؛ فَإِنَّ كُلَّ مُحْدَثَةٍ بِدْعَةٌ ، وَكُلَّ بِدْعَةٍ ضَلَالَةٌ" رَوَاهُ أَحْمَدُ ، وَأَبُوْدَاوُدَ ، وَالتِّرْمِذِىُّ وَابْنُ مَاجَةَ إِلَّا أَنَّهُمَا لَمْ يَذْكُرَا الصَّلَاةَ .

165 It is reported on the same authority that Allah's Messenger (peace and blessings of Allah be upon him) one day led us in prayer. He then turned his face towards us and gave us a very moving sermon which made our eyes welled up with tears and our hearts were softened. A person said: Allah's Messenger, (you have delivered us such a sermon) as if it were a farewell sermon. Thereupon he said: I exhort you to be God-conscious, to hear and to obey even if (your commander) is an Abyssinian slave, and he who amongst you would survive me, he would see great differences so you hold fast to my Sunnah and the practice of the rightly guided caliphs; adhere to it and hold it fastly and beware of the innovation for every innovation (in religion) is *bida'*,[1] and every *bida'*, is an error. (*Transmitted by Abu Dawud, Tirmidhi, Ibn Majah, but the last two did not make mention of the prayer*)

1. The term *bida'* has been explained differently by different writers but the general conclusion is that it is an innovation in religion which has neither the sanction of the Qurān nor that of the Sunnāh and which has been made a part and parcel of religion to such an extent that those who do not put into practice are supposed to have committed an act of omission.

١٦٦ـ وَعَنْ عَبْدِ اللهِ بْنِ مَسْعُودٍ، قَالَ: خَطَّ لَنَا رَسُولُ اللهِ ﷺ خَطًّا، ثُمَّ قَالَ: "هٰذَا سَبِيلُ اللهِ"، ثُمَّ خَطَّ خُطُوطًا عَنْ يَمِينِهِ وَعَنْ شِمَالِهِ وَقَالَ: "هٰذِهِ سُبُلٌ، عَلَى كُلِّ سَبِيلٍ مِنْهَا شَيْطَانٌ يَدْعُو إِلَيْهِ"، وَقَرَأَ: رَوَا إِنَّ هٰذَا صِرَاطِي مُسْتَقِيمًا، فَاتَّبِعُوهُ، الْآيَةَ. رَوَاهُ أَحْمَدُ وَالنَّسَائِيُّ وَالدَّارِمِيُّ.

166 'Abdullah b. Mas'ud reported that Allah's Messenger (peace and blessings of Allah be upon him) drew up a line for us and then said: That is the path shown by Allah. Thereafter he drew several other lines on his right and left sides and said: These are the paths on every side of which there is a devil calling towards it.[1] He then recited this verse: Verily this path of Mine is straight so adhere it (5 : 167).

(*Ahmad, Nisai and Darimi*)

1. There can be only one line between two points and all other lines drawn to join the two points—must diverge from the straight path. Similarly, the path of Truth is only one and any other line which does not conicide with one must diverge from the path of Truth.

١٦٧ - وَعَنْ عَبْدِ اللهِ بْنِ عَمْرِو، قَالَ : قَالَ رَسُولُ اللهِ ﷺ : "لَا يُؤْمِنُ أَحَدُكُمْ حَتَّى يَكُونَ هَوَاهُ تَبْعًا لِمَا جِئْتُ بِهِ" رَوَاهُ فِي "شَرْحِ السُّنَّةِ" وَ قَالَ النَّوَوِيُّ فِي "أَرْبَعِينِهِ" : هٰذَا حَدِيثٌ صَحِيحٌ رَوَيْنَاهُ فِي "كِتَابِ الْحُجَّةِ" بِإِسْنَادٍ صَحِيحٍ .

167 'Abdullah b. 'Amr reported Allah's Messenger (peace and blessings of Allah be upon him) as saying: None amongst you is a true believer unless his desires become subservient to what I have brought.

The author mentioned it in *Sharh ul-Sunna*, and al-Nawawi said in his *Araba'in*: This is a *sahih hadith* which we have transmitted in *Kitab-ul-Hujjah* through a reliable chain of transmission.

١٦٨ - وَعَنْ بِلَالِ بْنِ الْحَارِثِ الْمُزَنِيِّ، قَالَ : قَالَ رَسُولُ اللهِ ﷺ : "مَنْ أَحْيَا سُنَّةً مِنْ سُنَّتِي قَدْ أُمِيتَتْ بَعْدِي، فَإِنَّ لَهُ مِنَ الْأَجْرِ مِثْلَ أُجُورِ مَنْ عَمِلَ بِهَا مِنْ غَيْرِ أَنْ يَنْقُصَ مِنْ أُجُورِهِمْ شَيْئًا، وَمَنِ ابْتَدَعَ بِدْعَةً ضَلَالَةً لَا يَرْضَاهَا اللهُ وَرَسُولُهُ، كَانَ عَلَيْهِ مِنَ الْإِثْمِ، مِثْلَ آثَامِ مَنْ عَمِلَ بِهَا لَا يَنْقُصُ مِنْ أَوْزَارِهِمْ شَيْئًا" رَوَاهُ التِّرْمِذِيُّ .

168 Bilal b. Harith al-Muzani reported Allah's Messenger (peace and blessings of Allah be upon him) as saying: He who revived a Sunnah out of my Sunan which has died after me, for him is the reward like the reward of those who acted upon it, without any decrease in that reward and he who introduced some evil innovation which Allah and His Messenger did not approve has (burden of sin upon him) like the sins of one who acted according to it, without their sins being mitigated thereby in the least bit. (*Tirmidhi*)

١٦٩ - وَرَوَاهُ ابْنُ مَاجَهْ عَنْ كَثِيرِ بْنِ عَبْدِ اللهِ بْنِ عَمْرِو، عَنْ أَبِيهِ، عَنْ جَدِّهِ،

169 Tirmidhi transmitted it and Ibn Majah transmitted it from Kathir b. 'Abdullah b. 'Amr from his father from his grandfather.

١٧٠ـ وَعَنْ عَمْرِو بْنِ عَوْفٍ، قَالَ: قَالَ رَسُولُ اللهِ ﷺ: "إِنَّ الدِّينَ لَيَأْرِزُ إِلَى الْحِجَازِ كَمَا تَأْرِزُ الْحَيَّةُ إِلَى جُحْرِهَا، وَلَيَعْقِلَنَّ الدِّينُ مِنَ الْحِجَازِ مَعْقِلَ الْأُرْوِيَّةِ مِنْ رَأْسِ الْجَبَلِ، إِنَّ الدِّينَ بَدَأَ غَرِيبًا وَسَيَعُودُ كَمَا بَدَأَ، فَطُوبَى لِلْغُرَبَاءِ، وَهُمُ الَّذِينَ يُصْلِحُونَ مَا أَفْسَدَ النَّاسُ مِنْ بَعْدِي مِنْ سُنَّتِي." رَوَاهُ التِّرْمِذِيُّ.

170 **'Amr b. 'Auf** reported Allah's Messenger (peace and blessings of Allah be upon him) as saying: Verily ad-Din will recede to Hijaz as the serpent crawls back to its hole and ad-Din will find its abode in Hijaz as the mountain goat seeks refuge in the peak of the mountain, verily the Din was initiated amongst the strangers, and would revert to them as it started. Let there be glad tidings for the strangers and they are those persons who set right what the people had corrupted of my Sunnah. (*Tirmidhi*)

١٧١ـ وَعَنْ عَبْدِ اللهِ بْنِ عَمْرٍو، قَالَ: قَالَ رَسُولُ اللهِ ﷺ: "لَيَأْتِيَنَّ عَلَى أُمَّتِي كَمَا أَتَى عَلَى بَنِي إِسْرَائِيلَ حَذْوَ النَّعْلِ بِالنَّعْلِ، حَتَّى إِنْ كَانَ مِنْهُمْ مَنْ أَتَى أُمَّهُ عَلَانِيَةً، لَكَانَ فِي أُمَّتِي مَنْ يَصْنَعُ ذَلِكَ، وَإِنَّ بَنِي إِسْرَائِيلَ تَفَرَّقَتْ عَلَى ثِنْتَيْنِ وَسَبْعِينَ مِلَّةً، وَتَفْتَرِقُ أُمَّتِي عَلَى ثَلَاثٍ وَسَبْعِينَ مِلَّةً كُلُّهُمْ فِي النَّارِ إِلَّا مِلَّةً وَاحِدَةً." قَالُوا: مَنْ هِيَ يَا رَسُولَ اللهِ؟ قَالَ: "مَا أَنَا عَلَيْهِ وَأَصْحَابِي." رَوَاهُ التِّرْمِذِيُّ.

171 **'Abdullah b. 'Amr** reported Allah's Messenger (peace and blessings of Allah be upon him) as saying: There would exactly befall my Ummah (all those) evils which had befallen the people of Israil, so much so that if there was one amongst them who openly committed fornication with his mother there would be among my Ummah one who would do that and if

the people of Israel were fragmented into seventy-two sects
my Ummah would be fragmented into seventy-three sects.[1] All
of them would be in Hell Fire except one sect. They (the
Companions) said: Allah's Messenger, which is that? Whereupon he said: It is one to which I and my Companions
belong. (*Trimidhi*)

> 1. This does not mean exactly seventy-two or seventy-three but it only
> implies a fairly large number.

١٤٢- وَفِى رِوَايَةِ أَحْمَدَ، وَأَبِى دَاوُدَ، عَنْ مُعَاوِيَةَ: ثِنْتَانِ وَ سَبْعُونَ فِى
النَّارِ، وَوَاحِدَةٌ فِى الْجَنَّةِ، وَهِىَ الْجَمَاعَةُ، وَ إِنَّهُ سَيَخْرُجُ فِى أُمَّتِى أَقْوَامُ
تَتَجَارَى بِهِمْ تِلْكَ الْأَهْوَاءُ كَمَا يَتَجَارَى الْكَلْبُ بِصَاحِبِهِ، لَا يَبْقَى مِنْهُ
عِرْقٌ وَ لَا مَفْصِلٌ إِلَّا دَخَلَهُ:

172 In another version by *Ahmad* and *Abu Dawud* from Mu'awiya
(the wording is): Seventy-two will be in the Hell and one in
Paradise, and there would come out from my Ummah people
through which would run the vain desires, like hydrophobia
which infects its victim through and through and leaves not
a vein or a joint without its taint. (*Ahmad and Abu Dawud*)

١٤٣- وَعَنِ ابْنِ عُمَرَ، قَالَ: قَالَ رَسُولُ اللهِ ﷺ: إِنَّ اللهَ لَا يَجْمَعُ أُمَّتِى-
أَوْ قَالَ: أُمَّةَ مُحَمَّدٍ- عَلَى ضَلَالَةٍ، وَ يَدُ اللهِ عَلَى الْجَمَاعَةِ، وَمَنْ شَذَّ
شَذَّ فِى النَّارِ: رَوَاهُ التِّرْمِذِىُّ.

173 Ibn 'Umar reported Allah's Messenger (peace and blessings
of Allah be upon him) as saying: Verily my Ummah would
not agree (or he said the Ummah of Muhammad) on error and
the Hand of Allah is upon the community and he who sets
himself apart from it will be set apart in Hell Fire. (*Tirmidhi*)

١٤٤- وَعَنْهُ، قَالَ: قَالَ رَسُولُ اللهِ ﷺ: اِتَّبِعُوا السَّوَادَ الْأَعْظَمَ، فَإِنَّهُ
مَنْ شَذَّ شَذَّ فِى النَّارِ: رَوَاهُ (ابْنُ مَاجَةَ مِنْ حَدِيثِ أَنَسٍ)

174 It is reported on the same authority that Allah's Messenger
(peace and blessings of Allah be upon him) said: Follow the
great mass[1] for he who kept himself away from it in fact would
be thrown in Hell Fire. (*Ibn Majah*)

1. There is good deal of difference of opinion as to what the term Sawad Azam implies. The overwhelming majority of the scholars is of the view that As-Sawad al-Azam means the largest group of the learned scholars and pious persons whose opinions are held in high esteem in Islam.

١٤٥ـ وَعَنْ أَنَسٍ، قَالَ، قَالَ لِي رَسُولُ اللهِ ﷺ : "يَا بُنَيَّ ! إِنْ قَدَرْتَ أَنْ
تُصْبِحَ وَتُمْسِيَ وَلَيْسَ فِي قَلْبِكَ غِشٌّ لِأَحَدٍ فَافْعَلْ : ثُمَّ قَالَ : يَا بُنَيَّ !
وَذٰلِكَ مِنْ سُنَّتِي ، وَمَنْ أَحَبَّ سُنَّتِي فَقَدْ أَحَبَّنِي وَمَنْ أَحَبَّنِي كَانَ
مَعِي فِي الْجَنَّةِ " رَوَاهُ التِّرْمِذِيُّ .

175 Anas reported that Allah's Messenger (peace and blessings of Allah be upon him) said to me: My son, if you are in a position to pass your morning and evening keeping your heart free from malice against any one, then act according to it (this high ideal). He then said: My son, and that is my Sunnah and he who loves my Sunnah he in fact loves me and he who loves me, he would be with me in Paradise. (*Tirmidhi*)

١٤٦ـ وَعَنْ أَبِي هُرَيْرَةَ ، قَالَ : قَالَ رَسُولُ اللهِ ﷺ : "مَنْ تَمَسَّكَ بِسُنَّتِي عِنْدَ
فَسَادِ أُمَّتِي ، فَلَهُ أَجْرُ مِائَةِ شَهِيدٍ : رَوَاهُ

176 Abu Huraira reported Allah's Messenger (peace and blessings of Allah be upon him) as saying: He who held fast to my Sunnah in the period of turmoil of my people for him is the reward of a hundred martyrs. (*Baihaqi*)

١٤٧ـ وَعَنْ جَابِرٍ ، عَنِ النَّبِيِّ ﷺ حِينَ أَتَاهُ عُمَرُ فَقَالَ : إِنَّا نَسْمَعُ أَحَادِيثَ
مِنْ يَهُودٍ تُعْجِبُنَا ، أَفَتَرَى أَنْ نَكْتُبَ بَعْضَهَا ؛ فَقَالَ : "أَمُتَهَوِّكُونَ أَنْتُمْ
كَمَا تَهَوَّكَتِ الْيَهُودُ وَالنَّصَارَى ؟ ! لَقَدْ جِئْتُكُمْ بِهَا بَيْضَاءَ نَقِيَّةً ، وَلَوْ
كَانَ مُوسَى حَيًّا مَا وَسِعَهُ إِلَّا اتِّبَاعِي : رَوَاهُ أَحْمَدُ ، وَالْبَيْهَقِيُّ فِي كِتَابِ
"شُعَبِ الْإِيمَانِ "

177 Jabir reported that when 'Umar came to Allah's Messenger (peace and blessings of Allah be upon him), he said: We hear the narrations from the Jews which sound pleasing to us, so should we not write some of them; whereupon he said: Do you want to be baffled as were baffled the Jews and the Christians, I have brought to you (guidance) bright and pure and if Moses would have been alive by now there would have been no alternative left for him but to follow me.

(Transmitted by Ahmad, Baihaqi in Shu'ab-ul-Iman)

١٧٨ـ وَعَنْ أَبِي سَعِيْدٍ الْخُدْرِيِّ، قَالَ: قَالَ رَسُوْلُ اللهِ ﷺ "مَنْ أَكَلَ طَيِّبًا،

وَعَمِلَ فِي سُنَّةٍ، وَّ أَمِنَ النَّاسُ بَوَائِقَهُ، دَخَلَ الْجَنَّةَ" فَقَالَ رَجُلٌ: يَا

رَسُوْلَ اللهِ! إِنَّ هٰذَا الْيَوْمَ لَكَثِيْرٌ فِي النَّاسِ؛ قَالَ: "وَسَيَكُوْنُ فِي قُرُوْنٍ

بَعْدِيْ" رَوَاهُ التِّرْمِذِيُّ.

178 Abu Sa'id Khudri reported that Allah's Messenger (peace and blessings of Allah be upon him) said: He who eats lawfully earned food and acts according to (my Sunnah) and mankind is safe from any excess on his part would enter Paradise. Thereupon a person said: Allah's Messenger, verily in these times there are many of that description whereupon he (the Holy Prophet) said: And many such will there be in ages after me. (*Tirmidhi*)

١٧٩ـ وَعَنْ أَبِي هُرَيْرَةَ، قَالَ: قَالَ رَسُوْلُ اللهِ ﷺ "إِنَّكُمْ فِي زَمَانٍ مَنْ تَرَكَ

مِنْكُمْ عُشْرَ مَا أُمِرَ بِهِ هَلَكَ، ثُمَّ يَأْتِي زَمَانٌ مَنْ عَمِلَ مِنْهُمْ بِعُشْرِ مَا أُمِرَ

بِهِ نَجَا" رَوَاهُ التِّرْمِذِيُّ.

179 Abu Huraira reported Allah's Messenger (peace and blessings of Allah be upon him) as saying: (You are living) in a blessed age that he who abandons even one-tenth of that what he is prescribed, courts destruction; after this there will come a time when he who observes one-tenth of what is now prescribed would be saved. (*Tirmidhi*)

١٨٠ـ وَعَنْ أَبِي أُمَامَةَ، قَالَ: قَالَ رَسُوْلُ اللهِ ﷺ "مَا ضَلَّ قَوْمٌ بَعْدَ هُدًى

كَانُوْا عَلَيْهِ إِلَّا أُوْتُوا الْجَدَلَ" ثُمَّ قَرَأَ رَسُوْلُ اللهِ ﷺ هٰذِهِ الْآيَةَ:

(مَا ضَرَبُوْهُ لَكَ إِلَّا جَدَلًا بَلْ هُمْ قَوْمٌ خَصِمُوْنَ). رَوَاهُ أَحْمَدُ،

وَالتِّرْمِذِيُّ، وَابْنُ مَاجَهْ.

180 Abu Umama reported Allah's Messenger (peace and blessings of Allah be upon him) as saying: No people, who have once found the right way, ever go astray except through disputatiousness, then Allah's Messenger (peace and blessings of Allah be upon him) recited this verse: "They set it forth to thee only by way of disputation. Lo they are contentious people" (**43** : 58). (*Ahmad, Tirmidhi and Ibn Majah*)

١٨١- وَعَنْ أَنَسِ بْنِ مَالِكٍ ، أَنَّ رَسُولَ اللهِ ﷺ كَانَ يَقُولُ : لَا تُشَدِّدُوا عَلَى أَنْفُسِكُمْ فَيُشَدِّدَ اللهُ عَلَيْكُمْ، فَإِنَّ قَوْمًا شَدَّدُوا عَلَى أَنْفُسِهِمْ، فَشَدَّدَ اللهُ عَلَيْهِمْ، فَتِلْكَ بَقَايَاهُمْ فِي الصَّوَامِعِ وَالدِّيَارِ، رَهْبَانِيَّةً ابْتَدَعُوهَا مَا كَتَبْنَاهَا عَلَيْهِمْ، رَوَاهُ أَبُو دَاوُدَ.

181 Anas b. Malik reported Allah's Messenger (peace and blessings of Allah be upon him) as saying: Don't impose austerities on yourself, for in that case Allah would impose austerities upon you, for the people who imposed austerities upon themselves Allah imposed austerities upon them. Their survivors are to be found in cloisters and monasteries (then he quoted) "so far as monasticism is concerned it is they who have innovated it. We did not prescribe it for them' (57 : 27). (*Abu Dawud*)

١٨٢- وَعَنْ أَبِي هُرَيْرَةَ، قَالَ، قَالَ رَسُولُ اللهِ ﷺ : نَزَلَ الْقُرْآنُ عَلَى خَمْسَةِ أَوْجُهٍ : حَلَالٍ، وَحَرَامٍ، وَمُحْكَمٍ، وَمُتَشَابِهٍ، وَأَمْثَالٍ. فَأَحِلُّوا الْحَلَالَ، وَحَرِّمُوا الْحَرَامَ، وَاعْمَلُوا بِالْمُحْكَمِ، وَآمِنُوا بِالْمُتَشَابِهِ، وَاعْتَبِرُوا بِالْأَمْثَالِ" هَذَا لَفْظُ الْمَصَابِيحِ، وَرَوَى الْبَيْهَقِيُّ فِي "شُعَبِ الْإِيمَانِ" وَلَفْظُهُ : "فَاعْمَلُوا بِالْحَلَالِ، وَاجْتَنِبُوا الْحَرَامَ، وَاتَّبِعُوا الْمُحْكَمَ".

182 Abu Huraira reported Allah's Messenger (peace and blessings of Allah be upon him) as saying: The Qurān was revealed (containing injunctions) of five categories: Things lawful, things unlawful, clear and positive injunctions, allegories and parables, so hold lawful which (Allah has ordained) lawful for you and consider prohibited (what Allah has ordained so) and act according to the clear and positive injunctions and affirm faith in allegories and draw lessons from the parables. (*This is the wording of Al-Masabih, Baihaqi transmitted it in Shu'ab-ul-Iman, his wording being : Act according to what is lawful and avoid unlawful and follow what is clear and decisive*).

١٨٣ - وَعَنِ ابْنِ عَبَّاسٍ، قَالَ: قَالَ رَسُولُ اللّٰهِ ﷺ "اَلْأَمْرُ ثَلَاثَةٌ: أَمْرٌ بَيِّنٌ رُشْدُهُ فَاتَّبِعْهُ، وَأَمْرٌ بَيِّنٌ غَيُّهُ فَاجْتَنِبْهُ، وَأَمْرٌ اخْتُلِفَ فِيهِ فَكِلْهُ إِلَى اللّٰهِ عَزَّ وَجَلَّ" رَوَاهُ أَحْمَدُ.

183 Ibn 'Abbas reported Allah's Messenger (peace and blessings of Allah be upon him) as saying: Affairs are of three categories: There is an affair whose being right is quite obvious; do it. Then there is an affair whose being wrong is obvious; shun it. Then there may be an affair (the nature of which) is debatable. In that case you must resign it to Allah, the Exalted and Glorious. (*Ahmad*)

Section III   اَلْفَصْلُ الثَّالِثُ

١٨٤ - عَنْ مُعَاذِ بْنِ جَبَلٍ، قَالَ: قَالَ رَسُولُ اللّٰهِ ﷺ "إِنَّ الشَّيْطَانَ ذِئْبُ الْإِنْسَانِ كَذِئْبِ الْغَنَمِ، يَأْخُذُ الشَّاذَّةَ وَالْقَاصِيَةَ وَالنَّاحِيَةَ، وَإِيَّاكُمْ وَالشِّعَابَ، وَعَلَيْكُمْ بِالْجَمَاعَةِ وَالْعَامَّةِ" رَوَاهُ أَحْمَدُ.

184 Mua'dh b. Jabal reported Allah's Messenger (peace and blessings of Allah be upon him) as saying: Verily the satan is the wolf of a man just as the wolf is (the enemy) of flock. He seizes the solitary sheep going astray from the flock or going aside from the flock, so avoid the branching paths and it is essential for you to remain along with the community.
(*Ahmad*)

١٨٥ـ وَعَنْ أَبِي ذَرٍّ، قَالَ: قَالَ رَسُولُ اللهِ ﷺ: "مَنْ فَارَقَ الْجَمَاعَةَ شِبْرًا
فَقَدْ خَلَعَ رِبْقَةَ الْإِسْلَامِ مِنْ عُنُقِهِ؟ رَوَاهُ أَحْمَدُ، وَأَبُو دَاوُدَ.

185 **Abu Dharr** reported Allah's Messenger (peace and blessings
of Allah be upon him) as saying: He who separates from the
main body (of Ummah) by even a hand's breadth from the
community he throws off Islam from his neck.

(*Ahmad and Abu Dawud*)

١٨٦ـ وَعَنْ مَالِكِ بْنِ أَنَسٍ مُرْسَلًا، قَالَ: قَالَ رَسُولُ اللهِ ﷺ: "تَرَكْتُ فِيكُمْ
أَمْرَيْنِ لَنْ تَضِلُّوا مَا تَمَسَّكْتُمْ بِهِمَا: كِتَابَ اللهِ وَسُنَّةَ رَسُولِهِ؟ رَوَاهُ
فِي "الْمُوَطَّا".

186 **Malik b. Anas** reported it as a *mursal hadith* that Allah's
Messenger (peace and blessings of Allah be upon him) said:
I am leaving with you two things. You will never go astray
so long as you hold them tightly: The Book of Allah and the
Sunnah of His Messenger. (*Muwatta'*)

١٨٧ـ وَعَنْ غُضَيْفِ بْنِ الْحَارِثِ الثُّمَالِيِّ، قَالَ: قَالَ رَسُولُ اللهِ ﷺ: "مَا
أَحْدَثَ قَوْمٌ بِدْعَةً إِلَّا رُفِعَ مِثْلُهَا مِنَ السُّنَّةِ؛ فَتَمَسُّكُكَ بِسُنَّةٍ خَيْرٌ
مِنْ إِحْدَاثِ بِدْعَةٍ؟ رَوَاهُ أَحْمَدُ.

187 **Ghudaif b. al-Harith ath-Thumali** reported Allah's Messenger
(peace and blessings of Allah be upon him) as saying: Never
a people made innovation (in religion) that there was not
withdrawn from them the equal measure of Sunnah. Adher-
ing to Sunnah is better than making innovations. (*Ahmad*)

١٨٨ـ وَعَنْ حَسَّانَ، قَالَ: "مَا ابْتَدَعَ قَوْمٌ بِدْعَةً فِي دِينِهِمْ إِلَّا نَزَعَ اللهُ مِنْ
سُنَّتِهِمْ مِثْلَهَا، ثُمَّ لَا يُعِيدُهَا إِلَيْهِمْ إِلَى يَوْمِ الْقِيَامَةِ. رَوَاهُ الدَّارِمِيُّ.

188 It is reported on the authority of Hassan[1]: No people whosoever, made an innovation in their religion but Allah with-
drew the equal portion from their Sunnah and He would not
restore it to them till the Day of Resurrection. (*Darimi*)

1. He is not Hassan famous poet and the emiuent companion of the Holy Prophet but he is the son of Atiyya, the famous successor. He died in 130H.

١٨٩- وَعَنْ إِبْرَاهِيمَ بْنِ مَيْسَرَةَ، قَالَ: قَالَ رَسُولُ اللهِ ﷺ: "مَنْ وَقَّرَ صَاحِبَ بِدْعَةٍ، فَقَدْ أَعَانَ عَلَى هَدَمِ الْإِسْلَامِ" رَوَاهُ الْبَيْهَقِيُّ فِي شُعَبِ الْإِيمَانِ مُرْسَلًا.

189 Ibrahim b. Maisara reported Allah's Messenger (peace and blessings of Allah be upon him) as saying: He who showed respect to an innovator he in fact aided in the demolishing of Islam. (*Baihaqi transmitted it as Mursal in Shu'ab ul-Iman*)

١٩٠- وَعَنِ ابْنِ عَبَّاسٍ، قَالَ: مَنْ تَعَلَّمَ كِتَابَ اللهِ ثُمَّ اتَّبَعَ مَا فِيهِ هَدَاهُ اللهُ مِنَ الضَّلَالَةِ فِي الدُّنْيَا، وَوَقَاهُ يَوْمَ الْقِيَامَةِ سُوءَ الْحِسَابِ. وَفِي رِوَايَةٍ، قَالَ: مَنِ اقْتَدَى بِكِتَابِ اللهِ لَا يَضِلُّ فِي الدُّنْيَا وَلَا يَشْقَى فِي الْآخِرَةِ، ثُمَّ تَلَا هَذِهِ الْآيَةَ: (فَمَنِ اتَّبَعَ هُدَايَ فَلَا يَضِلُّ وَلَا يَشْقَى). رَوَاهُ رَزِينٌ

190 Ibn 'Abbas reported: He who learns the Book of Allah then follows what it contains, Allah safeguards him in the righteousness against error and safeguards him from the severe reckoning, on the Day of Resurrection. It is reported on the same authority that he who adhered to the Book of Allah would not go astray in this world and would not face hardship in the Hereafter. He then recited this verse: "He who followed the guidance is not led astray nor is afflicted with hardship" (20 : 123). (*Razin*)

١٩١- وَعَنِ ابْنِ مَسْعُودٍ، أَنَّ رَسُولَ اللهِ ﷺ قَالَ: "ضَرَبَ اللهُ مَثَلًا صِرَاطًا مُسْتَقِيمًا، وَعَنْ جَنْبَتَيِ الصِّرَاطِ سُورَانِ، فِيهِمَا أَبْوَابٌ مُفَتَّحَةٌ، وَ عَلَى الْأَبْوَابِ سُتُورٌ مُرْخَاةٌ، وَعِنْدَ رَأْسِ الصِّرَاطِ دَاعٍ يَقُولُ: إِسْتَقِيمُوا عَلَى الصِّرَاطِ وَلَا تَعَوَّجُوا، وَفَوْقَ ذَلِكَ دَاعٍ يَدْعُو، كُلَّمَا

هَمَّ عَبْدٌ أَنْ يَفْتَحَ شَيْئًا مِنْ تِلْكَ الْأَبْوَابِ قَالَ: وَيْحَكَ! لَا تَفْتَحْهُ، فَإِنَّكَ إِنْ تَفْتَحْهُ تَلِجْهُ" ثُمَّ فَسَّرَهُ فَأَخْبَرَ:"أَنَّ الصِّرَاطَ هُوَ الْإِسْلَامُ، وَأَنَّ الْأَبْوَابَ الْمُفَتَّحَةَ مَحَارِمُ اللهِ، وَأَنَّ السُّتُورَ الْمُرْخَاةَ حُدُودُ اللهِ، وَأَنَّ الدَّاعِيَ عَلَى رَأْسِ الصِّرَاطِ هُوَ الْقُرْآنُ، وَأَنَّ الـدَّاعِيَ مِنْ فَوْقِهِ وَاعِظُ اللهِ فِي قَلْبِ كُلِّ مُؤْمِنٍ: رَوَاهُ رَزِينٌ، رَوَاهُ أَحْمَدُ.

191 **Ibn Mas'ud** reported Allah's Messenger (peace and blessings of Allah be upon him) as saying: Allah has set forth a parable of a straight path and on the both sides of the path there are two enclosures in which there are open doors and there hang upon each door the curtains and there is at the extremity of the path an admonisher saying: Adhere to the path and don't go astray, and above that there is an announcer who announces as often as anyone intends to open the doors: Woe be to thee don't open it for if you open it you shall have to enter into it. He then explained (this parable) and said: Verily the path is Al-Islam and the open doors are the prohibitions made by Allah and the hanging curtains are the limits set by Allah and the announcer at the extremity of the path is the Qurān and the announcer over it is Allah's Preacher in every heart. (*Razin and Ahmad*)

١٩٢- وَالْبَيْهَقِيُّ فِي "شُعَبِ الْإِيمَانِ" عَنِ النَّوَّاسِ بْنِ سَمْعَانَ، وَكَذَا التِّرْمِذِيُّ عَنْهُ إِلَّا أَنَّهُ ذَكَرَ أَخْصَرَ مِنْهُ.

192 **Baihaqi** relates the same from Nawaz b. Sim'an from whom Tirmidhi has also related the same report, but briefly.

١٩٣- وَعَنِ ابْنِ مَسْعُودٍ، قَالَ: مَنْ كَانَ مُسْتَنًّا؛ فَلْيَسْتَنَّ بِمَنْ قَدْ مَاتَ فَإِنَّ الْحَيَّ لَا تُؤْمَنُ عَلَيْهِ الْفِتْنَةُ. أُولَئِكَ أَصْحَابُ مُحَمَّدٍ ﷺ كَانُوا أَفْضَلَ هَذِهِ الْأُمَّةِ. أَبَرَّهَا قُلُوبًا، وَأَعْمَقَهَا عِلْمًا، وَأَقَلَّهَا تَكَلُّفًا، إِخْتَارَهُمُ اللهُ لِصُحْبَةِ نَبِيِّهِ، وَلِإِقَامَةِ دِينِهِ، فَاعْرِفُوا لَهُمْ فَضْلَهُمْ

وَاتَّبِعُوهُمْ عَلَى أَثَرِهِمْ، وَتَمَسَّكُوا بِمَا اسْتَطَعْتُمْ مِنْ أَخْلَاقِهِمْ دَ

سِيَرِهِمْ، فَإِنَّهُمْ عَلَى الْهُدَى الْمُسْتَقِيمِ. رَوَاهُ رَزِينٌ.

193 Ibn Mas'ud reported: If one has to follow the practice
of another one he must follow the practice of one who is dead
for a living person is never immune from trial. Those (who
can be safely followed) are the companions of Muhammad
(peace and blessings of Allah be upon him) for they are best
of Ummah, purest of heart, most profound in knowledge
(of Islam), most unassuming. Allah chose them for the
companionship of His Apostle and for establishing the supre-
macy of his religion so acknowledge their merit, follow their
footsteps and hold fast to the best of your ability their morals
and their character for they are on the right guidance.

(*Razin*)

١٩٤- وَعَنْ جَابِرٍ، أَنَّ عُمَرَ بْنَ الْخَطَّابِ، رَضِيَ اللهُ عَنْهُمَا، أَنَّ رَسُولَ اللهِ

ﷺ بِنُسْخَةٍ مِنَ التَّوْرَاةِ، فَقَالَ: يَا رَسُولَ اللهِ! هٰذِهِ نُسْخَةٌ مِنَ

التَّوْرَاةِ، فَسَكَتَ فَجَعَلَ يَقْرَأُ وَوَجْهُ رَسُولِ اللهِ ﷺ يَتَغَيَّرُ. فَقَالَ

أَبُوْبَكْرٍ، ثَكِلَتْكَ الثَّوَاكِلُ! مَا تَرَى مَا بِوَجْهِ رَسُولِ اللهِ ﷺ؟! فَنَظَرَ

عُمَرُ إِلَى وَجْهِ رَسُولِ اللهِ ﷺ فَقَالَ: أَعُوْذُ بِاللهِ مِنْ غَضَبِ اللهِ وَ

غَضَبِ رَسُوْلِهِ، رَضِيْنَا بِاللهِ رَبًّا، وَبِالْإِسْلَامِ دِيْنًا، وَبِمُحَمَّدٍ نَبِيًّا.

فَقَالَ رَسُوْلُ اللهِ ﷺ: وَالَّذِيْ نَفْسُ مُحَمَّدٍ بِيَدِهِ، لَوْ بَدَالَكُمْ مُوْسَى

فَاتَّبَعْتُمُوْهُ وَتَرَكْتُمُوْنِيْ لَضَلَلْتُمْ عَنْ سَوَاءِ السَّبِيْلِ؛ وَلَوْ كَانَ حَيًّا

وَأَدْرَكَ نَبُوَّتِيْ لَاتَّبَعَنِيْ. رَوَاهُ الدَّارِمِيُّ

194 Jabir reported that 'Umar b. Khattab (may Allah be pleased
with him) brought to Allah's Messenger (peace and blessings
of Allah be upon him) a copy of the Torah and said: Allah's
Messenger, this is a copy of the Torah. He (Allah's Messenger)
(peace and blessings of Allah be upon him) kept quiet and he
(Hadrat 'Umar) began to read it and the (colour) of the

face of Allah's Messenger (peace and blessings of Allah be upon him) underwent a change, whereupon Abu Bakr said: Would that your mother mourn you, don't you see the face of Allah's Messenger? 'Umar saw the face of Allah's Messenger (peace and blessings of Allah be upon him) and said: I seek refuge with Allah from the wrath of Allah and the wrath of His Messenger. We are well pleased with Allah as Lord, with Islam as religion, with Muhammad as Prophet. Where-upon Allah's Messenger (peace and blessings of Allah be upon him) said: By Him in Whose hand is the life of Muhammad even if Moses were to appear before you and you would follow him leaving me aside you would certainly stray away with error; for if (Moses) had been alive (at this time) and had he found my prophetical ministry, he would have definitely followed me. (*Darimi*)

١٩٥ـ وَعَنْهُ، قَالَ: قَالَ رَسُولُ اللهِ ﷺ: "كَلَامِي لَا يَنْسَخُ كَلَامَ اللهِ، وَكَلَامُ اللهِ يَنْسَخُ كَلَامِي، وَكَلَامُ اللهِ يَنْسَخُ بَعْضُهُ بَعْضًا"

195 Jabir reported Allah's Messenger (peace and blessings of Allah be upon him) as saying: So far as my word it does not abrogate the word of Allah and the word of Allah abrogates my word, and one revelation of God may abrogate another[1].

1. What it means is that there is no contradiction between the Book of Allah and its definite implications as explained by the Holy Prophet (peace be upon him). What the Prophet has said and done is thus as important as the Book of Allah. So far as the abrogation of some of the verses of the Qurān is concerned, these have been made by Allah Himself. It also refers to the fact the former Books have been repealed by the Holy Qurān.

١٩٦ـ وَعَنِ ابْنِ عُمَرَ، قَالَ: قَالَ رَسُولُ اللهِ ﷺ: "إِنَّ أَحَادِيثَنَا يَنْسَخُ بَعْضُهَا بَعْضًا كَنَسْخِ الْقُرْآنِ"

196 Ibn 'Umar reported Allah's Messenger (peace and blessings of Allah be upon him) as saying: Some of our ahadith (traditions) abrogate the other ones like the abrogation of some verses of the Qurān.

١٩٧ - وَعَنْ أَبِي ثَعْلَبَةَ الْخُشَنِيِّ، قَالَ : قَالَ رَسُولُ اللهِ ﷺ : إِنَّ اللهَ فَرَضَ
فَرَائِضَ فَلَا تُضَيِّعُوهَا، وَحَرَّمَ حُرُمَاتٍ فَلَا تَنْتَهِكُوهَا، وَحَدَّ حُدُوداً
فَلَا تَعْتَدُوهَا، وَسَكَتَ عَنْ أَشْيَاءَ مِنْ غَيْرِ نِسْيَانٍ فَلَا تَبْحَثُوا عَنْهَا.
رَوَى الْأَحَادِيثَ الثَّلَاثَةَ الدَّارَقُطْنِيُّ.

197 Abi Tha'laba al-Khushani reported Allah's Messenger (peace
and blessings of Allah be upon him) as saying: Allah has
prescribed certain things obligatory, so don't miss them. He
has declared certain things forbidden so don't violate them.
He has set certain limits so don't transgress them (and He
has observed meaningful silence about certain things and
that He has not done out of forgetfulness. so don't enquire
about them. (*Dar Qutni*)

————————●————————

كِتَابُ الْعِلْمِ

Kitab-ul-'Ilm

(BOOK OF KNOWLEDGE)

THE BOOK OF KNOWLEDGE

CHAPTER 7

Section 1   اَلْفَصْلُ الْأَوَّلُ

١٩٨ـ عَنْ عَبْدِ اللهِ بْنِ عَمْرٍو، قَالَ: قَالَ رَسُولُ اللهِ ﷺ: "بَلِّغُوا عَنِّي وَلَوْ اٰيَةً، وَحَدِّثُوا عَنْ بَنِي إِسْرَائِيلَ وَلَا حَرَجَ، وَمَنْ كَذَبَ عَلَيَّ مُتَعَمِّدًا فَلْيَتَبَوَّأْ مَقْعَدَهُ مِنَ النَّارِ". رَوَاهُ الْبُخَارِيُّ.

198 'Abdullah b. 'Amr reported Allah's Messenger (peace and blessings of Allah be upon him) as saying: Transmit from me even though it is a single verse and transmit (the narrations) from Banu Israel and there is no harm (in doing it provided these are true) and he who deliberately lies about me let him seek his abode in Hell. (*Bukhari*)

١٩٩ـ وَعَنْ سَمُرَةَ بْنِ جُنْدُبٍ، وَالْمُغِيرَةِ بْنِ شُعْبَةَ، قَالَا: قَالَ رَسُولُ اللهِ ﷺ: "مَنْ حَدَّثَ عَنِّي بِحَدِيثٍ يُرَى أَنَّهُ كَذِبٌ، فَهُوَ أَحَدُ الْكَاذِبِينَ". رَوَاهُ مُسْلِمٌ.

199 Samura b. Jundub and al-Mughira b. Shu'ba reported Allah's Messenger (peace and blessings of Allah be upon him) as saying: He who narrated a tradition from me knowing it not to be so, will be one of the liars. (*Muslim*)

٢٠٠ـ وَعَنْ مُعَاوِيَةَ، قَالَ: قَالَ رَسُولُ اللهِ ﷺ: "مَنْ يُرِدِ اللهُ بِهِ خَيْرًا يُفَقِّهْهُ فِي الدِّينِ، وَإِنَّمَا أَنَا قَاسِمٌ وَاللهُ يُعْطِي". مُتَّفَقٌ عَلَيْهِ.

200 Mua'wiya reported Allah's Messenger (peace and blessings of Allah be upon him) as saying: He to whom Allah intends to show goodness He gives him the understanding of *Din*. I am the distributor (of Divine knowledge); the Giver is Allah. (*Agreed upon*)

٢٠١ - وَعَنْ اَبِى هُرَيْرَةَ، قَالَ: قَالَ رَسُولُ اللهِ ﷺ "اَلنَّاسُ مَعَادِنُ كَمَعَادِنِ
الذَّهَبِ وَ الْفِضَّةِ، خِيَارُهُمْ فِى الْجَاهِلِيَّةِ خِيَارُهُمْ فِى الْإِسْلَامِ إِذَا
فَقُهُوَا" رَوَاهُ مُسْلِمٌ.

201 Abu Huraira reported Allah's Messenger (peace and blessings
of Allah be upon him) as saying: Human beings are the
mines like the mines of gold and silver. The good amongst
them in ignorance are in fact good amongst them in Islam,
if they understand it. (*Muslim*)

٢٠٢ - وَعَنِ ابْنِ مَسْعُودٍ، قَالَ: قَالَ رَسُولُ اللهِ ﷺ "لَا حَسَدَ إِلَّا فِى اثْنَتَيْنِ:
رَجُلٌ اَتَاهُ اللهُ مَالًا فَسَلَّطَهُ عَلَى هَلَكَتِهِ فِى الْحَقِّ، وَ رَجُلٌ اَتَاهُ اللهُ الْحِكْمَةَ
فَهُوَ يَقْضِى بِهَا وَيُعَلِّمُهَا" مُتَّفَقٌ عَلَيْهِ.

202 Ibn Mas'ud reported Allah's Messenger (peace and blessings
of Allah be upon him) as saying: No envy is to be shown
but to only two (persons): the person whom Allah bestowed
riches empowering him to spend that in the path of righteousness and the person whom Allah gave wisdom with which he
judges and which he teaches to others. (*Agreed upon*)

٢٠٣ - وَعَنْ اَبِى هُرَيْرَةَ، قَالَ: قَالَ رَسُولُ اللهِ ﷺ "إِذَا مَاتَ الْإِنْسَانُ انْقَطَعَ
عَنْهُ عَمَلُهُ إِلَّا مِنْ ثَلَاثَةِ اَشْيَاءَ: صَدَقَةٍ جَارِيَةٍ، اَوْ عِلْمٍ يُنْتَفَعُ بِهِ،
اَوْ وَلَدٍ صَالِحٍ يَدْعُو لَهُ" رَوَاهُ مُسْلِمٌ.

203 Abu Huraira reported Allah's Messenger (peace and blessings
of Allah be upon him) as saying: When the man dies merit
ceases further to accrue from his actions, except from three
things viz : The ever-recurring *sadaqa*, the knowledge from
which the benefit is derived and the pious offspring who
invokes blessings upon him. (*Muslim*)

٢٠٤ - وَ عَنْهُ، قَالَ: قَالَ رَسُولُ اللهِ ﷺ "مَنْ نَفَّسَ عَنْ مُؤْمِنٍ
كُرْبَةً مِنْ كُرَبِ الدُّنْيَا، نَفَّسَ اللهُ عَنْهُ كُرْبَةً مِنْ كُرَبِ يَوْمِ الْقِيَامَةِ.

وَمَنْ يَسْتَرْ عَلَى مُعْسِرٍ يَسَّرَ اللهُ عَلَيْهِ فِى الدُّنْيَا وَالْآخِرَةِ. وَمَنْ سَتَرَ مُسْلِمًا

سَتَرَهُ اللهُ فِى الدُّنْيَا وَالْآخِرَةِ. وَاللهُ فِى عَوْنِ الْعَبْدِ مَا كَانَ الْعَبْدُ فِى

عَوْنِ أَخِيهِ. وَمَنْ سَلَكَ طَرِيقًا يَلْتَمِسُ فِيهِ عِلْمًا سَهَّلَ اللهُ لَهُ بِهِ

طَرِيقًا إِلَى الْجَنَّةِ. وَمَا اجْتَمَعَ قَوْمٌ فِى بَيْتٍ مِنْ بُيُوتِ اللهِ يَتْلُونَ كِتَابَ

اللهِ وَيَتَدَارَسُونَهُ بَيْنَهُمْ. إِلَّا نَزَلَتْ عَلَيْهِمُ السَّكِينَةُ، وَغَشِيَتْهُمُ الرَّحْمَةُ

وَحَفَّتْهُمُ الْمَلَائِكَةُ، وَذَكَرَهُمُ اللهُ فِيمَنْ عِنْدَهُ. وَمَنْ أَبْطَأَ بِهِ عَمَلُهُ لَمْ

يُسْرِعْ بِهِ نَسَبُهُ. رَوَاهُ مُسْلِمٌ.

204 It is reported on the same authority that Allah's Messenger (peace and blessings of Allah be upon him) said: He who helped in alleviating suffering of a believer from the distress of the world Allah would relieve him of distress on the Day of Resurrection. He who made things easy for one who is hard pressed Allah would make things easy for him in this world and the Hereafter and he who covers (the failings of) a Muslim, Allah would provide him covering in this world and in the Hereafter. Allah would come to the help of the servant as the servant had been coming to the help of his brother and he who would tread the path in search of knowledge Allah would pave his way to Paradise and no assembly is held in the House amongst the Houses of Allah reciting the Book of Allah or studying it amongst themselves that the tranquillity is not sent upon them and enveloping them with mercy and the Angels surround them and Allah making mention of them to those who are with Him. And he who is slow in doing good deed his genealogy will be of no avail to him. (*Muslim*)

٢٠٥ - وَعَنْهُ، قَالَ: قَالَ رَسُولُ اللهِ ﷺ: إِنَّ أَوَّلَ النَّاسِ يُقْضَى عَلَيْهِ

يَوْمَ الْقِيَامَةِ رَجُلٌ اسْتُشْهِدَ، فَأُتِىَ بِهِ فَعَرَّفَهُ نِعْمَتَهُ فَعَرَفَهَا،

فَقَالَ مَا عَمِلْتَ فِيهَا؛ قَالَ: قَاتَلْتُ فِيكَ حَتَّى اسْتُشْهِدْتُ. قَالَ:

كَذَبْتَ ؛ وَ لٰكِنَّكَ قَاتَلْتَ لِأَنْ يُقَالَ : جَرِيٌّ ، فَقَدْ قِيلَ . ثُمَّ أُمِرَ بِهِ

فَسُحِبَ عَلٰى وَجْهِهِ حَتّٰى أُلْقِيَ فِى النَّارِ . وَ رَجُلٌ تَعَلَّمَ الْعِلْمَ وَعَلَّمَهُ .

وَ قَرَأَ الْقُرْآنَ ، فَأُتِيَ بِهِ فَعَرَّفَهُ نِعَمَهُ فَعَرَفَهَا. قَالَ : فَمَا عَمِلْتَ فِيهَا؟

قَالَ : تَعَلَّمْتُ الْعِلْمَ وَعَلَّمْتُهُ ، وَقَرَأْتُ فِيكَ الْقُرْآنَ . قَالَ . كَذَبْتَ ؛ وَ

لٰكِنَّكَ تَعَلَّمْتَ الْعِلْمَ لِيُقَالَ : إِنَّكَ عَالِمٌ ، وَقَرَأْتَ الْقُرْآنَ لِيُقَالَ : هُوَ

قَارِئٌ ، فَقَدْ قِيلَ ، ثُمَّ أُمِرَ بِهِ فَسُحِبَ عَلٰى وَجْهِهِ حَتّٰى أُلْقِيَ فِى النَّارِ .

وَ رَجُلٌ وَسَّعَ اللهُ عَلَيْهِ وَأَعْطَاهُ مِنْ أَصْنَافِ الْمَالِ كُلِّهِ ، فَأُتِيَ بِهِ

فَعَرَّفَهُ نِعَمَهُ فَعَرَفَهَا . قَالَ : فَمَا عَمِلْتَ فِيهَا ؛ قَالَ : مَا تَرَكْتُ مِنْ سَبِيلٍ

تُحِبُّ أَنْ يُنْفَقَ فِيهَا إِلَّا أَنْفَقْتُ فِيهَا لَكَ . قَالَ : كَذَبْتَ ، وَ لٰكِنَّكَ فَعَلْتَ

لِيُقَالَ : هُوَ جَوَادٌ ؛ فَقَدْ قِيلَ ، ثُمَّ أُمِرَ بِهِ فَسُحِبَ عَلٰى وَجْهِهِ ثُمَّ أُلْقِيَ

فِى النَّارِ . رَوَاهُ مُسْلِمٌ

205 It is reported on the same authority that Allah's Messenger
(peace and blessings of Allah be upon him) said: Verily the
first person about whom the verdict will be given on the Day
of Resurrection will be a martyr. He would be brought (into
the presence of the Almighty) and He would recount him
the favours which were conferred upon him (in the world),
so that he would aknowledge them. He (God) would say:
What did you do (in return for them). He would say: I
fought in Thy cause and died as a martyr. Whereupon He
would say: You are telling a lie, you fought that you might
be called a hero and it was in fact said about you. Then
the command would be issued and he would be dragged
on his face and thrown in Hell-Fire. Then a person who
acquired knowledge and taught it and recited the Qur'ān
would be brought (in the presence of God) and he would be
reminded of the blessings (of Allah) and he would acknowledge them. He (God) would say: What did you perform
(as a token of thanksgiving)? He would say: I acquired
knowledge and then taught it and recited Qur'ān for Thy

pleasure. He (God) would say: You are telling a lie. You of course acquired knowledge so that you might be called a scholar and you recited the Qur'ān so that you might be called the reciter and you were in fact called so. Then command would be issued and he would be dragged and thrown into the Hell-Fire. Then a person whom Allah had made affluent and upon whom He had bestowed different kinds of riches would be brought forth and would be told of the favours he had received and he would acknowledge them and He (God) would say: What good act you performed (as a token of thanksgiving)? He would say: There is no cause for which I did not spend for Thee in which Thou desired me to spend. He (God) would say: You are telling a lie. You of course did it so that you might be called a generous person and it was in fact said about you. Then command would be issued about him and he would be dragged upon his face and thrown in the Hell-Fire. (*Muslim*)

٢٠٦ ـ وَعَنْ عَبْدِ اللهِ ابْنِ عَمْرٍ وَقَالَ : قَالَ رَسُولُ اللهِ ﷺ "إِنَّ اللهَ لَا يَقْبِضُ الْعِلْمَ اِنْتِزَاعًا يَنْتَزِعُهُ مِنَ الْعِبَادِ ، وَ لٰكِنْ يَقْبِضُ الْعِلْمَ بِقَبْضِ الْعُلَمَاءِ ، حَتّٰى إِذَا لَمْ يُبْقِ عَالِمًا ؛ اِتَّخَذَ النَّاسُ رُؤُوسًا جُهَّالًا ، فَسُئِلُوا فَأَفْتَوْا بِغَيْرِ عِلْمٍ ، فَضَلُّوا وَأَضَلُّوا" مُتَّفَقٌ عَلَيْهِ .

206 '**Abdullah b. 'Amr** reported Allah's Messenger (peace and blessings of Allah be upon him) having said: Allah will not cause extinction of knowledge by taking it away from the servants but He will cause extinction of knowledge by taking away the learned; so that when no learned man remains, the people would then take the illiterate as their leader. They would seek religious verdicts upon them and they would deliver them without knowledge and they would go astray and lead others into error. (*Agreed upon*)

٢٠٧ ـ وَعَنْ شَقِيقٍ كَانَ عَبْدُ اللهِ ابْنُ مَسْعُودٍ يُذَكِّرُ النَّاسَ فِي كُلِّ خَمِيسٍ فَقَالَ لَهُ رَجُلٌ : يَا أَبَا عَبْدِ الرَّحْمٰنِ ! لَوَدِدْتُ أَنَّكَ ذَكَّرْتَنَا فِي كُلِّ يَوْمٍ قَالَ ، أَمَا إِنَّهُ يَمْنَعُنِي مِنْ ذٰلِكَ أَنِّي أَكْرَهُ أَنْ أُمِلَّكُمْ ، وَ إِنِّي أَتَخَوَّلُكُمْ

بِالْمَوْعِظَةِ كَمَا كَانَ رَسُوْلُ اللهِ ﷺ يَتَخَوَّلُنَا بِهَا مَخَافَةَ السَّآمَةِ عَلَيْنَا.
مُتَّفَقٌ عَلَيْهِ

207 Shaqiq reported that 'Abdullah b. Mas'ud used to deliver
sermon to the people every Thursday. A person said to him:
Abu 'Abdur Rahman, I wish if you could deliver us sermon
every day. Whereupon he said: What prevents me from
doing so is the fact that I hate to annoy you, so I do not
address you frequently as the Allah's Messenger (peace and
blessings of Allah be upon him) did from fear lest it should
become burdensome for you.[1] (*Agreed upon*)

> 1. This hadith tells us that the preacher should be considerate in
> preaching and he should not thrust the sermons in the minds of the
> audience which may create hatred or aversion in them.

٢٠٨ - وَعَنْ أَنَسٍ، قَالَ: كَانَ النَّبِيُّ ﷺ إِذَا تَكَلَّمَ بِكَلِمَةٍ أَعَادَهَا ثَلَاثًا حَتَّى
تُفْهَمَ عَنْهُ، وَإِذَا أَتَى عَلَى قَوْمٍ فَسَلَّمَ عَلَيْهِمْ سَلَّمَ عَلَيْهِمْ ثَلَاثًا.
رَوَاهُ الْبُخَارِيُّ.

208 Anas reported that whenever Allah's Messenger (peace and blessings of Allah be upon him) spoke he repeated (the words)
thrice, so that they might be understood and whenever he
came to a people, he greeted them thrice with the words:
Assalam-o-'Alaikum (may there be peace upon you). (*Bukhari*)

٢٠٩ - وَعَنْ أَبِيْ مَسْعُوْدٍ الْأَنْصَارِيِّ، قَالَ: جَاءَ رَجُلٌ إِلَى النَّبِيِّ ﷺ
فَقَالَ: إِنَّهُ أُبْدِعَ بِيْ فَاحْمِلْنِيْ. فَقَالَ: مَا عِنْدِيْ. فَقَالَ رَجُلٌ: يَارَسُوْلَ
اللهِ! أَنَا أَدُلُّهُ عَلَى مَنْ يَحْمِلُهُ. فَقَالَ رَسُوْلُ اللهِ ﷺ: مَنْ دَلَّ عَلَى خَيْرٍ
فَلَهُ مِثْلُ أَجْرِ فَاعِلِهِ: رَوَاهُ مُسْلِمٌ.

209 Abu Mas'ud al-Ansari reported that a person came to Allah's
Messenger (peace and blessings of Allah be upon him) and
said: I am a destitute, provide me a ride. He (the Holy
Prophet) said: I do not possess it. A person said: Allah's
Messenger, I direct him to one who may be able to provide
him the mount. Whereupon Allah's Messenger (peace and

blessings of Allah be upon him) said: He who directs one to goodness for him is the reward equal to that of the doer of the good. (*Muslim*)

٢١٠ـ وَعَنْ جَرِيرٍ، قَالَ : كُنَّا فِي صَدْرِ النَّهَارِ عِنْدَ رَسُولِ اللهِ ﷺ ، فَجَاءَهُ قَوْمٌ عُرَاةٌ مُجْتَابِي النِّمَارِ أَوِ الْعَبَاءِ ، مُتَقَلِّدِي السُّيُوفِ ، عَامَّتُهُمْ مِنْ مُضَرَ ، بَلْ كُلُّهُمْ مِنْ مُضَرَ ، فَتَمَعَّرَ وَجْهُ رَسُولِ اللهِ ﷺ لِمَا رَأَى بِهِمْ مِنَ الْفَاقَةِ ، فَدَخَلَ ثُمَّ خَرَجَ ، فَأَمَرَ بِلَالاً فَأَذَّنَ ، وَ أَقَامَ فَصَلَّى ثُمَّ خَطَبَ فَقَالَ : « يَا أَيُّهَا النَّاسُ اتَّقُوا رَبَّكُمُ الَّذِي خَلَقَكُمْ مِنْ نَفْسٍ وَاحِدَةٍ إِلَى آخِرِ الْآيَةِ ﴿ إِنَّ اللهَ كَانَ عَلَيْكُمْ رَقِيبًا ﴾ ، وَ الْآيَةَ الَّتِي فِي الْحَشْرِ ﴿ اتَّقُوا اللهَ وَلْتَنْظُرْ نَفْسٌ مَا قَدَّمَتْ لِغَدٍ ﴾ ، تَصَدَّقَ رَجُلٌ مِنْ دِينَارِهِ ، مِنْ دِرْهَمِهِ ، مِنْ ثَوْبِهِ ، مِنْ صَاعِ بُرِّهِ ، مِنْ صَاعِ تَمْرِهِ ، حَتَّى قَالَ : وَ لَوْ بِشِقِّ تَمْرَةٍ » قَالَ : فَجَاءَ رَجُلٌ مِنَ الْأَنْصَارِ بِصُرَّةٍ كَادَتْ كَفُّهُ تَعْجِزُ عَنْهَا ، بَلْ قَدْ عَجَزَتْ ، ثُمَّ تَتَابَعَ النَّاسُ حَتَّى رَأَيْتُ كَوْمَيْنِ مِنْ طَعَامٍ وَ ثِيَابٍ حَتَّى رَأَيْتُ وَجْهَ رَسُولِ اللهِ ﷺ يَتَهَلَّلُ كَأَنَّهُ مُذْهَبَةٌ فَقَالَ رَسُولُ اللهِ ﷺ : « مَنْ سَنَّ فِي الْإِسْلَامِ سُنَّةً حَسَنَةً فَلَهُ أَجْرُهَا وَ أَجْرُ مَنْ عَمِلَ بِهَا مِنْ بَعْدِهِ مِنْ غَيْرِ أَنْ يُنْقَصَ مِنْ أُجُورِهِمْ شَيْءٌ ، وَ مَنْ سَنَّ فِي الْإِسْلَامِ سُنَّةً سَيِّئَةً كَانَ عَلَيْهِ وِزْرُهَا وَ وِزْرُ مَنْ عَمِلَ بِهَا مِنْ بَعْدِهِ مِنْ غَيْرِ أَنْ يُنْقَصَ مِنْ أَوْزَارِهِمْ شَيْءٌ » رَوَاهُ مُسْلِمٌ

210 **Jarir** reported: We were in the company of Allah's Messenger (peace and blessings of Allah be upon him) in the early hours of the morning that some people came there who were barefooted, naked, wearing striped woollen clothes or cloaks with their sword slung (round) their necks. Most of them, nay, all of them, belonged to the tribe of Muḍar. The colour of the face of Allah's Messenger (peace and blessings of Allah be upon him) underwent a change when he saw their famished

looks. He went in and then came out and then commanded
Bilal to pronounce Adhan and he pronounced Adhan and
Iqama and he observed prayer and then delivered the sermon
saying: "O people, fear your Lord Who created you from a
single being upto the verse Allah is ever Watcher for you".
(34 : 1). He then recited a verse of Surah Hashr: "Fear
Allah and let every one should consider that which he
sends forth for the morrow". (59 : 18). (Then the audience
began to vie with one another in giving charity). Some
persons donated a dinar, some dirham, some cloth, some
donated *sa'* of wheat, some a *sa'* of dates; till he (the Holy
Prophet) said: (Bring) even if it is half a date. Then a person
from amongst the Ansar came there with a money bag which
his hands could scarcely lift; in fact they could not. Then
the people followed continuously till I saw two heaps of
eatables and clothes, and I saw the face of Allah's Messenger
(peace and blessings of Allah be upon him) glistening as gold
(because of delight). The Messenger of Allah (peace and
blessings of Allah be upon him) said: He who sets a good
precedent in Islam, there is a reward for him for this (act of
goodness) and a reward for him also who acts according to
it subsequently, without any deduction from their rewards
and he who sets in Islam an evil precedent there is upon
him the burden of that, and the burden of him also who
acted upon it subsequently, without any deduction from
their burden. (*Muslim*)

٢١١ - وَعَنِ ابْنِ مَسْعُودٍ ، قَالَ : قَالَ رَسُولُ اللهِ ﷺ : "لَا تُقْتَلُ نَفْسٌ ظُلْمًا

إِلَّا كَانَ عَلَى ابْنِ آدَمَ الْأَوَّلِ كِفْلٌ مِنْ دَمِهَا ؛ لِأَنَّهُ أَوَّلُ مَنْ سَنَّ الْقَتْلَ :

مُتَّفَقٌ عَلَيْهِ . وَ سَنَذْكُرُ حَدِيثَ مُعَاوِيَةَ : "لَا يَزَالُ مِنْ أُمَّتِي" فِي بَابِ

ثَوَابِ هَذِهِ الْأُمَّةِ إِنْ شَاءَ اللهُ تَعَالَى -

211 Ibn Mas'ud reported Allah's Messenger (peace and blessings of
Allah be upon him) as saying: No life is taken unjustly but
the burden of its blood is laid upon the first son of Adam for
he was the first who introduced bloodshed. (*Agreed upon*).

We shall narrate the tradition from Mu'awiya: A Section
of my Ummah will continue, in the chapter: 'On the Reward
of this Ummah, if God so wills'.

Section II الْفَصْلُ الثَّانِى

٢١٢ - عَنْ كَثِيرِ بْنِ قَيْسٍ، قَالَ كُنْتُ جَالِسًا مَعَ أَبِى الدَّرْدَاءِ فِى مَسْجِدِ دِمَشْقَ
فَجَاءَ رَجُلٌ فَقَالَ: يَا أَبَا الدَّرْدَاءِ! إِنِّى جِئْتُكَ مِنْ مَدِينَةِ الرَّسُولِ ﷺ لِحَدِيثٍ
بَلَغَنِى أَنَّكَ تُحَدِّثُ عَنْ رَسُولِ اللَّهِ ﷺ مَا جِئْتُ لِحَاجَةٍ قَالَ: فَإِنِّى سَمِعْتُ
رَسُولَ اللَّهِ ﷺ يَقُولُ: "مَنْ سَلَكَ طَرِيقًا يَطْلُبُ فِيهِ عِلْمًا سَلَكَ اللَّهُ بِهِ طَرِيقًا مِنْ
طُرُقِ الْجَنَّةِ، وَإِنَّ الْمَلَائِكَةَ لَتَضَعُ أَجْنِحَتَهَا رِضًى لِطَالِبِ الْعِلْمِ وَإِنَّ الْعَالِمَ
يَسْتَغْفِرُ لَهُ مَنْ فِى السَّمَوَاتِ وَمَنْ فِى الْأَرْضِ وَالْحِيتَانُ فِى جَوْفِ الْمَاءِ، وَإِنَّ
فَضْلَ الْعَالِمِ عَلَى الْعَابِدِ كَفَضْلِ الْقَمَرِ لَيْلَةَ الْبَدْرِ عَلَى سَائِرِ الْكَوَاكِبِ،
وَإِنَّ الْعُلَمَاءَ وَرَثَةُ الْأَنْبِيَاءِ، وَإِنَّ الْأَنْبِيَاءَ لَمْ يُوَرِّثُوا دِينَارًا وَلَا
دِرْهَمًا، وَإِنَّمَا وَرَّثُوا الْعِلْمَ، فَمَنْ أَخَذَهُ أَخَذَ بِحَظٍّ وَافِرٍ. رَوَاهُ
أَحْمَدُ وَالتِّرْمِذِيُّ، وَأَبُو دَاوُدَ، وَابْنُ مَاجَةَ، وَالدَّارِمِيُّ، وَسَمَّاهُ
التِّرْمِذِيُّ قَيْسَ بْنَ كَثِيرٍ.

212 Kathir b. Qais reported: I was sitting in the company of Abu Darda in the mosque of Damascus that a man came there. He said: Abu Darda, I have come to you from the city of Allah's Messenger (peace and blessings of Allah be upon him); I have not come for any need (but to ascertain a hadith) for I have been told that you narrate it from Allah's Messenger (peace and blessings of Allah be upon him). Abu Darda said: I heard Allah's Messenger (peace and blessings of Allah be upon him) as saying: He who treads a path in the search of knowledge Allah will direct him to tread a path of the paths of Paradise and the Angels would accord welcome to the seeker of knowledge, and all that is found in Heaven and the Earth and even fish in the depth of water seek forgiveness for the scholar and the superiority of the scholar over a worshipper is like that of moon in the night when it is full over the rest of the stars and verily the scholars are the heirs of the Prophets

and verily the prophets do not leave behind them the **dinar**
and dirham. They only leave the knowledge as their heritage,
so whosoever acquires it, he acquires a huge fortune. (*Transmitted by Ahmad, Tirmidhi, by Abu Dawud: Ibn Majah, and
Darimi. Tirmidhi calling him Qais b. Kathir*).

٢١٣- وَعَنْ أَبِى أُمَامَةَ الْبَاهِلِى، قَالَ ذُكِرَ لِرَسُولِ اللهِ ﷺ رَجُلَانِ: أَحَدُهُمَا
عَابِدٌ وَالْأَخَرُ عَالِمٌ، فَقَالَ رَسُولُ اللهِ ﷺ: فَضْلُ الْعَالِمِ عَلَى الْعَابِدِ كَفَضْلِى
عَلَى أَدْنَاكُمْ، ثُمَّ قَالَ رَسُولُ اللهِ ﷺ: إِنَّ اللهَ وَمَلَائِكَتَهُ وَ أَهْلَ
السَّمٰوَاتِ وَ الْأَرْضِينَ حَتَّى النَّمْلَةَ فِى جُحْرِهَا، وَحَتَّى الْحُوتَ لَيُصَلُّونَ
عَلَى مُعَلِّمِ النَّاسِ الْخَيْرَ، رَوَاهُ التِّرْمِذِىُّ.

213 Abu Umama Al-Bahili reported that a mention was made to
Allah's Messenger (peace and blessings of Allah be upon him)
of two persons: the one being a devout, and the other being a
scholar; thereupon Allah's Messenger (peace and blessings of
Allah be upon him) said: The superiority of a scholar over
the devout is like my superiority over one who is of the lowest
rank amongst you. Allah's Messenger (peace and blessings of
Allah be upon him) said: Verily (for the scholars) Allah and
His Angels and the dwellers of the Heavens and of the earth
and even an ant in its hole and fish (in the depth of water)
invoke blessings on one who teaches people goodness. (*Tirmidhi*)

٢١٤- وَرَوَاهُ الدَّارِمِيُّ عَنْ مَكْحُولٍ مُرْسَلًا، وَلَمْ يَذْكُرْ رَجُلَانِ وَقَالَ:
"فَضْلُ الْعَالِمِ عَلَى الْعَابِدِ كَفَضْلِى عَلَى أَدْنَاكُمْ، ثُمَّ تَلَا هٰذِهِ الْأَيَةَ:
رَ إِنَّمَا يَخْشَى اللهَ مِنْ عِبَادِهِ الْعُلَمَاءُ" وَسَرَدَ الْحَدِيثَ إِلَى أَخِرِهِ.

214 Darimi transmitted it from Makhul in Mursal form but he
made no mention of two persons but simply said:
   The superiority of a scholar over the devout is like my
superiority over one who is lowest in rank amongst you. He
then recited this verse: "Those of His servants who are
scholars fear Allah" (**35** : 28).
   Then he went on with the tradition to the end.

٢١٥ـ وَعَنْ أَبِي سَعِيدِ إلْخُدْرِيِّ، قَالَ، قَالَ رَسُولُ اللهِ ﷺ: إِنَّ النَّاسَ لَكُمْ تَبَعٌ، وَإِنَّ رِجَالًا يَأْتُونَكُمْ مِنْ أَقْطَارِ الأَرْضِ يَتَفَقَّهُونَ فِي الدِّينِ فَإِذَا أَتَوْكُمْ فَاسْتَوْصُوا بِهِمْ خَيْرًا: رَوَاهُ التِّرْمِذِيُّ.

215 Abu Sa'id Khudri reported Allah's Messenger (peace and blessings of Allah be upon him) as saying: The mankind shall follow you and the people from the different parts of the earth would come to you in order to learn and acquire understanding of religion so when they come to you exhort them to do good. *(Tirmidhi)*

٢١٦ـ وَعَنْ أَبِي هُرَيْرَةَ، قَالَ، قَالَ رَسُولُ اللهِ ﷺ: الْكَلِمَةُ الْحِكْمَةُ، ضَالَّةُ الْحَكِيمِ، فَحَيْثُ وَجَدَهَا فَهُوَ أَحَقُّ بِهَا: رَوَاهُ التِّرْمِذِيُّ وَابْنُ مَاجَهُ، وَقَالَ التِّرْمِذِيُّ: هَذَا حَدِيثٌ غَرِيبٌ، وَإِبْرَاهِيمُ بْنُ الْفَضْلِ الرَّاوِى يُضَعَّفُ فِي الْحَدِيثِ.

216 Abu Huraira reported Allah's Messenger (peace and blessings of Allah be upon him) as saying: The word of wisdom is the lost property of a wise man so he has a better right to it (than any one else) wherever he finds it.
(Transmitted by Tirmidhi, Ibn Majah, Trimidhi said: This is a gharib tradition and Ibrahim b. Al-Fadl, the transmitter, is declared to be weak in transmission)

٢١٧ـ وَعَنِ ابْنِ عَبَّاسٍ، قَالَ: قَالَ رَسُولُ اللهِ ﷺ: فَقِيهٌ وَاحِدٌ أَشَدُّ عَلَى الشَّيْطَانِ مِنْ أَلْفِ عَابِدٍ: رَوَاهُ التِّرْمِذِيُّ، وَابْنُ مَاجَهُ.

217 Ibn 'Abbas reported Allah's Messenger (peace and blessings of Allah be upon him) as saying: A single scholar of religion is more formidable against a devil than a thousand devout persons. *(Tirmidhi and Ibn Majah)*

٢١٨ـ وَعَنْ أَنَسٍ، قَالَ: قَالَ رَسُولُ اللهِ ﷺ: طَلَبُ الْعِلْمِ فَرِيضَةٌ عَلَى كُلِّ مُسْلِمٍ، وَوَاضِعُ الْعِلْمِ عِنْدَ غَيْرِ أَهْلِهِ كَمُقَلِّدِ الْخَنَازِيرِ الْجَوْهَرَ وَاللُّؤْلُؤَ

وَالذَّهَبُ ؛ رَوَاهُ ابْنُ مَاجَةَ ، وَرَوَى الْبَيْهَقِيُّ فِي "شُعَبِ الْإِيمَانِ" إِلَى

قَوْلِهِ "مُسْلِمٍ" ؛ وَقَالَ : هٰذَا حَدِيثٌ مَتْنُهُ مَشْهُورٌ ، وَإِسْنَادُهُ ضَعِيفٌ

وَقَدْ رُوِيَ مِنْ أَوْجُهٍ كُلُّهَا ضَعِيفٌ .

218 **Anas** reported Allah's Messenger (peace and blessings of Allah be upon him) as saying: The seeking of knowledge is obligatory for every Muslim and the imparting of knowledge to the non-deserving is like putting on necklaces of jewels, pearls and gold around the necks of swine.

(Transmitted by Ibn Majah and Baihaqi in Shu'ab-ul-Iman upto the word "Muslim" saying: This is a hadith the text of which is quite well known but the chain of transmission is weak)

٢١٩ - وَعَنْ أَبِي هُرَيْرَةَ ، قَالَ ، قَالَ رَسُولُ اللهِ ﷺ : خَصْلَتَانِ لَا تَجْتَمِعَانِ

فِي مُنَافِقٍ ، حُسْنُ سَمْتٍ ، وَلَا فِقْهٌ فِي الدِّينِ" رَوَاهُ التِّرْمِذِيُّ .

219 **Abu Huraira** reported Allah's Messenger (peace and blessings of Allah be upon him) as saying: Two are the qualities which can never co-exist in a hypocrite: Good conduct and understanding of religion. *(Tirmidhi)*

٢٢٠ - وَعَنْ أَنَسٍ ، قَالَ : قَالَ رَسُولُ اللهِ ﷺ : مَنْ خَرَجَ فِي طَلَبِ الْعِلْمِ

فَهُوَ فِي سَبِيلِ اللهِ حَتَّى يَرْجِعَ" رَوَاهُ التِّرْمِذِيُّ ، وَالدَّارِمِيُّ .

220 **Anas** reported Allah's Messenger (peace and blessings of Allah be upon him) as saying: One who goes out to search for knowledge is (devoted) to the cause of Allah till he returns.

                                  (Tirmidhi and Darimi)

٢٢١ - وَعَنْ سَخْبَرَةَ الْأَزْدِيِّ ، قَالَ : قَالَ رَسُولُ اللهِ ﷺ : مَنْ طَلَبَ الْعِلْمَ كَانَ

كَفَّارَةً لِمَا مَضَى" رَوَاهُ التِّرْمِذِيُّ ، وَالدَّارِمِيُّ . وَقَالَ التِّرْمِذِيُّ : هٰذَا

حَدِيثٌ ضَعِيفُ الْإِسْنَادِ ، وَأَبُو دَاوُدَ الرَّاوِي يُضَعَّفُ .

221 **Sakhbara Al-Azdi** reported: He who acquires knowledge it is an expiation for his past sins.

(Tirmidhi and Darimi transmitted it. Tirmidhi said: This hadith has a weak chain of transmission and the transmitter is declared to be weak)

٢٢٢ - وَعَنْ أَبِي سَعِيدٍ الْخُدْرِيِّ، قَالَ: قَالَ رَسُولُ اللهِ ﷺ : "لَنْ يَشْبَعَ الْمُؤْمِنُ مِنْ خَيْرٍ يَسْمَعُهُ حَتَّى يَكُونَ مُنْتَهَاهُ الْجَنَّةَ". رَوَاهُ التِّرْمِذِيُّ.

222 Abu Sa'id Khudri reported Allah's Messenger (peace and blessings of Allah be upon him) as saying: A believer is never satiated with listening to the good things till he reaches Paradise. (*Tirmidhi*)

٢٢٣ - وَعَنْ أَبِي هُرَيْرَةَ، قَالَ: قَالَ رَسُولُ اللهِ ﷺ : "مَنْ سُئِلَ عَنْ عِلْمٍ عَلِمَهُ ثُمَّ كَتَمَهُ؛ أُلْجِمَ يَوْمَ الْقِيَامَةِ بِلِجَامٍ مِنْ نَارٍ". رَوَاهُ أَحْمَدُ، وَأَبُو دَاوُدَ، وَالتِّرْمِذِيُّ.

223 Abu Huraira reported Allah's Messenger (peace and blessings of Allah be upon him) as saying: Whosoever is sought knowledge from one who possesses it, but he conceals it, he would be made to wear on the Day of Resurrection the bridle of fire. (*Ahmad, Abu Dawud and Tirmidhi*)

٢٢٤ - وَرَوَاهُ ابْنُ مَاجَةَ عَنْ أَنَسٍ.

224 Transmitted by Ibn Majah on the authority of Anas.

٢٢٥ - وَعَنْ كَعْبِ بْنِ مَالِكٍ، قَالَ: قَالَ رَسُولُ اللهِ ﷺ : "مَنْ طَلَبَ الْعِلْمَ لِيُجَارِيَ بِهِ الْعُلَمَاءَ، أَوْ لِيُمَارِيَ بِهِ السُّفَهَاءَ، أَوْ يَصْرِفَ بِهِ وُجُوهَ النَّاسِ إِلَيْهِ، أَدْخَلَهُ اللهُ النَّارَ". رَوَاهُ التِّرْمِذِيُّ.

225 Ka'b b. Malik reported Allah's Messenger (peace and blessings of Allah be upon him) as saying: He who acquires knowledge in order to falling into polemics with other scholars and proving his superiority over them or to dispute with the ignorant persons or to attract the attention of the people, Allah would throw him in fire. (*Tirmidhi*)

٢٢٦ - وَرَوَاهُ ابْنُ مَاجَةَ عَنِ ابْنِ عُمَرَ.

226 Transmitted by Ibn Majah on the authority of Ibn 'Umar.

٢٢٧ - وَعَنْ أَبِي هُرَيْرَةَ، قَالَ: قَالَ رَسُولُ اللهِ ﷺ : "مَنْ تَعَلَّمَ عِلْمًا مِمَّا

يُبْتَغَى بِهِ وَجْهُ اللهِ ، لَا يَتَعَلَّمُهُ إِلَّا لِيُصِيبَ بِهِ عَرَضًا مِّنَ الدُّنْيَا ، لَمْ

يَجِدْ عَرْفَ الْجَنَّةِ يَوْمَ الْقِيَامَةِ ، يَعْنِى رِيحَهَا . رَوَاهُ أَحْمَدُ ، وَأَبُو

دَاؤدَ ، وَابْنُ مَاجَةَ .

227 Abu Huraira reported Allah's Messenger (peace and blessings of Allah be upon him) as saying: He who acquires knowledge the sole purpose of which is seeking the pleasure of Allah but he does not acquire it except for gaining worldly ends, he would not smell the odour of Paradise on the Day of Resurrection. (*Ahmad, Abu Dawud, Ibn Majah*)

٢٢٨ ـ وَعَنِ ابْنِ مَسْعُودٍ ، قَالَ : قَالَ رَسُولُ اللهِ ﷺ "نَضَّرَ اللهُ عَبْدًا سَمِعَ

مَقَالَتِى فَحَفِظَهَا وَوَعَاهَا وَأَدَّاهَا ؛ فَرُبَّ حَامِلِ فِقْهٍ غَيْرِ فَقِيهٍ ، وَرُبَّ

حَامِلِ فِقْهٍ إِلَى مَنْ هُوَ أَفْقَهُ مِنْهُ ثَلَاثٌ لَا يُغِلُّ عَلَيْهِنَّ قَلْبُ مُسْلِمٍ : إِخْلَاصُ

الْعَمَلِ لِلهِ ، وَالتَّصِيحَةُ لِلْمُسْلِمِينَ ، وَلُزُومُ جَمَاعَتِهِمْ ، فَإِنَّ دَعْوَتَهُمْ

تُحِيطُ مِنْ وَرَآئِهِمْ" رَوَاهُ الشَّافِعِيُّ وَالْبَيْهَقِيُّ فِى الْمَدْخَلِ .

228 Ibn Mas'ud reported Allah's Messenger (peace and blessings of Allah be upon him) as saying: May Allah be well pleased with the servant who heard our words, remembered them, retained them well and then passed them on to others. And how many scholars are there who are the scholars of religion without having understanding of it and how many scholars of religion are there who convey knowledge to those who are more well versed as compared to them. There are three things on account of which no rancour enters a Muslim heart, the sincerity of purpose for Allah's sake, seeking goodness for the Muslims and sticking to their main body, for their prayers encompass them all round.

(*Shafi' reported it and also Baihaqi in Al-Madkhal*)

٢٢٩ ـ وَرَوَاهُ أَحْمَدُ ، وَالتِّرْمِذِيُّ ، وَأَبُو دَاؤدَ ، وَابْنُ مَاجَةَ ، وَالدَّارِمِيُّ

عَنْ زَيْدِ بْنِ ثَابِتٍ ، إِلَّا أَنَّ التِّرْمِذِيَّ وَأَبَا دَاؤدَ لَمْ يَذْكُرَا "ثَلَاثٌ لَا يُغِلُّ

عَلَيْهِنَّ" إِلَى آخِرِهِ .

229 **Ahmad, Tirmidhi, Abu Dawud, Ibn Majah, Darimi** transmitted it from Zaid b. Thabit but Tirmidhi and Abu Dawud did not mention: There are three things on account of which no rancour enters to the end.

٢٣٠ ـ وَعَنِ ابْنِ مَسْعُودٍ، قَالَ : سَمِعْتُ رَسُوْلَ اللهِ ﷺ يَقُوْلُ: نَضَّرَ اللهُ امْرَأً سَمِعَ مِنَّا شَيْئًا فَبَلَّغَهُ كَمَا سَمِعَهُ، فَرُبَّ مُبَلَّغٍ أَوْعَى لَهُ مِنْ سَامِعٍ؛ رَوَاهُ التِّرْمِذِيُّ وَابْنُ مَاجَةَ.

230 **Ibn Mas'ud** reported: I heard Allah's Messenger (peace and blessings of Allah be upon him) as saying: May Allah be pleased with a person who heard a thing from us and then transmitted it to others as he had heard; for many a one to whom it is brought retains it better than one who heard it.

(*Tirmidhi and Ibn Majah*)

١٣١ ـ وَ رَوَاهُ الدَّارِمِيُّ عَنْ أَبِي الدَّرْدَاءِ.

231 **Darimi** transmitted this hadith from Abu Darda.

٢٣٢ ـ وَعَنِ ابْنِ عَبَّاسٍ، رَضِيَ اللهُ عَنْهُ، قَالَ : قَالَ رَسُوْلُ اللهِ ﷺ: إِتَّقُوا الْحَدِيْثَ عَنِّي إِلَّا مَا عَلِمْتُمْ، فَمَنْ كَذَبَ عَلَيَّ مُتَعَمِّدًا فَلْيَتَبَوَّأْ مَقْعَدَهُ مِنَ النَّارِ؛ رَوَاهُ التِّرْمِذِيُّ.

232 **Ibn 'Abbas** reported: Allah's Messenger (peace and blessings of Allah be upon him) as saying: Be mindful in transmitting a hadith from me. (Transmit) only that which you know (very well) for he who intentionally lies about me will find his abode in Hell-Fire. (*Tirmidhi*)

٢٣٣ ـ وَرَوَاهُ ابْنُ مَاجَةَ عَنِ ابْنِ مَسْعُودٍ وَجَابِرٍ، وَّ لَمْ يَذْكُرْ: إِتَّقُوا الْحَدِيْثَ عَنِّي إِلَّا مَا عَلِمْتُمْ؛

233 **Ibn Majah** transmitted it from Ibn Mas'ud and Jabir but he did not make mention: Be mindful in transmitting hadith from me, but only that which you know very well.

٢٣٤ - وَعَنِ ابْنِ عَبَّاسٍ، قَالَ: قَالَ رَسُولُ اللهِ ﷺ: "مَنْ قَالَ فِي الْقُرْآنِ بِرَأْيِهِ

فَلْيَتَبَوَّأْ مَقْعَدَهُ مِنَ النَّارِ" وَفِي رِوَايَةٍ: "مَنْ قَالَ فِي الْقُرْآنِ بِغَيْرِ عِلْمٍ

فَلْيَتَبَوَّأْ مَقْعَدَهُ مِنَ النَّارِ" رَوَاهُ التِّرْمِذِيُّ.

234 **Ibn 'Abbas** reported Allah's Messenger (peace and blessings of Allah be upon him) as saying: He who speaks about the Qur'ān on the basis of his personal opinion (only) would find his abode in Hell-Fire. In another version (the words are): He who speaks about the Qur'ān without sound knowledge of it would find his abode in Hell-Fire. (*Tirmidhi*)

٢٣٥ - وَعَنْ جُنْدُبٍ، قَالَ: قَالَ رَسُولُ اللهِ ﷺ: "مَنْ قَالَ فِي الْقُرْآنِ بِرَأْيِهِ

فَأَصَابَ فَقَدْ أَخْطَأَ" رَوَاهُ التِّرْمِذِيُّ، وَأَبُو دَاوُدَ.

235 **Jundub** reported Allah's Messenger (peace and blessings of Allah be upon him) as saying: He who speaks about the Qur'ān on the basis of his personal opinion (by any accord) he commits an error, even if he is right (because it is by accident that he arrives at the truth). (*Tirmidhi and Abu Dawud*)

٢٣٦ - وَعَنْ أَبِي هُرَيْرَةَ، قَالَ: قَالَ رَسُولُ اللهِ ﷺ: "أَلْمِرَاءُ فِي الْقُرْآنِ كُفْرٌ"

رَوَاهُ أَحْمَدُ، وَأَبُو دَاوُدَ.

236 **Abu Huraira** reported Allah's Messenger (peace and blessings of Allah be upon him) as saying: Disputation (in regard to the teachings of the Qur'ān) is a sort of unbelief.

(*Ahmad and Abu Dawud*)

٢٣٧ - وَعَنْ عَمْرِو بْنِ شُعَيْبٍ، عَنْ أَبِيهِ، عَنْ جَدِّهِ، قَالَ: سَمِعَ النَّبِيُّ ﷺ

قَوْمًا يَتَدَارَؤُونَ فِي الْقُرْآنِ، فَقَالَ: "إِنَّمَا هَلَكَ مَنْ كَانَ قَبْلَكُمْ بِهَذَا:

ضَرَبُوا كِتَابَ اللهِ بَعْضَهُ بِبَعْضٍ، وَإِنَّمَا نَزَلَ كِتَابُ اللهِ يُصَدِّقُ بَعْضُهُ بَعْضًا

بَعْضًا، فَلَا تُكَذِّبُوا بَعْضَهُ بِبَعْضٍ، فَمَا عَلِمْتُمْ مِنْهُ فَقُولُوا، وَمَا جَهِلْتُمْ

فَكِلُوهُ إِلَى عَالِمِهِ" رَوَاهُ أَحْمَدُ، وَابْنُ مَاجَةَ.

237 **'Amr b. Shu'aib** reported on the authority of his father who reported on the authority of his father that Allah's Apostle (peace and blessings of Allah be upon him) heard a people falling into disputation about the Qur'ān. Thereupon he said: It was because of this that those gone before you were perished. They set parts of the books against the others (whereas the fact is) that the Book of Allah has been revealed, one part confirming the others. Therefore, do not falsify some parts with the others and speak only that which you know and which you do not know refer it to one who knows it well. *(Ahmad and Ibn Majah)*

٢٣٨ - وَعَنِ ابْنِ مَسْعُودٍ، قَالَ : قَالَ رَسُولُ اللهِ ﷺ : أُنْزِلَ الْقُرْآنُ عَلَى سَبْعَةِ أَحْرُفٍ، لِكُلِّ آيَةٍ مِنْهَا ظَهْرٌ وَبَطْنٌ، وَلِكُلِّ حَدٍّ مُطَّلَعٌ ' رَوَاهُ فِي شَرْحِ السُّنَّةِ .

238 **Ibn Mas'ud** reported Allah's Messenger (peace and blessings of Allah be upon him) as saying: The Qur'ān was sent down in seven dialects. Every one of its verses has an explicit and implicit meaning and every interdiction is clearly defined.
(Reported in Sharh us-Sunna)

٢٣٩ - وَعَنْ عَبْدِ اللهِ بْنِ عَمْرٍو، قَالَ : قَالَ رَسُولُ اللهِ ﷺ : الْعِلْمُ ثَلَاثَةٌ : آيَةٌ مُحْكَمَةٌ، أَوْ سُنَّةٌ قَائِمَةٌ، أَوْ فَرِيضَةٌ عَادِلَةٌ، وَمَا كَانَ سِوَى ذٰلِكَ فَهُوَ فَضْلٌ ' رَوَاهُ أَبُو دَاوُدَ، وَابْنُ مَاجَةَ .

239 **'Abdullah b. 'Amr** reported Allah's Messenger (peace and blessings of Allah be upon him) as saying: The knowledge is constituted of three (categories): well defined verse or an established Sunnah or the obligatory duties and whatever is beyond it is superfluous. *(Abu Dawud and Ibn Majah)*

٢٤٠ - وَعَنْ عَوْفِ بْنِ مَالِكٍ الْأَشْجَعِيِّ، قَالَ : قَالَ رَسُولُ اللهِ ﷺ : لَا يَقُصُّ إِلَّا أَمِيرٌ أَوْ مَأْمُورٌ أَوْ مُخْتَالٌ ' رَوَاهُ أَبُو دَاوُدَ .

240 **'Auf b. Malik Al-Ashja'i** reported Allah's Messenger (peace and blessings of Allah be upon him) as saying: The sermon is delivered either by the ruler or by one who is deputed for this (purpose) or the vain person. *(Abu Dawud)*

٢٤١ - وَرَوَاهُ الدَّارِمِيُّ، عَنْ عَمْرِو بْنِ شُعَيْبٍ، عَنْ أَبِيهِ، عَنْ جَدِّهِ، وَفِي رِوَايَتِهِ

مَرَاءٌ بَدَلَ " أَوْ مُخْتَالٌ "

241 **Darimi** transmitted it from 'Amr b. Shu'aib from his father,
from his grandfather. A version has 'or a hypocrite' instead
of 'one who is vain.'

٢٤٢ - وَعَنْ أَبِي هُرَيْرَةَ، قَالَ: قَالَ رَسُولُ اللهِ ﷺ: " مَنْ أَفْتِيَ بِغَيْرِ عِلْمٍ

كَانَ إِثْمُهُ عَلَى مَنْ أَفْتَاهُ، وَمَنْ أَشَارَ عَلَى أَخِيهِ بِأَمْرٍ يَعْلَمُ أَنَّ الرُّشْدَ

فِي غَيْرِهِ فَقَدْ خَانَهُ " رَوَاهُ أَبُو دَاوُدَ.

242 **Abu Huraira** reported Allah's Messenger (peace and blessings
of Allah be upon him) as saying: He who was given a
religious verdict without (sound) scholarship, its sin would fall
on one who gave it and he who gave a counsel to his brother
about a matter knowing that the right course is otherwise, he
in fact committed treachery with him. (*Abu Dawud*)

٢٤٣ - وَعَنْ مُعَاوِيَةَ، قَالَ: إِنَّ النَّبِيَّ ﷺ نَهَى عَنِ الْأَغْلُوطَاتِ. رَوَاهُ

أَبُو دَاوُدَ.

243 **Mua'wiya** reported that Allah's Messenger (peace and blessings of Allah be upon him) forbade (bringing under discussion)
the misleading problems. (*Abu Dawud*)

٢٤٤ - وَعَنْ أَبِي هُرَيْرَةَ، قَالَ: قَالَ رَسُولُ اللهِ ﷺ: " تَعَلَّمُوا الْفَرَائِضَ وَ

الْقُرْآنَ وَعَلِّمُوا النَّاسَ فَإِنِّي مَقْبُوضٌ " رَوَاهُ التِّرْمِذِيُّ.

244 **Abu Huraira** reported Allah's Messenger (peace and blessings
of Allah be upon him) as saying: Learn the obligatory acts
and the Qur'ān and teach them to the people for I am a
mortal. (*Tirmidhi*)

٢٤٥ - وَعَنْ أَبِي الدَّرْدَاءِ، قَالَ: كُنَّا مَعَ رَسُولِ اللهِ ﷺ فَشَخَصَ بِبَصَرِهِ

إِلَى السَّمَاءِ ثُمَّ قَالَ: " هَذَا أَوَانٌ يُخْتَلَسُ فِيهِ الْعِلْمُ مِنَ النَّاسِ، حَتَّى لَا

يَقْدِرُوا مِنْهُ عَلَى شَيْءٍ " رَوَاهُ التِّرْمِذِيُّ.

245 Abu Darda reported: We were in the company of Allah's Messenger (peace and blessings of Allah be upon him) that he fixed his gaze on the sky and said: The time is come when knowledge[1] will be taken from the people, as they will be unable to acquire it. (*Tirmidhi*)

> 1. Knowledge here means Divine revelation which ceased with the Holy Prophet (peace and blessings of Allah be upon him)

٢٤٦ ـ وَعَنْ أَبِى هُرَيْرَةَ رِوَايَةً "يُوْشِكُ أَنْ تَضْرِبَ النَّاسُ أَكْبَادَ الْإِبِلِ يَطْلُبُوْنَ الْعِلْمَ، فَلَا يَجِدُوْنَ أَحَدًا أَعْلَمَ مِنْ عَالِمِ الْمَدِيْنَةِ" رَوَاهُ التِّرْمِذِيُّ فِى جَامِعِهِ . قَالَ ابْنُ عُيَيْنَةَ : إِنَّهُ مَالِكُ بْنُ أَنَسٍ، وَ مِثْلُهُ عَنْ عَبْدِ الرَّزَّاقِ ، قَالَ إِسْحٰقُ بْنُ مُوْسٰى ، وَسَمِعْتُ ابْنَ عُيَيْنَةَ أَنَّهُ قَالَ، هُوَ الْعُمَرِىُّ الزَّاهِدُ وَ إِسْمُهُ عَبْدُ الْعَزِيْزِ بْنُ عَبْدِ اللهِ

246 Abu Huraira reported: The time is nearby when people will urge their camels in search of knowledge and they will find none more learned than the scholar of Medina.

Tirmidhi transmitted it and he in his *Jami'* quotes Ibn 'Uyaina as saying: That it was Malik b. Anas (who was implied as the scholar of Medina), and the same view is expressed by Abdur Razzaq. Ishaq b. Musa reported: I heard Ibn 'Uyaina as saying: He meant Al-'Umri the pious whose name was 'Abdul 'Aziz b. 'Abdullah.

٢٤٧ ـ وَعَنْهُ ، فِيْمَا أَعْلَمُ عَنْ رَسُوْلِ اللهِ ﷺ ، قَالَ :"إِنَّ اللهَ عَزَّ وَجَلَّ يَبْعَثُ لِهٰذِهِ الْأُمَّةِ عَلٰى رَأْسِ كُلِّ مِائَةِ سَنَةٍ مَنْ يُجَدِّدُ لَهَا دِيْنَهَا: رَوَاهُ أَبُوْدَاوُدَ .

247 It is reported on the same authority: I have learnt Allah's Messengers (peace and blessings of Allah be upon him) to have said that Allah, the Exalted and Glorious would send to this Ummah of mine at the end of every century one (scholar or a group of scholars) who would give new life to its religion. (*Abu Dawud*)

٢٤٨ ـ وَعَنْ إِبْرَاهِيْمَ بْنِ عَبْدِ الرَّحْمٰنِ الْعُذْرِىِّ قَالَ : قَالَ رَسُوْلُ اللهِ ﷺ :"يَحْمِلُ هٰذَا الْعِلْمَ مِنْ كُلِّ خَلَفٍ عُدُوْلُهُ ، يَنْفُوْنَ عَنْهُ تَحْرِيْفَ الْغَالِيْنَ وَانْتِحَالَ

الْمُبْطِلِيْنَ، وَتَأْوِيْلَ الْجَاهِلِيْنَ" رَوَاهُ الْبَيْهَقِيُّ. فِيْ كِتَابِ الْمَدْخَلِ مُرْسَلًا.
وَسَنَذْكُرُ حَدِيْثَ جَابِرٍ" فَإِنَّمَا شِفَاءُ الْعِيِّ السُّؤَالُ" فِيْ بَابِ التَّيَمُّمِ
إِنْ شَاءَ اللهُ تَعَالَى.

248 **Ibrahim b. 'Abdur Rahman Al-'Udhri** reported Allah's Messenger (peace and blessings of Allah be upon him) as saying: In every successive century the authentic scholars would bear this knowledge who would rectify the distortions of the extremists, and the falsification of the falsifiers and the interpretations of the ignorant.   (*Baihaqi*)

    We shall mention Jabir's tradition: The only remedy for perplexities is to ask in the Chapter 'On Performing the Ablution with Sand', if God wills.

Section III   اَلْفَصْلُ الثَّالِثُ

٢٤٩- عَنِ الْحَسَنِ مُرْسَلًا، قَالَ: قَالَ رَسُوْلُ اللهِ ﷺ "مَنْ جَاءَهُ الْمَوْتُ
وَهُوَ يَطْلُبُ الْعِلْمَ لِيُحْيِيَ بِهِ الْإِسْلَامَ، فَبَيْنَهُ وَبَيْنَ النَّبِيِّيْنَ دَرَجَةٌ
وَّاحِدَةٌ فِي الْجَنَّةِ" رَوَاهُ الدَّارِمِيُّ.

249 **Hasan Basari** reported in Mursal form that Allan's Messenger (peace and blessings of Allah be upon him) said: He whom death overtakes while he is engaged in acquiring knowledge with a view to reviving Islam with the help of it there will be one degree between him and the Prophets in Paradise. (*Darimi*)

٢٥- وَعَنْهُ مُرْسَلًا، قَالَ: سُبِلَ رَسُوْلُ اللهِ ﷺ عَنْ رَجُلَيْنِ كَانَا فِيْ بَنِيْ
إِسْرَائِيْلَ: أَحَدُهُمَا كَانَ عَالِمًا يُصَلِّي الْمَكْتُوْبَةَ، ثُمَّ يَجْلِسُ فَيُعَلِّمُ النَّاسَ
الْخَيْرَ، وَالْآخَرُ يَصُوْمُ النَّهَارَ وَيَقُوْمُ اللَّيْلَ، أَيُّهُمَا أَفْضَلُ؟ قَالَ رَسُوْلُ
اللهِ ﷺ: "فَضْلُ هٰذَا الْعَالِمِ الَّذِيْ يُصَلِّي الْمَكْتُوْبَةَ ثُمَّ يَجْلِسُ فَيُعَلِّمُ النَّاسَ
الْخَيْرَ عَلَى الْعَابِدِ الَّذِيْ يَصُوْمُ النَّهَارَ وَيَقُوْمُ اللَّيْلَ كَفَضْلِيْ عَلَى أَدْنَاكُمْ:
رَوَاهُ الدَّارِمِيُّ.

250 It is reported on the same authority and in the form of Mursal that Allah's Messenger (peace and blessings of Allah be upon him) was asked about two persons of Banu Israel; one of whom was a scholar observing prescribed prayer then sitting and teaching the people goodness; the second one who observed fast by day and prayed during the night—who amongst them is superior. Thereupon Allah's Messenger (peace and blessings of Allah be upon him) said: The superiority of a scholar who observes the prescribed prayer and then sits down to teach people goodness over the worshipper who observes fast during the day and worships during the night, is like my superiority over the lowest in rank amongst you. (*Darimi*)

٢٥١ـ وَعَنْ عَلِيٍّ، رَضِيَ اللهُ عَنْهُ، قَالَ: قَالَ رَسُولُ اللهِ ﷺ: نِعْمَ الرَّجُلُ الْفَقِيهُ فِي الدِّينِ؛ إِنِ احْتِيجَ إِلَيْهِ نَفَعَ، وَإِنِ اسْتُغْنِيَ عَنْهُ أَغْنَى نَفْسَهُ. رَوَاهُ رَزِينٌ.

251 'Ali (Allah be pleased with him) reported Allah's Messenger (peace and blessings of Allah be upon him) having said: Good is the man who acquired understanding in religion and who benefits others if they need (his guidance) but if they do not seek his guidance he is satisfied (with his knowledge). (*Razin*)

٢٥٢ـ وَعَنْ عِكْرِمَةَ، أَنَّ ابْنَ عَبَّاسٍ قَالَ: حَدِّثِ النَّاسَ كُلَّ جُمْعَةٍ مَرَّةً، فَإِنْ أَبَيْتَ فَمَرَّتَيْنِ، فَإِنْ أَكْثَرْتَ فَثَلَاثَ مَرَّاتٍ، وَلَا تُمِلَّ النَّاسَ هٰذَا الْقُرْآنَ؛ وَلَا أُلْفِيَنَّكَ تَأْتِي الْقَوْمَ وَهُمْ فِي حَدِيثٍ مِنْ حَدِيثِهِمْ فَتَقُصُّ عَلَيْهِمْ فَتَقْطَعُ عَلَيْهِمْ حَدِيثَهُمْ فَتُمِلَّهُمْ؛ وَلَكِنْ أَنْصِتْ، فَإِذَا أَمَرُوكَ فَحَدِّثْهُمْ وَهُمْ يَشْتَهُونَهُ، وَانْظُرِ السَّجْعَ مِنَ الدُّعَاءِ فَاجْتَنِبْهُ، فَإِنِّي عَهِدْتُ رَسُولَ اللهِ صَلَّى اللهُ عَلَيْهِ وَسَلَّمَ وَأَصْحَابَهُ لَا يَفْعَلُونَ ذٰلِكَ. رَوَاهُ الْبُخَارِيُّ.

252 'Ikrima reported Ibn 'Abbas as saying: Talk to the people once every Friday but if they object then biweekly but if they demand more, then thrice and do not bore people with this Qur'ān and don't let me find you coming to the people while they are engaged in conversation (of their own interests) and you interrupt them by addressing them and so bore them. Keep silent and when they request you then talk to them and they will listen to (you) with interest and avoid rhymed prose in supplication for I know that Allah's Messenger (peace and blessings of Allah be upon him) and his companions did not use it. (*Bukhari*)

٢٥٣ - وَعَنْ وَاثِلَةَ بْنِ الْأَسْقَعِ، قَالَ: قَالَ رَسُولُ اللهِ ﷺ "مَنْ طَلَبَ الْعِلْمَ فَأَدْرَكَهُ ـ كَانَ لَهُ كِفْلَانِ مِنَ الْأَجْرِ؛ فَإِنْ لَمْ يُدْرِكْهُ، كَانَ لَهُ كِفْلٌ مِنَ الْأَجْرِ" رَوَاهُ الدَّارِمِيُّ.

253 Wathila b. Al-Asqa' reported Allah's Messenger (peace and blessings of Allah be upon him) as saying : He who sought knowledge and acquired it, he has two shares of reward (but if he sought it) but did not acquire it there is only one reward for him. (*Darimi*)

٢٥٤ - وَعَنْ أَبِي هُرَيْرَةَ، قَالَ: قَالَ رَسُولُ اللهِ ﷺ "إِنَّ مِمَّا يَلْحَقُ الْمُؤْمِنَ مِنْ عَمَلِهِ وَحَسَنَاتِهِ بَعْدَ مَوْتِهِ عِلْمًا عَلَّمَهُ وَنَشَرَهُ، وَوَلَدًا صَالِحًا تَرَكَهُ، أَوْ مُصْحَفًا وَرَّثَهُ، أَوْ مَسْجِدًا بَنَاهُ، أَوْ بَيْتًا لِابْنِ السَّبِيلِ بَنَاهُ، أَوْ نَهْرًا أَجْرَاهُ، أَوْ صَدَقَةً أَخْرَجَهَا مِنْ مَالِهِ فِي صِحَّتِهِ وَحَيَاتِهِ تَلْحَقُهُ مِنْ بَعْدِ مَوْتِهِ" رَوَاهُ ابْنُ مَاجَهْ وَالْبَيْهَقِيُّ فِي شُعَبِ الْإِيمَانِ"

254 Abu Huraira reported Allah's Messenger (peace and blessings of Allah be upon him) as saying: Verily what a believer continues to receive (in the form of reward) for his action and his virtues after his death is the knowledge which he acquired and then disseminated it; the pious son that he left behind him or a copy of the Qur'ān which he left as a legacy or the mosques that he got built or the inn that he got built for the wayfarers or the canal that he caused to flow or a *sadaqa* which he gave out of his property in the state when he was healthy and he was alive. (These are the acts of goodness the reward of which) reaches him even after his death.

(*Ibn Majah, Baihaqi in Shu'ab-ul-Iman*)

٢٥٥ - وَعَنْ عَائِشَةَ، أَنَّهَا قَالَتْ: سَمِعْتُ رَسُولَ اللهِ ﷺ يَقُولُ: "إِنَّ اللهَ عَزَّ وَجَلَّ أَوْحَى إِلَيَّ، أَنَّهُ مَنْ سَلَكَ مَسْلَكًا فِي طَلَبِ الْعِلْمِ، سَهَّلْتُ لَهُ طَرِيقَ الْجَنَّةِ؛ وَمَنْ سَلَبْتُ كَرِيمَتَيْهِ؛ أَثْبَتُهُ عَلَيْهِمَا الْجَنَّةَ؛ وَفَضْلُ فِي عِلْمٍ خَيْرٌ مِنْ فَضْلٍ فِي عِبَادَةٍ. وَمِلَاكُ الدِّينِ الْوَرَعُ" رَوَاهُ الْبَيْهَقِيُّ فِي "شُعَبِ الْإِيمَانِ"

255 'Aisha reported: I heard Allah's Messenger (peace and blessings of Allah be upon him) as saying: Verily Allah, the Exalted and Glorious, revealed to me this: He who treads a path for acquiring knowledge for him I shall make easy the path leading to Paradise, and if I deprive anyone of his eyesight I shall guarantee him the Paradise and the superiority of the knowledge is better than the superiority in worship and the basis of *Din* is the fear (of Allah). (*Baihaqi in Shu'ab-ul-Iman*)

٢٥٦ - وَعَنِ ابْنِ عَبَّاسٍ، قَالَ: تَدَارُسُ الْعِلْمِ سَاعَةً مِنَ اللَّيْلِ خَيْرٌ مِنْ إِحْيَائِهَا. رَوَاهُ الدَّارِمِيُّ.

256 Ibn 'Abbas reported acquiring of knowledge in company for an hour in the night is better than spending the whole night in prayer. (*Darimi*)

٢٥٧ - وَعَنْ عَبْدِ اللهِ بْنِ عَمْرٍو، أَنَّ رَسُولَ اللهِ ﷺ مَرَّ بِمَجْلِسَيْنِ فِي مَسْجِدٍ فَقَالَ: "كِلَاهُمَا عَلَى خَيْرٍ، وَأَحَدُهُمَا أَفْضَلُ مِنْ صَاحِبِهِ؛ أَمَّا هَؤُلَاءِ فَيَدْعُونَ اللهَ وَيَرْغَبُونَ إِلَيْهِ، فَإِنْ شَاءَ أَعْطَاهُمْ وَإِنْ شَاءَ مَنَعَهُمْ وَأَمَّا هَؤُلَاءِ فَيَتَعَلَّمُونَ الْفِقْهَ أَوِ الْعِلْمَ وَيُعَلِّمُونَ الْجَاهِلَ، فَهُمْ أَفْضَلُ وَإِنَّمَا بُعِثْتُ مُعَلِّمًا" ثُمَّ جَلَسَ فِيهِمْ. رَوَاهُ الدَّارِمِيُّ.

257 'Abdullah b. 'Amr reported that Allah's Messenger (peace and blessings of Allah be upon him) happened to pass by two groups (of Muslims) in the mosque and he said: Both of them are on good, but one being superior to the other, one group is supplicating Allah and praying Him and if He so wills He would confer upon them and if He so wills He would withhold and so far as those who are acquiring the understanding of religion and its knowledge and are busy in teaching the ignorant they are superior. Verily I have been sent as a teacher. He then sat down amongst them. (*Darimi*)

٢٥٨ ـ وَعَنْ أَبِي الدَّرْدَآءِ قَالَ : سُئِلَ رَسُولُ اللهِ ﷺ ، مَا حَدُّ الْعِلْمِ الَّذِى إِذَا بَلَغَهُ الرَّجُلُ كَانَ فَقِيهًا؟ فَقَالَ رَسُولُ اللهِ ﷺ : "مَنْ حَفِظَ عَلَى أُمَّتِى أَرْبَعِينَ حَدِيثًا فِى أَمْرِ دِينِهَا بَعَثَهُ اللهُ فَقِيهًا، وَكُنْتُ لَهُ يَوْمَ الْقِيَامَةِ شَافِعًا وَّ شَهِيدًا "

258 Abu al-Darda reported that Allah's Messenger (peace and blessings of Allah be upon him) was asked: What is the degree of knowledge which, when a man attains, makes him *faqih* (one who has a deep understanding of religion)? Allah's Messenger (peace and blessings of Allah be upon him) said: He who remembers (and then transmits) to my Ummah forty ahadith pertaining to religion, Allah would raise him as a *faqih* and I would be an intercessor and witness for him on the Day of Resurrection.

٢٥٩ ـ وَعَنْ أَنَسِ بْنِ مَالِكٍ ، قَالَ : قَالَ رَسُولُ اللهِ ﷺ : "هَلْ تَدْرُونَ مَنْ أَجْوَدُ جُودًا ؟ قَالُوا : اللهُ وَرَسُولُهُ أَعْلَمُ . قَالَ : "اللهُ تَعَالَى أَجْوَدُ جُودًا ، ثُمَّ أَنَا أَجْوَدُ بَنِى آدَمَ ، وَأَجْوَدُهُمْ مِّنْ بَعْدِى رَجُلٌ عَلِمَ عِلْمًا فَنَشَرَهُ ، يَأْتِى يَوْمَ الْقِيَامَةِ أَمِيرًا وَّحْدَهُ ، أَوْ قَالَ : أُمَّةً وَّاحِدَةً "

259 Anas b. Malik reported that Allah's Messenger (peace and blessings of Allah be upon him) said: Do you know who is most generous? They said: Allah and His Messenger know best. Whereupon he said: Allah is the most Generous, then I am most generous to mankind and the most generous persons after me would be the persons who would acquire knowledge and then disseminate it. He will come on the Day of Resurrection singly, like a ruler, or he said: As a single Ummah.

٢٦٠ـ وَعَنْهُ أَنَّ النَّبِيَّ ﷺ قَالَ: "مَنْهُومَانِ لَا يَشْبَعَانِ: مَنْهُومٌ فِي الْعِلْمِ لَا
يَشْبَعُ مِنْهُ وَمَنْهُومٌ فِي الدُّنْيَا لَا يَشْبَعُ مِنْهَا" رَوَى الْبَيْهَقِيُّ الْأَحَادِيثَ
الثَّلَاثَةَ فِي "شُعَبِ الْإِيمَانِ" وَقَالَ: قَالَ الْإِمَامُ أَحْمَدُ فِي حَدِيثِ أَبِي الدَّرْدَاءِ:
هٰذَا مَتْنٌ مَشْهُورٌ فِيمَا بَيْنَ النَّاسِ، وَلَيْسَ لَهُ إِسْنَادٌ صَحِيحٌ .

260 It is reported on the same authority that Allah's Apostle (peace and blessings of Allah be upon him) said: There are two avaricious persons who are never content; one greedy of knowledge who is never content and the greedy of the world (worldly riches and that of power) who is never content.
(*Baihaqi transmitted the three traditions in Shu'ab-ul-Iman and quoted Imam Ahmad as saying about hadith of Abud Darda: This is well known text amongst the people but it does not have a sound chain of transmission*).

٢٦١ـ وَعَنْ عَوْنٍ، قَالَ: قَالَ عَبْدُ اللهِ بْنُ مَسْعُودٍ: مَنْهُومَانِ لَا يَشْبَعَانِ صَاحِبُ
الْعِلْمِ، وَصَاحِبُ الدُّنْيَا، وَلَا يَسْتَوِيَانِ، أَمَّا صَاحِبُ الْعِلْمِ فَيَزْدَادُ رِضًى
لِلرَّحْمٰنِ، وَأَمَّا صَاحِبُ الدُّنْيَا فَيَتَمَادَى فِي الطُّغْيَانِ. ثُمَّ قَرَأَ عَبْدُ اللهِ: كَلَّا
إِنَّ الْإِنْسَانَ لَيَطْغَى أَنْ رَآهُ اسْتَغْنَى، قَالَ: وَقَالَ الْآخَرَ: إِنَّمَا يَخْشَى اللهَ
مِنْ عِبَادِهِ الْعُلَمَاءُ، رَوَاهُ الدَّارِمِيُّ .

261 'Aun reported that 'Abdullah b. Mas'ud said: There are two avaricious persons who are never contented. The man of learning and the man of world, but the two are not equal; the man of knowledge increases in submission to Allah and as for the man of the world, he becomes head-strong and defiant. 'Abdullah then recited: Nay man is surely rebellious when he sees himself free from want (46 : 6). Concerning the other he recited the verse: Surely those of His servants who are possessed of knowledge, fear Allah. (35: 28). (*Darimi*)

٢٦٢ـ وَعَنِ ابْنِ عَبَّاسٍ، قَالَ: قَالَ رَسُولُ اللهِ ﷺ: "إِنَّ أُنَاسًا مِنْ أُمَّتِي
سَيَتَفَقَّهُونَ فِي الدِّينِ وَيَقْرَؤُونَ الْقُرْآنَ، يَقُولُونَ: نَأْتِي الْأُمَرَاءَ فَنُصِيبُ

مِنْ دُنْيَاهُمْ وَ نَعْتَزِلُهُمْ بِدِيْنِنَا وَ لَا يَكُوْنُ ذٰلِكَ ، كَمَا لَا يُجْتَنٰى مِنَ الْقَتَادِ
إِلَّا الشَّوْكُ ، كَذَالِكَ لَا يُجْتَنٰى مِنْ قُرْبِهِمْ إِلَّا - قَالَ مُحَمَّدُ بْنُ الصَّبَّاحِ : كَأَنَّهُ
يَعْنِيْ - اَلْخَطَايَا : رَوَاهُ ابْنُ مَاجَةَ.

262 Ibn 'Abbas reported that Allah's Messenger (peace and blessings of Allah be upon him) said: Verily some persons from amongst my Ummah will acquire the understanding of religion and will recite the Qur'ān and would say: We will go to the men of authority and partake of their worldly (riches) and (then) withdraw from them with our religion. But it can't be; as nothing can be gathered from thorny trees except thorn, in like manner nothing can be gathered by drawing near to them except—Muhammad b. As-Sabbah said: (the same): *i.e.* sin and vice. (*Ibn Majah*)

٢٦٣ - وَعَنْ عَبْدِ اللهِ بْنِ مَسْعُودٍ ، قَالَ : لَوْ أَنَّ أَهْلَ الْعِلْمِ صَانُوا الْعِلْمَ
وَوَضَعُوهُ عِنْدَ أَهْلِهِ لَسَادُوا بِهِ أَهْلَ زَمَانِهِمْ وَلٰكِنَّهُمْ بَذَلُوْهُ لِأَهْلِ الدُّنْيَا
لِيَنَالُوْا بِهِ مِنْ دُنْيَاهُمْ ؛ فَهَانُوْا عَلَيْهِمْ . سَمِعْتُ نَبِيَّكُمْ ﷺ يَقُوْلُ :
"مَنْ جَعَلَ الْهُمُوْمَ هَمًّا وَّاحِدًا هَمَّ أَخِرَتِهِ ، كَفَاهُ اللهُ هَمَّ دُنْيَاهُ وَ مَنْ
تَشَعَّبَتْ بِهِ الْهُمُوْمُ رفِيْ أَحْوَالِ الدُّنْيَا ، لَمْ يُبَالِ اللهُ فِيْ أَيِّ أَوْدِيَتِهَا
هَلَكَ" رَوَاهُ ابْنُ مَاجَةَ.

263 'Abdullah b. Mas'ud reported: If the people of knowledge were to preserve it and impart it to those who are worthy of it they will most certainly be the leaders of their age by virtue of it, but they passed it on to the people of the world to attain thereby some portion of their world, so they fell into the estimation of their eyes. I heard your Apostle (peace and blessings of Allah be upon him) as saying: Whosoever centers all his thoughts upon one object viz. the thought of the Hereafter, God would suffice him with the worldly needs and he whose whole distraction is worldly ends, God does not care in what wilderness of the world he perishes. (*Ibn Majah*)

٢٦٤ - وَرَوَاهُ الْبَيْهَقِيُّ فِي "شُعَبِ الْإِيمَانِ" عَنِ ابْنِ عُمَرَ مِنْ قَوْلِهِ :"مَنْ جَعَلَ الْهُمُومَ"إِلَى آخِرِهِ .

264 And *Baihaqi* transmitted it in *Shu'ab-ul-Iman* from Ibn 'Umar beginning with "Whosoever makes the care" till the end of the hadith.

٢٦٥ - وَعَنِ الْأَعْمَشِ ، قَالَ : قَالَ رَسُولُ اللهِ ﷺ : "آفَةُ الْعِلْمِ النِّسْيَانُ ، وَ إِضَاعَتُهُ أَنْ تُحَدِّثَ بِهِ غَيْرَ أَهْلِهِ" رَوَاهُ الدَّارِمِيُّ مُرْسَلًا .

265 **Al-A'mash** reported Allah's Messenger (peace and blessings of Allah be upon him) as saying: The calamity of knowledge is its forgetfulness and its wastage is to impart it to those who are not worthy of it. (*Darimi transmitted it as mursal*)

٢٦٦ - وَعَنْ سُفْيَانَ ، أَنَّ عُمَرَ بْنَ الْخَطَّابِ ، رَضِيَ اللهُ عَنْهُ ، قَالَ لِكَعْبٍ :"مَنْ أَرْبَابُ الْعِلْمِ؟ قَالَ :الَّذِينَ يَعْمَلُونَ بِمَا يَعْلَمُونَ . قَالَ :فَمَا أَخْرَجَ الْعِلْمَ مِنْ قُلُوبِ الْعُلَمَاءِ؟ قَالَ :الطَّمَعُ . رَوَاهُ الدَّارِمِيُّ .

266 **Sufyan** reported that 'Umar b. Khattab (may Allah be pleased with him) said: Ka'b, who are the learned? He said: Those who act according to what they know. 'Umar said: What is that which drives out knowledge from the hearts of the learned? He said: Covetousness. (*Darimi*)

٢٦٧ - وَعَنِ الْأَحْوَصِ بْنِ حَكِيمٍ ، عَنْ أَبِيهِ ، قَالَ : سَأَلَ رَجُلٌ النَّبِيَّ ﷺ عَنِ الشَّرِّ، فَقَالَ :"لَا تَسْأَلُونِي عَنِ الشَّرِّ، وَاسْأَلُونِي عَنِ الْخَيْرِ" يَقُولُهَا ثَلَاثًا ، ثُمَّ قَالَ :"أَلَا إِنَّ شَرَّ الشَّرِّ شِرَارُ الْعُلَمَاءِ ، وَإِنَّ خَيْرَ الْخَيْرِ خِيَارُ الْعُلَمَاءِ" رَوَاهُ الدَّارِمِيُّ .

267 **Al-Ahwas b. Hakim** reported on the authority of his father that he asked Allah's Messenger (peace and blessings of Allah be upon him) about the evil. Whereupon he said: Don't ask me about evil but ask me about good. He repeated this thrice after which he said: Behold the worst beings are the wicked among the learned ones and the best are the virtuous among the learned. (*Darimi*)

٢٦٨ ـ وَعَنْ أَبِي الدَّرْدَاءِ، قَالَ : إِنَّ مِنْ أَشَرِّ النَّاسِ عِنْدَ اللهِ مَنْزِلَةً يَوْمَ
الْقِيَامَةِ : عَالِمٌ لَّا يَنْتَفِعُ بِعِلْمِهِ" رَوَاهُ الدَّارِمِيُّ .

268 Abu Darda said: The worst of men in the eye of Allah on
the Day of Resurrection would be the scholar who does not
derive benefit from his knowledge. (*Darimi*)

٢٦٩ ـ وَعَنْ زِيَادِ بْنِ حُدَيْرٍ، قَالَ : قَالَ لِي عُمَرُ : هَلْ تَعْرِفُ مَا يَهْدِمُ الْإِسْلَامَ؟
قَالَ : قُلْتُ : لَا ، قَالَ : يَهْدِمُهُ زَلَّةُ الْعَالِمِ ، وَجِدَالُ الْمُنَافِقِ بِالْكِتَابِ وَحُكْمُ
الْأَئِمَّةِ الْمُضِلِّينَ . رَوَاهُ الدَّارِمِيُّ .

269 Ziyad b Hudair reported: 'Umar said to me: Do you know
what demolishes Islam? I said: No. Whereupon he said:
It is the slip of a scholar and the disputation of the hypocrite
about the Book of the commands of the misguided rulers
which demolish it. (*Darimi*)

٢٧٠ ـ وَعَنِ الْحَسَنِ، قَالَ : أَلْعِلْمُ عِلْمَانِ : فَعِلْمٌ فِي الْقَلْبِ فَذَاكَ الْعِلْمُ
النَّافِعُ ، وَعِلْمٌ عَلَى اللِّسَانِ فَذَاكَ حُجَّةُ اللهِ عَزَّ وَجَلَّ عَلَى ابْنِ آدَمَ .
رَوَاهُ الدَّارِمِيُّ .

270 Hasan reported: The knowledge is of two types. Firstly
the knowledge perceived by heart and that is useful knowledge and the knowledge at tongue's (tip) and that is an
argument from Allah, the Exalted and Glorious, against the
children of Adam.[1] (*Darimi*)

1. What this means is that Allah would say on the Day of Resurrection
   that He had sent down the Divine Knowledge to the human race and
   that many people had acquired it but still they did not act according
   to it.

٢٧١ ـ وَعَنْ أَبِي هُرَيْرَةَ، قَالَ : حَفِظْتُ مِنْ رَسُولِ اللهِ ﷺ وِعَاءَيْنِ : فَأَمَّا
أَحَدُهُمَا فَبَثَثْتُهُ فِيكُمْ ، وَأَمَّا الْآخَرُ فَلَوْ بَثَثْتُهُ قُطِعَ هٰذَا الْبُلْعُومُ ـ يَعْنِي
مَجْرَى الطَّعَامِ ـ رَوَاهُ الْبُخَارِيُّ .

271 Abu Huraira reported: I have received from Allah's Messenger (peace and blessings of Allah be upon him) two vessels of learning (the contents of one I have distributed amongst you) but as to the other[1] if I were to make it public this throat (that is, his own) will be cut. (*Bukhari*)

1. This knowledge refers to the turmoil in the grip of which the Ummah was caught after the Holy Prophet (may peace and blessings of Allah be upon him). There is every possibility that the Holy Prophet (peace and blessings of Allah be upon him) might have made a pointed reference to the people who would be responsible for it. Abu Huraira, therefore, did not like to disclose this that it might lead to some serious troubles.

٢٧٢ـ وَعَنْ عَبْدِ اللهِ بْنِ مَسْعُودٍ، قَالَ يَا أَيُّهَا النَّاسُ ! مَنْ عَلِمَ شَيْئًا فَلْيَقُلْ بِهِ، وَمَنْ لَمْ يَعْلَمْ فَلْيَقُلْ: اَللهُ أَعْلَمُ، فَإِنَّ مِنَ الْعِلْمِ أَنْ تَقُوْلَ لِمَا لَا تَعْلَمُ: اَللهُ أَعْلَمُ. قَالَ اللهُ تَعَالَى لِنَبِيِّهِ: ﴿قُلْ مَا أَسْأَلُكُمْ عَلَيْهِ مِنْ أَجْرٍ وَمَا أَنَا مِنَ الْمُتَكَلِّفِيْنَ﴾، مُتَّفَقٌ عَلَيْهِ.

272 'Abdullah b. Mas'ud is reported to have said: O ye men, he who knows a thing he should talk about it and he who does not know he should simply say: It is Allah Who knows best, because this too is of knowledge that one should say about a thing, one does not know that Allah knows best, as Allah says to His Prophet: Say: I do not ask you any reward for it nor I am of those who affect. (38: 86). (*Agreed upon*)

٢٧٣ـ وَعَنِ ابْنِ سِيْرِيْنَ، قَالَ: إِنَّ هٰذَا الْعِلْمَ دِيْنٌ، فَانْظُرُوْا عَمَّنْ تَأْخُذُوْنَ دِيْنَكُمْ. رَوَاهُ مُسْلِمٌ.

273 Ibn Sirin reported: Verily this knowledge is the knowledge of religion (and, therefore, is of almost importance). You must carefully see from whom you are receiving the knowledge of your religion. (*Muslim*)

٢٧٤ـ وَعَنْ حُذَيْفَةَ، قَالَ: يَا مَعْشَرَ الْقُرَّاءِ ! إِسْتَقِيْمُوْا فَقَدْ سَبَقْتُمْ سَبْقًا بَعِيْدًا، وَإِنْ أَخَذْتُمْ يَمِيْنًا وَشِمَالًا لَقَدْ ضَلَلْتُمْ ضَلَالًا بَعِيْدًا. رَوَاهُ الْبُخَارِيُّ.

274 Abu Hudhaifa reported: O Ye reciters of the Qur'ān, keep to the straight path for you have been given a great precedence and if you stray to the right path or the left, verily you will stray away very far. (*Bukhari*)

٢٧٥- وَعَنْ أَبِى هُرَيْرَةَ، قَالَ: قَالَ رَسُولُ اللهِ ﷺ تَعَوَّذُوا بِاللهِ مِنْ جُبِّ الْحُزْنِ، قَالُوا: يَا رَسُولَ اللهِ! وَمَا جُبُّ الْحُزْنِ؟ قَالَ: وَادٍ فِى جَهَنَّمَ تَتَعَوَّذُ مِنْهُ جَهَنَّمُ كُلَّ يَوْمٍ أَرْبَعَ مِائَةِ مَرَّةٍ. قِيلَ: يَا رَسُولَ اللهِ! وَمَنْ يَدْخُلُهَا! قَالَ: أَلْقُرَّاءُ الْمُرَاؤُونَ بِأَعْمَالِهِمْ. رَوَاهُ التِّرْمِذِيُّ، وَكَذَا ابْنُ مَاجَهْ، وَزَادَ فِيهِ: وَإِنَّ مِنْ أَبْغَضِ الْقُرَّاءِ إِلَى اللهِ تَعَالَى الَّذِينَ يَزُورُونَ الْأُمَرَاءَ قَالَ الْمُحَارِبِيُّ: يَعْنِى الْجَوَرَةَ.

275 Abu Huraira reported Allah's Messenger (peace and blessings of Allah be upon him) as saying: Seek refuge with Allah from the well of sorrow. They said: Allah's Messenger, What is the well of sorrow? He said: It is a valley in Hell from which even Hell seeks refuge four hundred times every day. It was said to him: Allah's Messenger, who will enter it? Whereupon he said: The reciters of the Qur'ān who are hypocritical in their actions. (*Tirmidhi reported it and so Ibn Majah and he made this addition in it: Verily the most hateful in the eyes of Allah are those reciters who visit the rulers. Al-Muharibi said that he meant 'tyrants'*)

٢٧٦- وَعَنْ عَلِيٍّ، قَالَ: قَالَ رَسُولُ اللهِ ﷺ: يُوشِكُ أَنْ يَأْتِيَ عَلَى النَّاسِ زَمَانٌ لَا يَبْقَى مِنَ الْإِسْلَامِ إِلَّا اسْمُهُ، وَلَا يَبْقَى مِنَ الْقُرْآنِ إِلَّا رَسْمُهُ، مَسَاجِدُهُمْ عَامِرَةٌ وَهِيَ خَرَابٌ مِنَ الْهُدَى، عُلَمَاؤُهُمْ شَرٌّ مَنْ تَحْتَ أَدِيمِ السَّمَاءِ، مِنْ عِنْدِهِمْ تَخْرُجُ الْفِتْنَةُ، وَفِيهِمْ تَعُودُ. رَوَاهُ الْبَيْهَقِيُّ فِى "شُعَبِ الْإِيمَانِ".

276 'Ali reported Allah's Messenger (peace and blessings of Allah be upon him) as saying: There will come a time upon mankind when nothing will remain of Islam except its name only and nothing will remain of the Qur'ān except its ritual. Their mosques will be full but destitute of guidance. Their learned men will be the worst people under the heaven and strife will issue from and revert to them.

(Baihaqi, Shu'ab-ul-Iman)

٢٧٧ ـ وَعَنْ زِيَادِ بنِ لَبِيدٍ، قَالَ ذَكَرَ النَّبِيُّ ﷺ شَيْئًا، فَقَالَ: ذَاكَ عِنْدَ أَوَانِ ذَهَابِ الْعِلْمِ، قُلْتُ: يَا رَسُولَ اللهِ! وَكَيْفَ يَذْهَبُ الْعِلْمُ وَنَحْنُ نَقْرَأُ الْقُرْآنَ وَنُقْرِئُهُ أَبْنَاءَنَا، وَيُقْرِئُوهُ أَبْنَاءُنَا أَبْنَاءَهُمْ إِلَى يَوْمِ الْقِيَامَةِ؟ فَقَالَ: ثَكِلَتْكَ أُمُّكَ زِيَادُ! إِنْ كُنْتُ لَأَرَاكَ مِنْ أَفْقَهِ رَجُلٍ بِالْمَدِينَةِ! أَوَ لَيْسَ هٰذِهِ الْيَهُودُ وَالنَّصَارَى يَقْرَؤُونَ التَّوْرَاةَ وَالْإِنْجِيلَ لَا يَعْمَلُونَ بِشَيْءٍ مِمَّا فِيهِمَا؟! رَوَاهُ أَحْمَدُ، وَابْنُ مَاجَهْ، وَرَوَى التِّرْمِذِيُّ عَنْهُ نَحْوَهُ.

277 Ziyad b. Labid reported Allah's Messenger (peace and blessings of Allah be upon him) spoke of something and said: It will happen when knowledge will be no more. I said: Allah's Messenger, how will the knowledge vanish despite of the fact that we would be reciting the Qur'ān and teaching its recitation to our children and our children would teach its recitation to their children upto the Day of Resurrection. Thereupon he said: Ziyad, may your mother weep over you. I was of the opinion that you were the person having the greatest understanding of religion in Medina. Do these Jews and Christians not recite the Torah and the Bible but they do not act according to what is contained in them.

(Ahmad, Ibn Majah, Tirmidhi)

٢٧٨ ـ وَكَذَا الدَّارِمِيُّ عَنْ أَبِي أُمَامَةَ.

278 Darimi reported the same from Abu Umama.

٢٧٩ ـ وَعَنِ ابْنِ مَسْعُودٍ، قَالَ: قَالَ لِي رَسُولُ اللهِ ﷺ: تَعَلَّمُوا الْعِلْمَ وَ

عَلِّمُوهُ النَّاسَ ، تَعَلَّمُوا الْفَرَائِضَ وَعَلِّمُوهَا النَّاسَ ، تَعَلَّمُوا الْقُرْآنَ وَ
عَلِّمُوهُ النَّاسَ ! فَإِنِّي امْرُؤٌ مَقْبُوضٌ ، وَ الْعِلْمُ سَيَنْقَبِضُ ، وَ تَظْهَرُ الْفِتَنُ
حَتَّى يَخْتَلِفَ اثْنَانِ فِي فَرِيضَةٍ لَا يَجِدَانِ أَحَدًا يَفْصِلُ بَيْنَهُمَا ، رَوَاهُ
الدَّارِمِيُّ ، وَ الدَّارَ قُطْنِيُّ .

279 Ibn Mas'ud reported that Allah's Messenger (peace and blessings of Allah be upon him) said to him: Acquire the knowledge and impart it to the people. Acquire the knowledge of obligatory acts (especially pertaining to the inheritance) and teach it to the people, learn the Qur'ān and teach it to the people, for I am a person who has to depart this world and the knowledge will be taken away and turmoil will appear to such an extent that two persons will not agree in regard to the obligatory act and find none who would decide between them. (*Darimi and Daraqutni*)

٢٨٠ - وَعَنْ أَبِي هُرَيْرَةَ ، قَالَ : قَالَ رَسُولُ اللهِ ﷺ : مَثَلُ عِلْمٍ لَا يُنْتَفَعُ
بِهِ كَمَثَلِ كَنْزٍ لَا يُنْفَقُ مِنْهُ فِي سَبِيلِ اللهِ ، رَوَاهُ أَحْمَدُ ، وَ الدَّارِمِيُّ .

280 Abu Huraira reported Allah's Messenger (peace and blessings of Allah be upon him) as saying: The knowledge from which no benefit is derived is like a treasure out of which nothing is spent in the cause of Allah. (*Ahmad and Darimi*)

كِتَابُ الطَّهَارَةِ

Kitab-ul-Taharah
(THE BOOK OF PURIFICATION)

CHAPTER 8

Section I الفَصَلُ الأوَّل

٢٨١- عَنْ أَبِي مَالِكٍ الأَشْعَرِيِّ ، قَالَ : قَالَ رَسُولُ اللهِ ﷺ "أَلطُّهُورُ شَطْرُ
الإيمَانِ ، وَالْحَمْدُ للهِ تَمْلأُ الْمِيزَانَ ، وَسُبْحَانَ اللهِ وَ الْحَمْدُ للهِ
تَمْلأنِ – أَوْ تَمْلأُ – مَا بَيْنَ السَّمَاوَاتِ وَ الأَرْضِ ، وَالصَّلاةُ نُورٌ ،
وَ الصَّدَقَةُ بُرْهَانٌ ، وَالصَّبْرُ ضِيَاءٌ ، وَ الْقُرْآنُ حُجَّةٌ لَكَ أَوْ عَلَيْكَ .
كُلُّ النَّاسِ يَغْدُو : فَبَائِعٌ نَفْسَهُ فَمُعْتِقُهَا أَوْ مُوبِقُهَا" رَوَاهُ مُسْلِمٌ
وَ فِي رِوَايَةٍ : لَا آلَهَ إِلا اللهُ وَ اللهُ أَكْبَرَ ، تَمْلآنِ مَا بَيْنَ السَّمَاءِ
وَ الأَرْضِ" لَمْ أَجِدْ هَذِهِ الرِّوَايَةَ فِي "الصَّحِيحَيْنِ" : وَ لَا فِي كِتَابِ
الْحُمَيْدِيِّ ، وَ لَا فِي "الْجَامِعِ" ؛ وَ لَكِنْ ذَكَرَهَا الدَّارِمِيُّ بَدَلَ "سُبْحَانَ اللهِ
وَ الْحَمْدُ للهِ"

281 Abu Malik Al-Ash'ari reported Allah's Messenger (peace and blessings of Allah be upon him) as saying: Cleanliness is half of faith.[1] *Alhamdulillah* (Praise be to Allah) fills the scale and *Subhanallah* (Hallowed be Allah) and *Alhamdulillah* (Praise be to Allah) fill up what is between the heavens and the earth and prayer is light and charity is proof (of one's faith) and endurance is a brightness and the Qur'ān is proof on your belief or against you[2] and men go out early in the morning and sell[3] themselves thereby setting themselves free or destroying themselves. And in another version the words are: There is no god but Allah and Allah is the Greatest. (These two kalimahs) fill the space between heavens and earth. (*I, however, do not find this narration in Sahihain, in Al-Humaidis' Book or in the Jami' but Darimi mentioned it in the place of "Glory be to Allah, and Praise be to Allah"*)

1. Faith covers two aspects :
   (a) Purification of one's soul of evil thoughts and ideas and banishing from it the love of all false deities.

(b) Entertaining in one's heart the love of Allah alone.
Cleanliness is said to be half of faith because unless the work of purification of heart is not complete one cannot have full devotion to Allah. Thus half of faith is purification of the soul and half is devotion to Allah to the exclusion of devotion to any other godhood. If we take *Al-Tahur* in the sense of cleanliness of body then the word faith would imply prayer because prayer is the first visible expression of one's faith. We find in the Holy Qur'ān: Nor was Allah going to make your prayer go waste. (2 : 143). Here the Iman stands for prayer.

2. 'The Holy Qur'ān is a proof on your behalf or against you' means that your destiny would be determined by your attitude towards the Qur'ān. If you act according to the teachings embodied in the Holy Qar'ān with sincerity and devotion you would gain salvation but if you act contrary to them you will suffer disgrace and humiliation at the hand of Allah.

3. Life is a sort of trade in the sense that we barter our physical strength, our inborn and acquired qualities for certain desires and needs. If these desires or needs are moral and inspired by a spirit of piety and God-consciousness then we are doing profitable business which would ensure salvation in the Hereafter. But if we are mortgaging for vain desires and fancies we are ruining ourselves.

٢٨٢ - وَعَنْ أَبِى هُرَيْرَةَ ، قَالَ : قَالَ رَسُولُ اللهِ ﷺ : « أَلَا أَدُلُّكُمْ عَلَى مَا يَمْحُوا اللهُ بِهِ الْخَطَايَا . وَيَرْفَعُ بِهِ الدَّرَجَاتِ ؟» . قَالُوا : بَلَى يَا رَسُولَ اللهِ ! قَالَ : « إِسْبَاغُ الْوُضُوءِ عَلَى الْمَكَارِهِ ، وَكَثْرَةُ الْخُطَى إِلَى الْمَسَاجِدِ ، وَ انْتِظَارُ الصَّلَاةِ بَعْدَ الصَّلَاةِ ، فَذَلِكُمُ الرِّبَاطُ :

282 Abu Huraira reported that Allah's Messenger (peace and blessings of Allah be upon him) said: Should I not direct you to something by which Allah obliterates the sins and elevates (your) ranks. They said: Yes, Allah's Messenger with great (pleasure). Whereupon he said: Performing complete ablution despite odds, taking many steps for going to mosque and looking expectantly to the next time of prayer after the prayer has been said and that is a defence of frontier.

٢٨٣ - وَفِى حَدِيثِ مَالِكِ بْنِ أَنَسٍ : «فَذَلِكُمُ الرِّبَاطُ» فَذَلِكُمُ الرِّبَاطُ» رَدَّدَ، مَرَّتَيْنِ . رَوَاهُ مُسْلِمٌ . وَفِى رِوَايَةِ التِّرْمِذِيِّ : ثَلَاثًا .

283 In the tradition of Malik b. Anas (the words) are: That is the defence of the frontier, that is the defence of the frontier. He repeated it twice. (*Transmitted by Muslim and in Tirmidhi it is repeated thrice*)

٢٨٤ - وَعَنْ عُثْمَانَ ، رَضِيَ اللهُ عَنْهُ ، قَالَ : قَالَ رَسُولُ اللهِ ﷺ : "مَنْ تَوَضَّأَ فَأَحْسَنَ الْوُضُوءَ ، خَرَجَتْ خَطَايَاهُ مِنْ جَسَدِهِ حَتَّى تَخْرُجَ مِنْ تَحْتِ أَظْفَارِهِ" مُتَّفَقٌ عَلَيْهِ .

284 'Uthman (may Allah be pleased with him) reported Allah's Messenger (peace and blessings of Allah be upon him) said: He who performs ablution well, his sins are driven out from his body till they pour out even underneath his nails.

(*Agreed upon*)

٢٨٥ - وَعَنْ أَبِى هُرَيْرَةَ ، قَالَ : قَالَ رَسُولُ اللهِ ﷺ : "إِذَا تَوَضَّأَ الْعَبْدُ الْمُسْلِمُ ـ أَوِ الْمُؤْمِنُ ـ فَغَسَلَ وَجْهَهُ ، خَرَجَ مِنْ وَجْهِهِ كُلُّ خَطِيئَةٍ نَظَرَ إِلَيْهَا بِعَيْنَيْهِ مَعَ الْمَاءِ ، أَوْ مَعَ آخِرِ قَطْرِ الْمَاءِ ـ فَإِذَا غَسَلَ يَدَيْهِ خَرَجَ مِنْ يَدَيْهِ كُلُّ خَطِيئَةٍ كَانَ بَطَشَتْهَا يَدَاهُ مَعَ الْمَاءِ ـ أَوْ مَعَ آخِرِ قَطْرِ الْمَاءِ ـ فَإِذَا غَسَلَ رِجْلَيْهِ خَرَجَ كُلُّ خَطِيئَةٍ مَشَتْهَا رِجْلَاهُ مَعَ الْمَاءِ ـ أَوْ مَعَ آخِرِ قَطْرِ الْمَاءِ ـ حَتَّى يَخْرُجَ نَقِيًّا مِنَ الذُّنُوبِ" رَوَاهُ مُسْلِمٌ .

285 Abu Huraira reported Allah's Messenger (peace and blessings of Allah be upon him) as saying: When a bondman—a Muslim or a believer—washes his face (in the course of ablution) all sins that he committed with his eyes will be washed away from his face along with water or with the last drop of water and when he washes his feet, every sin towards which his feet walked would be washed away with water or with the last drop of water, with the result that he becomes pure of all sins.[1] (*Muslim*)

1. These are minor sins committed inadvertently as the next Hadith shows.

٢٨٦ - وَعَنْ عُثْمَانَ ، قَالَ : قَالَ رَسُولُ اللهِ ﷺ : "مَا مِنِ امْرِئٍ مُسْلِمٍ تَحْضُرُهُ صَلَاةٌ مَكْتُوبَةٌ ، فَيُحْسِنُ وُضُوءَهَا وَخُشُوعَهَا وَرُكُوعَهَا ؛

إِلَّا كَانَتْ كَفَّارَةً لِمَا قَبْلَهَا مِنَ الذُّنُوبِ، مَا لَمْ يُؤْتِ كَبِيرَةً، وَذَلِكَ الدَّهْرَ كُلَّهُ" رَوَاهُ مُسْلِمٌ.

286 **'Uthman** reported Allah's Messenger (peace and blessings of Allah be upon him) as saying: A Muslim who finds the time for the prescribed prayer and performs ablution well and offers prayer with devotion and humility it would be an expiation for his past sins so long he has not committed a major sin and that means for all time. (*Muslim*)

٢٨٧- وَعَنْهُ، أَنَّهُ تَوَضَّأَ فَأَفْرَغَ عَلَى يَدَيْهِ ثَلَاثًا، ثُمَّ تَمَضْمَضَ وَاسْتَنْثَرَ، ثُمَّ غَسَلَ وَجْهَهُ ثَلَاثًا، ثُمَّ غَسَلَ يَدَهُ الْيُمْنَى إِلَى الْمِرْفَقِ ثَلَاثًا، ثُمَّ غَسَلَ يَدَهُ الْيُسْرَى إِلَى الْمِرْفَقِ ثَلَاثًا، ثُمَّ مَسَحَ بِرَأْسِهِ، ثُمَّ غَسَلَ رِجْلَهُ الْيُمْنَى ثَلَاثًا، ثُمَّ الْيُسْرَى ثَلَاثًا، ثُمَّ قَالَ: رَأَيْتُ رَسُولَ اللهِ ﷺ تَوَضَّأَ نَحْوَ وُضُوئِي هَذَا، ثُمَّ قَالَ: "مَنْ تَوَضَّأَ وُضُوئِي هَذَا، ثُمَّ يُصَلِّي رَكْعَتَيْنِ لَا يُحَدِّثُ نَفْسَهُ فِيهِمَا بِشَيْءٍ، غُفِرَ لَهُ مَا تَقَدَّمَ مِنْ ذَنْبِهِ" مُتَّفَقٌ عَلَيْهِ. وَلَفْظُهُ لِلْبُخَارِيِّ.

287 It is reported on the same authority: He who performs ablution (by pouring water over his hands) thrice then rinsing his mouth and snuffing of water then washing his face thrice, then washing his right hand upto the elbow thrice then washing his left hand upto the elbow thrice, then wiping his head then washing his right foot thrice, then left foot thrice he then said: I have seen Allah's Messenger (peace and blessings of Allah be upon him) performing ablution like the ablution of mine. He then said: He who performs ablution like this ablution of mine and then offers two Rak'as without allowing his soul to be distracted, all his previous sins would be expiated. (*Agreed upon. And the wording is that of Bukhari*)

٢٨٨- وَعَنْ عُقْبَةَ بْنِ عَامِرٍ، قَالَ: قَالَ رَسُولُ اللهِ ﷺ: "مَا مِنْ مُسْلِمٍ يَتَوَضَّأُ، فَيُحْسِنُ وُضُوءَهُ، ثُمَّ يَقُومُ فَيُصَلِّي رَكْعَتَيْنِ، مُقْبِلاً عَلَيْهِمَا بِقَلْبِهِ وَوَجْهِهِ، إِلَّا وَجَبَتْ لَهُ الْجَنَّةُ" رَوَاهُ مُسْلِمٌ.

288 **'Uqba b. 'Amir** reported Allah's Messenger (peace and bless-ings of Allah be upon him) as saying: If any Muslim who performed ablution well, then stood to offer two Raka's (of prayer) with (the devotion) of heart and his face (set towards *Qibla*) the Paradise would be guaranteed for him. (*Muslim*)

٢٨٩- وَعَنْ عُمَرَ بْنِ الْخَطَّابِ، رَضِيَ اللهُ عَنْهُ، قَالَ: قَالَ رَسُولُ اللهِ ﷺ: "مَا
مِنْكُمْ مِنْ أَحَدٍ يَتَوَضَّأُ فَيُبْلِغُ - أَوْ فَيُسْبِغُ - الْوُضُوءَ، ثُمَّ يَقُولُ: أَشْهَدُ
أَنْ لَا إِلَهَ إِلَّا اللهُ، وَأَنَّ مُحَمَّدًا عَبْدُهُ وَرَسُولُهُ - وَفِي رِوَايَةٍ: أَشْهَدُ
أَنْ لَا إِلَهَ إِلَّا اللهُ، وَحْدَهُ لَا شَرِيكَ لَهُ، وَأَشْهَدُ أَنَّ مُحَمَّدًا عَبْدُهُ وَ
رَسُولُهُ - إِلَّا فُتِحَتْ لَهُ أَبْوَابُ الْجَنَّةِ الثَّمَانِيَةُ، يَدْخُلُ مِنْ أَيِّهَا
شَاءَ"؛ هَكَذَا رَوَاهُ مُسْلِمٌ فِي "صَحِيحِهِ"، وَالْحُمَيْدِيُّ فِي "أَفْرَادِ مُسْلِمٍ"،
وَكَذَا ابْنُ الْأَثِيرِ فِي "جَامِعِ الْأُصُولِ":

وَذَكَرَ الشَّيْخُ مُحْيِي الدِّينِ النَّوَوِيُّ فِي آخِرِ حَدِيثِ مُسْلِمٍ عَلَى مَا
رَوَيْنَاهُ، وَزَادَ التِّرْمِذِيُّ: "أَللَّهُمَّ اجْعَلْنِي مِنَ التَّوَّابِينَ وَاجْعَلْنِي
مِنَ الْمُتَطَهِّرِينَ":

وَالْحَدِيثُ الَّذِي رَوَاهُ مُحْيِي السُّنَّةِ فِي الصِّحَاحِ: "مَنْ تَوَضَّأَ فَأَحْسَنَ
الْوُضُوءَ" إِلَى آخِرِهِ، رَوَاهُ التِّرْمِذِيُّ فِي "جَامِعِهِ" بِعَيْنِهِ إِلَّا كَلِمَةَ "أَشْهَدُ
قَبْلَ أَنَّ مُحَمَّدًا":

289 **'Umar b. Khattab** (may Allah be pleased with him) reported Allah's Messenger (peace and blessings of Allah be upon him) as saying: If any one amongst you performs the ablution and performs it well and then says: I bear testimony to the fact that there is no god but Allah and Muhammad is His servant and His Messenger and in another version (the words are): I bear testimony to the fact that there is no god but Allah, the One Who has no associate with Him and I bear testimony to the fact that Muhammad is His servant and His Messenger, the eight gates of the Paradise will be open for him and he may enter through whichever of them he likes. (*Thus Muslim transmitted it in his Sahih and Al-Humaidi among the traditions given by Muslim but not by Bukhari as also did Ibn Al-Athir in Jami' al-Usul. Sheikh Mohyuddin Nawawi has make a mention of it at the end of Muslim tradition as we have transmitted it. And Tirmidhi has made this addition: Oh Allah, make me of the penitent and make me of those who seek purification. The tradition: He who performs ablution well upto the end which Muhyi as-Sunnah transmitted amongst the Sihah is transmitted identically by Tirmidhi in his Jami' except for: "I testify" before the words "that Muhammad"*)

٢٩٠ ـ وَعَنْ أَبِى هُرَيْرَةَ ، قَالَ : قَالَ رَسُولُ اللهِ ﷺ : إِنَّ أُمَّتِى يُدْعَوْنَ يَوْمَ الْقِيَامَةِ غُرًّا مُحَجَّلِينَ مِنْ آثَارِ الْوُضُوءِ . فَمَنِ اسْتَطَاعَ مِنْكُمْ أَنْ يُطِيلَ غُرَّتَهُ فَلْيَفْعَلْ . مُتَّفَقٌ عَلَيْهِ .

290 Abu Huraira reported Allah's Messenger (peace and blessings of Allah be upon him) as saying: The people of my Ummah would be called on the Day of Resurrection with white faces and hands and feet because of the effects of ablution so he who amongst you intends to enhance the whiteness let him do so. (*Agreed upon*)

٢٩١ ـ وَعَنْهُ ، قَالَ : قَالَ رَسُولُ اللهِ ﷺ : تَبْلُغُ الْحِلْيَةُ مِنَ الْمُؤْمِنِ حَيْثُ يَبْلُغُ الْوُضُوءُ . رَوَاهُ مُسْلِمٌ .

291 It is reported on the same authority that Allah's Messenger (peace and blessings of Allah be upon him) said: In a believer the embellishment would reach to the extent to which the (marks of ablution) reach. (*Muslim*)

Section II الْفَصْلُ الثَّانِى

٢٩٢ ـ عَنْ ثَوْبَانَ ، قَالَ : قَالَ رَسُولُ اللهِ ﷺ : اِسْتَقِيمُوا وَلَنْ تُحْصُوا وَ اعْلَمُوا أَنَّ خَيْرَ أَعْمَالِكُمُ الصَّلَاةَ ، وَلَا يُحَافِظُ عَلَى الْوُضُوءِ إِلَّا مُؤْمِنٌ . رَوَاهُ مَالِكٌ ، وَأَحْمَدُ ، وَابْنُ مَاجَةَ ، وَالدَّارِمِيُّ .

292 Thauban (Allah be pleased with him) reported Allah's Messenger (peace and blessings of Allah be upon him) as saying: Adhere to the righteousness which you will not be able to do completely and bear in mind the best act (amongst your deeds) to the prayer and none is so much particular about ablution but a believer.

(Transmitted by Malik, Ahmad, Ibn Majah, Darimi)

٢٩٣ - وَعَنِ ابْنِ عُمَرَ، قَالَ : قَالَ رَسُولُ اللهِ ﷺ : "مَنْ تَوَضَّأَ عَلَى طُهْرٍ، كُتِبَ لَهُ عَشْرُ حَسَنَاتٍ" رَوَاهُ التِّرْمِذِيُّ .

293 Ibn 'Umar reported Allah's Messenger (peace and blessings of Allah be upon him) as saying: He who performs ablution when he is already pure there would be recorded ten blessings for him. *(Tirmidhi)*

Section III   اَلْفَصْلُ الثَّالِثُ

٢٩٤ - عَنْ جَابِرٍ، قَالَ : قَالَ رَسُولُ اللهِ ﷺ : "مِفْتَاحُ الْجَنَّةِ الصَّلَاةُ، وَ مِفْتَاحُ الصَّلَاةِ الطُّهُورُ" رَوَاهُ أَحْمَدُ .

294 Jabir reported Allah's Messenger (peace and blessings of Allah be upon him) as saying: The key to Paradise is prayer and the key to prayer is cleanliness (Ablution). *(Ahmad)*

٢٩٥ - وَعَنْ شَبِيبِ بْنِ أَبِي رَوْحٍ، عَنْ رَجُلٍ مِنْ أَصْحَابِ رَسُولِ اللهِ ﷺ أَنَّ رَسُولَ اللهِ ﷺ صَلَّى صَلَاةَ الصُّبْحِ، فَقَرَأَ الرُّومَ، فَالْتَبَسَ عَلَيْهِ فَلَمَّا صَلَّى، قَالَ : "مَا بَالُ أَقْوَامٍ يُصَلُّونَ مَعَنَا لَا يُحْسِنُونَ الطُّهُورَ؟! وَإِنَّمَا يَلْبِسُ عَلَيْنَا الْقُرْآنَ أُولَئِكَ" رَوَاهُ النَّسَائِيُّ .

295 Shabib b. Abi Rauh reported on the authority of one of the companions of Allah's Messenger (peace and blessings of Allah be upon him) that Allah's Messenger (peace and blessings of Allah be upon him) observed the dawn prayer and he recited (Surah) Rum (30), and he felt somewhat confounded. When he had finished the prayer he said: What has happened to the people who pray without performing the ablution well. It is these who cause confusion to us while reciting the Qur'ān. (*Nasa'i*)

٢٩٦ - وَعَنْ رَجُلٍ مِنْ بَنِي سُلَيْمٍ، قَالَ: عَدَّهُنَّ رَسُوْلُ اللهِ ﷺ فِي يَدِيْ - أَوْ فِي يَدِهِ - قَالَ: "التَّسْبِيْحُ نِصْفُ الْمِيْزَانِ، وَالْحَمْدُ لِلّٰهِ يَمْلَؤُهُ، وَالتَّكْبِيْرُ يَمْلَأُ مَا بَيْنَ السَّمَاءِ وَالْأَرْضِ، وَالصَّوْمُ نِصْفُ الصَّبْرِ، وَالطُّهُوْرُ نِصْفُ الْإِيْمَانِ": رَوَاهُ التِّرْمِذِيُّ، وَقَالَ: هٰذَا حَدِيْثٌ حَسَنٌ.

296 A person from Bani Sulaim reported that Allah's Messenger (peace and blessings of Allah be upon him) counted them in my hand or in his hand saying: *Tasbih (Subhanallah)* is half the scale, praise be to Allah fills it (completely). *Allah-o-Akbar* (Allah is the Greatest) fills the space between the heaven and the earth, fasting is the half endurance and cleanliness is half of faith. (*Tirmidhi transmitted it and said, this is a Hasan tradition*)

٢٩٧ - وَعَنْ عَبْدِ اللهِ الصُّنَابِحِيِّ، قَالَ: قَالَ رَسُوْلُ اللهِ ﷺ: "إِذَا تَوَضَّأَ الْعَبْدُ الْمُؤْمِنُ فَمَضْمَضَ، خَرَجَتِ الْخَطَايَا مِنْ فِيْهِ، وَإِذَا اسْتَنْثَرَ، خَرَجَتِ الْخَطَايَا مِنْ أَنْفِهِ، وَإِذَا غَسَلَ وَجْهَهُ، خَرَجَتِ الْخَطَايَا مِنْ وَجْهِهِ، حَتَّى تَخْرُجَ مِنْ تَحْتِ أَشْفَارِ عَيْنَيْهِ، فَإِذَا غَسَلَ يَدَيْهِ، خَرَجَتِ الْخَطَايَا مِنْ تَحْتِ أَظْفَارِ يَدَيْهِ، فَإِذَا مَسَحَ بِرَأْسِهِ، خَرَجَتِ الْخَطَايَا مِنْ رَأْسِهِ حَتَّى تَخْرُجَ مِنْ أُذُنَيْهِ، فَإِذَا غَسَلَ رِجْلَيْهِ، خَرَجَتِ الْخَطَايَا مِنْ رِجْلَيْهِ، حَتَّى تَخْرُجَ مِنْ (تَحْتِ) أَظْفَارِ رِجْلَيْهِ، ثُمَّ كَانَ مَشْيُهُ إِلَى الْمَسْجِدِ وَصَلَاتُهُ نَافِلَةً لَهُ": رَوَاهُ مَالِكٌ وَالنَّسَائِيُّ.

297 'Abdullah as-Sunabihi reported Allah's Messenger (peace and blessings of Allah be upon him) as saying: When a believing servant performs ablution and rinses his mouth the sins go out from his mouth and when he snuffs up water the sins go out

from his nose and when he washes his face the sins go out
from his face till they go out even from under his eye-lashes
and as he washes his hands the sins go out from under his
finger nails and when he wipes his head the sins go out from
his head till they go out from his ears and when he washes his
feet his sins go out from his feet till they go out from under
the nails of his feet. Then his walking to the mosque and his
prayer would be a source of extra blessings for him.

(*Malik, Nasa'i*)

٢٩٨ - وَعَنْ أَبِى هُرَيْرَةَ، أَنَّ رَسُولَ اللهِ ﷺ أَتَى الْمَقْبَرَةَ فَقَالَ: "أَلسَّلَامُ
عَلَيْكُمْ دَارَ قَوْمٍ مُؤْمِنِينَ، وَإِنَّآ إِنْ شَآءَ اللهُ بِكُمْ لَاحِقُونَ، وَدِدْتُ
أَنَّا قَدْ رَأَيْنَا إِخْوَانَنَا؟ قَالُوا: أَوَلَسْنَا إِخْوَانَكَ يَا رَسُولَ اللهِ؟ قَالَ:
"أَنْتُمْ أَصْحَابِى، وَإِخْوَانُنَا الَّذِينَ لَمْ يَأْتُوا بَعْدُ" فَقَالُوا: كَيْفَ تَعْرِفُ
مَنْ لَمْ يَأْتِ بَعْدُ مِنْ أُمَّتِكَ يَا رَسُولَ اللهِ؟ فَقَالَ: "أَرَأَيْتَ لَوْ أَنَّ رَجُلاً
لَهُ خَيْلٌ غُرٌّ مُحَجَّلَةٌ، بَيْنَ ظَهْرَىْ خَيْلٍ دُهْمٍ بُهْمٍ، أَلَا يَعْرِفُ خَيْلَهُ؟
قَالُوا: بَلَى، يَا رَسُولَ اللهِ! قَالَ: "فَإِنَّهُمْ يَأْتُونَ غُرًّا مُحَجَّلِينَ مِنَ الْوُضُوءِ
وَأَنَا فَرَطُهُمْ عَلَى الْحَوْضِ" رَوَاهُ مُسْلِمٌ.

298 Abu Huraira reported that Allah's Messenger (peace and
blessings of Allah be upon him) came to the graveyard and
said: Peace be upon you! The abode of the believing people
and we, if God so wills, are about to join you and I love to
see my brothers. They (the bystanders) said: Allah's
Messenger aren't we your brothers. He said: You are my
companions, you are my companions, and our brothers are
those who have, so far, not come into the world. They said:
Messenger of Allah, how would you recognize those persons of
your Ummah who have not yet been born; whereupon he
said: Suppose man had horses with white blazes on forehead
and legs among horses which were all black, would he not
recognize his own horses? They said: Certainly, Messenger
of Allah, certainly (he would recognize them). He said:
They would come with white faces and arms and legs because

of ablution and I will arrive at the cistern ahead of them.

(*Muslim*)

٢٩٩- وَعَنْ أَبِي الدَّرْدَاءِ ، قَالَ : قَالَ رَسُولُ اللهِ ﷺ : أَنَا أَوَّلُ مَنْ يُؤْذَنُ

لَهُ بِالسُّجُودِ يَوْمَ الْقِيَامَةِ ، وَأَنَا أَوَّلُ مَنْ يُؤْذَنُ لَهُ أَنْ يَرْفَعَ رَأْسَهُ ، فَأَنْظُرُ

إِلَى مَا بَيْنَ يَدَيَّ ، فَأَعْرِفُ أُمَّتِي مِنْ بَيْنِ الْأُمَمِ ، وَمِنْ خَلْفِي مِثْلَ ذٰلِكَ ،

وَعَنْ يَمِينِي مِثْلَ ذٰلِكَ ، وَعَنْ شِمَالِي مِثْلَ ذٰلِكَ ، فَقَالَ رَجُلٌ : يَا رَسُولَ اللهِ

كَيْفَ تَعْرِفُ أُمَّتَكَ مِنْ بَيْنِ الْأُمَمِ فِيمَا بَيْنَ نُوحٍ إِلَى أُمَّتِكَ ؟ قَالَ : هُمْ

غُرٌّ مُحَجَّلُونَ مِنْ أَثَرِ الْوُضُوءِ ، لَيْسَ أَحَدٌ كَذٰلِكَ غَيْرُهُمْ ، وَأَعْرِفُهُمْ

أَنَّهُمْ يُؤْتَوْنَ كُتُبَهُمْ بِأَيْمَانِهِمْ ، وَأَعْرِفُهُمْ تَسْعَى بَيْنَ أَيْدِيهِمْ

ذُرِّيَّتُهُمْ ، رَوَاهُ أَحْمَدُ .

299 Abu Darda reported Allah's Messenger (peace and blessings of Allah be upon him) as saying: I shall be the first who would be permitted to fall in prostration on the Day of Resurrection and I would be the first to whom the permission would be given to raise his head. I shall then look what would be in front of me, and recognize my Ummah amongst the other Ummahs and I shall do the same behind me, on my right hand and on my left. A person said: Allah's Messenger, how would you recognize your Ummah among the peoples from Noah's time onwards. He said: They (the people of my Ummah) will have white faces, arms and legs because of the traces of ablution and none besides them would be like them and I would recognize them because they would be given their scrolls in their right hands and I shall recognize them with their posterity (going) before them. (*Ahmid*)

———————●◆●———————

CHAPTER 9

WHAT MAKES THE ABLUTION ESSENTIAL?

Section I أَلْفَصْلُ الْأَوَّلُ

٣٠٠ـ عَنْ أَبِي هُرَيْرَةَ، قَالَ: قَالَ رَسُولُ اللهِ ﷺ: "لَا تُقْبَلُ صَلَاةٌ مَنْ أَحْدَثَ حَتَّى يَتَوَضَّأَ" مُتَّفَقٌ عَلَيْهِ .

300 Abu Huraira reported Allah's Messenger (peace and blessings of Allah be upon him) as saying: The prayer would not be accepted from one who needs ablution[1] till he performs ablution. (*Agreed upon*)

> 1. We have translated *ahdatha* as one who needs ablution whereas in its present context it means one who has broken the wind or as one who has voided excrement.

٣٠١ـ وَعَنِ ابْنِ عُمَرَ، قَالَ: قَالَ رَسُولُ اللهِ ﷺ: "لَا تُقْبَلُ صَلَاةٌ بِغَيْرِ طُهُورٍ، وَلَا صَدَقَةٌ مِنْ غُلُولٍ" رَوَاهُ مُسْلِمٌ .

301 Ibn 'Umar reported Allah's Messenger (peace and blessings of Allah upon him) as saying: No prayer is accepted without purification and no charity is accepted out of ill-gotten wealth. (*Muslim*)

٣٠٢ـ وَعَنْ عَلِيٍّ، قَالَ: كُنْتُ رَجُلًا مَذَّاءً، فَكُنْتُ أَسْتَحْيِي أَنْ أَسْأَلَ النَّبِيَّ ﷺ لِمَكَانِ ابْنَتِهِ، فَأَمَرْتُ الْمِقْدَادَ، فَسَأَلَهُ، فَقَالَ يَغْسِلُ ذَكَرَهُ وَ يَتَوَضَّأُ" مُتَّفَقٌ عَلَيْهِ .

302 'Ali reported: I was the person whose prostatic fluid[1] flowed readily and I felt shy of asking Allah's Messenger (peace and blessings of Allah be upon him) because of the position of his daughther.[2] I, therefore, asked Miqdad (to ask him on my behalf) and he asked. The Holy Prophet (peace and blessings of Allah be upon him) said: He should wash his male organ and perform ablution. (*Agreed upon*)

1. There is a difference between the Arabic words *Madhi* (prostatic fluid) and *Mani* (semen). The former comes in watery form before copulation and the latter comes out after copulation in thick form. In case of the former, ablution is necessary and in case of the latter bath is obligatory.

2. 'Ali (may Allah be pleased with him) was the son-in-law of the Holy Prophet and he felt shy of asking anything pertaining to sex problems directly from his father-in-law.

٣٠٣ - وَعَنْ أَبِي هُرَيْرَةَ، قَالَ: قَالَ رَسُولُ اللهِ ﷺ: تَوَضَّؤُوا مِمَّا مَسَّتِ النَّارُ. رَوَاهُ مُسْلِمٌ.

قَالَ الشَّيْخُ الْإِمَامُ الْأَجَلُّ مُحْيِي السُّنَّةِ، رَحِمَهُ اللهُ، هٰذَا مَنْسُوخٌ بِحَدِيثِ ابْنِ عَبَّاسٍ:

303 Abu Huraira reported Allah's Messenger (peace and blessings of Allah be upon him) as saying: Perform ablution because of anything touched by fire. (*Muslim transmitted it. The Shaikh Al-Imam Muhyi as-Sunnah (may Allah have mercy upon him) said that this is abrogated by the tradition of Ibn 'Abbas who stated:*)

٣٠٤ - قَالَ: إِنَّ رَسُولَ اللهِ ﷺ أَكَلَ كَتِفَ شَاةٍ ثُمَّ صَلَّى وَ لَمْ يَتَوَضَّأْ. مُتَّفَقٌ عَلَيْهِ.

304 That Allah's Messenger (peace and blessings of Allah be upon him) ate a shoulder of mutton then observed prayer without performing ablution. (*Agreed upon*)

٣٠٥ - وَعَنْ جَابِرِ بْنِ سَمُرَةَ، أَنَّ رَجُلاً سَأَلَ رَسُولَ اللهِ ﷺ: أَنَتَوَضَّأُ مِنْ لُحُومِ الْغَنَمِ؟ قَالَ: إِنْ شِئْتَ فَتَوَضَّأْ، وَإِنْ شِئْتَ فَلَا تَتَوَضَّأْ. قَالَ: أَنَتَوَضَّأُ مِنْ لُحُومِ الْإِبِلِ؟ قَالَ: نَعَمْ! فَتَوَضَّأْ مِنْ لُحُومِ الْإِبِلِ. قَالَ: أُصَلِّي فِي مَرَابِضِ الْغَنَمِ؟ قَالَ: نَعَمْ؛ قَالَ: أُصَلِّي فِي مَبَارِكِ الْإِبِلِ؟ قَالَ: لَا. رَوَاهُ مُسْلِمٌ.

305 Jabir b. Samura reported that a person asked Allah's Messenger (peace and blessings of Allah be upon him): Should we perform ablution after eating mutton, whereupon he said:

You may perform ablution if you so like and you may not perform ablution if you so desire. He said: Should we perform ablution after eating the flesh of the camel; whereupon he said: Yes. Do perform ablution after eating the flesh[1] of the camel. He said: Should I observe prayer in the fold of the flock.[2] He said: Yes. He again said: Should I observe prayer where the camels lie down. He said: No. (*Muslim*)

1. There is a difference of opinion amongst the jurists about this matter. Some of the scholars of *ahadith* are of the opinion that the eating of the camel's flesh does not break the ablution, but according to others, for example Imam Ahmad b. Hanbal, Ishaque b. Rahwai Yahya and Mundar, it does break. The question naturally arises why such exception is made for the flesh of the camel. Various reasons have been put forward for this. Maulana Shabbir Ahmad 'Uthmani deems its offensive smell to be the main cause of it. Shah Waliullah Dehlwi has given a different view. His argument is that the eating of camel's flesh had been forbidden in the Torah and all other Apostles of Bani Israel agreed to it but it was permissible for the followers of Muhammad (may peace be upon him) and ablution was enjoined upon them as an expression of thankfulness to the Lord for this favour. Similarly, other scholars have given other arguments. The most plausible reason is that given by Maulana Shabbir Ahmad 'Uthmani that this order of ablution after eating the flesh of camel is one of the main phases through which new converts had to pass for learning the laws of purification. Firstly, ablution was made obligatory for everyone who ate food touched by fire. This was done in order to accustom people to the habit of purification. Later on concession was granted in this matter but it was ordained to continue this practice of ablution in case of camel's flesh and subsequently the full concession was given. (For detailed study, see *Fath-ul-Mulhim*, Vol. I, page 490, Shah Waliullah, *Hujjat Allah al-Balighah*, Vol. I, page 177).

2. Different are the conditions in the folds of sheep and camels. The sheep and goats are small and meek animals and one feels no danger from them, and, therefore, one has no cause to fear them. But this is not the case of the camels. They at times become violent and one has to exercise great care in living by their sides. Prayer in their folds is a cause of distraction.

٣٠٤ ـ وَعَنْ أَبِي هُرَيْرَةَ، قَالَ: قَالَ رَسُولُ اللهِ ﷺ: "إِذَا وَجَدَ أَحَدُكُمْ فِي بَطْنِهِ شَيْئًا، فَأَشْكَلَ عَلَيْهِ أَخْرَجَ مِنْهُ شَيْءٌ أَمْ لاَ. فَلاَ يَخْرُجَنَّ مِنَ الْمَسْجِدِ حَتَّى يَسْمَعَ صَوْتًا أَوْ يَجِدَ رِيحًا: رَوَاهُ مُسْلِمٌ.

306 Abu Huraira reported Allah's Messenger (peace and blessings of Allah be upon him) as saying: When any one of you feels something in his stomach and he harbours doubt whether anything has issued from that or not, he should not get out of the mosque, unless, he has heard the voice (of wind break) or sensed its smell. (*Muslim*)

$$ ٣٠٧ - وَعَنْ عَبْدِ اللهِ بْنِ عَبَّاسٍ، قَالَ: إِنَّ رَسُوْلَ اللهِ ﷺ شَرِبَ لَبَنًا فَمَضْمَضَ، وَقَالَ: إِنَّ لَهُ دَسَمًا، مُتَّفَقٌ عَلَيْهِ. $$

307 'Abdullah b. 'Abbas reported that Allah's Messenger (peace and blessings of Allah be upon him) took milk and he rinsed his mouth and said: It contains greaziness. (*Agreed upon*)

$$ ٣٠٨ - وَعَنْ بُرَيْدَةَ: أَنَّ النَّبِيَّ ﷺ صَلَّى الصَّلَوَاتِ يَوْمَ الْفَتْحِ بِوُضُوْءٍ وَاحِدٍ، وَمَسَحَ عَلَى خُفَّيْهِ، فَقَالَ لَهُ عُمَرُ: لَقَدْ صَنَعْتَ الْيَوْمَ شَيْئًا لَمْ تَكُنْ تَصْنَعُهُ! فَقَالَ: عَمْدًا صَنَعْتُهُ يَا عُمَرُ، رَوَاهُ مُسْلِمٌ. $$

308 Buraida reported that Allah's Messenger (peace and blessings of Allah be upon him) observed several prayers on the Day of Victory (of Mecca) with one ablution and he wiped over his socks; whereupon 'Umar said to him: Today, you have done a thing which you did not do (before). Thereupon he said: 'Umar, it is intentionally that I have done that. (*Muslim*)

$$ ٣٠٩ - وَعَنْ سُوَيْدِ بْنِ النُّعْمَانِ: أَنَّهُ خَرَجَ مَعَ رَسُوْلِ اللهِ ﷺ عَامَ خَيْبَرَ حَتَّى إِذَا كَانُوْا بِالصَّهْبَاءِ - وَهِيَ مِنْ أَدْنَى خَيْبَرَ- صَلَّى الْعَصْرَ، ثُمَّ دَعَا بِالْأَزْوَادِ، فَلَمْ يُؤْتَ إِلَّا بِالسَّوِيْقِ، فَأَمَرَ بِهِ فَثُرِّيَ، فَأَكَلَ رَسُوْلُ اللهِ ﷺ وَأَكَلْنَا، ثُمَّ قَامَ إِلَى الْمَغْرِبِ، فَمَضْمَضَ وَمَضْمَضْنَا، ثُمَّ صَلَّى وَ لَمْ يَتَوَضَّأْ. رَوَاهُ الْبُخَارِيُّ. $$

309 Suwaid b. al-Nu'man reported that he went out with Allah's Messenger (peace and blessings of Allah be upon him) in the year (of the conquest) of Khaibar till they reached as-Sahba and that is near Khaibar. He (the Holy Prophet) performed

the afternoon prayer. He then sent for food. Nothing
was procured (to him) as food, but a small quantity of flour.
He then ordered and it was moistened. Allah's Messenger
(peace and blessings of Allah be upon him) ate that and we
also ate that. He then got up for sunset prayer, and he
rinsed his mouth and we too rinsed our mouths. He then
observed prayer but did not perform ablution. (*Bukhari*)

Section II الْفَصْلُ الثَّانِي

٣١٠ـ عَنْ أَبِي هُرَيْرَةَ، قَالَ : قَالَ رَسُولُ اللهِ ﷺ : "لَا وُضُوءَ إِلَّا مِنْ صَوْتٍ
أَوْ رِيحٍ" رَوَاهُ أَحْمَدُ، وَالتِّرْمِذِيُّ.

310 Abu Huraira reported Allah's Messenger (peace and blessings
of Allah be upon him) as saying: No ablution is necessary
except in case of sound (of the wind) or (foul smell of the
wind). (*Ahmad, Tirmidhi*)

٣١١ـ وَعَنْ عَلِيٍّ، قَالَ : سَأَلْتُ رَسُولَ اللهِ ﷺ مِنَ الْمَذْيِ، فَقَالَ : "مِنَ الْمَذْيِ
الْوُضُوءُ، وَمِنَ الْمَنِيِّ الْغُسْلُ" رَوَاهُ التِّرْمِذِيُّ.

311 'Ali reported: I asked Allah's Messenger (peace and blessings of Allah be upon him) about the emission of prostatic
fluid?[1] Whereupon he said: (The emission of) prostatic
fluid necessitates ablution whereas the seminal emission necessitates bathing. (*Tirmidhi*)

1. The guidance was sought indirectly as mentioned in *hadith* No. 302.

٣١٢ـ وَعَنْهُ، قَالَ : قَالَ رَسُولُ اللهِ ﷺ : "مِفْتَاحُ الصَّلَاةِ الطُّهُورُ، وَتَحْرِيمُهَا
التَّكْبِيرُ، وَتَحْلِيلُهَا التَّسْلِيمُ" رَوَاهُ أَبُو دَاوُدَ، وَالتِّرْمِذِيُّ، وَالدَّارِمِيُّ.

312 It is reported on the same authority that Allah's Messenger
(peace and blessings of Allah be upon him) said: The key
to prayer is purity. The *Takbir* (saying Allah-o-Akbar),
(Allah is the Greatest) makes it a sacred state (making lawful
things unlawful) and salutation (saying Assalamo-'alaikum
for ending the prayer) brings that state to a close (and thus

lawful things are again made lawful).

(Abu Dawud, Tirmidhi, Darimi)

٣١٣ـ وَرَوَاهُ ابْنُ مَاجَهْ عَنْهُ وَعَنْ أَبِى سَعِيدٍ.

313 **Ibn Majah** has reported it on the same authority ('Ali) and Abu Sa'id.

٣١٤ـ وَعَنْ عَلِيِّ بْنِ طَلْقٍ، قَالَ: قَالَ رَسُولُ اللهِ ﷺ "إِذَا فَسَا أَحَدُكُمْ فَلْيَتَوَضَّأْ، وَلَا تَأْتُوا النِّسَاءَ فِى أَعْجَازِهِنَّ" رَوَاهُ التِّرْمِذِىُّ، وَأَبُودَاوُدَ.

314 **'Ali b. Talq** reported Allah's Messenger (peace and blessings of Allah be upon him) as saying: When any one of you breaks wind he should perform ablution; and come not to the women from their backside. (*Tirmidhi and Abu Dawud*)

٣١٥ـ وَعَنْ مُعَاوِيَةَ بْنِ أَبِى سُفْيَانَ، أَنَّ النَّبِىَّ ﷺ قَالَ: إِنَّمَا الْعَيْنَانِ وِكَآءُ السَّهِ، فَإِذَا نَامَتِ الْعَيْنُ إِسْتَطْلَقَ الْوِكَآءُ" رَوَاهُ الدَّارِمِىُّ.

315 **Mu'awiya b. Abu Sufyan** reported Allah's Apostle (peace and blessings of Allah be upon him) as saying: (Ablution becomes essential) for one who goes to sleep, for when one (closes) one's eyes (in sleep) the leather straps (of his anus) are loosened. (*Darimi*)

٣١٦ـ وَعَنْ عَلِيٍّ، قَالَ: قَالَ رَسُولُ اللهِ ﷺ "وِكَآءُ السَّهِ الْعَيْنَانِ، فَمَنْ نَامَ فَلْيَتَوَضَّأْ" رَوَاهُ أَبُودَاوُدَ.

قَالَ الشَّيْخُ الإِمَامُ مُحْيِى السُّنَّةِ، رَحِمَهُ اللهُ: هٰذَا فِى غَيْرِ الْقَاعِدِ لِمَا صَحَّ.

316 **'Ali** reported Allah's Messenger (peace and blessings of Allah be upon him) as saying: (With the closing) of eyes (in sleep) the leather straps of the anus (are loosened), so he who sleeps, he should perform ablution. (*Abu Dawud*)

(*Al-Sheikh al-Imam Muhyi as-Sunnah (may Allah have mercy upon him) said: This does not refer to one who is sitting because of the sound traditions.*)

٣١٧ـ عَنْ أَنَسٍ، قَالَ: كَانَ أَصْحَابُ رَسُولِ اللهِ ﷺ يَنْتَظِرُونَ الْعِشَاءَ حَتَّى تَخْفِقَ رُؤُوسُهُمْ، ثُمَّ يُصَلُّونَ وَلَا يَتَوَضَّأُونَ. رَوَاهُ أَبُوْدَاوُدَ، وَالتِّرْمِذِيُّ إِلَّا أَنَّهُ ذَكَرَ: فِيهِ يَنَامُونَ بَدَلَ: يَنْتَظِرُونَ الْعِشَاءَ حَتَّى تَخْفِقَ رُؤُوسُهُمْ.

317 Anas reported: The companions of Allah's Messenger (peace and blessings of Allah be upon him) waited for the night prayer till they dozed and they observed prayer and did not perform ablution. (*Transmitted by Abu Dawud, Tirmidhi, but Tirmidhi said: 'They slept' instead of saying that they dozed while waiting for night prayer*)

٣١٨ـ وَعَنِ ابْنِ عَبَّاسٍ، قَالَ: قَالَ رَسُولُ اللهِ ﷺ " إِنَّ الْوُضُوءَ عَلَى مَنْ نَامَ مُضْطَجِعًا، فَإِنَّهُ إِذَا اضْطَجَعَ اسْتَرْخَتْ مَفَاصِلُهُ ": رَوَاهُ التِّرْمِذِيُّ، وَأَبُو دَاوُدَ.

318 Ibn 'Abbas reported Allah's Messenger (peace and blessings of Allah be upon him) as saying: Ablution is necessary for one who sleeps lying down because when he lies down his joints are relaxed.[1] (*Tirmidhi and Abu Dawud*)

1. The state of mind is different when a man dozes in a sitting posture or goes to sleep in the bed. In the sitting posture he is half awake and half sleep, and, therefore, he can well perceive whether his ablution is broken or not. When he is in a sound sleep in the bed he becomes completely forgetful of the state of his body and, there-fore, ablution becomes obligatory for him for performing prayer.

٣١٩ـ وَعَنْ بُسْرَةَ، قَالَتْ: قَالَ رَسُولُ اللهِ ﷺ " إِذَا مَسَّ أَحَدُكُمْ ذَكَرَهُ، فَلْيَتَوَضَّأْ ": رَوَاهُ مَالِكٌ، وَأَحْمَدُ، وَأَبُوْدَاوُدَ، وَالتِّرْمِذِيُّ، وَالنَّسَائِيُّ، وَابْنُ مَاجَةَ، وَالدَّارِمِيُّ.

319 Busra reported Allah's Messenger (peace and blessings of Allah be upon him) as saying: When anyone of you touches the sexual organ he must perform ablution. (*Malik, Ahmad, Abu Dawud, Nasai', Ibn Majah and Darimi*)

٣٢٠ - وَعَنْ طَلِقِ بْنِ عَلِيٍّ، قَالَ سُئِلَ رَسُولُ اللهِ ﷺ عَنْ مَسِّ الرَّجُلِ ذَكَرَهُ
بَعْدَ مَا يَتَوَضَّأُ. قَالَ: " وَهَلْ هُوَ إِلَّا بَضْعَةٌ مِنْهُ؟" رَوَاهُ أَبُو دَاوُدَ، وَ
التِّرْمِذِيُّ، وَالنَّسَائِيُّ، وَرَوَى ابْنُ مَاجَةَ نَحْوَهُ.

قَالَ الشَّيْخُ الْإِمَامُ مُحْيِ السُّنَّةِ، رَحِمَهُ اللهُ: هٰذَا مَنْسُوخٌ؛ إِلَّا أَنَّ
أَبَا هُرَيْرَةَ أَسْلَمَ بَعْدَ قُدُومِ طَلِقٍ.

320 Talq b. 'Ali reported: Allah's Messenger (peace and blessings of Allah be upon him) was asked about a man touching his sexual organ after performing ablution whereupon he said: What is it but a part of him. (*Darimi, Tirmidhi, Nasai', Ibn Majah*)

(*Sheikh Imam Muhyi-as-Sunnah* (*may Allah have mercy upon him*) *said: This* (hadith) *is abrogated one because Abu Huraira accepted Islam after Talq came.*)

٣٢١ - وَقَدْ رَوَى أَبُو هُرَيْرَةَ عَنْ رَسُولِ اللهِ ﷺ، قَالَ: "إِذَا أَفْضَى أَحَدُكُمْ
بِيَدِهِ إِلَى ذَكَرِهِ لَيْسَ بَيْنَهُ وَبَيْنَهَا شَيْءٌ فَلْيَتَوَضَّأْ". رَوَاهُ الشَّافِعِيُّ وَ
الدَّارَ قُطْنِيُّ.

321 Abu Huraira reported Allah's Messenger (peace and blessings of Allah be upon him) as saying: If anyone touches his sexual organ without there being anything between it and that (hand) then he should perform ablution.[1]

(*Transmitted by Shaf'i and Daraqutni*)

1. The general view is that if someone touches the male organ with his naked hand, the ablution is broken and he must perform ablution, but if one touches the sexual organ over the cloth he should better wash his hand and ablution is not essential.

٣٢٢ - وَرَوَاهُ النَّسَائِيُّ عَنْ بُسْرَةَ: إِلَّا أَنَّهُ لَمْ يَذْكُرْ: "لَيْسَ بَيْنَهُ وَ
بَيْنَهَا شَيْءٌ".

322 Nasai' reported from Busra but made no mention of this: There is nothing between it (hand) and that (sexual organ).

٣٢٣ - وَعَنْ عَائِشَةَ، قَالَتْ: كَانَ النَّبِيُّ ﷺ يُقَبِّلُ بَعْضَ أَزْوَاجِهِ ثُمَّ يُصَلِّي
وَلَا يَتَوَضَّأُ. رَوَاهُ أَبُو دَاوُدَ، وَالتِّرْمِذِيُّ، وَالنَّسَائِيُّ، وَابْنُ مَاجَهْ.
وَقَالَ التِّرْمِذِيُّ: لَا يَصِحُّ عِنْدَ أَصْحَابِنَا بِحَالٍ إِسْنَادُ عُرْوَةَ عَنْ عَائِشَةَ
وَأَيْضًا إِسْنَادُ إِبْرَاهِيمَ التَّيْمِيِّ عَنْهَا.
وَقَالَ أَبُو دَاوُدَ: هَذَا مُرْسَلٌ، وَإِبْرَاهِيمُ التَّيْمِيُّ لَمْ يَسْمَعْ مِنْ عَائِشَةَ.

323 'Aisha reported that Allah's Messenger (peace and blessings of Allah be upon him) kissed one of his wives and then observed prayer without performing ablution. (*Transmitted by Abu Dawud, Tirmidhi, Nasai', Ibn Majah but Tirmidhi said: The isnad of 'Urwa from 'Aisha is in no way sound in the opinion of our traditionalists and the same applies to the isnad of Ibrahim-At-Taimi from her. Abu Dawud said: This is mursal hadith and that Ibrahim At-Taimi did not hear it from 'Aisha*)

٣٢٤ - وَعَنِ ابْنِ عَبَّاسٍ، قَالَ: أَكَلَ رَسُولُ اللهِ ﷺ كَتِفًا ثُمَّ مَسَحَ يَدَهُ بِمَسِيحٍ
كَانَ تَحْتَهُ، ثُمَّ قَامَ فَصَلَّى. رَوَاهُ أَبُو دَاوُدَ، وَابْنُ مَاجَهْ.

324 Ibn 'Abbas reported that Allah's Messenger (peace and blessings of Allah be upon him) ate the meat of the shoulder and after wiping his hand with cloth on which he was sitting he got up and prayed. (*Abu Dawud and Ibn Majah*)

٣٢٥ - وَعَنْ أُمِّ سَلَمَةَ، أَنَّهَا قَالَتْ: قَرَّبْتُ إِلَى النَّبِيِّ ﷺ جَنْبًا مَشْوِيًّا فَأَكَلَ
مِنْهُ، ثُمَّ قَامَ إِلَى الصَّلَاةِ وَلَمْ يَتَوَضَّأْ. رَوَاهُ أَحْمَدُ.

325 Umm Salamah reported: I offered roasted meat to the Prophet (may peace and blessings of Allah be upon him), he ate it and then got up for prayer without performing ablution.[1]

1. Only rinsing of the mouth is enough and there is no need of ablution after taking the meat.

Section III الْفَصْلُ الثَّالِثُ

٣٢٦ ـ عَنْ أَبِي رَافِعٍ ، قَالَ : أَشْهَدُ لَقَدْ كُنْتُ أَشْوِى لِرَسُولِ اللهِ ﷺ بَطْنَ
الشَّاةِ ، ثُمَّ صَلَّى وَلَمْ يَتَوَضَّأْ . رَوَاهُ مُسْلِمٌ .

326 Abu Rafi' reported: I testify that I roasted the inside of a
sheep (liver) for Allah's Messenger (peace and blessings of
Allah be upon him). He then observed prayer without performing ablution. (*Muslim*)

٣٢٧ ـ وَعَنْهُ ، قَالَ : أُهْدِيَتْ لَهُ شَاةٌ ، فَجَعَلَهَا فِي الْقِدْرِ ، فَدَخَلَ رَسُولُ اللهِ ﷺ
فَقَالَ : مَا هٰذَا يَا أَبَا رَافِعٍ ؟ فَقَالَ : شَاةٌ أُهْدِيَتْ لَنَا يَا رَسُولَ اللهِ ! فَطَبَخْتُهَا
فِي الْقِدْرِ . قَالَ : نَاوِلْنِي الذِّرَاعَ يَا أَبَا رَافِعٍ ! نَاوَلْتُهُ الذِّرَاعَ . ثُمَّ قَالَ :
نَاوِلْنِي الذِّرَاعَ الْآخَرَ ، نَاوَلْتُهُ الذِّرَاعَ الْآخَرَ . ثُمَّ قَالَ : نَاوِلْنِي الْآخَرَ
فَقَالَ : يَا رَسُولَ اللهِ إِنَّمَا لِلشَّاةِ ذِرَاعَانِ . فَقَالَ لَهُ رَسُولُ اللهِ ﷺ : أَمَا
إِنَّكَ لَوْ سَكَتَّ لَنَاوَلْتَنِي ذِرَاعًا ذِرَاعًا مَا سَكَتَّ ؟ ثُمَّ دَعَا بِمَاءٍ فَتَمَضْمَضَ
فَاهُ ، وَغَسَلَ أَطْرَافَ أَصَابِعِهِ ، ثُمَّ قَامَ فَصَلَّى ، ثُمَّ عَادَ إِلَيْهِمْ ، فَوَجَدَ
عِنْدَهُمْ لَحْمًا بَارِدًا ، فَأَكَلَ ، ثُمَّ دَخَلَ الْمَسْجِدَ فَصَلَّى وَلَمْ يَمَسَّ مَاءً .
رَوَاهُ أَحْمَدُ .

327 It is reported on the same authority that he was presented a
sheep and he put it in an earthen pot (and placed it on fire
to be cooked), that Allah's Messenger (peace and blessings of
Allah be upon him) happened to come there and he said:
Abu Rafi', what is this? He said: Allah's Messenger, it is
sheep which was presented to us and I cooked it in the
earthen pot. He said: Abu Rafi' give me the foreleg. So I
gave him the foreleg. He said: Give me the other foreleg;
and I gave him the other foreleg. He then said: Give me the
other foreleg; whereupon Abu Rafi' said: Allah's Messenger:
The sheep has only two forelegs. Thereupon Allah's Messen-

ger (peace and blessings of Allah be upon him) said: Had
you remained silent you would have managed to give me one
foreleg after another as long as you had observed silence.[1]
He then called for water and rinsed his mouth and washed
the tips of his fingers then got up and observed prayer, then
came back to them and found that they had condensed meat.
He ate, then entered the mosque, observed prayer and did
not touch water. (*Ahmad*)

1. It must have been the miracle of Allah's Apostle (peace and blessings
of Allah be upon him).

٣٢٨ ـ وَرَوَاهُ الدَّارِمِيُّ عَنْ أَبِي عُبَيدٍ إِلَّا أَنَّهُ لَمْ يَذْكُرْ ، ثُمَّ دَعَا بِمَاءٍ

إِلَى آخِرِهِ .

328 Darimi reported it on the authority of Abu 'Ubaid but he
did not make mention of this: He called for water upto
the end.

٣٢٩ ـ وَعَنْ أَنَسِ بنِ مَالِكٍ ، قَالَ : كُنْتُ أَنَا وَأُبَيٌّ وَأَبُو طَلْحَةَ جُلُوسًا نَأْكُلُ

لَحْمًا وَخُبْزًا ، ثُمَّ دَعَوْتُ بِوَضُوءٍ ، فَقَالَا : لِمَ تَتَوَضَّأُ ، فَقُلْتُ : لِهٰذَا

الطَّعَامِ الَّذِي أَكَلْنَا. فَقَالَا : أَتَتَوَضَّأُ مِنَ الطَّيِّبَاتِ ؟! لَمْ يَتَوَضَّأْ مِنْهُ مَنْ

هُوَ خَيْرٌ مِنْكَ . رَوَاهُ أَحْمَدُ .

329 Anas b. Malik reported: I, Ubayy, Abu Talha were sitting
and were busy in eating the meat and bread. I called for
water (to perform ablution). They said: Why do you
perform ablution. I said: It is because for the food that we
took. They said: Do you perform ablution after eating
things which are good. He (*i.e.* the Holy Prophet, peace and
blessings of Allah be upon him) who was (infinitely) better
than you did not perform ablution (because of the eating of
good things). (*Ahmad*)

٣٣٠ ـ وَعَنِ ابنِ عُمَرَ ، كَانَ يَقُولُ : قُبْلَةُ الرَّجُلِ امْرَأَتَهُ وَجَسُّهَا بِيَدِهِ مِنَ

الْمُلَامَسَةِ. وَمَنْ قَبَّلَ امْرَأَتَهُ أَوْ جَسَّهَا بِيَدِهِ ، فَعَلَيْهِ الْوُضُوءُ. رَوَاهُ

مَالِكٌ ، وَالشَّافِعِيُّ .

330 Ibn 'Umar reported: A man's kiss to his wife and touching her with his hand actuated by sexual lust, in such a case, he who kisses his wife and touches her with his hands ablution becomes necessary for him. (*Malik and Shafi'i*)

٣٣١- وَعَنِ ابْنِ مَسْعُودٍ، كَانَ يَقُولُ: مِنْ قُبْلَةِ الرَّجُلِ امْرَأَتَهُ الْوُضُوءُ. رَوَاهُ مَالِكٌ.

331 Ibn Masu'd reported: Ablution is necessary when a man kisses his wife (actuated with sexual lust). (*Malik*)

٣٣٢- وَعَنِ ابْنِ عُمَرَ، أَنَّ عُمَرَ بْنَ الْخَطَّابِ، رَضِيَ اللهُ عَنْهُ، قَالَ: إِنَّ الْقُبْلَةَ مِنَ اللَّمْسِ، فَتَوَضَّؤُوا مِنْهَا.

332 Ibn 'Umar reported that 'Umar b. Khattab (may Allah be pleased with him) said: A kiss actuated by sexual lust necessitates ablution. (*Daraqutni*)

٣٣٣- وَعَنْ عُمَرَ بْنِ عَبْدِ الْعَزِيزِ، عَنْ تَمِيمٍ الدَّارِيِّ، قَالَ، قَالَ رَسُولُ اللهِ ﷺ: "الْوُضُوءُ مِنْ كُلِّ دَمٍ سَائِلٍ" رَوَاهُمَا الدَّارَقُطْنِيُّ، وَقَالَ: عُمَرُ بْنُ عَبْدِ الْعَزِيزِ لَمْ يَسْمَعْ مِنْ تَمِيمٍ الدَّارِيِّ وَلَا رَآهُ، وَيَزِيدُ بْنُ خَالِدٍ، وَيَزِيدُ بْنُ مُحَمَّدٍ مَجْهُولَانِ.

333 'Umar b. 'Abdul 'Aziz told on the authority of Tamim Ad-Dari that Allah's Messenger (peace and blessings of Allah be upon him) said: Ablution must be performed because of the flow of blood. (*Daraqutni transmitted these two traditions saying: 'Umar b. 'Abdul 'Aziz neither heard from Tamim Ad-Dari nor saw him and that Yazid b. Khalid and Yazid b. Muhammad are unknown*)

CHAPTER 10

HOW TO ACT WHILE RELIEVING ONESELF

Section I الْفَصْلُ الْأَوَّلُ

٣٣٤ ـ عَنْ أَبِى أَيُّوبَ الْأَنْصَارِيِّ ، قَالَ : قَالَ رَسُولُ اللهِ ﷺ : إِذَا أَتَيْتُمُ الْغَائِطَ فَلَا تَسْتَقْبِلُوا الْقِبْلَةَ ، وَلَا تَسْتَدْبِرُوهَا ، وَلٰكِنْ شَرِّقُوا أَوْ غَرِّبُوا ، مُتَّفَقٌ عَلَيْهِ

قَالَ الشَّيْخُ الْإِمَامُ مُحْيِى السُّنَّةِ ، رَحِمَهُ اللهُ : هٰذَا الْحَدِيثُ فِى الصَّحْرَاءِ ، وَأَمَّا فِى الْبُنْيَانِ ، فَلَا بَأْسَ لِمَا رُوِىَ :

334. Hadrat Abu Ayub Ansari reported Allah's Messenger (peace and blessings of Allah be upon him) as saying: When you come to privy neither turn your face nor turn your back towards *Qiblah* but keep *Qiblah* towards the East or the West.[1]

(*Agreed upon*)

(*Sheikh Imam Mohyi as-Sunnah stated:* This hadith relates to the desert but so far as the built up area is concerned it does not matter as it has been narrated in the following hadith).

1. The scholars of hadith have resolved the apparent contradiction between the two ahadith by saying: It is forbidden to face *Qiblah* or to turn one's back towards it when one goes out for relieving one's self in the wilderness or desert where one can easily avoid it, but in a built up area or enclosures one is permitted to do so.

٣٣٥ ـ عَنْ عَبْدِ اللهِ بْنِ عُمَرَ ، قَالَ : ارْتَقَيْتُ فَوْقَ بَيْتِ حَفْصَةَ لِبَعْضِ حَاجَتِى فَرَأَيْتُ رَسُولَ اللهِ ﷺ يَقْضِى حَاجَتَهُ مُسْتَدْبِرَ الْقِبْلَةِ مُسْتَقْبِلَ الشَّامِ ، مُتَّفَقٌ عَلَيْهِ .

335 '**Abdullah b. 'Umar** reported : I went up to the roof of the house of Hafsa for some need and I saw Allah's Messenger (peace and blessings of Allah be upon him) relieving himself facing Syria with his back to *Qiblah*. (*Agreed upon*)

٣٣٦ - وَعَنْ سَلْمَانَ ، قَالَ : نَهَانَا - يَعْنِي رَسُوْلَ اللّٰهِ ﷺ - أَنْ نَسْتَقْبِلَ
الْقِبْلَةَ لِغَائِطٍ أَوْ بَوْلٍ ، أَوْ أَنْ نَسْتَنْجِيَ بِالْيَمِيْنِ ، أَوْ أَنْ نَسْتَنْجِيَ بِأَقَلَّ مِنْ
ثَلَاثَةِ أَحْجَارٍ ، أَوْ أَنْ نَسْتَنْجِيَ بِرَجِيْعٍ أَوْ بِعَظْمٍ رَوَاهُ مُسْلِمٌ .

336 Salman reported that Allah's Messenger (peace and blessings
of Allah be upon him) forbade us to face *Qiblah* (while relieving ourselves) in the desert or while urinating or washing
ourselves with right hand or clean ourselves with less than
three pebbles or clean ourselves with the dung or with the
help of bone. (*Muslim*)

٣٣٧ - وَعَنْ أَنَسٍ ، قَالَ : كَانَ رَسُوْلُ اللّٰهِ ﷺ إِذَا دَخَلَ الْخَلَاءَ يَقُوْلُ : "اللّٰهُمَّ
إِنِّي أَعُوْذُ بِكَ مِنَ الْخُبْثِ وَ الْخَبَائِثِ" مُتَّفَقٌ عَلَيْهِ

337 Anas reported that whenever Allah's Messenger (peace and
blessings of Allah be upon him) entered the privy he used to
say : O Allah, I seek refuge with Thee from impurities and
evil spirits. (*Agreed upon*)

٣٣٨ - وَعَنِ ابْنِ عَبَّاسٍ ، قَالَ : مَرَّ النَّبِيُّ ﷺ بِقَبْرَيْنِ ، فَقَالَ : "إِنَّهُمَا يُعَذَّبَانِ
وَمَا يُعَذَّبَانِ فِي كَبِيْرٍ ؛ أَمَّا أَحَدُهُمَا فَكَانَ لَا يَسْتَتِرُ مِنَ الْبَوْلِ - وَ فِي
رِوَايَةٍ لِمُسْلِمٍ : لَا يَسْتَنْزِهُ مِنَ الْبَوْلِ - وَ أَمَّا الْآخَرُ فَكَانَ يَمْشِي بِالنَّمِيْمَةِ
ثُمَّ أَخَذَ جَرِيْدَةً رَطْبَةً ، فَشَقَّهَا بِنِصْفَيْنِ ، ثُمَّ غَرَزَ فِي كُلِّ قَبْرٍ وَاحِدَةً . قَالُوْا :
يَا رَسُوْلَ اللّٰهِ : لِمَ صَنَعْتَ هٰذَا ؛ فَقَالَ : لَعَلَّهُ يُخَفَّفُ عَنْهُمَا مَا يَيْبَسَا "
مُتَّفَقٌ عَلَيْهِ .

338 Ibn 'Abbas reported that Allah's Messenger (peace and blessings of Allah be upon him) happened to pass by the side of two
graves and he remarked : Verily they are being tormented,
but they are not being tormented for anything serious. One
of them did not observe care in keeping himself safe from the
urine, and so far as the other is concerned, he used to carry
tales. He then took hold of a fresh twig and split it into two

parts and planted them on each grave. They (the companions around him) said : Allah's Messenger, what for have you done it? Whereupon he said : There may be some relief in their punishment as long as these (twigs) do not wither.

(Agreed upon)

٣٣٩ - وَعَنْ أَبِى هُرَيْرَةَ، قَالَ : قَالَ رَسُولُ اللهِ ﷺ : "إِتَّقُوا اللَّاعِنَيْنِ" قَالُوا : وَمَا اللَّاعِنَانِ يَا رَسُولَ اللهِ؟ قَالَ : "أَلَّذِى يَتَخَلَّى فِى طَرِيقِ النَّاسِ أَوْ فِى ظِلِّهِمْ" رَوَاهُ مُسْلِمٌ.

339 Abu Huraira reported Allah's Messenger (peace and blessings of Allah be upon him) as saying : Guard against two invokers of curse. They said : Allah's Messenger, what are these causes of curse? Whereupon he said : Relieving one's self in the paths of the people or where they enjoy shade. *(Muslim)*

٣٤٠ - وَعَنْ أَبِى قَتَادَةَ، قَالَ : قَالَ رَسُولُ اللهِ ﷺ : "إِذَا شَرِبَ أَحَدُكُمْ فَلَا يَنْتَقِسْ فِى الْإِنَاءِ، وَإِذَا أَتَى الْخَلَاءَ، فَلَا يَمَسَّ ذَكَرَهُ بِيَمِينِهِ، وَلَا يَتَمَسَّحْ بِيَمِينِهِ" مُتَّفَقٌ عَلَيْهِ.

340 Abu Qatada reported Allah's Messenger (peace and blessings of Allah be upon him) as saying : When anyone of you drinks he should not breathe in the vessel and when he goes to the privy he should not touch his male organ with his right hand or wipe with his right hand. *(Agreed upon)*

٣٤١ - وَعَنْ أَبِى هُرَيْرَةَ، قَالَ : قَالَ رَسُولُ اللهِ ﷺ : "مَنْ تَوَضَّأَ فَلْيَسْتَنْثِرْ، وَمَنِ اسْتَجْمَرَ فَلْيُوتِرْ" مُتَّفَقٌ عَلَيْهِ.

341 Abu Huraira reported Allah's Messenger (peace and blessings of Allah be upon him) as saying : He who performs ablution he must clean his nose and when anyone uses sods (to clean one's private part) he should make use of odd numbers (not less than three). *(Agreed upon)*

٣٤٢ - وَعَنْ أَنَسٍ، قَالَ : كَانَ رَسُولُ اللهِ ﷺ يَدْخُلُ الْخَلَاءَ، فَأَحْمِلُ أَنَا وَغُلَامٌ إِدَاوَةً مِنْ مَاءٍ وَعَنَزَةً يَسْتَنْجِى بِالْمَاءِ" مُتَّفَقٌ عَلَيْهِ.

342 Anas reported : When Allah's Messenger (peace and blessings of Allah be upon him) went out for relieving himself I
and a servant used to carry a small water skin filled with
water and a staff[1] too. He cleaned himself with water.

(Agreed upon)

1. As it was the habit of Allah's Messenger (peace and blessings of Allah
be upon him) to go very far off place into the desert for relieving
himself, the staff was, therefore carried with him. *Attaliq-as-Sabih
'Ala Mishkat fil Masabih* by M. Idris Kandhalvi, Vol. I, p. 192.

Section II اَلْفَصْلُ الثَّانِي

٣٤٣ـ عَنْ أَنَسٍ، قَالَ: كَانَ النَّبِيُّ ﷺ إِذَا دَخَلَ الْخَلَاءَ نَزَعَ خَاتَمَهُ. رَوَاهُ
أَبُوْ دَاوُدَ، وَالنَّسَائِيُّ، وَالتِّرْمِذِيُّ، وَقَالَ: هٰذَا حَدِيْثٌ حَسَنٌ صَحِيْحٌ
غَرِيْبٌ.

وَقَالَ أَبُوْ دَاوُدَ: هٰذَا حَدِيْثٌ مُنْكَرٌ وَفِيْ رِوَايَتِهِ: وَضَعَ بَدَلَ نَزَعَ.

343 Anas reported as saying: When Allah's Messenger (peace
and blessings of Allah be upon him) entered into privy he
took off his ring. *(Abu Dawud and Tirmidhi transmitted it.
Tirmidhi said: This is a Hasan Sahih gharib hadith and Abu
Dawud said: This is a munkar[1] hadith; and in his narration (the
wording is) : "He laid down" instead of "he took off.")*

1. A Munkar hadith is that in which a weak narrator narrates it in
contravention to a very sound narrator.

٣٤٤ـ وَعَنْ جَابِرٍ، قَالَ: كَانَ النَّبِيُّ ﷺ إِذَا أَرَادَ الْبَرَازَ انْطَلَقَ حَتَّى لَا يَرَاهُ
أَحَدٌ. رَوَاهُ أَبُوْ دَاوُدَ.

344 Jabir reported that when Allah's Apostle (peace and blessings
of Allah be upon him) intended to go for call of nature he
proceeded on till nobody could see him. *(Abu Dawud)*

٣٤٥ـ وَعَنْ أَبِيْ مُوْسَى، قَالَ: كُنْتُ مَعَ النَّبِيِّ ﷺ ذَاتَ يَوْمٍ فَأَرَادَ أَنْ يَبُوْلَ
فَأَتَى دَمِثًا فِيْ أَصْلِ جِدَارٍ، فَبَالَ. ثُمَّ قَالَ: إِذَا أَرَادَ أَحَدُكُمْ أَنْ يَبُوْلَ
فَلْيَرْتَدْ لِبَوْلِهِ: رَوَاهُ أَبُوْ دَاوُدَ.

345 Abu Musa reported : I was along with Allah's Messenger (peace and blessings of Allah be upon him) one day and he intended to pass water. So he went to some soft ground at the foot of a wall and urinated and then said : When any-one of you intends to urinate he should look (for) a place like this for urinating. (*Abu Dawud*)

٣٤٥- وَعَنْ أَنَسٍ ، قَالَ :كَانَ النَّبِيُّ ﷺ إِذَا أَرَادَ الْحَاجَةَ لَمْ يَرْفَعْ ثَوْبَهُ حَتَّى يَدْنُوَ مِنَ الْأَرْضِ. رَوَاهُ التِّرْمِذِيُّ ، وَأَبُوْدَاوُدَ ، وَالدَّارِمِيُّ .

346 Anas reported that when Allah's Apostle (peace be upon him) wanted to relieve himself he did not lift his garment, till he was near the ground. (*Tirmidhi, Abu Dawud and Darimi*)

٣٤٧- وَعَنْ أَبِيْ هُرَيْرَةَ ، قَالَ : قَالَ رَسُوْلُ اللهِ ﷺ : إِنَّمَا أَنَا لَكُمْ مِثْلُ الْوَالِدِ لِوَلَدِهِ ، أُعَلِّمُكُمْ ، إِذَا أَتَيْتُمُ الْغَائِطَ ، فَلَا تَسْتَقْبِلُوا الْقِبْلَةَ ، وَلَا تَسْتَدْبِرُوْهَا ؛ وَأَمَرَ بِثَلَاثَةِ أَحْجَارٍ . وَنَهَى عَنِ الرَّوْثِ وَالرُّمَّةِ . وَ نَهَى أَنْ يَسْتَطِيْبَ الرَّجُلُ بِيَمِيْنِهِ . رَوَاهُ ابْنُ مَاجَةَ ، وَالدَّارِمِيُّ .

347 Abu Huraira reported Allah's Messenger (peace and blessings of Allah be upon him) as saying : I am unto you as a father is to his son. So I teach you that whenever you go to the desert (for relieving yourselves) don't face *Qiblah* and don't turn back towards it, and he (the Holy Prophet) commanded to use three sods for (cleansing) the private parts and he forbade to use dung or the bones and he forbade that a person should clean himself with his right hand. (*Ibn Majah and Darimi*)

٣٤٨- وَعَنْ عَائِشَةَ ، قَالَتْ : كَانَتْ يَدُ رَسُوْلِ اللهِ ﷺ الْيُمْنَى لِطُهُوْرِهِ وَطَعَامِهِ ، وَكَانَتْ يَدُهُ الْيُسْرَى لِخَلَائِهِ وَمَا كَانَ مِنْ أَذًى . رَوَاهُ أَبُوْدَاوُدَ .

348 'A'isha reported that Allah's Messenger (peace and blessings of Allah be upon him) used his right hand for ablution and for dining and his left hand (for cleansing) his private parts with sods or water and for any other thing disagreeable.

(*Abu Dawud*)

٣٤٩- وَعَنْهَا، قَالَتْ، قَالَ رَسُولُ اللهِ ﷺ: إِذَا ذَهَبَ أَحَدُكُمْ إِلَى الْغَائِطِ
فَلْيَذْهَبْ مَعَهُ بِثَلَاثَةِ أَحْجَارٍ يَسْتَطِيبُ بِهِنَّ، فَإِنَّهَا تُجْزِى عَنْهُ رَوَاهُ
أَحْمَدُ، وَأَبُو دَاوُدَ، وَالنَّسَائِيُّ، وَالدَّارِمِيُّ.

349 It is reported on the same authority that Allah's Messenger
(peace and blessings of Allah be upon him) said: Whenever
anyone of you goes to the desert for relieving himself he should
carry with him (at least) three sods with which he should
cleanse oneself. They are sufficient for him.

(*Ahmad, Abu Dawud, Nasai', Darimi*)

٣٥٠- وَعَنِ ابْنِ مَسْعُودٍ، قَالَ: قَالَ رَسُولُ اللهِ ﷺ: لَا تَسْتَنْجُوا بِالرَّوْثِ
وَلَا بِالْعِظَامِ، فَإِنَّهَا زَادُ إِخْوَانِكُمْ مِنَ الْجِنِّ، رَوَاهُ التِّرْمِذِيُّ وَالنَّسَائِيُّ
إِلَّا أَنَّهُ لَمْ يَذْكُرْ: زَادُ إِخْوَانِكُمْ مِنَ الْجِنِّ.

350 Ibn Mas'ud reported Allah's Messenger (peace and blessings
of Allah be upon him) as saying: Don't cleanse yourself with
dung or with bones for that is the food of your brothers from
amongst jinn. (*Transmitted by Tirmidhi, Nasai' with this exception that he did not make mention of : The food of your brothers
from amongst the jinn*)

٣٥١- وَعَنْ رُوَيْفِعِ بْنِ ثَابِتٍ، قَالَ، قَالَ لِي رَسُولُ اللهِ ﷺ: يَا رُوَيْفِعُ! لَعَلَّ الْحَيَاةَ
سَتَطُولُ بِكَ بَعْدِي، فَأَخْبِرِ النَّاسَ أَنَّ مَنْ عَقَدَ لِحْيَتَهُ، أَوْ تَقَلَّدَ وَتَرًا،
أَوِ اسْتَنْجَى بِرَجِيعِ دَابَّةٍ، أَوْ عَظْمٍ؛ فَإِنَّ مُحَمَّدًا بَرِىءٌ مِنْهُ رَوَاهُ
أَبُو دَاوُدَ.

351 Ruwaifi' b. Thabit reported that Allah's Messenger (peace and
blessings of Allah be upon him) said to me: Ruwaifi',
you would perhaps live long after me so tell people that if anyone
ties his beard[1] or wears round his neck a string to ward off
the evil eye or cleanse himself with the dung of animals or
with the bones, Muhammad has nothing to do with him.

(*Abu Dawud*)

1. This was done to make the hair artificially curly.

٣٥٢ - وَعَنْ أَبِيْ هُرَيْرَةَ ، رَضِيَ اللهُ عَنْهُ ، قَالَ : قَالَ رَسُوْلُ اللهِ ﷺ : مَنِ
اكْتَحَلَ فَلْيُوْتِرْ ، مَنْ فَعَلَ فَقَدْ أَحْسَنَ ، وَمَنْ لَّا فَلَا حَرَجَ . وَمَنِ اسْتَجْمَرَ
فَلْيُوْتِرْ ، مَنْ فَعَلَ فَقَدْ أَحْسَنَ ، وَمَنْ لَّا فَلَا حَرَجَ ، وَمَنْ أَكَلَ فَمَا تَخَلَّلَ ،
فَلْيَلْفِظْ ، وَمَا لَاكَ بِلِسَانِهِ فَلْيَبْتَلِعْ ، مَنْ فَعَلَ فَقَدْ أَحْسَنَ ، وَمَنْ لَّا
فَلَا حَرَجَ . وَمَنْ أَتَى الْغَائِطَ فَلْيَسْتَتِرْ ، وَ مَنْ لَمْ يَجِدْ إِلَّا أَنْ يَجْمَعَ
كَثِيْبًا مِنْ رَمْلٍ فَلْيَسْتَدْبِرْهُ ، فَإِنَّ الشَّيْطَانَ يَلْعَبُ بِمَقَاعِدِ بَنِيْ آدَمَ ،
مَنْ فَعَلَ فَقَدْ أَحْسَنَ ، وَ مَنْ لَّا فَلَا حَرَجَ ؛ رَوَاهُ أَبُوْ دَاوُدَ ، وَابْنُ مَاجَةَ ،
وَالدَّارِمِيُّ .

352 Abu Huraira reported Allah's Messenger (peace and blessings
of Allah be upon him) as saying: If anyone applies collyrium
he should do it an odd number of times, and if one has done
that he has done well and he who has not done that there is
no harm in it and he who uses sods to cleanse himself, let him
use their odd number and he who has done that he has done
well and he who has not done that, there is no harm in it and
whoever takes food let him throw away what he removes with
a tooth pick and swallow what he removes with his tongue.
If anyone does so he has done well, but if not, there is no
harm. If one goes to relieve himself he should conceal himself and if all he can do is to collect a heap of sand he should
sit with his back towards it, because the satan plays with
private parts of the children of Adam and he who has done
that he has done well and he who has not done that, there is
no harm. *(Abu Dawud, Ibn Majah, Darimi)*

٣٥٢ - وَعَنْ عَبْدِ اللهِ بْنِ مُغَفَّلٍ ، قَالَ : قَالَ رَسُوْلُ اللهِ ﷺ " لَا يَبُوْلَنَّ أَحَدُكُمْ
فِيْ مُسْتَحِمِّهِ ، ثُمَّ يَغْتَسِلُ فِيْهِ ، أَوْ يَتَوَضَّأُ فِيْهِ . فَإِنَّ عَامَّةَ الْوَسْوَاسِ
مِنْهُ ؛ رَوَاهُ أَبُوْ دَاوُدَ ، وَالتِّرْمِذِيُّ ، وَ النَّسَائِيُّ ؛ إِلَّا أَنَّهُمَا لَمْ يَذْكُرَا
ثُمَّ يَغْتَسِلُ فِيْهِ ، أَوْ يَتَوَضَّأُ فِيْهِ ؛

353 **'Abdullah b. Mughaffal** reported Allah's Messenger (peace and blessings of Allah be upon him) as saying: None of you should pass urine at the bathing[1] place and then take bath or perform ablution in it for there arise evil promptings from it. *(Transmitted by Abu Dawud, Tirmidhi, Nasai', but they did not make mention of this: Then take bath in it or perform ablution there)*

1. The Holy Prophet (may peace and blessings of Allah be upon him) has forbidden to pass urine in the bath rooms or bathing places for it creates evil promptings in the minds of the people which cause doubts whether he has performed bath well or not. The state of piety is the state of certainty and not that of doubt. The Holy Prophet has, therefore, warned his followers against doing anything which may create doubts in the minds of the people and thus disturb the state of certainty.

٣٥٢ - وَعَنْ عَبْدِ اللهِ بْنِ سَرْجِسَ، قَالَ: قَالَ رَسُولُ اللهِ ﷺ: لَا يَبُولَنَّ أَحَدُكُمْ

فِي جُحْرٍ؛ رَوَاهُ أَبُو دَاوُدَ، وَالنَّسَائِيُّ

354 **'Abdullah b. Sarjis** reported that Allah's Messenger (peace and blessings of Allah be upon him) said: None of you should urinate in a hole.[2] *(Abu Dawud, Nasai')*

2. The holes are the living places of reptiles and there is every likelihood that when anyone urinates in the hole, the reptile may come and harm that person or a harmless reptile may be troubled by urination.

٣٥٥ - وَعَنْ مُعَاذٍ، قَالَ: قَالَ رَسُولُ اللهِ ﷺ: إِتَّقُوا الْمَلَاعِنَ الثَّلَاثَةَ: الْبَرَازَ

فِي الْمَوَارِدِ، وَقَارِعَةِ الطَّرِيقِ، وَالظِّلِّ؛ رَوَاهُ أَبُو دَاوُدَ، وَابْنُ مَاجَةَ

355 **Mu'adh** reported Allah's Messenger (peace and blessings of Allah be upon him) as saying: Guard against three things which may induce cursing. Relieving oneself in watering places and in the thoroughfares and under the shades.

(Abu Dawud and Ibn Majah)

٣٥٦ - وَعَنْ أَبِي سَعِيدٍ، قَالَ: قَالَ رَسُولُ اللهِ ﷺ: لَا يَخْرُجِ الرَّجُلَانِ يَضْرِبَانِ

الْغَائِطَ كَاشِفَيْنِ عَنْ عَوْرَتِهِمَا يَتَحَدَّثَانِ، فَإِنَّ اللهَ يَمْقُتُ عَلَى ذَلِكَ؛ رَوَاهُ

أَحْمَدُ، وَأَبُو دَاوُدَ، وَابْنُ مَاجَةَ

356 Abu Sa'id reported Allah's Messenger (peace and blessings of Allah be upon him) as saying: No two men should come to the privy exposing their parts and be busy in conversation for Allah hates it. (*Ahmad, Abu Dawud and Ibn Majah*)

٣٥٦ ـ وَعَنْ زَيْدِ بْنِ أَرْقَمَ ، قَالَ : قَالَ رَسُولُ اللهِ ﷺ "إِنَّ هَذِهِ الْحُشُوشَ
مُحْتَضَرَةٌ ، فَإِذَا أَتَى أَحَدُكُمُ الْخَلَاءَ ، فَلْيَقُلْ : أَعُوذُ بِاللهِ مِنَ الْخُبْثِ
وَ الْخَبَائِثِ" رَوَاهُ أَبُو دَاوُدَ ، وَ ابْنُ مَاجَهْ

357 Zaid b. Arqam reported Allah's Messenger (peace and blessings of Allah be upon him) as saying: Verily these privies are haunted, so when anyone of you comes to the privy he should say: I seek refuge with Allah from the impurity and evil spirits. (*Abu Dawud and Ibn Majah*)

٣٥٨ ـ وَعَنْ عَلِيٍّ ، قَالَ : قَالَ رَسُولُ اللهِ ﷺ : "سِتْرُ مَا بَيْنَ أَعْيُنِ الْجِنِّ وَ
عَوْرَاتِ بَنِي آدَمَ إِذَا دَخَلَ أَحَدُهُمُ الْخَلَاءَ أَنْ يَقُولَ : بِسْمِ اللهِ" رَوَاهُ
التِّرْمِذِيُّ ، وَ قَالَ : هَذَا حَدِيثٌ غَرِيبٌ ، وَ إِسْنَادُهُ لَيْسَ بِقَوِيٍّ ٠

358 'Ali reported Allah's Messenger (peace and blessings of Allah be upon him) as saying: The covering between the eyes of Jinn and the private parts of the sons of Adam as one of them enters the privy is that he should say: In the name of Allah. (*This hadith has been transmitted by Tirmidhi and said: It is a gharib hadith and its isnad is not sound.*)

٣٥٩ ـ وَعَنْ عَائِشَةَ ، قَالَتْ كَانَ النَّبِيُّ ﷺ إِذَا خَرَجَ مِنَ الْخَلَاءِ قَالَ :
"غُفْرَانَكَ" رَوَاهُ التِّرْمِذِيُّ ، وَ ابْنُ مَاجَهْ ، وَ الدَّارِمِيُّ

359 'A'isha reported that when Allah's Apostle (peace and blessings of Allah be upon him) came out from the privy. He said: (I seek) forgiveness from Thee. (*Tirmidhi, Ibn Majah and Darimi*)

٣٦٠ ـ وَعَنْ أَبِي هُرَيْرَةَ ، قَالَ : كَانَ النَّبِيُّ ﷺ إِذَا أَتَى الْخَلَاءَ أَتَيْتُهُ بِمَاءٍ
فِي تَوْرٍ أَوْ رَكْوَةٍ ، فَاسْتَنْجَى ، ثُمَّ مَسَحَ يَدَهُ عَلَى الْأَرْضِ ، ثُمَّ أَتَيْتُهُ
بِإِنَاءٍ آخَرَ ، فَتَوَضَّأَ" رَوَاهُ أَبُو دَاوُدَ ، وَ رَوَى الدَّارِمِيُّ وَ النَّسَائِيُّ مَعْنَاهُ٠

360 Abu Huraira reported : When Allah's Apostle (peace and blessings of Allah be upon him) came out from the privy I brought water for him in a pot or in a water skin and he used to wash himself or he cleansed himself. He then rubbed his hands on the earth. I then brought another vessel (full of water) and he performed ablution with it.

(Abu Dawud, Darimi and Nasai')

٣٦١ - وَعَنِ الْحَكَمِ بْنِ سُفْيَانَ، قَالَ. كَانَ النَّبِيُّ ﷺ إِذَا بَالَ تَوَضَّأَ وَنَضَحَ فَرْجَهُ. رَوَاهُ أَبُو دَاؤُدَ، وَ النَّسَائِيُّ.

361 Hakam b. Sufyan reported that when Allah's Apostle (peace and blessings of Allah be upon him) urinated, he performed ablution. He sprinkled water over his private parts.

(Abu Dawud and Nasai')

٣٦٢ - وَعَنْ أُمَيْمَةَ بِنْتِ رُقَيْقَةَ، قَالَتْ: كَانَ لِلنَّبِيِّ ﷺ قَدَحٌ مِنْ عِيدَانٍ تَحْتَ سَرِيرِهِ يَبُولُ فِيهِ بِاللَّيْلِ. رَوَاهُ أَبُو دَاؤُدَ، وَ النَّسَائِيُّ.

362 Umaima, daughter of Ruqaiqa reported that Allah's Apostle (peace and blessings of Allah be upon him) had a bed pan of wood beneath his cot in which he passed the urine at night.

(Abu Dawud and Nasai')

٣٦٣ - وَعَنْ عُمَرَ، قَالَ : رَآنِي النَّبِيُّ ﷺ وَ أَنَا أَبُولُ قَائِمًا، فَقَالَ : يَاعُمَرُ لَا تَبُلْ قَائِمًا ؛ فَمَا بُلْتُ قَائِمًا بَعْدُ. رَوَاهُ التِّرْمِذِيُّ، وَ ابْنُ مَاجَةَ.

قَالَ الشَّيْخُ الْإِمَامُ مُحْيِي السُّنَّةِ، رَحِمَهُ اللهُ : قَدْ صَحَّ.

363 'Umar reported that Allah's Apostle (peace and blessings of Allah be upon him) saw me passing urine while standing, thereupon he said: 'Umar, don't urinate while standing. And afterwards I never passed urine while standing.

(Tirmidhi and Ibn Majah)

٣٦٤ - عَنْ حُذَيْفَةَ، قَالَ أَتَى النَّبِيُّ ﷺ سُبَاطَةَ قَوْمٍ، فَبَالَ قَائِمًا. مُتَّفَقٌ عَلَيْهِ. قِيلَ : كَانَ ذَلِكَ لِعُذْرٍ

364 *As-Sheikh Al-Imam Muhyi as-Sunnah (may Allah have mercy upon him) said : There is a sound tradition on the authority of Hudaifa* who said: That Allah's Apostle (peace and blessings of Allah be upon him) came to the sweepings of the people and he passed water while standing. It was said: He did that because of (genuine) excuse.[1]

> 1. The plausible excuse according to some of the scholars of hadith was that there was no fit place to sit in. The second excuse was as it has been reported on the authority of Abu Huraira that he had a wound in his ankle and he could not sit. Then Imam Shafi'i has also reported that some of the Arabs cured the pain in their sides by urinating while standing and the Holy Prophet (peace and blessings of Allah be upon him) did this because he had been also suffering from this pain. (*At-Taliq-us-Sabih*, Vol. 1, p. 198).

Section III ٱلْفَصْلُ الثَّالِثُ

٣٦٥ ـ عَنْ عَائِشَةَ . رَضِيَ اللهُ عَنْهَا ، قَالَتْ : مَنْ حَدَّثَكُمْ أَنَّ النَّبِيَّ ﷺ كَانَ يَبُولُ قَائِمًا فَلَا تُصَدِّقُوهُ ؛ مَا كَانَ يَبُولُ إِلَّا قَاعِدًا . رَوَاهُ أَحْمَدُ ، وَالتِّرْمِذِيُّ ، وَالنَّسَائِيُّ .

365 There is a report from 'Ā'isha (may Allah be pleased with her) that she said : He who narrated to you that Allah's Apostle (peace and blessings of Allah be upon him) used to pass water while standing don't testify him. He was not used to urinate while standing.[2] (*Ahmad, Nasa'i, Tirmidhi*)

> 2. That the Holy Prophet passed water while sitting is an established fact, if he did otherwise it was an exception rather than routine of his life.

٣٦٦ ـ وَعَنْ زَيْدِ بْنِ حَارِثَةَ ، عَنِ النَّبِيِّ ﷺ : إِنَّ جِبْرِيلَ أَتَاهُ فِي أَوَّلِ مَا أُوحِيَ إِلَيْهِ ، نَعَلَّمَهُ الْوُضُوءَ وَالصَّلَاةَ ، فَلَمَّا فَرَغَ مِنَ الْوُضُوءِ أَخَذَ غُرْفَةً مِنَ الْمَاءِ ، فَنَضَحَ بِهَا فَرْجَهُ" رَوَاهُ أَحْمَدُ ، وَالدَّارَ قُطْنِيُّ .

366 Zaid b. Harith reported Allah's Messenger (peace and blessings of Allah be upon him) as saying: When Gibraiel came

to him at the time of first revelation he taught him (the Holy
Prophet) to perform ablution[1] and observe prayer. When he
finished the ablution he took hold of a vessel containing water
and sprinkled it over his private parts.   (*Ahmad, Daraqutni*)

   1. Gabriel had come to Allah's Messenger (peace and blessings of Allah
      be upon him) in human form, and taught him the complete process of
      performing ablution and observing prayer.

٣٦٧ - وَعَنْ أَبِى هُرَيْرَةَ ، رَضِىَ اللهُ عَنْهُ، قَالَ : قَالَ رَسُولُ اللهِ ﷺ : جَاءَنِى
جِبْرِيلُ، فَقَالَ : يَا مُحَمَّدُ إِذَا تَوَضَّأْتَ فَانْتَضِحْ " رَوَاهُ التِّرْمِذِيُّ ، وَقَالَ :
هَذَا حَدِيثٌ غَرِيبٌ . وَسَمِعْتُ مُحَمَّدًا ـ يَعْنِى الْبُخَارِىَّ ـ يَقُولُ :
الْحَسَنُ بْنُ عَلِىٍّ الْهَاشِمِىُّ الرَّاوِى مُنْكَرُ الْحَدِيثِ .

367 Abu Huraira reported that Allah's Messenger (peace and
blessings of Allah be upon him) said: Gabriel came to me
and said: When you perform ablution sprinkle water over
yourself.   (*Transmitted by Tirmidhi and he said: This is a gharib
tradition and I heard Muhammad (i.e., Bukhari) as saying: That
the tradition of Al-Hasan b. 'Ali Al-Hashimi the transmitter, are
Munkar*)

٣٦٨ - وَعَنْ عَائِشَةَ ، رَضِىَ اللهُ عَنْهُمَا، قَالَتْ : بَالَ رَسُولُ اللهِ ﷺ : فَقَامَ
عُمَرُ خَلْفَهُ بِكُوزٍ مِنْ مَاءٍ ، فَقَالَ : مَا هَذَا يَا عُمَرُ ؟ قَالَ : مَاءٌ تَتَوَضَّأُ
بِهِ . قَالَ : مَا أُمِرْتُ كُلَّمَا بُلْتُ أَنْ أَتَوَضَّأَ ، وَلَوْ فَعَلْتُ لَكَانَتْ سُنَّةً ؟ رَوَاهُ
أَبُو دَاوُدَ ، وَابْنُ مَاجَهَ .

368 'A'isha reported that Allah's Messenger (peace and blessings
of Allah be upon him) passed water and 'Umar stood behind
him with a jug of water; whereupon he (the Holy Prophet)
said: 'Umar, what is this?   He said: This is water for your
ablution; whereupon he said: I have not been directed
that whenever I pass urine I should make ablution. Had I
done it, it would have become a Sunnah (binding practice for
followers).   (*Abu Dawud and Ibn Majah*)

٣٦٩ - وَعَنْ أَبِى أَيُّوبَ ، وَجَابِرٍ ، وَأَنَسٍ ، أَنَّ هَذِهِ الْآيَةَ لَمَّا نَزَلَتْ : ﴿فِيهِ
رِجَالٌ يُحِبُّونَ أَنْ يَتَطَهَّرُوا ، وَ اللهُ يُحِبُّ الْمُطَّهِّرِينَ﴾ ، قَالَ رَسُولُ
اللهِ ﷺ " يَا مَعْشَرَ الْأَنْصَارِ ! إِنَّ اللهَ قَدْ أَثْنَى عَلَيْكُمْ فِى الطُّهُورِ ، فَمَا طُهُورُكُمْ؟
قَالُوا : نَتَوَضَّأُ لِلصَّلَاةِ ، وَ نَغْتَسِلُ مِنَ الْجَنَابَةِ ، وَ نَسْتَنْجِى بِالْمَاءِ . قَالَ :
" فَهُوَ ذَاكَ ، فَعَلَيْكُمُوهُ " رَوَاهُ ابْنُ مَاجَةَ

369 Abu Ayub, Jabir and Anas reported that when this verse was
revealed: Wherein there are men desirous of growing in purity
for Allah loves all who purify themselves (9: 108) Thereupon
Allah's Messenger (peace and blessings of Allah be upon him)
said: O people of Ansar verily Allah has praised you for
your purification. (What is nature of your purification).
They said: We perform ablution for prayer, take bath after
seminal emission and cleanse ourselves with water. He said:
That is it, so keep on doing it. (*Ibn Majah*)

٣٧٠ - وَعَنْ سَلْمَانَ ، قَالَ : بَعْضُ الْمُشْرِكِينَ ، وَهُوَ يَسْتَهْزِئُ : إِنِّى لَأَرَى صَاحِبَكُمْ
يُعَلِّمُكُمْ حَتَّى الْخَرَاءَةَ . قُلْتُ : أَجَلْ ! أَمَرَنَا أَنْ لَا نَسْتَقْبِلَ الْقِبْلَةَ ، وَلَا
نَسْتَنْجِى بِأَيْمَانِنَا ، وَ لَا نَكْتَفِى بِدُونِ ثَلَاثَةِ أَحْجَارٍ لَيْسَ فِيهَا رَجِيعٌ وَلَا
عَظْمٌ . رَوَاهُ مُسْلِمٌ ، وَأَحْمَدُ وَ اللَّفْظُ لَهُ .

370 Salman reported that a polytheist remarked: I find that
your master teaches you even the (manner of) excrement. I
said: yes. He has commanded us that we should not face
Qiblah (while relieving ourselves); we should not cleanse ourselves with our right hand and we should not be contented
with less than three sods and there should be no dung or
bone. (*Muslim and Ahmad*)

١٣٧١ - وَعَنْ عَبْدِ الرَّحْمَنِ بْنِ حَسَنَةَ ، قَالَ : خَرَجَ عَلَيْنَا رَسُولُ اللهِ ﷺ وَ
فِى يَدِهِ الدَّرَقَةُ فَوَضَعَهَا ، ثُمَّ جَلَسَ فَبَالَ إِلَيْهَا . فَقَالَ بَعْضُهُمْ : انْظُرُوا

إِلَيْهِ يَبُوْلُ كَمَا تَبُوْلُ الْمَرْأَةُ. فَسَمِعَهُ النَّبِيُّ ﷺ ، فَقَالَ: وَيْحَكَ! أَمَا
عَلِمْتَ مَا أَصَابَ صَاحِبَ بَنِيْ إِسْرَآئِيْلَ: كَانُوْا إِذَا أَصَابَهُمُ الْبَوْلُ
قَرَضُوْهُ بِالْمَقَارِيْضِ ، نَهَاهُمْ ، فَعُذِّبَ فِيْ قَبْرِهِ " رَوَاهُ أَبُوْدَاوُدَ ، وَ
ابْنُ مَاجَهَ.

371 **'Abdur Rahman b. Hasana** reported that Allah's Messenger (peace and blessings of Allah be upon him) came to them with an armour. He laid it down and then sat and passed water facing towards it. Some of them said: Look he is passing water just as a woman passes water. Allah's Messenger (peace and blessings of Allah be upon him) heard it and said: Woe be to thee. Do you know what happened to the ruler of Bani Israel. When urine fell upon them, they cut that part with pair of scissors, and he prohibited them but he was punished in his grave. (*Abu Dawud and Ibn Majah*)

٣٧٢ - وَرَوَاهُ النَّسَآئِيُّ عَنْهُ عَنْ أَبِيْ مُوْسَى

372 This hadith has been transmitted on the authority of **Abu Musa** and is recorded in *Nasai'*.

٣٧٣ - وَعَنْ مَرْوَانَ الْأَصْفَرِ ، قَالَ: رَأَيْتُ ابْنَ عُمَرَ أَنَاخَ رَاحِلَتَهُ مُسْتَقْبِلَ
الْقِبْلَةِ ، ثُمَّ جَلَسَ يَبُوْلُ إِلَيْهَا. فَقُلْتُ: يَا أَبَا عَبْدِ الرَّحْمَنِ! أَلَيْسَ قَدْ نُهِيَ
عَنْ هٰذَا ؛ قَالَ : بَلْ إِنَّمَا نُهِيَ عَنْ ذٰلِكَ فِي الْفَضَآءِ ، فَإِذَا كَانَ بَيْنَكَ وَبَيْنَ
الْقِبْلَةِ شَيْءٌ يَسْتُرُكَ فَلَا بَأْسَ. رَوَاهُ أَبُوْدَاوُدَ.

373 **Marwan b. Asfar** reported: I saw Ibn 'Umar leading his camel by the nose-string towards the direction of *Qiblah*. He then made his camel sit and urinated facing towards it (the camel). I said: 'Abdur Rahman: Has this not been forbidden. He said: No, that is forbidden only in open field and when there is anything between you and *Qiblah* to cover it there is no harm in it.

٣٧٤ـ وَعَنْ أَنَسٍ، قَالَ: كَانَ النَّبِيُّ ﷺ إِذَا خَرَجَ مِنَ الْخَلَاءِ قَالَ: "أَلْحَمْدُ لِلَّهِ الَّذِي أَذْهَبَ عَنِّي الْأَذَى وَعَافَانِي". رَوَاهُ ابْنُ مَاجَهَ.

374 **Anas** reported that when Allah's Messenger (peace and blessings of Allah be upon him) came out from privy, he said: Praise be to Allah Who has removed injurious things from me and kept me in health. *(Ibn Majah)*

٣٧٥ـ وَعَنِ ابْنِ مَسْعُودٍ، قَالَ: لَمَّا قَدِمَ وَفْدُ الْجِنِّ عَلَى النَّبِيِّ ﷺ قَالُوا: يَا رَسُولَ اللهِ! إِنَّهُ أَمَنْتَكَ أَنْ يَسْتَنْجُوا بِعَظْمٍ أَوْ رَوْثَةٍ أَوْ حُمَمَةٍ؛ فَإِنَّ اللهَ جَعَلَ لَنَا فِيهَا رِزْقًا. فَنَهَانَا رَسُولُ اللهِ ﷺ عَنْ ذَلِكَ. رَوَاهُ أَبُو دَاوُدَ.

375 **Ibn Mas'ud** reported that when a delegation of Jinn came to Allah's Apostle (peace and blessings of Allah be upon him), they said: Allah's Messenger, prohibit your people from cleansing themselves with bone or dung or with charcoal. Allah has made therein our provision; thereupon Allah's Messenger (peace and blessings of Allah be upon him) prohibited us (from their use). *(Abu Dawud)*

CHAPTER 11

PERTAINING TO TOOTH BRUSH (*MISWAK*)

Section I الْفَصْلُ الْأَوَّلُ

٣٧٦ ـ عَنْ أَبِى هُرَيْرَةَ ، رَضِىَ اللهُ عَنْهُ ، قَالَ : قَالَ رَسُولُ اللهِ ﷺ : لَوْلَا
أَنْ أَشُقَّ عَلَى أُمَّتِى لَأَمَرْتُهُمْ بِتَأْخِيرِ الْعِشَاءِ ، وَ بِالسِّوَاكِ عِنْدَ كُلِّ
صَلَاةٍ . مُتَّفَقٌ عَلَيْهِ .

376 Abu Huraira (may Allah be pleased with him) reported
Allah's Messenger (peace and blessings of Allah be upon him)
as saying: If it were not burdensome for (the people of) my
Ummah, I would have ordered them (to observe) night prayer
late and use *miswak* (tooth brush) at every prayer.

(*Agreed upon*)

٣٧٧ ـ وَعَنْ شُرَيْحِ بْنِ هَانِئٍ ، قَالَ : سَأَلْتُ عَائِشَةَ : بِأَىِّ شَىْءٍ كَانَ يَبْدَأُ
رَسُولُ اللهِ ﷺ إِذَا دَخَلَ بَيْتَهُ ؟ قَالَتْ : بِالسِّوَاكِ . رَوَاهُ مُسْلِمٌ .

377 Shuraih b. Hani reported: I asked 'Ā'isha what thing did
Allah's Messenger (peace and blessings of Allah be upon him)
start doing first on entering the house. She said: (He started
with the use) of *miwak*. (*Muslim*)

٣٧٨ ـ وَعَنْ حُذَيْفَةَ ، قَالَ : كَانَ النَّبِىُّ ﷺ إِذَا قَامَ لِلتَّهَجُّدِ مِنَ اللَّيْلِ يَشُوصُ
فَاهُ بِالسِّوَاكِ . مُتَّفَقٌ عَلَيْهِ .

378 Hudhaifa reported that when Allah's Apostle (peace and
blessings of Allah be upon him) got up for Tahajjud prayer,
he rinsed his mouth with *miswak*. (*Agreed upon*)

٣٧٩ ـ وَعَنْ عَائِشَةَ ، رَضِىَ اللهُ عَنْهَا ، قَالَتْ : قَالَ رَسُولُ اللهِ ﷺ : عَشْرٌ
مِنَ الْفِطْرَةِ : قَصُّ الشَّارِبِ ، وَ إِعْفَاءُ اللِّحْيَةِ ، وَ السِّوَاكُ ، وَ اسْتِنْشَاقُ
الْمَاءِ ، وَ قَصُّ الْأَظْفَارِ ، وَ غَسْلُ الْبَرَاجِمِ ، وَ نَتْفُ الْإِبِطِ ، وَحَلْقُ الْعَانَةِ

وَ انْتِقَاصُ الْمَاءِ — يَعْنِى الْإِسْتِنْجَاءَ — قَالَ الرَّاوِى : وَنَسِيتُ الْعَاشِرَةَ

إِلَّا أَنْ تَكُونَ الْمَضْمَضَةَ . رَوَاهُ مُسْلِمٌ

وَ فِى رِوَايَةٍ : "الْخِتَانُ" بَدَلَ :"إِعْفَاءُ اللِّحْيَةِ" : لَمْ أَجِدْ هٰذِهِ

الرِّوَايَةَ فِى "الصَّحِيْحَيْنِ" وَلَا فِى كِتَابِ "الْحُمَيْدِيِّ" :

وَ لٰكِنْ ذَكَرَهَا صَاحِبُ "الْجَامِعِ" وَكَذَا الْخَطَّابِيُّ فِى "مَعَالِمِ السُّنَنِ" :

379 **'A'isha** (may Allah be pleased with her) reported Allah's Messenger (peace and blessings of Allah be upon him) as saying: Ten are (the acts quite close to) the *Fitrah*[1] the clipping of moustache, growing of long beard, use of *miswak*; snuffing up water in the nostrils; cutting of nails; washing of joints; removing of hair under the armpits; and the shaving of pubes; *intiqas* i.e. cleansing private parts of oneself with water. The narrator said: I have forgotten the tenth but it may have been rinsing the mouth. (*Muslim*)

And in a version there is "circumcision" instead of "growin of long beard". I have not found this narration in two Sahihs or in Humaidi's book but the author of *Jami'* i.e. *Al-Jami' Al-Usul* mentioned it as did Khattabi in *Ma'alim as-Sunan.*

1. It is very difficult to render the Arabic term *fitrah* into English. On some occasions, it denotes original constitution or disposition, with which a child comes into the world, as contrasted with qualities or inclinations acquired during life. On other occasion, it implies the spiritual inclination inherent in man in his unspoilt state. In the above mentioned hadith *fitrah* stands for the Sunnah of Allah's Apostles; for in a hadith transmitted on the authority of Abu 'Awana, there is a word Sunnah instead of *fitrah*. The conduct of the Apostles is quite close to nature. Some of the commentators have explained this word as the religion of Islam, since it is given to man by the same Lord Who has created nature and thus both nature and Islam are quite akin to each other. Some of the scholars are of the view that *fitrah* here implies the inner sense of cleanliness in a man which is a proof of his moral and mental health.

٣٨٠ - عَنْ أَبِى دَاؤُدَ بِرِوَايَةِ عَتَّارِ بْنِ يَاسِرٍ

380 Abu Dawud narrated on the authority of 'Ammar b. Yāsir.

Section II الْفَصْلُ الثَّانِي

٣٨١ـ عَنْ عَائِشَةَ، قَالَتْ: قَالَ رَسُوْلُ اللهِ ﷺ: أَسِّوَاكُ مَطْهَرَةٌ لِلْفَمِ، مَرْضَاةٌ لِلرَّبِّ " رَوَاهُ الشَّافِعِيُّ، وَ أَحْمَدُ، وَ الدَّارِمِيُّ، وَ النَّسَائِيُّ، وَ رَوَاهُ الْبُخَارِيُّ فِيْ "صَحِيْحِهِ" بِلَا إِسْنَادٍ.

381 **'A'isha** reported Allah's Messenger (peace and blessings of Allah be upon him) as saying: *Miswak* is the purifier of the mouth and (the means of) earning the pleasure of the Lord. (*Transmitted by Shafi'i, Ahmad, Darimi, Nasa'i and Bukhari transmitted in his Sahih without the chain of transmission.*)

٣٨٢ـ وَعَنْ أَبِيْ أَيُّوْبَ، قَالَ: قَالَ رَسُوْلُ اللهِ ﷺ: أَرْبَعٌ مِنْ سُنَنِ الْمُرْسَلِيْنَ: أَلْحَيَاءُ ـ وَ يُرْوَى الْخِتَانُ ـ، وَ التَّعَطُّرُ، وَالسِّوَاكُ، وَالنِّكَاحُ: رَوَاهُ التِّرْمِذِيُّ.

382 **Abu Ayyub** reported Allah's Messenger (peace and blessings of Allah be upon him) having said: Four are the characteristics (which may be called) the *Sunan* (the practices) of messengers of Allah: Modesty, but some say: Circumcision; the use of perfume, *miswak* and marriage. (*Tirmidhi*)

٣٨٣ـ وَعَنْ عَائِشَةَ، قَالَتْ: كَانَ النَّبِيُّ ﷺ لَا يَرْقُدُ مِنْ لَيْلٍ وَّ لَا نَهَارٍ فَيَسْتَيْقِظُ، إِلَّا يَتَسَوَّكُ قَبْلَ أَنْ يَتَوَضَّأَ. رَوَاهُ أَحْمَدُ وَأَبُوْ دَاوُدَ.

383 **'A'isha** reported that never did Allah's Apostle (peace and blessings of Allah be upon him) get up after sleep by night or by day without using *miswak* before performing ablution.
(*Ahmad and Abu Dawud*)

٣٨٤ـ وَعَنْهَا، قَالَتْ: كَانَ النَّبِيُّ ﷺ يَسْتَاكُ، فَيُعْطِيْنِي السِّوَاكَ لِأَغْسِلَهُ، فَأَبْدَأُ بِهِ فَأَسْتَاكُ، ثُمَّ أَغْسِلُهُ وَ أَدْفَعُهُ إِلَيْهِ. رَوَاهُ أَبُوْ دَاوُدَ.

384 It is reported on the same authority that Allah's Messenger (peace and blessings of Allah be upon him) used *miswak* and then he gave the *miswak* to me so that I should wash it. I first used it myself then washed it and then handed it over to him. *(Abu Dawud)*

Section III اَلْفَصْلُ الثَّالِثُ

٣٨٥ ـ وَعَنِ ابْنِ عُمَرَ، أَنَّ النَّبِيَّ ﷺ قَالَ: "أَرَانِي فِي الْمَنَامِ أَتَسَوَّكُ بِسِوَاكٍ،
فَجَاءَنِي رَجُلَانِ أَحَدُهُمَا أَكْبَرُ مِنَ الْآخَرِ، فَنَاوَلْتُ السِّوَاكَ الْأَصْغَرَ مِنْهُمَا،
فَقِيلَ لِي: كَبِّرْ، فَدَفَعْتُهُ إِلَى الْأَكْبَرِ مِنْهُمَا. مُتَّفَقٌ عَلَيْهِ .

385 **Ibn 'Umar** reported that Allah's Apostle (peace and blessings of Allah be upon him) said: I saw in a dream that I was using a *miswak* that there came to me two persons; one of them older than the other. I handed over the *miswak* to the younger amongst them. It was said to me (I had a Divine suggestion to give that to) the older one and so I passed it on to the older one amongst them. *(Agreed upon)*

٣٨٦ ـ وَعَنْ أَبِي أُمَامَةَ، أَنَّ رَسُولَ اللهِ ﷺ قَالَ: "مَا جَاءَنِي جِبْرِيلُ عَلَيْهِ
السَّلَامُ قَطُّ إِلَّا أَمَرَنِي بِالسِّوَاكِ، لَقَدْ خَشِيتُ أَنْ أُحْفِيَ مُقَدَّمَ فِيَّ". رَوَاهُ
أَحْمَدُ .

386 **Abu Umama** reported Allah's Messenger (peace and blessings of Allah be upon him) as saying: Never did Gabriel come to me without commanding me to use *miswak* with the result that I was afraid of chafing the front of my mouth. *(Ahmad)*

٣٨٤ ـ وَعَنْ أَنَسٍ، قَالَ: قَالَ رَسُولُ اللهِ ﷺ، لَقَدْ أَكْثَرْتُ عَلَيْكُمْ فِي
السِّوَاكِ". رَوَاهُ الْبُخَارِيُّ .

387 **Anas** reported Allah's Messenger (peace and blessings of Allah be upon him) as saying: I have very much stressed upon you the use of *miswak*. *(Bukhari)*

٣٨٨ ـ وَعَنْ عَائِشَةَ ، رَضِيَ اللهُ عَنْهَا ، قَالَتْ ، كَانَ رَسُوْلُ اللهِ ﷺ يَسْتَنُّ وَ
عِنْدَهُ رَجُلَانِ ، أَحَدُهُمَا أَكْبَرُ مِنَ الْأَخَرِ ، فَأُوْحِىَ إِلَيْهِ فِىْ فَضْلِ السِّوَاكِ
أَنْ كَبِّرْ ، أَعْطِ السِّوَاكَ أَكْبَرَهُمَا . رَوَاهُ أَبُوْ دَاؤدَ .

388 ‘Ā’isha (may Allah be pleased with her) reported that Allah's
Messenger (peace and blessings of Allah be upon him) was
using *miswak* and there were two persons with him: One of
them was older than the other, and he (the Holy Prophet)
received revelation pertaining to the merit of *miswak* and (to
observe the order of preference) for the older one and to
give *miswak* to the older one. (*Abu Dawud*)

٣٨٩ ـ وَعَنْهَا ، قَالَتْ ، قَالَ رَسُوْلُ اللهِ ﷺ : تَفْضُلُ الصَّلَاةُ الَّتِىْ يُسْتَاكُ لَهَا
عَلَى الصَّلَاةِ الَّتِىْ لَا يُسْتَاكُ لَهَا سَبْعِيْنَ ضِعْفًا . رَوَاهُ الْبَيْهَقِىُّ فِىْ
" شُعَبِ الْإِيْمَانِ "

389 It is reported on the same authority that Allah's Messenger
(peace and blessings of Allah be upon him) said: The preference for prayer (with ablution) in which *miswak* is used to
prayer (with ablution) in which it is not used, is seventy
times. (*Baihaqi in Shu‘ab-ul-Iman*)

٣٩٠ ـ وَعَنْ أَبِىْ سَلَمَةَ ، عَنْ زَيْدِ بْنِ خَالِدٍ الْجُهَنِىِّ ، قَالَ : سَمِعْتُ رَسُوْلَ اللهِ
ﷺ يَقُوْلُ : " لَوْ لَا أَنْ أَشُقَّ عَلَى أُمَّتِىْ ، لَأَمَرْتُهُمْ بِالسِّوَاكِ عِنْدَ كُلِّ صَلَاةٍ
وَ لَأَخَّرْتُ صَلَاةَ الْعِشَاءِ إِلَى ثُلُثِ اللَّيْلِ " قَالَ : فَكَانَ زَيْدُ بْنُ خَالِدٍ يَشْهَدُ
الصَّلَوَاتِ فِى الْمَسْجِدِ وَ سِوَاكُهُ عَلَى أُذُنِهِ مَوْضِعَ الْقَلَمِ مِنْ أُذُنِ
الْكَاتِبِ . لَا يَقُوْمُ إِلَى الصَّلَاةِ إِلَّا اسْتَنَّ ، ثُمَّ رَدَّهُ إِلَى مَوْضِعِهِ . رَوَاهُ
التِّرْمِذِىُّ ، وَ أَبُوْ دَاؤدَ إِلَّا أَنَّهُ لَمْ يَذْكُرْ : " وَلَأَخَّرْتُ صَلَاةَ الْعِشَاءِ
إِلَى ثُلُثِ اللَّيْلِ " وَ قَالَ التِّرْمِذِىُّ : هٰذَا حَدِيْثٌ حَسَنٌ صَحِيْحٌ .

390 Abu Salama reported Zaid b. Khalid Al-Juhani as saying: I
heard Allah's Messenger (peace and blessings of Allah be upon

him) as saying: If it were not burdensome upon my Ummah I would have commanded them to use *miswak* at every prayer and to delay in night prayer till the third part of the night is over. Zaid b. Khalid attended prayers in the mosque with his *miswak* over his ears, the place where the scribe places his pen on the ear, and he did not pray without using *miswak*. After that he placed it at its proper place. (*Transmitted by Tirmidhi, Abu Dawud, but with this exception that he made no mention : I would have delayed the night prayer to a third part of the night. Tirmidhi stated : this is a hasan sahih hadith*)

CHAPTER 12
THE SUNNAN OF *WUDŪ* (ABLUTION)
Section I الْفَصْلُ الْأَوَّلُ

٣٩١ ـ عَنْ أَبِي هُرَيْرَةَ ، قَالَ : قَالَ رَسُولُ اللهِ ﷺ : "إِذَا اسْتَيْقَظَ أَحَدُكُمْ
مِنْ نَوْمِهِ فَلَا يَغْمِسْ يَدَهُ فِي الْإِنَاءِ حَتَّى يَغْسِلَهَا ثَلَاثًا ، فَإِنَّهُ لَا يَدْرِي أَيْنَ
بَاتَتْ يَدُهُ" ؛ مُتَّفَقٌ عَلَيْهِ.

391 Abu Huraira reported Allah's Massenger (peace and blessings of Allah be upon him) as saying : When anyone of you wakes up from the sleep, he should not dip his hand in the utensil, till he has washed it, for he does not know as to where his hand had spent the night.   (*Agreed upon*)

٣٩٢ ـ وَعَنْهُ ، قَالَ : قَالَ رَسُولُ اللهِ ﷺ : "إِذَا اسْتَيْقَظَ أَحَدُكُمْ مِنْ مَنَامِهِ
فَتَوَضَّأَ فَلْيَسْتَنْثِرْ ثَلَاثًا ، فَإِنَّ الشَّيْطَانَ يَبِيتُ عَلَى خَيْشُومِهِ : مُتَّفَقٌ عَلَيْهِ.

392 It is reported on the same authority that Allah's Messenger (peace and blessings of Allah be upon him) said: When any-one amongst you wakes up from his sleep, and performs ablution he should clean his nose thrice, for the Satan spends the night in the interior of his nostrils.[1]   (*Agreed upon*)

1. The presence of impurities in the nostrils has very unwholesome effect on the mind and the sensibilities of a man, and he sees nightmare in sleep (Shah Waliullah, *Hujjatullah al-Balighah*, Vol. I, p. 1457).

٣٩٣ ـ وَقِيلَ لِعَبْدِ اللهِ بْنِ زَيْدِ بْنِ عَاصِمٍ : كَيْفَ كَانَ رَسُولُ اللهِ ﷺ يَتَوَضَّأُ؟ فَدَعَا
بِوَضُوءٍ فَأَفْرَغَ عَلَى يَدَيْهِ فَغَسَلَ يَدَيْهِ مَرَّتَيْنِ مَرَّتَيْنِ ، ثُمَّ
مَضْمَضَ وَاسْتَنْثَرَ ثَلَاثًا ، ثُمَّ غَسَلَ وَجْهَهُ ثَلَاثًا ، ثُمَّ غَسَلَ يَدَيْهِ
مَرَّتَيْنِ مَرَّتَيْنِ إِلَى الْمِرْفَقَيْنِ ، ثُمَّ مَسَحَ رَأْسَهُ بِيَدَيْهِ ، فَأَقْبَلَ بِهِمَا
وَأَدْبَرَ ، بَدَأَ بِمُقَدَّمِ رَأْسِهِ ، ثُمَّ ذَهَبَ بِهِمَا إِلَى قَفَاهُ ، ثُمَّ رَدَّهُمَا حَتَّى
رَجَعَ إِلَى الْمَكَانِ الَّذِي بَدَأَ مِنْهُ ، ثُمَّ غَسَلَ رِجْلَيْهِ ـ رَوَاهُ مَالِكٌ ، وَ
النَّسَائِيُّ. وَلِأَبِي دَاوُدَ نَحْوَهُ ذَكَرَهُ صَاحِبُ "الْجَامِعِ" :

393 It was said to 'Abdullah b. Zaid: How did Allah's Messenger
(peace and blessings of Allah be upon him) perform ablution?
He called for water of ablution and poured it upon his hands
and washed both his hands twice.   He then rinsed the mouth
and cleaned the nose thrice.   He then washed his face thrice.
He then washed his hands upto the elbow twice; He then
wiped his head with his hands (first) bringing them forward
and then bringing them back, starting from the front part of
his head and then taking them back to the nape of the neck
and then returning to the place from where he started.   He
then washed his feet.   (*Transmitted by Malik, Nasa'i and Abu
Dawud.   The author of al Jami' mentioned it likewise.*)

٣٩٢ ـ وَفِي الْمُتَّفَقِ عَلَيْهِ : قِيلَ لِعَبْدِ اللهِ بْنِ زَيْدِ بْنِ عَاصِمٍ : تَوَضَّأْ لَنَا

وُضُوءَ رَسُولِ اللهِ ﷺ ، فَدَعَا بِإِنَاءٍ ، فَأَكْفَأَ مِنْهُ عَلَى يَدَيْهِ ، فَغَسَلَهُمَا

ثَلَاثًا ، ثُمَّ أَدْخَلَ يَدَهُ فَاسْتَخْرَجَهَا ، فَمَضْمَضَ وَاسْتَنْشَقَ مِنْ كَفٍّ

وَاحِدٍ ، فَعَلَ ذَلِكَ ثَلَاثًا ، ثُمَّ أَدْخَلَ يَدَهُ فَاسْتَخْرَجَهَا فَغَسَلَ وَجْهَهُ

ثَلَاثًا ، ثُمَّ أَدْخَلَ يَدَهُ فَاسْتَخْرَجَهَا ، فَغَسَلَ يَدَيْهِ إِلَى الْمِرْفَقَيْنِ مَرَّتَيْنِ

مَرَّتَيْنِ ، ثُمَّ أَدْخَلَ يَدَهُ فَاسْتَخْرَجَهَا ، فَمَسَحَ بِرَأْسِهِ ، فَأَقْبَلَ بِيَدِهِ وَأَدْبَرَ

ثُمَّ غَسَلَ رِجْلَيْهِ إِلَى الْكَعْبَيْنِ ، ثُمَّ قَالَ : هَكَذَا كَانَ وُضُوءُ رَسُولِ اللهِ صَلَّى

اللهُ عَلَيْهِ وَسَلَّمَ .

وَفِي رِوَايَةٍ : فَأَقْبَلَ بِهِمَا وَأَدْبَرَ ، بَدَأَ بِمُقَدَّمِ رَأْسِهِ ، ثُمَّ ذَهَبَ

بِهِمَا إِلَى قَفَاهُ ، ثُمَّ رَدَّهُمَا حَتَّى رَجَعَ إِلَى الْمَكَانِ الَّذِي بَدَأَ مِنْهُ ،

ثُمَّ غَسَلَ رِجْلَيْهِ

وَفِي رِوَايَةٍ : فَمَضْمَضَ وَاسْتَنْشَقَ وَاسْتَنْثَرَ ثَلَاثًا بِثَلَاثِ

غُرُفَاتٍ مِنْ مَاءٍ .

وَفِي أُخْرَى : فَمَضْمَضَ وَاسْتَنْشَقَ مِنْ كَفَّةٍ وَاحِدَةٍ ، فَفَعَلَ

ذٰلِكَ ثَلَاثًا .

وَفِى رِوَايَةٍ لِلْبُخَارِىِّ : نَمَسَحَ رَأْسَهُ فَأَقْبَلَ بِهِمَا وَ أَدْبَرَ مَرَّةً وَّاحِدَةً ،

ثُمَّ غَسَلَ رِجْلَيْهِ إِلَى الْكَعْبَيْنِ .

وَفِى أُخْرٰى لَهُ : فَمَضْمَضَ وَ اسْتَنْثَرَ ثَلَاثَ مَرَّاتٍ مِنْ غُرْفَةٍ وَّاحِدَةٍ .

394 In the version of *Bukhari* and *Muslim* (the words are): It was said to 'Abdullah b. Zaid b. 'Asim: Perform ablution for us (similar) to the ablution (performed) by Allah's Messenger (peace and blessings of Allah be upon him). (In response to our request) he called for water and poured some out of that upon his hands and washed (each one of them) thrice. He then put his hand in water and then brought it out (filling his palm with water), and then rinsed (his mouth) and snuffed up water (in the nose) from the palm of one hand. He did this thrice. He again put his hand (in water) and then brought it out and washed his face thrice. He again put his hand in water and brought it out (filling his palm with water) and washed his each hand upto the elbow twice. He again put his hand (in water) and brought it out and then wiped his head. He (first moved) his hand forward and (then) backward. He then washed his feet upto the ankles and said: This is how Allah's Messenger (peace and blessings of Allah be upon him) performed the ablution.

In a version (the wording is): He moved them (his hands) to the front and the back., he started with the front of his head and then took them back to the nape of his neck. He then returned them till he reached the place from which he began. Then he washed his feet.

In a version (the words are): He rinsed (his mouth) snuffed up water (in the nose) and cleaned (his nostrils) thrice with three handfuls of water.

In another version (the words are): He rinsed (his mouth) snuffed up (water in the nostrils) with one palm and he did this thrice. And in the version of *Bukhari* (the words are): He wiped his hand, and brought (his hands) forward and then (moved) them) backward once. He then washed his feet upto the ankles.

And in another version (of *Bukhari*, the words are): He rinsed (his mouth) and cleaned (his nostrils) three times from one handful (of water).

٣٩٥ - وَعَنْ عَبْدِ اللهِ بنِ عَبَّاسٍ ، قَالَ : تَوَضَّأَ رَسُولُ اللهِ ﷺ مَرَّةً مَرَّةً لَمْ يَزِدْ عَلَى هٰذَا . رَوَاهُ الْبُخَارِيُّ .

395 'Abdullah b. 'Abbas reported: Allah's Messenger (peace and blessings of Allah be upon him) performed ablution (washing the parts of the body) only one time and he made no addition to that. (*Bukhari*)

٣٩٦ - وَعَنْ عَبْدِ اللهِ بنِ زَيْدٍ : أَنَّ النَّبِيَّ ﷺ تَوَضَّأَ مَرَّتَيْنِ مَرَّتَيْنِ . رَوَاهُ الْبُخَارِيُّ .

396 'Abdullah b. Zaid reported that as Allah's Apostle (peace and blessings of Allah be upon him) performed ablution, he (washed the different parts of his body) twice. (*Bukhari*)

٣٩٧ - وَعَنْ عُثْمَانَ ، رَضِيَ اللهُ عَنْهُ ، أَنَّهُ تَوَضَّأَ بِالْمَقَاعِدِ ، فَقَالَ : أَلَا أُرِيكُمْ وُضُوءَ رَسُولِ اللهِ ﷺ ؟ فَتَوَضَّأَ ثَلَاثًا ثَلَاثًا . رَوَاهُ مُسْلِمٌ .

397 'Uthman (may Allah be pleased with him) performed ablution at a place (of sitting at Medina) and said: Should I not show you the ablution of Allah's Messenger (peace and blessings of Allah be upon him) and he performed ablution thrice[1] (i.e. he washed every part of his sacred body thrice). (*Muslim*)

1. We see that the Holy Prophet, while performing ablution, at times washed the different parts of his body once and at times twice and on most of the occasions thrice. The most desirable number is thrice, but once or twice are also permissible.

٣٩٨ - وَعَنْ عَبْدِ اللهِ بنِ عَمْرٍو ، قَالَ : رَجَعْنَا مَعَ رَسُولِ اللهِ ﷺ مِنْ مَكَّةَ إِلَى الْمَدِينَةِ ، حَتَّى إِذَا كُنَّا بِمَاءٍ بِالطَّرِيقِ تَعَجَّلَ قَوْمٌ عِنْدَ الْعَصْرِ ، فَتَوَضَّؤُوا وَهُمْ عِجَالٌ ، فَانْتَهَيْنَا إِلَيْهِمْ وَأَعْقَابُهُمْ تَلُوحُ لَمْ يَمَسَّهَا الْمَاءُ ، فَقَالَ رَسُولُ اللهِ ﷺ : وَيْلٌ لِلْأَعْقَابِ مِنَ النَّارِ ، أَسْبِغُوا الْوُضُوءَ " رَوَاهُ مُسْلِمٌ .

398 'Abdullah b. 'Amr reported: We returned from Mecca to Medina along with Allah's Messenger (peace and blessings of Allah be upon him) till when we (found) water in the way the people made haste at the time of afternoon (prayer) in performing ablution and they were those who hastened (to do so). And when we reached them, their heels were dry (as if) water had not touched them. Thereupon Allah's Messenger (peace and blessings of Allah be upon him) said: Woe to the heels because of Hell Fire. Perform ablution well. (*Muslim*)

٣٩٩ ـ وَعَنِ الْمُغِيْرَةِ بْنِ شُعْبَةَ، قَالَ: إِنَّ النَّبِيَّ ﷺ تَوَضَّأَ فَمَسَحَ بِنَاصِيَتِهِ
وَعَلَى الْعِمَامَةِ وَعَلَى الْخُفَّيْنِ، رَوَاهُ مُسْلِمٌ.

399 Mughira b. Shu'ba reported that Allah's Apostle (peace and blessings of Allah be upon him) performed ablution, wiping his forehead, and then (taking his hand) over the turban and then over his two inner-shoes. (*Muslim*)

Section II   اَلْفَصْلُ الثَّانِيْ

٤٠٠ ـ وَعَنْ عَائِشَةَ، قَالَتْ: كَانَ النَّبِيُّ ﷺ يُحِبُّ التَّيَمُّنَ مَا اسْتَطَاعَ فِيْ شَأْنِهِ
كُلِّهِ: فِيْ طُهُوْرِهِ وَتَرَجُّلِهِ وَتَنَعُّلِهِ. مُتَّفَقٌ عَلَيْهِ.

400 'A'isha reported that Allah's Apostle (peace and blessings of Allah be upon him) loved to begin with his right hand side all his affairs, as far as it lay in his power: In his purification, combing his hair, and putting on his sandals. (*Agreed upon*)

٤٠١ ـ عَنْ أَبِيْ هُرَيْرَةَ، قَالَ: قَالَ رَسُوْلُ اللهِ ﷺ: إِذَا لَبِسْتُمْ وَإِذَا تَوَضَّأْتُمْ
فَابْدَؤُوْا بِأَيَامِنِكُمْ، رَوَاهُ أَحْمَدُ، وَأَبُوْ دَاوُدَ.

401 Abu Huraira reported Allah's Messenger (peace and blessings of Allah be upon him) as saying: Whenever you dress and whenever you perform ablution, begin from your right side.
(*Ahmad and Abu Dawud*)

٤٠٢ ـ وَعَنْ سَعِيْدِ بْنِ زَيْدٍ، قَالَ: قَالَ رَسُوْلُ اللهِ ﷺ: لَا وُضُوْءَ لِمَنْ لَمْ يَذْكُرِ
اسْمَ اللهِ عَلَيْهِ، رَوَاهُ التِّرْمِذِيُّ، وَابْنُ مَاجَةَ.

402 Sa'd b. Zaid reported Allah's Messenger (peace and blessings of Allah be upon him) as saying: No ablution (is perfect) for which (while performing) the name of Allah is not mentioned. (*Tirmidhmi and Ibn Majah*)

م.ٯ - وَرَوَاهُ أَحْمَدُ، وَأَبُوْ دَاوُدَ عَنْ أَبِىْ هُرَيْرَةَ

403 (The above mentioned hadith) is transmitted by Ahmad, Abu Dawud on the authority of Abu Huraira.

م.ٯ - وَالدَّارِمِىُّ عَنْ أَبِىْ سَعِيْدِ الْخُدْرِىِّ ،عَنْ أَبِيْهِ ،وَزَادُوْا فِىْ أَوَّلِهِ ؟ لَا
صَلَاةَ لِمَنْ لَا وُضُوْءَ لَهُ ؟

404 And Darimi from Abu Sa'id al-Khudri, from his father, and they made this addition in the beginning: One is not (supposed) to have observed prayer who has not performed ablution.

٥.م - وَعَنْ لَقِيْطِ بْنِ صَبِرَةَ، قَالَ . قُلْتُ يَا رَسُوْلَ اللهِ! أَخْبِرُوْنِىْ عَنِ الْوُضُوْءَ
قَالَ ؟ أَسْبِغِ الْوُضُوْءَ، وَخَلِّلْ بَيْنَ الْأَصَابِع ، وَبَالِغْ فِى الْإِسْتِنْشَاقِ إِلَّا أَنْ
تَكُوْنَ صَائِمًا. رَوَاهُ أَبُوْ دَاوُدَ، وَ التِّرْمِذِىُّ ،وَ النَّسَائِىُّ ،وَ رَوَى ابْنُ مَاجَّةَ،
وَ الدَّارِمِىُّ إِلَى قَوْلِهِ ؟ بَيْنَ الْأَصَابِع ؟

405 Laqit b. Sabira reported: I said: Allah's Messenger (peace and blessings of Allah be upon him)! Tell me about ablution. Thereupon he said: Perform ablution complete (in all respect), and let water flow between the fingers, and snuff up water (in the nostrils) well except when you are observing fast. (*Transmitted by Abu Dawud, Tirmidhi, Nasai', Ibn Majah and Darimi upto the words: Between the fingers*)

م.ٯ - وَعَنِ ابْنِ عَبَّاسٍ ،قَالَ : قَالَ رَسُوْلُ اللهِ ﷺ ؟ إِذَا تَوَضَّأْتَ فَخَلِّلْ بَيْنَ
أَصَابِع يَدَيْكَ وَ رِجْلَيْكَ ؟ رَوَاهُ التِّرْمِذِىُّ . وَ رَوَى ابْنُ مَاجَّةَ نَحْوَهُ. وَ
قَالَ التِّرْمِذِىُّ : هٰذَا حَدِيْثٌ غَرِيْبٌ .

406 Ibn 'Abbas reported Allah's Messenger (peace and blessings of Allah be upon him) as saying: Whenever you perform

ablution, let the water flow between the fingers of your hands
and of your toes. (*Transmitted by Tirmidhi, Ibn Majah and
Tirmidhi said : This is a gharib hadith.*)

٤٠٧ - وَعَنِ الْمُسْتَوْرِدِ بْنِ شَدَّادٍ، قَالَ دَأَيْتُ رَسُوْلَ اللهِ ﷺ إِذَا تَوَضَّأَ
يَدْلُكُ أَصَابِعَ رِجْلَيْهِ بِخِنْصِرِهِ . رَوَاهُ التِّرْمِذِيُّ ، وَ أَبُوْ دَاوُدَ ، وَ
ابْنُ مَاجَةَ .

407 Mustawrid b. Shaddad reported: I saw that when Allah's
Messenger (peace and blessings of Allah be upon him) performed ablution, he rubbed the fingers of his feet with the
little finger (of his hand).

　　　　　　　　　　　(*Tirmidhi, Abu Dawud and Ibn Majah*)

٤٠٨ - وَعَنْ أَنَسٍ ، قَالَ : كَانَ رَسُوْلُ اللهِ ﷺ إِذَا تَوَضَّأَ أَخَذَ كَفًّا مِنْ مَاءٍ
فَأَدْخَلَهُ تَحْتَ حَنَكِهِ ، فَخَلَّلَ بِهِ لِحْيَتَهُ ، وَ قَالَ : "هٰكَذَا أَمَرَنِيْ رَبِّيْ" رَوَاهُ
أَبُوْ دَاوُدَ .

408 Anas reported that whenever Allah's Messenger (peace and
blessings of Allah be upon him) performed ablution, he took
a handful of water, and inserted it beneath his chin and let it
flow in his beard and said: This is how Allah has commanded[1] me. (*Abu Dawud*)

　　1. This shows that the Holy Prophet received the command of God
　　　　besides the Qur'ān also.

٤٠٩ - وَعَنْ عُثْمَانَ رَضِيَ اللهُ عَنْهُ : أَنَّ النَّبِيَّ ﷺ كَانَ يُخَلِّلُ لِحْيَتَهُ . رَوَاهُ
التِّرْمِذِيُّ وَ الدَّارِمِيُّ .

409 'Uthman (may Allah be pleased with him) reported that
Allah's Apostle (peace and blessings of Allah be upon him)
let the water flow through his beard. (*Tirmidhi and Darimi*)

٤١٠ - وَعَنْ أَبِيْ حَيَّةَ ، قَالَ : رَأَيْتُ عَلِيًّا تَوَضَّأَ نَغْسَلَ كَفَّيْهِ حَتَّى
أَنْقَاهُمَا ، ثُمَّ مَضْمَضَ ثَلَاثًا ، وَ اسْتَنْشَقَ ثَلَاثًا ، وَ غَسَلَ وَجْهَهُ

ثَلَاثًا، وَ ذِرَاعَيْهِ ثَلَاثًا، وَ مَسَحَ بِرَأْسِهِ مَرَّةً، ثُمَّ غَسَلَ قَدَمَيْهِ
إِلَى الْكَعْبَيْنِ، ثُمَّ قَامَ فَأَخَذَ فَضْلَ طُهُورِهِ فَشَرِبَهُ وَ هُوَ قَائِمٌ، ثُمَّ
قَالَ أَحْبَبْتُ أَنْ أُرِيَكُمْ كَيْفَ كَانَ طُهُورُ رَسُولِ اللهِ ﷺ. رَوَاهُ
التِّرْمِذِيُّ، وَ النَّسَائِيُّ.

410 Abu Hayya reported: I saw 'Ali performing ablution. He washed the palms of his hands till he cleaned them. He then rinsed (the mouth) thrice, and then snuffed up (water in the nostrils) thrice, and washed his face thrice, and forearm thrice and wiped his head once. He then washed his feet upto the ankles. He then stood up and then taking hold of the remaining part (of the water of ablution) took it, while standing. Then he said: It was my pleasure to show you how the Messenger of Allah (peace and blessings be upon him) performed his ablution. (*Tirmidhi and Nasa'i*)

٤١١ - وَ عَنْ عَبْدِ خَيْرٍ، قَالَ: نَحْنُ جُلُوسٌ تَنْظُرُ إِلَى عَلِيٍّ حِينَ تَوَضَّأَ، فَأَدْخَلَ
يَدَهُ الْيُمْنَى فَمَلَأَ فَمَهُ، فَمَضْمَضَ وَ اسْتَنْشَقَ، وَ نَثَرَ بِيَدِهِ الْيُسْرَى،
فَعَلَ هَذَا ثَلَاثَ مَرَّاتٍ، ثُمَّ قَالَ: مَنْ سَرَّهُ أَنْ يَنْظُرَ إِلَى طُهُورِ رَسُولِ
اللهِ ﷺ، فَهَذَا طُهُورُهُ، رَوَاهُ الدَّارِمِيُّ.

411 'Abd Khair reported: We were sitting and watching 'Ali as he performed ablution. He inserted his right hand (in water and then taking a handful) filled his mouth (with water). Then he rinsed (his mouth) and snuffed up (water in the nostrils) and then ejected the (mucus) with his left hand. He did that thrice and then said: He who is pleased to see (how) Allah's Messenger (peace and blessings of Allah be upon him) performed ablution (he should know) that this was (his method) of performing ablution. (*Darimi*)

٤١٢ - وَ عَنْ عَبْدِ اللهِ بْنِ زَيْدٍ، قَالَ: رَأَيْتُ رَسُولَ اللهِ ﷺ مَضْمَضَ وَاسْتَنْشَقَ
مِنْ كَفٍّ وَاحِدٍ، فَعَلَ ذَلِكَ ثَلَاثًا، رَوَاهُ أَبُو دَاوُدَ وَ التِّرْمِذِيُّ.

412 'Abdullah b. Zaid reported: I saw Allah's Messenger (peace
and blessings of Allah be upon him) rinsing his mouth and
snuffing up water (in his nostrils) with one palm and he did
it thrice. (*Abu Dawud, Tirmidhi*)

٤١٣ - وَعَنِ ابْنِ عَبَّاسٍ ، أَنَّ النَّبِيَّ ﷺ مَسَحَ بِرَأْسِهِ ، وَأُذُنَيْهِ : بَاطِنِهِمَا

بِالسَّبَّاحَتَيْنِ ، وَظَاهِرِهِمَا بِإِبْهَامَيْهِ . رَوَاهُ النَّسَائِيُّ ،

413 Ibn 'Abbas reported that Allah's Apostle (peace and blessings
of Allah be upon him) wiped his head and inside of his ears
with forefingers, and their exterior with his thumbs. (*Nasa'i*)

٤١٤ - وَعَنِ الرُّبَيِّعِ بِنْتِ مُعَوِّذٍ : أَنَّهَا رَأَتِ النَّبِيَّ ﷺ يَتَوَضَّأُ ، قَالَتْ

فَمَسَحَ رَأْسَهُ مَا أَقْبَلَ مِنْهُ وَ مَا أَدْبَرَ ، وَ صُدْغَيْهِ . وَ أُذُنَيْهِ مَرَّةً

وَاحِدَةً .

وَفِي رِوَايَةٍ ، أَنَّهُ تَوَضَّأَ فَأَدْخَلَ إِصْبَعَيْهِ فِي جُحْرَى أُذُنَيْهِ :

رَوَاهُ أَبُو دَاوُدَ .

وَرَوَى التِّرْمِذِيُّ الرِّوَايَةَ الأُولَى ، وَ أَحْمَدُ وَ ابْنُ مَاجَةَ الثَّانِيَةَ .

414 Rubayyi' bint Mu'awwidh reported that she saw Allah's Apostle
(peace and blessings of Allah be upon him) performing ablution. She (further) said that he wiped his head—its front
and back, and his temples and his ears once.
    In another version (the words are): He performed ablution
(and in his method of performing) inserted his fingers in the
holes of his ears. (*Abu Dawud and Tirmidhi transmitted the first
version and Ahmad and Ibn Majah, the second one.*)

٤١٥ - وَعَنْ عَبْدِ اللهِ بْنِ زَيْدٍ : أَنَّهُ رَأَى النَّبِيَّ ﷺ تَوَضَّأَ ، وَأَنَّهُ مَسَحَ

رَأْسَهُ بِمَاءٍ غَيْرِ فَضْلِ يَدَيْهِ . رَوَاهُ التِّرْمِذِيُّ وَرَوَاهُ مُسْلِمٌ مَعَ

زَوَائِدَ .

415 'Abdullah b. Zaid reported that he saw Allah's Apostle (peace
and blessings of Allah be upon him) perform ablution and he

wiped his head with water not left over (i.e. freshly taken after washing his) hands[1] (*Tirmidhi and Muslim transmitted it with additions.*)

1. The person performing ablution should dip his hand and get it wet, while wiping over the head, and should not deem those drops of water sufficient for wiping his head which had been left upon his hands while washing them.

٤١٦ - وَعَنْ أَبِى أُمَامَةَ ، ذَكَرَ وُضُوءَ رَسُولِ اللهِ ﷺ ، قَالَ : وَكَانَ يَمْسَحُ

الْمَاقَيْنِ ، وَ قَالَ : اَلْأُذُنَانِ مِنَ الرَّأْسِ . رَوَاهُ ابْنُ مَاجَةَ ، وَ أَبُو دَاوُدَ ،

وَ التِّرْمِذِيُّ . وَ ذَكَرَا . قَالَ حَمَّادٌ : قَالَ لَا أَدْرِى : أَلْأُذُنَانِ مِنَ الرَّأْسِ مِنْ

قَوْلِ أَبِى أُمَامَةَ أَمْ مِنْ قَوْلِ رَسُولِ اللهِ ﷺ

416 Abu Umama while making a mention of the ablution of Allah's Messenger (peace and blessings of Allah be upon him) said: He used to wipe the corners of his eyes[2] and he also said: The ears form a part of the head. (*Transmitted by Ibn Majah, Abu Dawud, Tirmidhi, (and the last two) mentioned that Hammad had said : I do not know whether (the words): The ears form a part of the head is the statement of Abu Umama or the words of Allah's Messenger*[3] *(peace and blessings of Allah be upon him).*

2. *Maq* (ماق) is that corner of the eye which is near the nose and ear.
3. The editor of *Mishkat* Muhammad Nasir-ud-Din al-Bani states: I say it makes no difference (how this hadith has been transmitted to us). It is, however, a fact that it is a Sahih hadith as it has been transmitted on the authority of a group of the companions directly from the Holy Prophet, and one amongst them is Ibn 'Abbas (p. 131).

٤١٧ - وَعَنْ عَمْرِو بْنِ شُعَيْبٍ ، عَنْ أَبِيهِ ، عَنْ جَدِّهِ ، قَالَ : جَاءَ أَعْرَابِيٌّ

إِلَى النَّبِيِّ ﷺ يَسْأَلُهُ عَنِ الْوُضُوءِ ، فَأَرَاهُ ثَلَاثًا ثَلَاثًا ، ثُمَّ قَالَ : هَكَذَا

الْوُضُوءُ ، فَمَنْ زَادَ عَلَى هٰذَا فَقَدْ أَسَاءَ وَ تَعَدَّى وَ ظَلَمَ . رَوَاهُ النَّسَائِيُّ ،

وَ ابْنُ مَاجَةَ . وَ رَوَى أَبُو دَاوُدَ مَعْنَاهُ .

417 'Amr b. Shu'aib reported on the authority of his father who reported it on the authority of his father that he said: A desert Arab came to Allah's Apostle (peace and blessings of

Allah be upon him) and asked him about ablution. He
demonstrated (washing each part of his body) thrice, and
then said: That is (the method) of the ablution. And he
who did more than this, he has done wrong, transgressed the
limit and has oppressed (himself). (*Transmitted by Nasa'i, Ibn
Majah, and Abu Dawud transmitted something to the same effect.*)

٤١٨ - وَ عَنْ عَبْدِ اللهِ بْنِ الْمُغَفَّلِ، أَنَّهُ سَمِعَ ابْنَهُ يَقُولُ: أَللّهُمَّ إِنِّي
أَسْأَلُكَ الْقَصْرَ الْأَبْيَضَ عَنْ يَمِينِ الْجَنَّةِ. قَالَ: أَيْ بُنَيَّ سَلِ اللهَ
الْجَنَّةَ، وَ تَعَوَّذْ بِهِ مِنَ النَّارِ؛ فَإِنِّي سَمِعْتُ رَسُولَ اللهِ ﷺ يَقُولُ:
إِنَّهُ سَيَكُونُ فِي هٰذِهِ الْأُمَّةِ قَوْمٌ يَعْتَدُونَ فِي الطُّهُورِ وَ الدُّعَاءِ رَوَاهُ
أَحْمَدُ، وَ أَبُو دَاوُدَ، وَ ابْنُ مَاجَهْ.

418 ‘**Abdullah b. Mughaffal** reported that he heard his son say:
O Allah, I beg of Thee a white palace in the right side of
Paradise; whereupon he said: Sonny, (only) beg Paradise
from Allah, and seek refuge (with Him) from Hell Fire, for I
heard Allah's Messenger (peace and blessings of Allah be
upon him) as saying: There would be people amongst this
Ummah who would fail to observe moderation in purification
and supplication. (*Ahmad, Abu Dawud and Ibn Majah*)

٤١٩ - وَ عَنْ أُبَيِّ بْنِ كَعْبٍ، عَنِ النَّبِيِّ ﷺ، قَالَ: إِنَّ لِلْوُضُوءِ شَيْطَانًا يُقَالُ
لَهُ: الْوَلَهَانُ، فَاتَّقُوا وَسْوَاسَ الْمَاءِ رَوَاهُ التِّرْمِذِيُّ، وَ ابْنُ مَاجَهْ.
وَ قَالَ التِّرْمِذِيُّ: هٰذَا حَدِيثٌ غَرِيبٌ، وَ لَيْسَ إِسْنَادُهُ بِالْقَوِيِّ عِنْدَ
أَهْلِ الْحَدِيثِ، لِأَنَّا لَا نَعْلَمُ أَحَدًا أَسْنَدَهُ غَيْرَ خَارِجَةَ، وَ هُوَ
لَيْسَ بِالْقَوِيِّ عِنْدَ أَصْحَابِنَا.

419 Ubayy b. Ka‘b reported Allah's Apostle (peace and blessings
of Allah be upon him) as saying: There is a Satan in ablution,
called al-Walahan, so be on your guard against the evil
promptings of (wasting) water. (*Tirmidhi, Ibn Majah and
Tirmidhi said : This is a gharib hadith, and its isnad is not*

authentic according to the scholars of hadith; for we know none who traced it up (to the Holy Prophet) except Kharija, and he is not authentic according to our scholars)

٤٢٠ ـ وَ عَنْ مُعَاذِ بِنْ جَبَلٍ ، قَالَ رَأَيْتُ رَسُولَ اللهِ ﷺ إِذَا تَوَضَّأَ مَسَحَ

وَجْهَهُ بِطَرَفِ ثَوْبِهِ . رَوَاهُ التِّرْمِذِيُّ .

420 Mu'adh b. Jabal reported: I saw Allah's Messenger (peace and blessings of Allah be upon him) wiping his face with the hem of his garment as he performed ablution. (*Tirmidhi*)

٤٢١ ـ وَ عَنْ عَائِشَةَ ، رَضِيَ اللهُ عَنْهَا ، قَالَتْ : كَانَتْ لِرَسُولِ اللهِ ﷺ

خِرْقَةٌ يَتَنَشَّفُ بِهَا أَعْضَاءَهُ بَعْدَ الْوُضُوءِ . رَوَاهُ التِّرْمِذِيُّ ، وَقَالَ هٰذَا

حَدِيثٌ لَيْسَ بِالْقَائِمِ ، وَ أَبُو مُعَاذٍ الرَّاوِى ضَعِيفٌ عِنْدَ أَهْلِ الْحَدِيثِ .

421 'A'isha reported that Allah's Messenger (peace and blessings of Allah be upon him) had a cloth with which he dried his limbs after ablution. (*Transmitted by Tirmidhi who said: This is a tradition which is not valid and Abu Mu'adh, the transmitter is considered to be a weak transmitter in the eyes of scholars of hadith*)

Section III ‌اَلْفَصْلُ الثَّالِثُ

٤٢٢ ـ عَنْ ثَابِتِ بْنِ أَبِى صَفِيَّةَ ، قَالَ : قُلْتُ لِأَبِى جَعْفَرٍ ـ هُوَ مُحَمَّدٌ الْبَاقِرُ ـ

حَدَّثَكَ جَابِرٌ : أَنَّ النَّبِيَّ ﷺ تَوَضَّأَ مَرَّةً مَرَّةً ، وَ مَرَّتَيْنِ وَ مَرَّتَيْنِ ، وَ

ثَلَاثًا وَ ثَلَاثًا ؛ قَالَ : نَعَمْ . رَوَاهُ التِّرْمِذِيُّ ، وَ ابْنُ مَاجَهْ

422 Thabit b. Abi Safiyya reported: I said to Abi Ja'far i.e. Muhammad Baqir, whether Jabir had narrated it to him that Allah's Apostle (peace and blessings of Allah be upon him) performed the ablution (at times cf washing the different parts of his body) once, and (sometimes) twice, and (sometimes) thrice. He said: Yes.[1] (*Tirmidhi, Ibn Majah*)

1. Washing of the parts of body once is the bare minimum, and thrice is excellent. (*Nail-ul-Autar*).

٤٢٣ ـ وَعَنْ عَبْدِ اللهِ بْنِ زَيْدٍ ، قَالَ : إِنَّ رَسُوْلَ اللهِ ﷺ تَوَضَّأَمَرَّتَيْنِ مَرَّتَيْنِ ، وَقَالَ : هُوَ نُوْرٌ عَلَى نُوْرٍ .

423 **'Abdullah b. Zaid** reported that Allah's Messenger (peace and blessings of Allah be upon him) performed the ablution (by washing the concerned parts of his body) twice and said: That is light upon light.

٤٢٤ ـ وَعَنْ عُثْمَانَ ، رَضِيَ اللهُ عَنْهُ ، قَالَ : إِنَّ رَسُوْلَ اللهِ ﷺ تَوَضَّأَ ثَلَاثًا ثَلَاثًا ، وَقَالَ : هٰذَا وُضُوْئِيْ وَ وُضُوْءُ الْأَنْبِيَاءِ قَبْلِيْ ، وَ وُضُوْءُ إِبْرَاهِيْمَ . رَوَاهُمَا رَزِيْنٌ ، وَ النَّوَوِيُّ ضَعَّفَ الثَّانِيَ فِيْ شَرْحِ مُسْلِمٍ .

424 **'Uthman** (may Allah be pleased with him) reported that Allah's Messenger (peace and blessings of Allah be upon him) performed ablution by washing thrice and remarked: That is my ablution and the ablution of the Apostles (gone) before me, and the ablution of Ibrahim. (*Razin transmitted these two (ahadith) but Nawawi in his commentary of the Muslim has declared the second one to be weak*[1])

> 1. Muhammad Nasir-ud-Din Albani states: "The words : 'light upon light' do not seem to be part of hadith as Hafiz al-Mundhari has asserted in *Targhib*. This may be the statement of later (scholars). *Muslim*, p. 132.

٤٢٥ ـ وَعَنْ أَنَسٍ ، قَالَ : كَانَ رَسُوْلُ اللهِ ﷺ يَتَوَضَّأُ لِكُلِّ صَلَاةٍ ، وَ كَانَ أَحَدُنَا يَكْفِيْهِ الْوُضُوْءُ مَا لَمْ يُحْدِثْ . رَوَاهُ الدَّارِمِيُّ .

425 **Anas** reported that Allah's Messenger (peace and blessings of Allah be upon him) used to perform ablution for every prayer, but one amongst us would deem the ablution sufficient (for more than one prayers) so long as it did not break. (*Darimi*)

٤٢٦ ـ وَعَنْ مُحَمَّدِ بْنِ يَحْيَى بْنِ حَبَّانَ ، قَالَ : قُلْتُ لِعُبَيْدِ اللهِ بْنِ عَبْدِ اللهِ بْنِ عُمَرَ : أَرَأَيْتَ وُضُوْءَ عَبْدِ اللهِ بْنِ عُمَرَ لِكُلِّ صَلَاةٍ طَاهِرًا كَانَ أَوْ غَيْرَ طَاهِرٍ ، عَمَّنْ أَخَذَهُ ؛ فَقَالَ : حَدَّثَتْهُ أَسْمَاءُ بِنْتُ زَيْدِ بْنِ الْخَطَّابِ أَنَّ

عَبْدُ اللهِ بْنُ حَنْظَلَةَ بْنِ أَبِي عَامِرٍ الْغَسِيْلِ، حَدَّثَتْهَا أَنَّ رَسُوْلَ اللهِ ﷺ
كَانَ أُمِرَ بِالْوُضُوْءِ لِكُلِّ صَلَاةٍ طَاهِراً كَانَ أَوْ غَيْرَ طَاهِرٍ، فَلَمَّا شَقَّ ذٰلِكَ
عَلَى رَسُوْلِ اللهِ ﷺ أُمِرَ بِالسِّوَاكِ عِنْدَ كُلِّ صَلَاةٍ، وَّ وُضِعَ عَنْهُ الْوُضُوْءُ
إِلَّا مِنْ حَدَثٍ. قَالَ: فَكَانَ عَبْدُ اللهِ: يَرَى أَنَّ بِهِ قُوَّةً عَلَى ذٰلِكَ فَفَعَلَهُ
حَتَّى مَاتَ. رَوَاهُ أَحْمَدُ.

426 Muhammad b. Yahya b. Hibban reported: I said to 'Ubaidullah b. 'Abdullah b. 'Umar: From where did 'Abdullah b.
'Umar get (this habit of) performing ablution for each prayer
whether he needed an ablution or not. He said: 'Asma bint
Zaid b. Khattab had reported that 'Abdullah b. Hanzala b.
Abu 'Amir al-Ghasil had told her that Allah's Messenger
(peace and blessings of Allah be upon him) had been commanded to perform ablution for every prayer whether he
needed that or not, but when it proved to be hard for Allah's
Messenger (peace and blessings of Allah be upon him) he was
commanded to use *miswak* for every prayer, and the (command) of performing ablution (for every prayer) was set aside,
but in case when ablution was needed[1] He (the narrator)
said that 'Abdullah found in himself the power to do that, so
he did that (i.e. he performed ablution) for every prayer, till
he died. (*Ahmad*)

1. This was the personal opinion of Ḥaḍrat 'Abdullah b. 'Umar, and not
something obligatory for a Muslim.

٤٢٧. وَعَنْ عَبْدِ اللهِ بْنِ عَمْرِو بْنِ الْعَاصِ ﷺ أَنَّ النَّبِيَّ ﷺ مَرَّ بِسَعْدٍ
وَهُوَ يَتَوَضَّأُ، فَقَالَ: "مَا هٰذَا السَّرَفُ يَا سَعْدُ؟" قَالَ: أَفِي الْوُضُوْءِ
سَرَفٌ؟! قَالَ: "نَعَمْ! وَإِنْ كُنْتَ عَلَى نَهْرٍ جَارٍ." رَوَاهُ أَحْمَدُ، وَابْنُ
مَاجَهْ.

427 'Abdullah b. 'Amr b. al-'Aas reported that Allah's Apostle
(peace and blessings of Allah be upon him) happened to pass
by Sa'd as he was performing ablution. Whereupon he said:
Sa'd what is this extravagance. He said: Can there be

any idea of extravagance in ablution? Whereupon he (the Holy Prophet) said: Yes, even if you are by the side of flowing river. (*Ibn Majah*)

٤٢٨ـ وَ عَنْ أَبِى هُرَيْرَةَ، وَ ابْنِ مَسْعُوْدٍ، وَ ابْنِ عُمَرَ،عَنِ النَّبِيِّ ﷺ،
قَالَ : مَنْ تَوَضَّأَ وَ ذَكَرَ اسْمَ اللهِ ، فَإِنَّهُ يُطَهِّرُ جَسَدَهُ كُلَّهُ ، وَمَنْ
تَوَضَّأَ وَ لَمْ يَذْكُرِ اسْمَ اللهِ ؛ لَمْ يُطَهِّرْ إِلَّا مَوْضِعَ الْوُضُوْءِ :

428 Abu Huraira and Ibn Mas'ud and Ibn 'Umar reported that Allah's Apostle (peace and blessings of Allah be upon him) said: He who performed ablution and mentioned the name of Allah, he in fact made his whole body pure and he who performed ablution, but did not mention the name of Allah, he in fact did not purify (his whole body) but only (those parts which he washed) by performing ablution.

٤٢٩ـ وَ عَنْ أَبِى رَافِعٍ ، قَالَ : كَانَ رَسُوْلُ اللهِ ﷺ إِذَا تَوَضَّأَ وَضَّوَءَ
الصَّلَاةِ حَرَّكَ خَاتَمَهُ فِىْ أَصْبُعِهِ . رَوَاهُمَا الدَّارَ قُطْنِيُّ ، وَ رَوَى
ابْنُ مَاجَةَ الْأَخِيْرَ :

429 Abu Rafi' reported: When Allah's Messenger (peace and blessings of Allah be upon him) performed ablution he moved his ring round his finger. (*Daraqutni transmitted the two traditions and Ibn Majah transmitted the second one.*)

———●►———

CHAPTER 13

PERTAINING TO BATHING

Section I الْفَصْلُ الأَوَّلُ

٤٣٠ - عَنْ أَبِي هُرَيْرَةَ، قَالَ : قَالَ رَسُولُ اللهِ ﷺ : إِذَا جَلَسَ أَحَدُكُمْ
بَيْنَ شُعَبِهَا الأَرْبَعِ، ثُمَّ جَهَدَهَا ، فَقَدْ وَجَبَ الْغُسْلُ وَ إِنْ لَمْ يُنْزِلْ.
مُتَّفَقٌ عَلَيْهِ.

430 Abu Huraira reported Allah's Messenger (peace and blessings of Allah be upon him) as saying: When any one of you sits between the four parts of her body and then makes effort (i.e. the man cohabits with the woman) the bathing becomes obligatory (for both of them) even if there is no orgasm.   (*Agreed upon*)

٤٣١ - وَعَنْ سَعِيدٍ، قَالَ : قَالَ رَسُولُ اللهِ ﷺ : إِنَّمَا الْمَاءُ مِنَ الْمَاءِ.
رَوَاهُ مُسْلِمٌ.

قَالَ الشَّيْخُ الإِمَامُ مُحْيِي السُّنَّةِ ، رَحِمَهُ اللهُ : هٰذَا مَنْسُوخٌ.

431 Sa'id reported Allah's Messenger (peace and blessings of Allah be upon him) as saying: Verily the (use of) water becomes essential, only in case of (the emission of) watery substance (semen). (*Muslim*)
Al-Sheikh al-Imam Muhyi as-Sunna (may Allah be merciful to him) said: It is abrogated one.

٤٣٢ - وَ قَالَ ابْنُ عَبَّاسٍ : إِنَّمَا الْمَاءُ مِنَ الْمَاءِ ، فِي الإِحْتِلامِ. رَوَاهُ
التِّرْمِذِيُّ ، وَلَمْ أَجِدْهُ فِي "الصَّحِيحَيْنِ".

432 Ibn 'Abbas said: (The essentiality of the use of) water in case of (the emission of) watery substance (semen) applies to wet dream. (*Tirmidhi transmitted it, but I have not found it in Sahihain.*)

٤٣٣ - وَ عَنْ أُمِّ سَلَمَةَ ، قَالَتْ : قَالَتْ أُمُّ سُلَيْمٍ، يَا رَسُولَ اللهِ ! إِنَّ
اللهَ لَا يَسْتَحْيِي مِنَ الْحَقِّ ؛ فَهَلْ عَلَى الْمَرْأَةِ مِنْ غُسْلٍ إِذَا احْتَلَمَتْ؟
قَالَ : نَعَمْ ، إِذَا رَأَتِ الْمَاءَ" فَغَطَّتْ أُمُّ سَلَمَةَ وَجْهَهَا . وَ قَالَتْ :
يَا رَسُولَ اللهِ ! أَوَ تَحْتَلِمُ الْمَرْأَةُ ؟ قَالَ " نَعَمْ ، تَرِبَتْ يَمِينُكِ ، فَبِمَ
يُشْبِهُهَا وَلَدُهَا ؟" . مُتَّفَقٌ عَلَيْهِ .

433 Umm Salama reported that Umm Sulaim said: Allah's
Messenger! Verily Allah is not ashamed of Truth. Is bathing
necessary for a woman when she sees the wet dream? He said:
Yes. When she sees the watery substance (flowing out of her
vagina). Umm Salama covering her face said: Allah's
Messenger, does the woman also see the wet dream? He (the
Holy Prophet) said: Yes. Let your hand be besmeared with
dust. In what way does her child resemble her. (*Agreed upon*)

٤٣٤ - وَ زَادَ مُسْلِمٌ بِرِوَايَةِ أُمِّ سُلَيْمٍ : "إِنَّ مَاءَ الرَّجُلِ غَلِيظٌ أَبْيَضُ،
وَ مَاءَ الْمَرْأَةِ رَقِيقٌ أَصْفَرُ، فَمِنْ أَيِّهِمَا عَلَا أَوْ سَبَقَ يَكُونُ مِنْهُ
الشَّبَهُ "

434 Muslim added to the version of Umm Sulaim: Man's discharge (i.e. sperm) is thick and white and the discharge of
woman is thin and yellow; so the resemblance comes from
the one whose genes prevail or dominate.[1]

1. Various explanations of this statement have been given by writers,
old and new. We quote two. One given by Muhammad Asad:
"The Prophet's answer raises the very complex problem of heredity.
Modern science has not yet decided as to the exact connection between
the details of a sexual act and characteristics of the offspring resulting
therefrom....It has certainly an indirect import on the conceptions for
it is a physiological expression of the degree or quality of the woman's
emotion during the act; and it goes without saying that in a highly
developed organism like the human body's emotional conditions must,
to a great extent, influence the reproductive processes. Moreover,
it is quite possible that the popular expression *ma ar-rajul* and *ma
al-mar'ah* do not refer, in this context, merely to the ejaculation of the
sperm on the part of the man and the vaginal secretion of the woman,

but to the genetic processes in entirety. This brings us considerably nearer to an understanding of the problem........ The above utterance of the Holy Prophet's would thus imply that the sex of the offspring is determined by the greater vigour of either of the parents at the time of mating. This idea is supported by one of the most influential modern theories in this domain, namely, that propounded by the biologist Girou, who connects the sex of the offspring with that of the more vigorous parent". (Sahih al-Bukhari's translation, Vol. V, 4th instalment, p. 242).

The recent researches in Genetics are embodied in the following words: Experiments with plants and animals, and particularly Goldschmidst's experiment, on the gypsy moth Lymantria, have shown that the sex of an individual is not the result of either pure male or pure female tendencies. Rather, in the development of either sex, both male and female determiners are at work; stronger male to the female ones in the origin of males and reverse in the origin of females. We may assume that some balance theory of sex holds for man. Perhaps human male has genes for maleness not only in the y-chromosome but also in the x-chromosome, or the autosomes, or in both of these; and, in addition, genes for femaleness in y-chromosome or autosomes, or in both. He is the male because male determiners 'outweigh' the female ones. Conversely, although a human female presumably has genes for both maleness and femaleness in the absence of strong male-determining factor carried by the y-chromosome, the female determiners outweigh the males ones". (Curt Stern, *Principles of Human Genetics*, p. 401).

٤٣٥ - وَعَنْ عَائِشَةَ ، قَالَتْ كَانَ رَسُولُ اللهِ ﷺ إِذَا اغْتَسَلَ مِنَ الْجَنَابَةِ بَدَأَ فَغَسَلَ يَدَيْهِ ، ثُمَّ يَتَوَضَّأُ كَمَا يَتَوَضَّأُ لِلصَّلَاةِ ، ثُمَّ يُدْخِلُ أَصَابِعَهُ فِي الْمَاءِ ، فَيُخَلِّلُ بِهَا أُصُولَ شَعْرِهِ ، ثُمَّ يَصُبُّ عَلَى رَأْسِهِ ثَلَاثَ غَرَفَاتٍ بِيَدَيْهِ ، ثُمَّ يُفِيضُ الْمَاءَ عَلَى جِسْدِهِ كُلِّهِ مُتَّفَقٌ عَلَيْهِ . وَفِي رِوَايَةٍ لِمُسْلِمٍ بَدَأَ فَيَغْسِلُ يَدَيْهِ قَبْلَ أَنْ يُدْخِلَهُمَا الْإِنَاءَ . ثُمَّ يُفْرِغُ بِيَمِينِهِ عَلَى شِمَالِهِ ، فَيَغْسِلُ فَرْجَهُ ، ثُمَّ يَتَوَضَّأُ

435 'Ā'isha reported that when Allah's Messenger (peace and blessings of Allah be upon him) took a bath, because of cohabitation, he first washed his hands, and then performed ablution as is done for prayer. He then inserted his fingers

in water (in order to moisten them) and then moved them to
the roots of his hair, and then poured three handfuls on his
head and then poured water over his whole body. (*Agreed upon*)

And in a version of *Muslim* (the words are): He first
washed his hands before inserting them in the vessel, then
poured water with his right hand over his left hand, then
washed his private parts, and then performed ablution.

٤٣٦ - وَعَنِ ابْنِ عَبَّاسٍ، قَالَ: قَالَتْ مَيْمُونَةُ: وَضَعْتُ لِلنَّبِيِّ ﷺ غُسْلًا
فَسَتَرْتُهُ بِثَوْبٍ، وَصَبَّ عَلَى يَدَيْهِ، فَغَسَلَهُمَا، ثُمَّ صَبَّ بِيَمِينِهِ
عَلَى شِمَالِهِ، فَغَسَلَ فَرْجَهُ، فَضَرَبَ بِيَدِهِ الْأَرْضَ فَمَسَحَهَا، ثُمَّ
غَسَلَهَا، فَمَضْمَضَ وَاسْتَنْشَقَ، وَغَسَلَ وَجْهَهُ وَذِرَاعَيْهِ، ثُمَّ صَبَّ
عَلَى رَأْسِهِ، وَأَفَاضَ عَلَى جَسَدِهِ، ثُمَّ تَنَحَّى فَغَسَلَ قَدَمَيْهِ، فَنَاوَلْتُهُ
ثَوْبًا فَلَمْ يَأْخُذْهُ، فَانْطَلَقَ وَهُوَ يَنْفُضُ يَدَيْهِ . مُتَّفَقٌ عَلَيْهِ، وَلَفْظُهُ
لِلْبُخَارِيِّ

436 **Ibn 'Abbas** reported Maimuna (the wife of the Holy Prophet)
as saying: I placed (the vessel) containing water for Allah's
Apostle (peace and blessings of Allah be upon him) for taking
bath and provided him privacy with the help of cloth
(curtain). He poured water on his hands and washed them.
He then poured (water) on his left hand with the help of
right hand, and then washed his private parts. He then
struck his (left) hand against the earth and rubbed it and then
washed it. He then rinsed his mouth and snuffed water (in
his nostrils) and then washed his face and forearms. He then
poured water on his head and then let it flow over his body.
He then moved aside and washed his feet. I tried to give him
a garment (a cloth like towel) but he did not take that. He went
on shaking his hands. (*Agreed upon and the wording is of Bukhari*)

٤٣٧ - وَعَنْ عَائِشَةَ، قَالَتْ: إِنَّ امْرَأَةً مِنَ الْأَنْصَارِ سَأَلَتْ رَسُولَ اللهِ
ﷺ عَنْ غُسْلِهَا مِنَ الْمَحِيضِ، فَأَمَرَهَا كَيْفَ تَغْتَسِلُ، ثُمَّ قَالَ: خُذِي

فِرْصَةً مِنْ مَسْكٍ ، فَتَطَهَّرِى بِهَا ، قَالَتْ : كَيْفَ أَتَطَهَّرُ بِهَا ؟ فَقَالَ : تَطَهَّرِى

بِهَا ؟ قَالَتْ : كَيْفَ أَتَطَهَّرُ بِهَا ؟ قَالَ : سُبْحَانَ اللهِ ! تَطَهَّرِى بِهَا ؟ فَاجْتَذَبْتُهَا

إِلَيَّ فَقُلْتُ لَهَا : تَبَتَّعِى بِهَا أَثَرَ الدَّمِ . مُتَّفَقٌ عَلَيْهِ .

437 **'A'isha** reported that a woman from amongst the Ansar asked Allah's Messenger (peace and blessings of Allah be upon him) how to wash herself after menstruation. He told her how to wash herself and added: Take a piece of cotton cloth (soaked) with musk, and purify yourself with it. She said: How should I purify myself with it? He said: Purify yourself with it. She again said: How should I purify myself with it. Whereupon he said: Praise be to Allah, purify yourself with it. I dragged herself to my side and said to her: Apply this (cotton) to wipe the trace of blood. (*Agreed upon*)

٤٣٨ـ وَعَنْ أُمِّ سَلَمَةَ ، قَالَتْ : قُلْتُ يَا رَسُولَ اللهِ ! إِنِّى امْرَأَةٌ أَشُدُّ ضَفْرَ

رَأْسِى ، أَفَأَنْقُضُهُ لِغُسْلِ الْجَنَابَةِ ؟ فَقَالَ : لَا ، إِنَّمَا يَكْفِيكِ أَنْ تَحْثِى

عَلَى رَأْسِكِ ثَلَاثَ حَثَيَاتٍ ، ثُمَّ تُفِيضِينَ عَلَيْكِ الْمَاءَ ، فَتَطْهُرِينَ .

رَوَاهُ مُسْلِمٌ .

438 **Umm Salama** reported that she said: Allah's Messenger, I am a woman with closely plaited hair on my head, am I required to undo it for taking a bath, because of sexual intercourse? Whereupon he said: No, it is enough for you to pour three handfuls of water (on your head) and then let the water flow on you (on the body) and you would be purified. (*Muslim*)

٤٣٩ـ وَعَنْ أَنَسٍ ، قَالَ : كَانَ النَّبِىُّ ﷺ ، يَتَوَضَّأُ بِالْمُدِّ ، وَيَغْتَسِلُ

بِالصَّاعِ إِلَى خَمْسَةِ أَمْدَادٍ . مُتَّفَقٌ عَلَيْهِ .

439 **Anas** reported that Allah's Apostle (peace and blessings of Allah be upon him) used to perform ablution with a *mudd*[1] (of water) and he took a bath with a *Sa'*[2] upto five *mudds*.

(*Agreed upon*)

1. *Mudd* is equal to a quarter of a seer.
2. *Sa'* is equal to four *mudds* or three seers and a half.
(For detail: See *Auzan-i-Shariyya* by Mufti Muhammad Shafi').

٤٤٠ـ وَعَنْ مُعَاذَةَ، قَالَتْ: قَالَتْ عَائِشَةُ: كُنْتُ أَغْتَسِلُ أَنَا وَرَسُولُ
اللهِ ﷺ مِنْ إِنَاءٍ وَاحِدٍ بَيْنِيْ وَبَيْنَهُ، فَيُبَادِرُنِيْ، حَتَّى أَقُوْلَ: دَعْ لِيْ
دَعْ لِيْ. قَالَتْ: وَهُمَا جُنُبَانِ. مُتَّفَقٌ عَلَيْهِ.

440 **Mua‘dh** reported that ‘A’isha said: I and Allah's Messenger
(peace and blessings of Allah be upon him) took a bath from
one vessel (placed) between me and him and he would get
ahead of me, so I would say: Spare (some water) for me,
spare (some water) for me and she (further) said: And they
had had a sexual intercourse. (*Agreed upon*)

Section II ٱلْفَصْلُ الثَّانِيْ

٤٤١ـ عَنْ عَائِشَةَ، قَالَتْ: سُئِلَ رَسُولُ اللهِ ﷺ عَنِ الرَّجُلِ يَجِدُ الْبَلَلَ
وَلَا يَذْكُرُ احْتِلَامًا. قَالَ: "يَغْتَسِلُ"، وَعَنِ الرَّجُلِ الَّذِيْ يَرَى أَنَّهُ
قَدِ احْتَلَمَ وَلَا يَجِدُ بَلَلًا. قَالَ: "لَا غُسْلَ عَلَيْهِ". قَالَتْ أُمُّ سُلَيْمٍ:
هَلْ عَلَى الْمَرْأَةِ تَرَى ذٰلِكَ غُسْلٌ؟ قَالَ نَعَمْ، إِنَّ النِّسَاءَ شَقَائِقُ الرِّجَالِ."
رَوَاهُ التِّرْمِذِيُّ، وَأَبُوْ دَاوُدَ. وَرَوَى الدَّارِمِيُّ، وَابْنُ مَاجَةَ، إِلَى قَوْلِهِ
"لَا غُسْلَ عَلَيْهِ".

441 **‘A’isha** reported that Allah's Messenger (peace and blessings
of Allah be upon him) was asked about a person who would
notice moisture but would not remember having seen a wet
dream. He said: He should take a bath. And (he was
asked again) about a person who thought as if he had seen a
wet dream but would find no moisture. He said: He is
under no obligation to take a bath. Umm Sulaim said:
Does the woman also see that which necessitates[1] a bath for
her. He said: Yes, the women are of the same nature as the
male persons. (*Tirmidhi, Abu Dawud and Darimi, Ibn Majah*

transmitted upto the words: He is under no obligation to take a bath.)

1. The sexual dreams i.e. experiencing of orgasm is not so common with
women. What actually happens with women is that because of vaginal
secretions from bartholins' glands or due to "sweating reaction"
occurring on the walls of vagina their clothes are soiled (Ruth and
Edward Brecher, ed. *An Analysis of Human Sexual Response*, p. 24)

٤٤٢ ـ وَعَنْهَا، قَالَتْ، قَالَ رَسُولُ اللهِ ﷺ: إِذَا جَاوَزَ الْخِتَانُ الْخِتَانَ،
وَجَبَ الْغُسْلُ، فَعَلْتُهُ أَنَا وَرَسُولُ اللهِ ﷺ فَاغْتَسَلْنَا. رَوَاهُ التِّرْمِذِيُّ
وَابْنُ مَاجَةَ.

442 **'Ā'isha** reported that Allah's Messenger (peace and blessings
of Allah be upon him) said: When the circumsized parts by-
pass one another, taking of a bath becomes necessary. I and
Allah's Messenger (peace and blessings of Allah be upon him)
did that and then we took bath. (*Tirmidhi and Ibn Majah*)

٤٤٣ ـ وَعَنْ أَبِى هُرَيْرَةَ، قَالَ، قَالَ رَسُولُ اللهِ ﷺ: تَحْتَ كُلِّ شَعْرَةٍ
جَنَابَةٌ فَاغْسِلُوا الشَّعْرَ، وَأَنْقُوا الْبَشَرَةَ. رَوَاهُ أَبُوْدَاوُدَ، وَالتِّرْمِذِيُّ
وَابْنُ مَاجَةَ. وَقَالَ التِّرْمِذِيُّ: هٰذَا حَدِيْثٌ غَرِيْبٌ، وَالْحَارِثُ بْنُ
وَجِيْهٍ إِلزَّاوِى وَهُوَ شَيْخٌ، لَيْسَ بِذَاكَ.

443 **Abu Huraira** reported Allah's Messenger (peace and blessings
of Allah be upon him) as saying: There is an effect of
janaba under every hair so wash the hair, cleanse the skin.
(*Transmitted by Abu Dawud, Tirmidhi and Ibn Majah and Tirmidhi
said: This is a gharib hadith and Harith b. Wajih who is the
transmitter is an aged person and thus cannot be fully relied upon.*)

٤٤٤ ـ وَعَنْ عَلِيٍّ، رَضِىَ اللهُ عَنْهُ، قَالَ: قَالَ رَسُولُ اللهِ ﷺ: مَنْ تَرَكَ
مَوْضِعَ شَعْرَةٍ مِنْ جَنَابَةٍ لَمْ يَغْسِلْهَا فُعِلَ بِهَا كَذَا وَكَذَا مِنَ النَّارِ
وَقَالَ عَلِيٌّ: فَمِنْ ثَمَّ عَادَيْتُ رَأْسِى، فَمِنْ ثَمَّ عَادَيْتُ رَأْسِى، فَمِنْ ثَمَّ
عَادَيْتُ رَأْسِى، ثَلَاثًا رَوَاهُ أَبُوْدَاوُدَ، وَأَحْمَدُ، وَالدَّارِمِيُّ، إِلَّا أَنَّهُمَا
لَمْ يُكَرِّرَا، فَمِنْ ثَمَّ عَادَيْتُ رَأْسِى.

444 'Ali (may Allah be pleased with him) reported that Allah's Messenger (peace and blessings of Allah be upon him) said: He who spares even a spot of hair as he is *iunubi* and does not wash it, he shall have to suffer (the pangs of) Hell-Fire, to the same extent (that he has not washed the hair). 'Ali said: It was because of this (grim warning) that I became enemy of my hair; and it was because of this that I cut my hair; and it was because of this that I cut my hair and he said it thrice. (*Abu Dawud, Ahmad and Darimi transmitted it but Ahmad and Abu Dawud did not repeat these words: It was because of this that I became enemy of my hair.*)

٤٤٥ - وَعَنْ عَائِشَةَ ، رَضِيَ اللهُ عَنْهَا ، قَالَتْ : كَانَ رَسُولُ اللهِ ﷺ لَا يَتَوَضَّأُ بَعْدَ الْغُسْلِ . رَوَاهُ أَبُو دَاوُدَ ، وَ التِّرْمِذِيُّ ، وَ النَّسَائِيُّ ، وَ ابْنُ مَاجَةَ .

445 'A'isha (may Allah be pleased with her) reported that Allah's Messenger (peace and blessings of Allah be upon him) did not perform ablution after taking a bath. (*Abu Dawud, Tirmidhi, Nasai' and Ibn Majah*)

٤٤٦ - وَ عَنْهَا ، قَالَتْ : كَانَ النَّبِيُّ ﷺ يَغْسِلُ رَأْسَهُ بِالْخِطْمِيِّ وَهُوَ جُنُبٌ يَجْتَزِئُ بِذٰلِكَ وَ لَا يَصُبُّ عَلَيْهِ الْمَاءَ ، رَوَاهُ أَبُو دَاوُدَ .

446 It is reported on the same authority that Allah's Messenger (peace and blessings of Allah be upon him) used to wash his head with marsh-mallow after having sexual intercourse. He considered it to be sufficient and did not pour water over it. (*Abu Dawud*)

٤٤٧ - وَ عَنْ يَعْلَى ، قَالَ : إِنَّ رَسُولَ اللهِ ﷺ رَأَى رَجُلًا يَغْتَسِلُ بِالْبَرَازِ فَصَعِدَ الْمِنْبَرَ ، فَحَمِدَ اللهَ ، وَ أَثْنَى عَلَيْهِ ، ثُمَّ قَالَ : إِنَّ اللهَ حَيِيٌّ سِتِّيرٌ يُحِبُّ الْحَيَاءَ وَ السَّتْرَ ، فَإِذَا اغْتَسَلَ أَحَدُكُمْ ، فَلْيَسْتَتِرْ . رَوَاهُ أَبُو دَاوُدَ ، وَ النَّسَائِيُّ وَ فِي رِوَايَتِهِ ، قَالَ : إِنَّ اللهَ سِتِّيرٌ ، فَإِذَا أَرَادَ أَحَدُكُمْ أَنْ يَغْتَسِلَ فَلْيَتَوَارَ بِشَيْءٍ .

447 Ya'la reported that Allah's Messenger (peace and blessings of Allah be upon him) saw a person taking a bath in an open place. He mounted the pulpit and praised Allah and extolled Him, then said: Verily Allah is highly Modest and Veiling and He loves modesty and privacy, so when anyone of you intends to take a bath he should draw a curtain around him. (*Transmitted by Abu Dawud, Nasa'i but in Nasa'i's version he said: Verily Allah is Concealed and if any one amongst you intends to take a bath he should hide himself with something*).

٤٤٨ ـ عَنْ أُبَيِّ بْنِ كَعْبٍ ، قَالَ ، إِنَّمَا كَانَ الْمَاءُ مِنَ الْمَاءِ رُخْصَةً فِي أَوَّلِ الْإِسْلَامِ ، ثُمَّ نُهِيَ عَنْهَا . رَوَاهُ التِّرْمِذِيُّ ، وَ أَبُو دَاؤدَ ، وَ الدَّارِميُّ .

448 Ubayy b. Ka'b reported: It was a concession in the early days of Islam that bathing became necessary (only in the case), when watery (thing was emitted because of sexual intercourse), but later on it was withdrawn.[1]

> 1. In early days of Islam the general practice in regard to bathing because of sexual intercourse was, that there should necessarily be seminal emission, and if there was no seminal emission the bath did not become obligatory. It was a sort of concession which was withdrawn in the later period and taking of bath became essential, even without seminal emission. (*Mirqat*, Vol. II, page 39).

٤٤٩ ـ وَ عَنْ عَلِيٍّ ، قَالَ : جَاءَ رَجُلٌ إِلَى النَّبِيِّ ﷺ فَقَالَ إِنِّي اغْتَسَلْتُ مِنَ الْجَنَابَةِ ، وَ صَلَّيْتُ الْفَجْرَ ، فَرَأَيْتُ قَدْرَ مَوْضِعِ الظُّفْرِ لَمْ يُصِبْهُ الْمَاءُ . فَقَالَ رَسُولُ اللهِ ﷺ : لَوْ كُنْتَ مَسَحْتَ عَلَيْهِ بِيَدِكَ أَجْزَأَكَ . رَوَاهُ ابْنُ مَاجَةَ .

449 'Ali reported: There came a person to Allah's Apostle (peace and blessings of Allah be upon him) and said: I took a bath because of sexual intercourse[1] and then observed the dawn prayer and saw a spot to the extent of the place of nail, where water had not reached. Thereupon Allah's Messenger (peace and blessings of Allah be upon him) said: Had you rubbed over it with your (wet) hand[2], it would have sufficed for you.
(*Ibn Majah*)

1. The word *al-Janaba* used in the text has been translated as: Because of sexual intercourse. This word is generally translated into English as sexual defilement or sexual impurity. This rendering is not correct. There is no idea of sexual defilement in Islam. The word *al-Janaba* which is a noun from *janaba* means to remain aside. Since a person who has done sexual intercourse is commanded to remain away from prayer and the recitation of the Qur'ān, unless he has taken a bath, he is, therefore, called *junubi*. He is not in the least defiled.

2. If you had done that while taking a bath, it would have been sufficient, but since he had not that at that time, it was an omission on his part, which required that he should take a bath again and repeat the prayer. (*Mirqat*, Vol. II, p. 40).

٥٧ـ وَعَنِ ابْنِ عُمَرَ، قَالَ: كَانَتِ الصَّلَاةُ خَمْسِينَ، وَالْغُسْلُ مِنَ الْجَنَابَةِ
سَبْعَ مَرَّاتٍ، وَغَسْلُ الْبَوْلِ مِنَ الثَّوْبِ سَبْعَ مَرَّاتٍ. فَلَمْ يَزَلْ رَسُولُ
اللهِ ﷺ يَسْأَلُ، حَتَّى جُعِلَتِ الصَّلَاةُ خَمْسًا، وَغَسْلُ الْجَنَابَةِ مَرَّةً،
وَغَسْلُ الثَّوْبِ مِنَ الْبَوْلِ مَرَّةً. رَوَاهُ أَبُو دَاوُدَ.

450 Ibn 'Umar reported: (Originally) there were fifty (obligatory) prayers and taking of a bath seven times because of sexual intercourse, and washing of the garment seven times for puri-fying it from urine. Allah's Messenger (peace and blessings of Allah be upon him) continued asking (Allah for remission) till prayers were (reduced) to five[1], and taking of a bath only to one time because of *janaba* and washing of garment only one time for purifying it from urine. (*Abu Dawud*)

1. It was during Prophet's ascent to heaven that fifty daily prayers were prescribed at the outset which were reduced to five by Allah on Prophet's request before his coming back on the earth.

CHAPTER 14

PERTAINING TO MEETING[1] WITH ONE WHO IS *JUNUBI* AND WHAT IS PERMITTED

Section I أَلْفَصْلُ الْأَوَّلُ

١٥١ - عَنْ أَبِي هُرَيْرَةَ (رَضِيَ اللهُ عَنْهُ ، قَالَ : لَقِيَنِي رَسُولُ اللهِ ﷺ وَأَنَا
جُنُبٌ ، فَأَخَذَ بِيَدِي ، فَمَشَيْتُ مَعَهُ حَتَّى قَعَدَ ، فَانْسَلَلْتُ ، فَأَتَيْتُ
الرَّحْلَ ، فَاغْتَسَلْتُ ، ثُمَّ جِئْتُ ، وَهُوَ قَاعِدٌ . فَقَالَ "أَيْنَ كُنْتَ يَا أَبَا هُرَيْرَةَ؟
فَقُلْتُ لَهُ . فَقَالَ "سُبْحَانَ اللهِ! إِنَّ الْمُؤْمِنَ لَا يَنْجُسُ" هـٰذَا لَفْظُ
الْبُخَارِيِّ ، وَلِمُسْلِمٍ مَعْنَاهُ ، وَزَادَ بَعْدَ قَوْلِهِ: فَقُلْتُ لَهُ: لَقَدْ لَقِيْتَنِي وَأَنَا
جُنُبٌ ، فَكَرِهْتُ أَنْ أُجَالِسَكَ حَتَّى أَغْتَسِلَ . وَكَذَا الْبُخَارِيُّ فِي رِوَايَةٍ
أُخْرَى .

451 Abu Huraira (may Allah be pleased with him) reported: Allah's Messenger (peace and blessings of Allah be upon him) (happened) to meet me as I was in a state of *janaba*. He took hold of my hand. I went along with him till he sat down. I slipped away (from that place) and came to my dwelling place and took a bath and then came (back) to him and found him sitting. He (the Holy Prophet) said: Abu Huraira where you have been? I told him (what the matter was); whereupon he said: Glory be to Allah, a believer is not defiled.[2] (*This is Bukhari's wording and Muslim's version is to the same effect but there is an addition after the words 'I said to him'* : *You (happened) to meet me as I was in the state of janaba, so I did not like that I should sit with you till I had taken a bath*)

1. The word *mukhalata* included sitting in the company of another person, talking with him, greeting him and shaking hands with him.
2. The soul of man is purified by belief in Allah and His Prophets and other articles of faith and taking to the path of righteousness and

religious piety. The seminal emission does not pollute him. He is, even in this very state, pure, because his soul is purified by his belief in Islam. He is barred from prayer and recitation of the Holy Qur'ān and entering into the mosque simply to make him conscious of the immeasurably high spiritual value of these acts of devotion to Allah. So far as man as a human being is concerned no person is defiled, not even a non-believer, because the Lord has created man in the best make (xcv : 4), and then he lowered himself by his own misdeeds. Man as such is the recipient of the special favours of the Lord. The Holy Qur'ān says:

And surely We have honoured the children of Adam, and We carry them in the land and the sea, and We provide them with good things, and We have made them to excel highly most of them whom We have created (xvii : 70).

This verse of the Holy Qur'an makes it clear that man has received the greatest honour from the Lord and he is created pure and is not defiled and polluted; it is his wrong beliefs and vicious acts that make him unclean. The verse of the Holy Qur'ān (ix : 28) in which the polytheists have been declared as unclean, points to their evil beliefs and practices. The jurists of Islam have elaborated this point and have drawn the conclusion that no man as a man is impure or defiled. It is because of his idolatrous beliefs and evil deeds that he becomes defiled. Imam Shawkani has given sound arguments in support of his opinion. "The Muslims have been permitted to marry the women of the People of the Book; they have been allowed to use their utensils provided they do not contain impurities of the forbidden things; they can accept their gifts, etc. All these facts go to prove that the Holy Prophet never treated them as inherently defiled and polluted persons, for if he had thought them so, he would have never come into contact with them. He called them unclean for their wrong beliefs and acts" (*Nail-ul-Awtar*, Vol. I, pp. 20, 21).

٤٥٢ - وَعَنِ ابْنِ عُمَرَ، قَالَ ذَكَرَ عُمَرُ بْنُ الْخَطَّابِ لِرَسُولِ اللهِ ﷺ أَنَّهُ
تُصِيبُهُ الْجَنَابَةُ مِنَ اللَّيْلِ ، فَقَالَ لَهُ رَسُولُ اللهِ ﷺ : تَوَضَّأْ، وَاغْسِلْ
ذَكَرَكَ ، ثُمَّ نَمْ ؛ مُتَّفَقٌ عَلَيْهِ .

452 Ibn 'Umar reported that 'Umar b. Al-Khatab said to Allah's Messenger (peace and blessings of Allah be upon him) that he became *junubi* during the night. Thereupon Allah's Messenger (peace and blessings of Allah be upon him) said to him: Perform ablution, wash your sexual organ and then go to sleep. (*Agreed upon*)

٣٥٣ ـ وَعَنْ عَائِشَةَ ، رَضِيَ اللهُ عَنْهَا ، قَالَتْ : كَانَ النَّبِيُّ ﷺ إِذَا كَانَ
جُنُبًا فَأَرَادَ أَنْ يَأْكُلَ ، أَوْ يَنَامَ ، تَوَضَّأَ وُضُوءَهُ لِلصَّلَاةِ . مُتَّفَقٌ عَلَيْهِ

453 'A'isha (may Allah be pleased with her) reported that whenever Allah's Apostle (peace and blessings of Allah be upon
him) intended to eat (something) or to go to sleep while he
was in a state of *janaba*, he performed ablution like the
ablution of prayer. (*Agreed upon*)

٣٥٤ ـ وَعَنْ أَبِي سَعِيدٍ لِخُدْرِيِّ ، قَالَ : قَالَ رَسُولُ اللهِ ﷺ ، إِذَا أَتَى أَحَدُكُمْ
أَهْلَهُ ، ثُمَّ أَرَادَ أَنْ يَعُودَ ، فَلْيَتَوَضَّأْ بَيْنَهُمَا وُضُوءًا . رَوَاهُ مُسْلِمٌ

454 Abu Sa'id Al-Khudri reported that Allah's Messenger (peace
and blessings of Allah be upon him) said: When anyone
amongst you has a sexual intercourse with his wife and then he
intends to repeat it, he should perform ablution. (*Muslim*)

٣٥٥ ـ وَعَنْ أَنَسٍ ، قَالَ : كَانَ النَّبِيُّ ﷺ يَطُوفُ عَلَى نِسَائِهِ بِغُسْلٍ وَّاحِدٍ
رَوَاهُ مُسْلِمٌ

455 Anas reported that Allah's Apostle (peace and blessings of
Allah be upon him) used to have a sexual intercourse with his
wives with a single[1] bath. (*Muslim*)

    1. The Holy Prophet (peace and blessings of Allah be upon him) did not
    take a bath after every intercourse. He simply performed ablution
    and took a bath at the end.

٣٥٦ ـ وَعَنْ عَائِشَةَ ، قَالَتْ : كَانَ النَّبِيُّ ﷺ يَذْكُرُ اللهَ عَزَّ وَجَلَّ عَلَى
كُلِّ أَحْيَانِهِ . رَوَاهُ مُسْلِمٌ
وَحَدِيثُ ابْنِ عَبَّاسٍ سَنَذْكُرُهُ فِي كِتَابِ الْأَطْعِمَةِ ، إِنْ شَاءَ
اللهُ تَعَالَى

456 'A'isha (may Allah be pleased with her) reported that the
Apostle of Allah (peace and blessings of Allah be upon him)
used to remember Allah at all moments.[1] (*Muslim*)

We shall mention the tradition of Ibn 'Abbas in the Book of Foods if Allah, the Exalted, so wills.

1. This means that one is always permitted to glorify the Lord, remember Him and extol Him with his tongue. There is, however, a difference of opinion whether one can recite the Holy Qur'an in a state of *janaba* or in case of menses of a woman. The general view is that it is not permitted. It is also forbidden to remember Allah while one is in the privy or is busy in sexual intercourse. (*Fath-ul-Mulhim*, Vol. I, p. 498).

Section II   الْفَصْلُ الثَّانِیْ

٧٥٤ ـ عَنِ ابْنِ عَبَّاسٍ ، قَالَ : اغْتَسَلَ بَعْضُ أَزْوَاجِ النَّبِیِّ ﷺ فِیْ جَفْنَةٍ . فَأَرَادَ رَسُوْلُ اللهِ ﷺ أَنْ یَّتَوَضَّأَ مِنْهُ ، فَقَالَتْ : یَا رَسُوْلَ اللهِ إِنِّیْ كُنْتُ جُنُبًا . فَقَالَ : "إِنَّ الْمَاءَ لَا یَجْنُبُ" ، رَوَاهُ التِّرْمِذِیُّ ، وَ أَبُوْ دَاوُدَ ، وَ ابْنُ مَاجَةَ . وَ رَوَى الدَّارِمِیُّ نَحْوَهُ ـ

457 Ibn 'Abbas reported that a wife of Allah's Apostle (peace and blessings of Allah be upon him) took a bath in a big bowl. Then the Messenger of Allah (peace and blessings of Allah be upon him) intended to perform ablution from that. She said : Allah's Messenger, I was a *junubi*. Whereupon he said : The water does not become impure.[1] (*Tirmidhi, Abu Dawud, Ibn Majah and Darimi as something similar*)

1. When a person does not become impure because of the sexual intercourse how can then water become impure, because it has been used by a *junubi*.

٧٥٨ ـ وَ فِیْ "شَرْحِ السُّنَّةِ" "عَنْهُ" ، عَنْ مَیْمُوْنَةَ ، بِلَفْظِ "الْمَصَابِیْحِ"

458 In *Sharh As-Sunnah* it is given from him who transmitted it from Maimuna with the wording in *Al-Masabih*.

٧٥٩ ـ وَ عَنْ عَائِشَةَ ، قَالَتْ ، كَانَ رَسُوْلُ اللهِ ﷺ یَغْتَسِلُ مِنَ الْجَنَابَةِ ، ثُمَّ یَسْتَدْفِئُ بِیْ قَبْلَ أَنْ أَغْتَسِلَ ، رَوَاهُ ابْنُ مَاجَةَ ، وَرَوَى التِّرْمِذِیُّ نَحْوَهُ . وَ فِیْ "شَرْحِ السُّنَّةِ" بِلَفْظِ "الْمَصَابِیْحِ"

459 **'A'isha** reported: Allah's Messenger (peace and blessings of Allah be upon him) used to take a bath because of sexual intercourse and then warm himself with me before I would take a bath. (*Ibn Majah and Tirmidhi transmitted something similar in 'Sharh As-Sunna' as is given with the wording in 'Al-Masabih'*)

٤٦٠ ـ وَعَنْ عَلِيٍّ، قَالَ : كَانَ النَّبِيُّ ﷺ يَخْرُجُ مِنَ الْخَلَاءِ فَيُقْرِئُنَا الْقُرْآنَ،

وَ يَأْكُلُ مَعَنَا اللَّحْمَ، وَ لَمْ يَكُنْ يَحْجُبُهُ ـ أَوْ يَحْجُزُهُ ـ عَنِ الْقُرْآنِ شَيْءٌ

لَيْسَ الْجَنَابَةَ. رَوَاهُ أَبُو دَاوُدَ، وَ النَّسَائِيُّ. وَ رَوَى ابْنُ مَاجَةَ نَحْوَهُ .

460 **'Ali** reported that Allah's Messenger (peace and blessings of Allah be upon him) used to come out of privy, and recited the Qur'ān to us and ate meat with us and nothing kept him away or restrained him (from the recitation of the Qur'ān) but *janaba*. (*Abu Dawud, Nasa'i and Ibn Majah transmitted something similar*)

٤٦١ ـ وَعَنِ ابْنِ عُمَرَ، قَالَ : قَالَ رَسُولُ اللهِ ﷺ : "لَا تَقْرَأُ الْحَائِضُ وَ لَا

الْجُنُبُ شَيْئًا مِنَ الْقُرْآنِ" رَوَاهُ التِّرْمِذِيُّ .

461 **Ibn 'Umar** reported Allah's Messenger (peace and blessings of Allah be upon him) as saying: The menstruating women and the *junubi* should not recite anything from the Qur'ān.
(*Tirmidhi*)

٤٦٢ ـ وَعَنْ عَائِشَةَ، قَالَتْ : قَالَ رَسُولُ اللهِ ﷺ : وَجِّهُوا هٰذِهِ الْبُيُوتَ

عَنِ الْمَسْجِدِ فَإِنِّي لَا أُحِلُّ الْمَسْجِدَ لِحَائِضٍ وَ لَا جُنُبٍ" رَوَاهُ أَبُو دَاوُدَ

462 **'A'isha** (may Allah be pleased with her) reported that Allah's Messenger (peace and blessings of Allah be upon him) said: Turn the faces of these houses from the mosque for I do not make (the entry of) a menstruating woman or a *junubi* person permissible in the mosque. (*Abu Dawud*)

٤٦٣ ـ وَعَنْ عَلِيٍّ، قَالَ : قَالَ رَسُولُ اللهِ ﷺ : "لَا تَدْخُلُ الْمَلَائِكَةُ بَيْتًا فِيهِ

صُورَةٌ وَ لَا كَلْبٌ وَ لَا جُنُبٌ" رَوَاهُ أَبُو دَاوُدَ، وَ النَّسَائِيُّ

463 **'Ali** reported Allah's Messenger (peace and blessings of Allah be upon him) as saying: The Angels do not enter the house wherein there is a picture or a dog or one who is *junubi*.[1]

(Abu Dawud, and Nasa'i)

1. Here the word *junubi* has a special significance. In this Hadith *Junubi* implies a person who is habitual in avoiding bath to the extent that even the time of obligatory prayer is over. Every person who is in the state of *janaba* does not come within the orbit of this law. We learn from the records of hadith that the Holy Prophet at times slept after the intercourse only with ablution and without taking a bath. (*Mirqat*, Vol. II, p. 47).

٤٦٢ - وَ عَنْ عَمَّارِ بْنِ يَاسِرٍ، قَالَ: قَالَ رَسُولُ اللهِ ﷺ "ثَلَاثَةٌ لَا تَقْرَبُهُمُ الْمَلَائِكَةُ: جِيفَةُ الْكَافِرِ، وَ الْمُتَضَمِّخُ بِالْخَلُوقِ، وَ الْجُنُبُ إِلَّا أَنْ يَتَوَضَّأَ" رَوَاهُ أَبُو دَاوُدَ.

464 **'Ammar b. Yasir** reported that Allah's Messenger (peace and blessings of Allah be upon him) said: Three (are the persons) to whom the Angels do not draw near: the dead body of a non-believer, one who is smeared with *khaluq*[1], and *junubi* who has not performed ablution. (*Abu Dawud*)

1. It is a liquid perfume, prepared out of saffron in which the yellow and red colours dominate. The Holy Prophet has prohibited its use, for it is a perfume fit for the women as he said: The perfume (fit) for the male is one in which the odour is smelt, but its colour is not significant, and the perfume for the women is one in which the colour is significant but odour is not strikingly smelt.

٤٦٥ - وَ عَنْ عَبْدِ اللهِ بْنِ أَبِي بَكْرِ بْنِ مُحَمَّدِ بْنِ عَمْرِو بْنِ حَزْمٍ: أَنَّ فِي الْكِتَابِ الَّذِي كَتَبَهُ رَسُولُ اللهِ ﷺ لِعَمْرِو بْنِ حَزْمٍ "أَنْ لَا يَمَسَّ الْقُرْآنَ إِلَّا طَاهِرٌ" رَوَاهُ مَالِكٌ وَ الدَّارَ قُطْنِيُّ.

465 **'Abdullah b. Abi Bakr b. Muhammad b. 'Amr b. Hazm** reported that in the letter that Allah's Messenger (peace and blessings of Allah be upon him) wrote to 'Amr b. Hazm, (he directed): None should touch the Qur'ān, but one who is pure.

(Malik and Daraqutni)

٤٦٦ - وَ عَنْ نَافِعٍ ، قَالَ : إِنْطَلَقْتُ مَعَ ابْنِ عُمَرَ فِى حَاجَةٍ ، فَقَضَى ابْنُ
عُمَرَ حَاجَتَهُ ، وَ كَانَ مِنْ حَدِيثِهِ يَوْمَئِذٍ أَنْ قَالَ : مَرَّ رَجُلٌ فِى سِكَّةٍ
مِنَ السِّكَكِ ، فَلَقِىَ رَسُولَ اللهِ ﷺ وَ قَدْ خَرَجَ مِنْ غَائِطٍ أَوْ بَوْلٍ ، فَسَلَّمَ
عَلَيْهِ ، فَلَمْ يَرُدَّ عَلَيْهِ ، حَتَّى إِذَا كَادَ الرَّجُلُ أَنْ يَتَوَارَى فِى السِّكَّةِ ،
ضَرَبَ رَسُولُ اللهِ ﷺ بِيَدَيْهِ عَلَى الْحَائِطِ وَ مَسَحَ بِهِمَا وَجْهَهُ ، ثُمَّ
ضَرَبَ ضَرْبَةً أُخْرَى . فَمَسَحَ ذِرَاعَيْهِ ، ثُمَّ رَدَّ عَلَى الرَّجُلِ السَّلَامَ ، وَ
قَالَ : "إِنَّهُ لَمْ يَمْنَعْنِى أَنْ أَرُدَّ عَلَيْكَ السَّلَامَ إِلَّا أَنِّى لَمْ أَكُنْ عَلَى طُهْرٍ"
رَوَاهُ أَبُو دَاوُدَ .

466 **Nafi'** reported: I accompanied Ibn 'Umar who wanted to
relieve himself. After doing that, he, in the course of talk
on that day, said that a person happened to go about a street
amongst the streets (of the town) that he met Allah's Messenger (peace and blessings of Allah be upon him) as he had
come out of privy or had (just) passed water. He (that
person) greeted him (the Holy Prophet) saying *Asslamo a'laikum*
but he (the Holy Prophet) did not respond till the man was
about to disappear in the street that Allah's Messenger (peace
and blessings of Allah be upon him) struck his hands on the
wall and wiped his face with them. He then struck (his hands
on the wall) for second time and wiped his forearms and then
responded to the greeting of that person and said: Verily
nothing prevented me to respond to your greeting, but (the
fact) that I had not performed ablution.[1]   (*Abu Dawud*)

   1. The original words are لم اكن على طهر but here we have translated it : 'I
   had not performed ablution, keeping into consideration the fact that
   not to speak of the sacred personality of the Holy Prophet, even a
   believer is not impure. Here the word طهر stands for ablution, as he
   performed Tayammum—a substitute for the ablution in case of the
   unavailability of water or any other hinderance.
   The second point to be noted is that in hadith No. 456, we have
   learnt that Allah's Apostle (peace and blessings of Allah be upon him)
   remembered Allah, the Exalted, at all moments, but here we are being
   told that he avoided even the responding of greeting while he had not

performed ablution. Both the actions are correct in their own way. In the ordinary routine it is permissible to remember Allah, and greet and mix up with people even when a believer has not performed ablution but what is expected of him as an ideal and the high standard of purity is that he should move about after having performed ablution, thus lifting himself high in spiritual mood.

٤٦٧ - وَعَنِ الْمُهَاجِرِ بِنِ قُنْفُذٍ : أَنَّهُ أَتَى النَّبِيَّ ﷺ وَهُوَ يَبُولُ ، فَسَلَّمَ عَلَيْهِ ، فَلَمْ يَرُدَّ عَلَيْهِ حَتَّى تَوَضَّأَ ، ثُمَّ اعْتَذَرَ إِلَيْهِ ، وَقَالَ : "إِنِّي كَرِهْتُ أَنْ أَذْكُرَ اللهَ إِلَّا عَلَى طُهْرٍ ، رَوَاهُ أَبُوْدَاؤُدَ . وَرَوَى النَّسَائِيُّ إِلَى قَوْلِهِ : حَتَّى تَوَضَّأَ . وَقَالَ : فَلَمَّا تَوَضَّأَ رَدَّ عَلَيْهِ .

467 Al-Muhajir b. Qunfuz reported that he came to Allah's Apostle (peace and blessings of Allah be upon him) as he was passing water, and greeted him, but he made no response to him, till he performed ablution. He then made an apology to him saying: I felt reluctant[1] that I should remember Allah without ablution. (*Abu Dawud*)

(*Nasa'i transmitted it upto the words: Till he performed ablution, he said: Then when he had performed ablution he responded to him*).

1. The word كرهت used in the text can be translated as: I did not like or I disapproved but the context in which this word has been used implies that what I have mentioned above. This word also substantiates the point explained in the previous note that it is permissible to remember Allah even without ablution, but it is highly laudable to do so with ablution.

Section III   أَلْفَصْلُ الثَّالِثُ

٤٦٨ - عَنْ أُمِّ سَلَمَةَ ، رَضِيَ اللهُ عَنْهَا ، قَالَتْ : كَانَ رَسُولُ اللهِ يَجْنُبُ ، ثُمَّ يَنَامُ ، ثُمَّ يَنْتَبِهُ ، ثُمَّ يَنَامُ . رَوَاهُ أَحْمَدُ .

468 Umm Salama (may Allah be pleased with her) reported that Allah's Messenger (peace and blessings of Allah be upon him) used to have sexual intercourse, and then go to sleep. He would then startle, and then again go to sleep. (*Ahmad*)

٤٦٩ ـ وَعَنْ شُعْبَةَ، قَالَ: إِنَّ ابْنَ عَبَّاسٍ رَضِيَ اللهُ عَنْهُ كَانَ إِذَا اغْتَسَلَ مِنَ الْجَنَابَةِ، يُفْرِغُ بِيَدِهِ الْيُمْنَى عَلَى يَدِهِ الْيُسْرَى سَبْعَ مِرَارٍ، ثُمَّ يَغْسِلُ فَرْجَهُ، فَنَسِيَ مَرَّةً كَمْ أَفْرَغَ، نَسَأَلَنِي. فَقُلْتُ: لَا أَدْرِي. فَقَالَ: لَا أُمَّ لَكَ! وَمَا يَمْنَعُكَ أَنْ تَدْرِيَ؛ ثُمَّ يَتَوَضَّأُ وُضُوءَهُ لِلصَّلَاةِ، ثُمَّ يُفِيضُ عَلَى جِلْدِهِ الْمَاءَ، ثُمَّ يَقُولُ: هَكَذَا كَانَ رَسُولُ اللهِ ﷺ يَتَطَهَّرُ. رَوَاهُ أَبُو دَاوُدَ.

469 Shu'ba reported that when Ibn 'Abbas (may Allah be pleased with him) took a bath, because of *janaba* (seminal emission) he poured water with his right hand over his left hand seven times. He then washed his private part. He once forgot as to how many times he had poured (water) so he asked me (about it). I said: I do not know. Whereupon he said: May you miss your mother, what prevented you from knowing it. He then performed ablution—one performed for prayer and then poured water over his skin and then said: This is how Allah's Messenger (peace and blessings of Allah be upon him) took a bath. (*Abu Dawud*)

٤٧٠ ـ وَعَنْ أَبِي رَافِعٍ، قَالَ: إِنَّ رَسُولَ اللهِ ﷺ طَافَ ذَاتَ يَوْمٍ عَلَى نِسَائِهِ، يَغْتَسِلُ عِنْدَ هَذِهِ، وَعِنْدَ هَذِهِ، قَالَ: فَقُلْتُ لَهُ: يَا رَسُولَ اللهِ! أَلَا تَجْعَلُهُ غُسْلًا وَاحِدًا أَخِرًا؛ قَالَ: هَذَا أَزْكَى وَأَطْيَبُ وَأَطْهَرُ. رَوَاهُ أَحْمَدُ، وَأَبُو دَاوُدَ.

470 Abu Rafi'[1] reported that one day Allah's Messenger (peace and blessings of Allah be upon him) went about his wives taking a bath after intercourses with each. I said to him: Allah's Messenger, why don't you take a bath once at the end? Whereupon he said: It is purer, better and more virtuous. (*Ahmad and Abu Dawud*)

1. Abu Rafi' (may Allah be pleased with him) was the slave of the Holy Prophet who lived with him in his house and thus knew all his activities within the family.

٤٧١ - وَعَنِ الْحَكَمِ بْنِ عَمْرٍو، قَالَ: نَهَى رَسُولُ اللهِ ﷺ أَنْ يَتَوَضَّأَ الرَّجُلُ

بِفَضْلِ طَهُورِ الْمَرْأَةِ. رَوَاهُ أَبُو دَاوُدَ، وَابْنُ مَاجَهْ، وَالتِّرْمِذِيُّ وَ

زَادَ: أَوْ قَالَ: بِسُؤْرِهَا وَقَالَ: هَذَا حَدِيثٌ حَسَنٌ صَحِيحٌ.

471 Hakam b. 'Amr reported that Allah's Messenger (peace and blessings of Allah be upon him) forbade that a person should perform ablution with water spared by a woman while taking a bath. (*Abu Dawud, Ibn Majah, Tirmidhi and he made this addition*) : Or he said : Or by her left over. And he said : It is a Hasan Sahih hadith.

٤٧٢ - وَعَنْ حُمَيْدٍ الْحِمْيَرِيِّ، قَالَ: لَقِيتُ رَجُلًا صَحِبَ النَّبِيَّ ﷺ

أَرْبَعَ سِنِينَ، كَمَا صَحِبَهُ أَبُو هُرَيْرَةَ، قَالَ: نَهَى رَسُولُ اللهِ

أَنْ تَغْتَسِلَ الْمَرْأَةُ بِفَضْلِ الرَّجُلِ، أَوْ يَغْتَسِلَ الرَّجُلُ بِفَضْلِ الْمَرْأَةِ. زَادَ

مُسَدَّدٌ: وَلْيَغْتَرِفَا جَمِيعًا. رَوَاهُ أَبُو دَاوُدَ، وَالنَّسَائِيُّ، وَزَادَ أَحْمَدُ فِي أَوَّلِهِ:

نَهَى أَنْ يَمْتَشِطَ أَحَدُنَا كُلَّ يَوْمٍ أَوْ يَبُولَ فِي مُغْتَسَلٍ:

472 Humaid al-Himayri reported: I met a person (who had the privilege) of companionship of four years with Allah's Apostle (peace and blessings of Allah be upon him) just as Abu Huraira had. He said that Allah's Messenger (peace and blessings of Allah be upon him) forbade that a woman should take a bath with the water spared by a man, or a man should take bath with water spared by a woman[1] (while taking a bath). Musaddad made this addition : They should use it together. Abu Dawud and Nasa'i transmitted it, and Ahmad added at the beginning : He forbade anyone of us to use a comb every day or to pass water in a bath room.

1. Apparently there seems to be contradiction between the two categories of ahadith : one in which the Holy Prophet clearly stated that water does not become impure because of its use by a *junubi* see hadith No. 457, but here in ahadith No. 471, 472 we find a sort of prohibition in using water spared either by a man or woman from bath. The scholars of ahadith have reconciled the two statements by saying that what hadith No. 457 states is a religious verdict to the effect that water does not become impure after its use by a *junubi* and one is

permitted to take a bath or perform ablution with it. So far as the prohibition in ahadith No. 471, 472 is concerned it is not an absolute prohibition, but something permissible though undesirable and not very agreeable which is known in Shari'ah as حرمت تنزیہی . This shows that abstention under the category of ahadith No. 471, 472, is something very excellent and desirable, and what falls under the category of hadith No. 457 is permissible. The apparent contradiction between the two types of ahadith is not irresolvable. It is a difference between permissible and highly excellent. See Imam Shawkani's *Nail-ul-Awtar*, Vol. I, p. 37).

٤٧٣ - وَ رَوَاهُ ابْنُ مَاجَةَ عَنْ عَبْدِ اللهِ بْنِ سَرْجِسٍ

473 Ibn Majah transmitted it from 'Abdullah b. Sarjis.

CHAPTER 15
PERTAINING TO WATER

Section I أَلْفَصْلُ الْأَوَّلُ

٤٧٤ - عَنْ أَبِي هُرَيْرَةَ ، رَضِيَ اللهُ عَنْهُ ، قَالَ : قَالَ رَسُولُ اللهِ ﷺ لَا

يَبُولَنَّ أَحَدُكُمْ فِي الْمَاءِ الدَّائِمِ الَّذِى لَا يَجْرِى ، ثُمَّ يَغْتَسِلُ فِيهِ .

مُتَّفَقٌ عَلَيْهِ

وَ فِي رِوَايَةٍ لِمُسْلِمٍ ، قَالَ : لَا يَغْتَسِلْ أَحَدُكُمْ فِي الْمَاءِ الدَّائِمِ

وَ هُوَ جُنُبٌ " قَالُوا : كَيْفَ يَفْعَلُ يَا أَبَا هُرَيْرَةَ ؟ قَالَ : يَتَنَاوَلُهُ تَنَاوُلًا .

474 **Abu Huraira** reported Allah's Messenger (peace and blessings
of Allah be upon him) as saying: None amongst you should
urinate in standing water (that which does not flow) and then
wash in it (*Agreed upon*), and in a version by *Muslim*, he said:
None of you should take a bath in a standing water while he
is a *junubi*.[1] They said: Abu Huraira, then how it to be
done? He said : It has to be taken out in handfuls.

1. The word *junub* means aside or remote what it signifies is that one
   who has sexual intercourse is on the side or remote from prayer.
   (Imam Raghib). The word *junub* may also convey the sense of lying
   on the side of one's wife and thus it is a metaphorical expression for
   sexual act. The necessity of taking a bath arises in case of emission of
   seminal fluid due to sexual intercourse or *pollutio nocturna*.

٤٧٥ - وَعَنْ جَابِرٍ . قَالَ : نَهَى رَسُولُ اللهِ ﷺ أَنْ يُبَالَ فِي الْمَاءِ الرَّاكِدِ .

رَوَاهُ مُسْلِمٌ .

475 **Jabir** reported that Allah's Messenger (peace and blessings of
Allah be upon him) forbade urinating in stagnant water.

(*Muslim*)

٤٧٦ - وَعَنِ السَّائِبِ بْنِ يَزِيدَ ، قَالَ : ذَهَبَتْ بِي خَالَتِي إِلَى النَّبِيِّ ﷺ

، فَقَالَتْ : يَا رَسُولَ اللهِ إِنَّ ابْنَ أُخْتِي وَجِعٌ ، فَمَسَحَ رَأْسِي ، وَدَعَا لِي

بِالْبَرَكَةِ . ثُمَّ تَوَضَّأَ ، فَشَرِبْتُ مِنْ وَضُوئِهِ ، ثُمَّ قُمْتُ خَلْفَ ظَهْرِهِ ،

فَنَظَرْتُ إِلَى خَاتَمِ النُّبُوَّةِ بَيْنَ كَتِفَيْهِ مِثْلَ زِرِّ الْحَجَلَةِ . مُتَّفَقٌ عَلَيْهِ .

476 As-Sa'ib b. Yazid reported: My mother's sister took me to Allah's Messenger (peace and blessings of Allah be upon him) and said: Allah's Messenger, my sister's son is ill. He wiped my head, invoked blessings upon me and then performed ablution and I drank some of water left from his ablution, and I stood up behind his back and looked to his seal of prophecy between his shoulders like the button on a bride's pavilion.

(Agreed upon)

٤٧٧ ـ عَنِ ابْنِ عُمَرَ، قَالَ : سُئِلَ رَسُولُ اللهِ ﷺ عَنِ الْمَاءِ يَكُونُ فِي الْفَلَاةِ مِنَ الْأَرْضِ وَ مَا يَنُوبُهُ مِنَ الدَّوَابِّ وَ السِّبَاعِ، فَقَالَ : " إِذَا كَانَ الْمَاءُ قُلَّتَيْنِ لَمْ يَحْمِلِ الْخَبَثَ " رَوَاهُ أَحْمَدُ، وَ أَبُو دَاوُدَ، وَ التِّرْمِذِيُّ، وَ النَّسَائِيُّ، وَ الدَّارِمِيُّ، وَ ابْنُ مَاجَةَ. وَ فِي أُخْرَى لِأَبِي دَاوُدَ : " فَإِنَّهُ لَا يَنْجُسُ "

477 Ibn 'Umar reported that Allah's Messenger (peace and blessings of Allah be upon him) was asked about water in desert and which is frequented by animals and wild beasts. He said: When the water is of the volume of two big pitchers it bears no impurity. *(Abu Dawud, Tirmidhi, Nasa'i and Ibn Majah transmitted it).*

In other version by Abu Dawud (the words are: It does not become unclean.)

٤٧٨ ـ وَعَنْ أَبِي سَعِيدٍ الْخُدْرِيِّ، قَالَ : قِيلَ يَا رَسُولَ اللهِ! أَنَتَوَضَّأُ مِنْ بِئْرِ بُضَاعَةَ، وَ هِيَ بِئْرٌ يُلْقَى فِيهَا الْحِيَضُ، وَ لُحُومُ الْكِلَابِ، وَ النَّتْنُ؛ فَقَالَ رَسُولُ اللهِ ﷺ : " إِنَّ الْمَاءَ طَهُورٌ لَا يُنَجِّسُهُ شَيْءٌ " رَوَاهُ أَحْمَدُ، وَ التِّرْمِذِيُّ، وَ أَبُو دَاوُدَ، وَ النَّسَائِيُّ.

478 Abu Sai'd Khudri reported: It was said to Allah's Messenger (peace and blessings of Allah be upon him) whether they should perform ablution in well of Buda'a[1] (it was a well known well of Medina)—a well in which there are thrown the menstrual rags, the flesh of the dogs and the stinking things. Allah's Messenger (peace and blessings of Allah be upon him)

said: Verily water is pure and nothing makes it unclean.
(Ahmad, Tirmidhi, and Ibn Dawud and Nasa'i)

1. Shah Wali Ullah of Delhi has discussed in detail about this well of Buda'a. He says: It is wrong to presume that all those impurities for instance, menstrual rags, the flesh of dogs and the stinking things remained in that well, and with this despicable condition of uncleanliness the Holy Prophet (peace and blessings of Allah be upon him) was asked whether it was permissible to use water of this well. The fact is that the impurities unintentionally fell in this well as we find in our days, and these were constantly brought out even in the pre-Islamic days. After the advent of Islam the companions of the Holy Prophet were anxious to know the position of the purity of this well in which impurities had been falling off and on in the pre-Islamic days. They were under the impression that keeping in view the peculiar conditions of this well Allah's Apostle (peace and blessings of Allah be upon him) might make a special announcement about it. But the Holy Prophet simply told them that water is pure. What he wanted to say was that there is no special rule for the purity of water contained in this well. It, however, does not mean that all these impurities were intentionally retained in the well and no attempt was made to purify the water from them. *(Hujjatullahil-Baligha*, Vol. I, p. 194).

٤٧٩ - وَعَنْ أَبِي هُرَيْرَةَ، قَالَ: سَأَلَ رَجُلٌ رَسُولَ اللهِ ﷺ فَقَالَ: يَا رَسُولَ اللهِ! إِنَّا نَرْكَبُ الْبَحْرَ، وَ نَحْمِلُ مَعَنَا الْقَلِيلَ مِنَ الْمَاءِ، فَإِنْ تَوَضَّأْنَا بِهِ عَطِشْنَا، أَفَنَتَوَضَّأُ بِمَاءِ الْبَحْرِ؟ فَقَالَ رَسُولُ اللهِ ﷺ: "هُوَ الطَّهُورُ مَاؤُهُ، وَ الْحِلُّ مَيْتَتُهُ" رَوَاهُ مَالِكٌ، وَ التِّرْمِذِيُّ، وَالنَّسَائِيُّ، وَ ابْنُ مَاجَةَ وَ الدَّارِمِيُّ.

479 Abu Huraira reported: A person asked Allah's Messenger (peace and blessings of Allah be upon him): Allah's Messenger, we sail in the sea and carry with us small quantity of water, so if we perform ablution with it, we would feel thirsty. Can we then perform ablution with sea water? Thereupon Allah's Messenger (peace and blessings of Allah be upon him) said: Its water is pure and even what dies a natural death in it is also lawful[1] (is fit for eating). *(Malik, Tirmidhi, Nasai', Ibn Majah and Darimi)*

1. According to Imam Shafi'i every animal living in water is lawful. Imam Abu Hanifa is, however, of the opinion that fish is only lawful and the animals which are of the nature of the unlawful animals on the

land and air are unlawful in sea viz. sea dogs, sea hogs etc. So far
as the lawful slaughter of the sea animals is concerned, one does
not need it when they are brought out from water, they are supposed
to be lawfully slaughtered and their eating becomes permissible. It
should be borne in mind that when a sea animal dies a natural death
in water, its eating is no doubt permissible, but one should avoid
it as one is liable to contact disease from which the sea animal had
been suffering and it is on this ground that Imam Abu Hanifa deems
it to be unlawful.

٤٨٠ - وَعَنْ أَبِي زَيْدٍ، عَنْ عَبْدِ اللهِ بْنِ مَسْعُودٍ ﷺ أَنَّ النَّبِيَّ ﷺ قَالَ لَهُ
لَيْلَةَ الْجِنِّ "مَا فِي إِدَاوَتِكَ؟ قَالَ : نَبِيذٌ. قُلْتُ : نَبِيذٌ. قَالَ : تَمْرَةٌ طَيِّبَةٌ وَ
مَاءٌ طَهُورٌ" رَوَاهُ أَبُو دَاوُدَ، وَزَادَ أَحْمَدُ، وَالتِّرْمِذِيُّ نَتَوَضَّأُ مِنْهُ.
وَقَالَ التِّرْمِذِيُّ : أَبُو زَيْدٍ مَجْهُولٌ، وَصَحَّ :

480 Abu Zaid reported on the authority of 'Abdullah b. Mas'ud
that Allah's Apostle (peace and blessings of Allah be upon
him) said to him on the night of Jinn[1]: What is in your
second vessel? I ('Abdullah b. Mas'ud) said: It is *nabidh*[2].
Whereupon he (the Holy Prophet) said : The date is good
and water is purified. (*Transmitted by Abu Dawud, Ahmad
and Tirmidhi made this addition: He performed ablution with it
and Tirmidhi said that Abu Zaid is not known and (following) is a
sound tradition*)

1. Night of Jinn implies that night in which some Jinn took an oath of
   allegiance to the Holy Prophet and embraced Islam. They also listened
   to him reciting the Qur'ān. The Holy Prophet (peace and blessings
   of Allah be upon him) saw this night when after Abu Talib's death,
   he went to Taif to propagate his message but was driven out. Returning to Mecca he spent a night in the valley of Nakhla and a company
   of Jinn visited him. There is a pointed reference to this incident in
   Surah Jinn (72) and the words are:
   Say, it has been revealed to me that a party of Jinn listened, so they
   said: Surely we have heard a wonderful Qur'ān—guiding to the right
   way - so we believe in it and we shall not associate anyone with our
   Lord. (72 : 1-2)
2. *Nabidh* is a drink which is prepared by mixing up dates with water.

٤٨١ - عَنْ عَلْقَمَةَ، عَنْ عَبْدِ اللهِ بْنِ مَسْعُودٍ، قَالَ لَمْ أَكُنْ لَيْلَةَ الْجِنِّ
مَعَ رَسُولِ اللهِ ﷺ. رَوَاهُ مُسْلِمٌ.

481 **'Alqama** transmitted on the authority of 'Abdullah b. Mas'ud that he said: I was not along with Allah's Messenger (peace and blessings of Allah be upon him) on the night of Jinn.

(Muslim)

٢٨٢ - وَعَنْ كَبْشَةَ بِنْتِ كَعْبِ بْنِ مَالِكٍ - وَكَانَتْ تَحْتَ ابْنِ أَبِي قَتَادَةَ - أَنَّ أَبَا قَتَادَةَ دَخَلَ عَلَيْهَا، فَسَكَبَتْ لَهُ وَضُوْءًا، فَجَاءَتْ هِرَّةٌ تَشْرَبُ مِنْهُ فَأَصْغَى لَهَا الْإِنَاءَ حَتَّى شَرِبَتْ، قَالَتْ كَبْشَةُ: فَرَآنِيْ أَنْظُرُ إِلَيْهِ، فَقَالَ: أَتَعْجَبِيْنَ يَا ابْنَةَ أَخِيْ؟! قَالَتْ: فَقُلْتُ: نَعَمْ. قَالَ: إِنَّ رَسُوْلَ اللهِ ﷺ قَالَ: "إِنَّهَا لَيْسَتْ بِنَجَسٍ، إِنَّهَا مِنَ الطَّوَّافِيْنَ عَلَيْكُمْ أَوِ الطَّوَّافَاتِ" رَوَاهُ مَالِكٌ، وَأَحْمَدُ، وَالتِّرْمِذِيُّ، وَأَبُوْ دَاوُدَ، وَالنَّسَائِيُّ، وَابْنُ مَاجَةَ، وَالدَّارِمِيُّ.

482 **Kabsha,** the daughter of Ka'b b. Malik (and) the wife of the son of Abu Qatada reported that Abu Qatada visited her and she poured water for him for performing ablution. (It was at this time) that a cat came and drank out of that. He inclined the vessel towards her till she drank. Kabsha said: He saw me gazing at him and said: The daughter of my brother,[1] are you surprised? She reported: I said: Yes. He said that Allah's Messenger (peace and blessings of Allah be upon him) had said: It is not unclean since it (cat) is of those male and female animals which frequently go around you. (*Malik, Ahmad, Tirmidhi, Abu Dawud, Nasa'i Ibn Majah and Darimi*)

1. She was not the daughter of the brother of Abu Qatada, but owing to the customs of marrying the cousins prevalent amongst the Arabs and taking the cousins as brothers because of blood relation, they often applied the designation of uncle's son or uncle's daughter or brother's son or brother's daughter to husband and wife even in cases where this relationship did not exist.

٢٨٣ - وَعَنْ دَاوُدَ بْنِ صَالِحِ بْنِ دِيْنَارٍ، عَنْ أُمِّهِ، أَنَّ مَوْلَاتَهَا أَرْسَلَتْهَا بِهَرِيْسَةٍ إِلَى عَائِشَةَ. قَالَتْ: فَوَجَدْتُهَا تُصَلِّيْ، فَأَشَارَتْ إِلَيَّ أَنْ ضَعِيْهَا نَجَاءَتْ هِرَّةٌ، فَأَكَلَتْ مِنْهَا. فَلَمَّا انْصَرَفَتْ عَائِشَةُ مِنْ صَلَاتِهَا، أَكَلَتْ

مِنْ حَيْثُ أَكَلَتِ الْهِرَّةَ. فَقَالَتْ: إِنَّ رَسُولَ اللهِ ﷺ قَالَ: إِنَّهَا لَيْسَتْ
بِنَجِسٍ، إِنَّهَا مِنَ الطَّوَّافِينَ عَلَيْكُمْ" وَ إِنِّي رَأَيْتُ رَسُولَ اللهِ ﷺ يَتَوَضَّأُ
بِفَضْلِهَا. رَوَاهُ أَبُو دَاوُدَ.

483 Dawud b. Salih b. Dinar reported his mother having said that
her mistress sent her to 'Ā'isha with some *Harisa*.[1] She said:
I found her engaged in prayer. She pointed towards me that
I should place that there. A cat came and ate out of it.
When 'Ā'isha had concluded her prayer, she ate from the
place where the cat had eaten. She said that Allah's Messenger (peace and blessings of Allah be upon him) had stated
that it was not unclean. It is one of those who (frequently) go
around you and she further added: I have seen Allah's Messenger (peace and blessings of Allah be upon him) performing
ablution with (water) spared by her. (*Abu Dawud*)

1. It is a food prepared by mixing mutton and flour.

٤٨٤ - وَعَنْ جَابِرٍ، قَالَ: سُئِلَ رَسُولُ اللهِ ﷺ: أَنَتَوَضَّأُ بِمَا أَفْضَلَتِ
الْحُمُرُ؟ قَالَ: "نَعَمْ، وَ بِمَا أَفْضَلَتِ السِّبَاعُ كُلُّهَا" رَوَاهُ فِي "شَرْحِ
السُّنَّةِ"

484 Jabir reported that Allah's Messenger (peace and blessings of
Allah be upon him) was thus asked: Should we perform
ablution with (water) left by asses, he said: Yes; and all that
the beasts of prey leave.[2] (*Baghawi transmitted it in Sharh as-
Sunnah*).

2. This hadith forms the basis of Imam Shafi'i's contention that left over
of all the beasts is pure except that of dog and swine. Imam Hanifa is,
however, of the opinion that the left over of all the beasts is unclean
as the saliva falls in water which is unclean. The fact is that the water
is clean in the case when it is found in wilderness or desert in very large
quantity, i.e. in the form of lakes or rivers, but the water found in the
houses in small quantity becomes unclean when the beasts drink out
of that. (*Mirqat*, Vol. II, p. 62).

٤٨٥ - وَ عَنْ أُمِّ هَانِئٍ، قَالَتْ: اغْتَسَلَ رَسُولُ اللهِ ﷺ هُوَ وَ مَيْمُونَةُ
فِي قَصْعَةٍ فِيهَا أَثَرُ الْعَجِينِ. رَوَاهُ النَّسَائِيُّ، وَ ابْنُ مَاجَهْ

485 Umm Hani reported that Allah's Messenger (peace and blessings of Allah be upon him) and Maimuna took a bath from bowl wherein there was the trace of dough-paste.

(Nasa'i and Ibn Majah)

Section II اَلْفَصْلُ الثَّانِی

٤٨٦ - عَنْ يَحْيَى بْنِ عَبِيدِ الرَّحْمَنِ ، قَالَ : إِنَّ عُمَرَ خَرَجَ فِی رَكْبٍ فِيهِمْ عَمْرُو
بْنُ الْعَاصِ حَتَّى وَرَدُوا حَوْضًا . فَقَالَ عَمْرُو : يَا صَاحِبَ الْحَوْضِ ! هَلْ
تَرِدُ حَوْضَكَ السِّبَاعُ ؟ فَقَالَ عُمَرُ بْنُ الْخَطَّابِ : يَا صَاحِبَ الْحَوْضِ ! لَا
تُخْبِرْنَا ، وَإِنَّا نَرِدُ عَلَى السِّبَاعِ وَ تَرِدُ عَلَيْنَا . رَوَاهُ مَالِكٌ .

486 Yahya b. 'Abdur Rahman reported that 'Umar set out with a party of riders and there was amongst them 'Amr b. al-'As till they came to a cistern. 'Amr said: Owner of the cistern, do the beasts of prey come down to it. Thereupon 'Umar b. Khattab said: Owner of the cistern, don't inform us about this[1] for we go down to what beasts of prey (leave) and they come down to us (what we leave for them). *(Malik)*

> 1. What this means is that we should not make unnecessary enquiries about things which are obviously lawful. It was a big cistern and so drinking of water even by beasts did not pollute it, hence there was no need to probe into the matter.

٤٨٧ - وَزَادَ رَزِينٌ ، قَالَ : زَادَ بَعْضُ الرُّوَاةِ فِی قَوْلِ عُمَرَ : وَإِنِّی سَمِعْتُ
رَسُولَ اللهِ ﷺ يَقُولُ : "لَهَا مَا أَخَذَتْ فِی بُطُونِهَا ، وَ مَا بَقِیَ فَمَقُولُنَا
طَهُورٌ وَ شَرَابٌ" .

487 And Razin made an addition saying: That some of the transmitters have made this addition in the words of 'Umar : I heard Allah's Messenger (peace and blessings of Allah be upon him) as saying: They have their share in what they have taken down in their bellies and what has been left out of that is clean and (fit) for drinking.[1]

1. According to an eminent scholar Mirak Shah this statement of Haḍrat 'Umar is not a religious verdict, as one does not find any statement of the Holy Prophet to this effect. According to Imam Shafi'i it is correct. The three Imams, however, agree on the point that there is nothing harmful in using this water as it is based on the personal observation of Haḍrat 'Umar b. Khattab. (*Mazahir-i-Haqq*, Vol. I, p. 160.)

٢٨٨ ـ وَعَنْ أَبِى سَعِيدٍ إِلْخُدْرِيِّ : أَنَّ رَسُوْلَ اللّٰهِ ﷺ سُئِلَ عَنِ الْحِيَاضِ الَّتِى بَيْنَ مَكَّةَ وَ الْمَدِيْنَةِ تَرِدُهَا السِّبَاعُ وَ الْكِلَابُ وَ الْحُمُرُ عَنِ الطُّهُوِ مِنْهَا. فَقَالَ "لَهَا مَا حَمَلَتْ فِىْ بُطُوْنِهَا، وَ لَنَا مَا غَبَرَ طَهُوْرٌ". رَوَاهُ ابْنُ مَاجَهَ.

488 **Abu Sa'id Khudri** reported that Allah's Messenger (peace and blessings of Allah be upon him) was asked about the cleanliness of the cistern situated between Mecca and Medina and where the beasts, dogs and asses came down. He said: For them is that which they have taken to their bellies and we have what is left (from them) and it is pure. (*Ibn Majah*)

٢٨٩ ـ وَعَنْ عُمَرَ بْنِ الْخَطَّابِ ، رَضِىَ اللّٰهُ عَنْهُ ، قَالَ لَا تَغْتَسِلُوْا بِالْمَاءِ الْمُشَمَّسِ : فَإِنَّهُ يُوْرِثُ الْبَرَصَ . رَوَاهُ الدَّارَ قُطْنِىّ .

489 **'Umar b. Khattab** (may Allah be pleased with him) said: Do not take a bath in water exposed to the sun, for it results in leprosy. (*Daraqutni*)

CHAPTER 16
CLEANSING OF IMPURITIES

Section I أَلْفَصَّلُ الْأَوَّلُ

٤٩٠ ـ عَنْ أَبِي هُرَيْرَةَ، قَالَ: قَالَ رَسُولُ اللهِ ﷺ: "إِذَا شَرِبَ الْكَلْبُ فِي إِنَاءِ أَحَدِكُمْ، فَلْيَغْسِلْهُ سَبْعَ مَرَّاتٍ" مُتَّفَقٌ عَلَيْهِ.

وَفِي رِوَايَةٍ لِمُسْلِمٍ: "طُهُورُ إِنَاءِ أَحَدِكُمْ إِذَا وَلَغَ فِيهِ الْكَلْبُ أَنْ يَغْسِلَهُ سَبْعَ مَرَّاتٍ أُوْلَاهُنَّ بِالتُّرَابِ."

490 **Abu Huraira** reported Allah's Messenger (peace and blessings of Allah be upon him) as saying: When a dog licks a utensil belonging to any one of you he must wash it seven times.

(Agreed upon)

In a version by *Muslim* he said: When a dog licks water in a utensil belonging to any one of you he should wash it seven times using the clay first time.

٤٩١ ـ وَعَنْهُ، قَالَ: قَامَ أَعْرَابِيٌّ، فَبَالَ فِي الْمَسْجِدِ، فَتَنَاوَلَهُ النَّاسُ. فَقَالَ لَهُمُ النَّبِيُّ ﷺ: "دَعُوهُ وَهَرِيقُوا عَلَى بَوْلِهِ سَجْلاً مِنْ مَاءٍ ـ أَوْ ذَنُوبًا مِنْ مَاءٍ ـ فَإِنَّمَا بُعِثْتُمْ مُيَسِّرِينَ، وَلَمْ تُبْعَثُوا مُعَسِّرِينَ." رَوَاهُ الْبُخَارِيُّ.

491 It is reported on the same authority that a desert Arab stood up and urinated in the mosque. The people took hold of him. Allah's Messenger (peace and blessings of Allah be upon him) said: Leave him and pour a bucketful of water upon his urine, for you have been sent to make things easy and you have not been sent to make them difficult. *(Bukhari)*

٤٩٢ ـ وَعَنْ أَنَسٍ، قَالَ: بَيْنَمَا نَحْنُ فِي الْمَسْجِدِ مَعَ رَسُولِ اللهِ ﷺ، إِذْ جَاءَ أَعْرَابِيٌّ، فَقَامَ يَبُولُ فِي الْمَسْجِدِ. فَقَالَ أَصْحَابُ رَسُولِ اللهِ ﷺ:

مَهُ مَعَهُ . فَقَالَ رَسُولُ اللهِ ﷺ : "لَا تُزْرِمُوهُ ، دَعُوهُ" فَتَرَكُوهُ حَتَّى بَالَ

ثُمَّ إِنَّ رَسُولَ اللهِ ﷺ دَعَاهُ ، فَقَالَ لَهُ : "إِنَّ هٰذِهِ الْمَسَاجِدَ لَا تَصْلُحُ

لِشَىءٍ مِنْ هٰذَا الْبَوْلِ وَ الْقَذَرِ ، إِنَّمَا هِىَ لِذِكْرِ اللهِ ، وَ الصَّلَاةِ ، وَقِرَاءَةِ

الْقُرْآنِ" أَوْ كَمَا قَالَ رَسُولُ اللهِ ﷺ . قَالَ ، وَ أَمَرَ رَجُلاً مِنَ الْقَوْمِ ،

نَجَاءَ بِدَلْوٍ مِنْ مَاءٍ ، فَسَنَّهُ عَلَيْهِ . مُتَّفَقٌ عَلَيْهِ

492 **Anas** reported: As we were sitting in the mosque along with Allah's Messenger (peace and blessings of Allah be upon him) a desert Arab came. He stood up and urinated in the mosque. Thereupon the companions of Allah's Messenger (peace and blessings of Allah be upon him) said (grimly): Stop, stop. Upon this Allah's Messenger (peace and blessings of Allah be upon him) said: Don't interrupt his urination, leave him alone. So they left him till he urinated. Then Allah's Messenger (peace and blessings of Allah be upon him) called him and said to him: Verily these are the mosques and, therefore, it is not proper (to throw) anything as urine or filth in them. Verily these are meant for the remembrance of Allah, for the prayer and the recitation of the Qur'ān or Allah's Messenger (peace and blessings of Allah be upon him) said something like it. He (Anas) said that he commanded a person from the people to bring a bucketful of water. He brought that and poured it over it. (*Agreed upon*)

٤٩٣ - وَ عَنْ أَسْمَاءَ بِنْتِ أَبِى بَكْرٍ ، قَالَتْ : سَأَلَتِ امْرَأَةٌ رَسُولَ اللهِ

ﷺ فَقَالَتْ : يَا رَسُولَ اللهِ ! أَرَأَيْتَ إِحْدَانَا إِذَا أَصَابَ ثَوْبَهَا الدَّمُ

مِنَ الْحِيضَةِ ، كَيْفَ تَصْنَعُ ؟ فَقَالَ رَسُولُ اللهِ ﷺ : إِذَا أَصَابَ ثَوْبَ

إِحْدَاكُنَّ الدَّمُ مِنَ الْحِيضَةِ فَلْتَقْرُصْهُ ، ثُمَّ لِتَنْضَحْهُ بِمَاءٍ ثُمَّ لِتُصَلِّ

فِيهِ" مُتَّفَقٌ عَلَيْهِ .

493 **Asma'**, the daughter of Abu Bakr, reported that a woman asked Allah's Messenger (peace and blessings of Allah be upon him) as saying: Allah's Messenger, what according to your opinion one should do when one of us has upon her garments the drops of menstrual blood? Whereupon Allah's Messenger (peace and blessings of Allah be upon him) said: When the menstrual blood falls upon the garment of anyone of you she should rub it and then sprinkle water on it and observe prayer with it. (*Agreed upon*)

٤٩٤ - وَعَنْ سُلَيْمَانَ بْنِ يَسَارٍ، قَالَ : سَأَلْتُ عَائِشَةَ عَنِ الْمَنِيِّ يُصِيبُ الثَّوْبَ . فَقَالَتْ : كُنْتُ أَغْسِلُهُ مِنْ ثَوْبِ رَسُولِ اللهِ ، فَيَخْرُجُ إِلَى الصَّلَاةِ وَأَثَرُ الْغَسْلِ فِي ثَوْبِهِ . مُتَّفَقٌ عَلَيْهِ .

494 Sulaiman b. Yasar reported: I asked 'A'isha about the (drops of semen) which get on to a garment. She said: I used to wash it from the garment of Allah's Messenger (peace and blessings of Allah be upon him) and he went out for prayer with the mark of washing on his garment. (*Agreed upon*)

٤٩٥ - وَعَنِ الْأَسْوَدِ وَهَمَّامٍ، عَنْ عَائِشَةَ، قَالَتْ : كُنْتُ أَفْرُكُ الْمَنِيَّ مِنْ ثَوْبِ رَسُولِ اللهِ ﷺ . رَوَاهُ مُسْلِمٌ .

495 Aswad and Hammam reported 'A'isha having said: I used to scrape off the (drops) of semen from the garment of Allah's Messenger (peace and blessings of Allah be upon him).

(*Muslim*)

٤٩٦ - وَبِرِوَايَةِ عَلْقَمَةَ وَالْأَسْوَدِ، عَنْ عَائِشَةَ نَحْوَهُ، وَفِيهِ : ثُمَّ يُصَلِّي فِيهِ .

496 'Alqama and Aswad narrated a hadith like this on the authority of 'A'isha and there are (in that hadith, the words): He then observed prayer with the (garment).

٤٩٧ - وَعَنْ أُمِّ قَيْسٍ بِنْتِ مِحْصَنٍ : أَنَّهَا أَتَتْ بِابْنٍ لَهَا صَغِيرٍ لَمْ يَأْكُلِ الطَّعَامَ إِلَى رَسُولِ اللهِ ﷺ ، فَأَجْلَسَهُ رَسُولُ اللهِ ﷺ فِي حِجْرِهِ، فَبَالَ عَلَى ثَوْبِهِ ، فَدَعَا بِمَاءٍ، فَنَضَحَهُ، وَلَمْ يَغْسِلْهُ . مُتَّفَقٌ عَلَيْهِ .

497 Umm Qais, the daughter of Miḥṣan, reported that she came to Allah's Messenger (peace and blessings of Allah be upon him) along with her babe who was not yet weaned. Allah's

Messenger (peace and blessings of Allah be upon him) seated him in his lap. He pissed on his garment. He called for water, and sprinkled this on it (his garment) and did not wash it (thoroughly).[1] (*Agreed upon*)

1. According to Imam Abu Hanifa washing is essential in case the garment is soiled with urine. The verb لم يغسل according to the Hanafi scholars, does not mean: He did not wash it at all, but it means that he did not wash it thoroughly. (*Mirqat*, Vol. II, p. 70)

٢٩٨ - وَعَنْ عَبْدِ اللهِ بْنِ عَبَّاسٍ، قَالَ: سَمِعْتُ رَسُولَ اللهِ ﷺ يَقُولُ: إِذَا دُبِغَ الْإِهَابُ فَقَدْ طَهُرَ. رَوَاهُ مُسْلِمٌ.

498 'Abdullah b. 'Abbas reported: I heard Allah's Messenger (peace and blessings of Allah be upon him) as saying: When the skin is tanned, it becomes pure.[2] (*Muslim*)

2. According to Imam Abu Hanifa, any kind of skin becomes pure by tanning except that of swine (because of its utmost impurity). Imam Shafi'i excepted the skin of dog also. The skin of man is no way permitted to be tanned and used.

٢٩٩ - وَعَنْهُ، قَالَ: تُصُدِّقَ عَلَى مَوْلَاةٍ لِمَيْمُونَةَ بِشَاةٍ، فَمَاتَتْ، فَمَرَّ بِهَا رَسُولُ اللهِ ﷺ، فَقَالَ: "هَلَّا أَخَذْتُمْ إِهَابَهَا فَدَبَغْتُمُوهُ، فَانْتَفَعْتُمْ بِهِ!"، فَقَالُوا: إِنَّهَا مَيْتَةٌ، فَقَالَ: "إِنَّمَا حُرِّمَ أَكْلُهَا" مُتَّفَقٌ عَلَيْهِ.

499 It is reported on the same authority that a sheep was given in charity to the freed slave girl of Maimuna, but it died. Allah's Messenger (peace and blessings of Allah be upon him) happened to pass by it (and seeing that lying waste) said: Why did you not take its skin, and tan it and make use of it? They (the companions of the Holy Prophet) said: That is carcass. Thereupon he said: It is its eating which has been forbidden.
(*Agreed upon*)

٥٠٠ - وَعَنْ سَوْدَةَ زَوْجِ النَّبِيِّ ﷺ، قَالَتْ: مَاتَتْ لَنَا شَاةٌ، فَدَبَغْنَا مَسْكَهَا، ثُمَّ مَا زِلْنَا نَنْبِذُ فِيهِ حَتَّى صَارَ شَنًّا. رَوَاهُ الْبُخَارِيُّ.

500 Sawda, the wife of Allah's Apostle (peace and blessings of Allah be upon him), said: A sheep of ours died. We tanned its skin (and then made water skin out of that) and continued to preserve *nabidh* in that, till it was worn out. (*Bukhari*)

Section II اَلْفَصْلُ الثَّانِی

١٠٥ - عَنْ لُبَابَةَ بِنْتِ الْحَارِثِ، قَالَتْ: كَانَ الْحُسَيْنُ بْنُ عَلِیٍّ، رَضِیَ اللهُ
عَنْهُمَا، فِی حِجْرِ رَسُولِ اللهِ ﷺ، فَبَالَ عَلٰی ثَوْبِهِ. فَقُلْتُ: اِلْبَسْ ثَوْبًا،
وَأَعْطِنِی إِزَارَكَ حَتّٰی أَغْسِلَهُ، قَالَ: "إِنَّمَا یُغْسَلُ مِنْ بَوْلِ الْأُنْثٰی، وَ
یُنْضَحُ مِنْ بَوْلِ الذَّكَرِ". رَوَاهُ أَحْمَدُ، وَأَبُوْ دَاوُدَ، وَابْنُ مَاجَةَ.

501 Lubaba, the daughter of Harith, said: Husain b. 'Ali (may Allah
be pleased with both of them) was sitting in the lap of Allah's
Messenger (peace and blessings of Allah be upon him) and he
pissed upon his garment. I said: Put on (another) garment,
and give it to me so that I may wash it. He said: Washing (of
garment) is required in case of the urine of a female child, whereas sprinkling (is enough) in case of the urine of a male child.
                               (Ahmad, Abu Dawud, Ibn Majah)

٢٠٥ - وَفِی رِوَایَةٍ لِأَبِی دَاوُدَ، وَ النَّسَائِیِّ، عَنْ أَبِی السَّمْحِ، قَالَ: "یُغْسَلُ
مِنْ بَوْلِ الْجَارِیَةِ، وَ یُرَشُّ مِنْ بَوْلِ الْغُلَامِ."

502 In a version of **Abu Dawud,** and **Nasa'i** from Abu Samh, he
is reported to have said: It should be washed in case of the
urine of a girl and sprinkled in case of the urine of a boy.

٣٠٥ - وَعَنْ أَبِی هُرَیْرَةَ، قَالَ: قَالَ رَسُولُ اللهِ ﷺ: "إِذَا وَطِئَ أَحَدُكُمْ
بِنَعْلِهِ الْأَذٰی، فَإِنَّ التُّرَابَ لَهُ طَهُورٌ". رَوَاهُ أَبُوْ دَاوُدَ.
وَلِابْنِ مَاجَةَ مَعْنَاهُ.

503 Abu Huraira reported that Allah's Messenger (peace and
blessings of Allah be upon him) said: When any one of you
treads with his shoes upon an impurity, (it becomes pure)
since the dust serves as a purifier for that. *(Abu Dawud, and
Ibn Majah has transmitted something similar.)*

٥٠٤ ـ وَعَنْ أُمِّ سَلَمَةَ، قَالَتْ لَهَا امْرَأَةٌ: إِنِّي امْرَأَةٌ أُطِيلُ ذَيْلِي، وَ
أَمْشِي فِي الْمَكَانِ الْقَذِرِ. قَالَتْ: قَالَ رَسُولُ اللهِ ﷺ: "يُطَهِّرُهُ مَا بَعْدَهُ"
رَوَاهُ مَالِكٌ، وَأَحْمَدُ، وَالتِّرْمِذِيُّ. وَأَبُو دَاوُدَ وَالدَّارِمِيُّ ۚ قَالَا:
الْمَرْأَةُ أُمُّ وَلَدٍ لِإِبْرَاهِيمَ بْنِ عَبْدِ الرَّحْمَنِ بْنِ عَوْفٍ.

504 Umm Salamah reported that a woman said to her: I have a
shirt which is long and I walk in filthy places. She reported
that Allah's Messenger (peace and blessings of Allah be upon
him) said: What comes after it cleanses[1] it. (*Transmitted by
Malik, Ahmad, Tirmidhi. And Abu Dawud and Darimi said: That
woman was the Umm Walad[2] belonging to Ibrahim b. 'Abdur
Rahman b. 'Auf.*)

1. What this means is that the dust of the road cleanses the impurity stuck
   to the lower border of the shirt because of walking in impurity.
2. Literally it means the mother of a boy, but it is a technical term in the
   Shari'ah of Islam which means a slave-woman who has given birth to
   a child from the master and thus secured her freedom after his death.

٥٠٥ ـ وَعَنِ الْمِقْدَامِ بْنِ مَعْدِيَ كَرِبَ، قَالَ: نَهَى رَسُولُ اللهِ ﷺ عَنْ
لُبْسِ جُلُودِ السِّبَاعِ، وَالرُّكُوبِ عَلَيْهَا. رَوَاهُ أَبُو دَاوُدَ وَالنَّسَائِيُّ.

505 Al-Miqdam b. Ma'dikarib reported that Allah's Messenger
(peace and blessings of Allah be upon him) prohibited wearing the skins of beasts of prey or using them as saddles.

(*Abu Dawud and Nasa'i*)

٥٠٦ ـ وَعَنْ أَبِي الْمَلِيحِ بْنِ أُسَامَةَ، عَنْ أَبِيهِ، عَنِ النَّبِيِّ ﷺ: نَهَى عَنْ
جُلُودِ السِّبَاعِ. رَوَاهُ أَحْمَدُ، وَأَبُو دَاوُدَ، وَالنَّسَائِيُّ، وَزَادَ التِّرْمِذِيُّ،
وَالدَّارِمِيُّ: أَنْ تُفْتَرَشَ.

506 Abul Malih b. Usama reported on the authority of his father
that Allah's Apostle (peace and blessings of Allah be upon
him) forbade wearing of the skins of all the beasts of prey.
(*Transmitted by Ahmad, Abu Dawud, Nasa'i and Tirmidhi and
Darimi made this addition that they may not be used as carpets*)

٥٠٧ـ وَعَنْ أَبِى الْمَلِيْحِ : أَنَّهُ كَرِهَ ثَمَنَ جُلُوْدِ السِّبَاعِ . رَوَاهُ التِّرْمِذِيُّ
فِى اللِّبَاسِ مِنْ "جَامِعِهِ" وَ سَنَدُهُ جَيِّلٌ .

507 Abul Malih reported that he (the Holy Prophet) disapproved (the transaction and as a result of that) making the payment of the skins of beasts of prey. (*Transmitted by Tirmidhi in his Jami' under the head 'Dress' and the chain of transmission is sound.*)

٥٠٨ـ وَعَنْ عَبْدِ اللهِ بْنِ عُكَيْمٍ ، قَالَ : أَتَانَا كِتَابُ رَسُوْلِ اللهِ ﷺ :
"أَنْ لَّا تَنْتَفِعُوْا مِنَ الْمَيْتَةِ بِإِهَابٍ ، وَّ لَا عَصَبٍ" رَوَاهُ التِّرْمِذِيُّ
وَ أَبُوْ دَاؤُدَ ، وَ النَّسَائِيُّ ، وَ ابْنُ مَاجَةَ .

508 'Abdullah b. 'Ukaim reported : There came to us the letter of Allah's Messenger (peace and blessings of Allah be upon him) to the effect that the skin of the dead animal or (its) sinews should not be made use of (without tanning). (*Tirmidhi, Abu Dawud, Nasa'i and Ibn Majah*)

٥٠٩ـ وَعَنْ عَائِشَةَ ، رَضِيَ اللهُ عَنْهَا ، أَنَّ رَسُوْلَ اللهِ ﷺ أَمَرَ أَنْ
يُسْتَمْتَعَ بِجُلُوْدِ الْمَيْتَةِ إِذَا دُبِغَتْ . رَوَاهُ مَالِكٌ ، وَ أَبُوْ دَاؤُدَ .

509 'A'isha (may Allah be pleased with her) reported that Allah's Messenger (peace and blessings of Allah be upon him) commanded us to make use of the skins of the dead animals after these were tanned. (*Malik and Abu Dawud*)

٥١٠ـ وَعَنْ مَيْمُوْنَةَ ، قَالَتْ : مَرَّ عَلَى النَّبِيِّ ﷺ رِجَالٌ مِّنْ قُرَيْشٍ
يَجُرُّوْنَ شَاةً لَّهُمْ مِثْلَ الْحِمَارِ ، فَقَالَ لَهُمْ رَسُوْلُ اللهِ ﷺ : "لَوْ
أَخَذْتُمْ إِهَابَهَا" قَالُوْا : إِنَّهَا مَيْتَةٌ . فَقَالَ رَسُوْلُ اللهِ ﷺ : "يُطَهِّرُهَا
الْمَاءُ وَ الْقَرَظُ" رَوَاهُ أَحْمَدُ ، وَ أَبُوْ دَاؤُدَ .

510 Maimuna reported that some persons from Quraish happened to pass by Allah's Messenger (peace and blessings of Allah be upon him) dragging a sheep of theirs as an ass. Allah's Messenger (peace and blessings of Allah be upon him) said to

them: I wish if you were to make use of its hide. They said:
It is dead. Thereupon Allah's Messenger (peace and blessings
of Allah be upon him) said: Water and leaves of the *mimosa
flava* purify it. (*Ahmad and Abu Dawud*)

٥١١ - وَعَنْ سَلَمَةَ بِنِ الْمُحَبِّقِ، قَالَ إِنَّ رَسُولَ اللهِ ﷺ جَاءَ فِي غَزْوَةِ
تَبُوكَ عَلَى أَهْلِ بَيْتٍ، فَإِذَا قِرْبَةٌ مُعَلَّقَةٌ، فَسَأَلَ الْمَاءَ . فَقَالُوا:
يَا رَسُولَ اللهِ! إِنَّهَا مَيْتَةٌ . فَقَالَ: "دِبَاغُهَا طُهُورُهَا" رَوَاهُ أَحْمَدُ،
وَأَبُو دَاوُدَ .

511 Salama bint Muhabbaq reported that Allah's Messenger (peace
and blessings of Allah be upon him) came (back) from the expedition of Tabuk to the members of a family that he found a
small water-skin being suspended there. He asked for water
and they said : Allah's Messenger, it (has been prepared out
of the skin) of dead (animal). He said: Its tanning is its
purification. (*Ahmad and Abu Dawud.*)

Section III   أَلْفَصْلُ الثَّالِثُ

٥١٢ - عَنِ امْرَأَةٍ مِنْ بَنِي عَبْدِ الْأَشْهَلِ، قَالَتْ: قُلْتُ يَا رَسُولَ اللهِ!
إِنَّ لَنَا طَرِيقًا إِلَى الْمَسْجِدِ مُنْتِنَةً، فَكَيْفَ نَفْعَلُ إِذَا مُطِرْنَا؟ فَقَالَ:
"أَلَيْسَ بَعْدَهَا طَرِيقٌ هِيَ أَطْيَبُ مِنْهَا؟" قُلْتُ: بَلَى. قَالَ: "فَهٰذِهِ بِهٰذِهِ"
رَوَاهُ أَبُو دَاوُدَ .

512 A woman from the tribe of 'Abd al-Ashhal reported ; I
said: Allah's Messenger, our roads leading to the mosque
have a stenching smell so what we should do (with our clothes)
when it is raining in our (habitations). He said: Is there
not after that a road more pleasant one. I said: Yes.
Whereupon he said: It makes amend for that. (*Abu Dawud*)

٥١٣ - وَعَنْ عَبْدِ اللهِ بْنِ مَسْعُودٍ، قَالَ كُنَّا نُصَلِّي مَعَ رَسُولِ اللهِ ﷺ وَلَا
نَتَوَضَّأُ مِنَ الْمَوْطِئِ . رَوَاهُ التِّرْمِذِيُّ .

513 'Abdullah b. Mas'ud reported: We used to observe prayer along with Allah's Messenger (peace and blessings of Allah be upon him) and we did not perform ablution because of treading on anything. (*Tirmidhi*)

٥١٣ - وَعَنِ ابْنِ عُمَرَ، قَالَ: كَانَتِ الْكِلَابُ تُقْبِلُ وَ تُدْبِرُ فِي الْمَسْجِدِ
فِي زَمَانِ رَسُولِ اللهِ ﷺ ، فَلَمْ يَكُوْنُوْا يَرُشُّونَ شَيْئًا مِّنْ ذٰلِكَ
رَوَاهُ الْبُخَارِيُّ .

514 'Abdullah b. 'Umar reported that the dogs used (to roam about) in and out of the mosque during the lifetime of Allah's Messenger (peace and blessings of Allah be upon him) but they (the companions) did not sprinkle anything because of that (the movement of the dogs). (*Bukhari*)

٥١٥ - وَعَنِ الْبَرَاءِ (بْنِ عَازِبٍ)، قَالَ : قَالَ رَسُولُ اللهِ ﷺ : "لَا بَأْسَ
بِبَوْلِ مَا يُؤْكَلُ لَحْمُهُ ":

515 Al-Bara' b. 'Azib reported: There is no harm in the urine of that animal the flesh of which is (lawfully) eaten.

٥١٦ - وَفِي رِوَايَةِ جَابِرٍ. قَالَ : "مَا أُكِلَ لَحْمُهُ فَلَا بَأْسَ بِبَوْلِهِ" رَوَاهُ
أَحْمَدُ ، وَ الدَّارَ قُطْنِيُّ

516 It is reported on the authority of **Jabir** that he said: (The animal) the flesh of which (is lawful) to eat there is no harm (uncleanliness) in its urine. (*Ahmad and Daraqutni*)

CHAPTER 17
PERTAINING TO THE WIPING OVER THE SOCKS

Section I الْفَصَلُ الْأَوَّلُ

٥١٧ ـ عَنْ شُرَيْحِ بْنِ هَانِئٍ ، قَالَ : سَأَلْتُ عَلِيَّ بْنَ أَبِى طَالِبٍ رَضِىَ اللهُ
عَنْهُ ، عَنِ الْمَسْحِ عَلَى الْخُفَّيْنِ ، فَقَالَ : جَعَلَ رَسُولُ اللهِ ﷺ ـ ثَلَاثَةَ
أَيَّامٍ وَلَيَالِيْهِنَّ لِلْمُسَافِرِ ، وَيَوْمًا وَّلَيْلَةً لِّلْمُقِيْمِ ، رَوَاهُ مُسْلِمٌ .

517 Shuraih b. Hani said: I asked 'Ali b. Abu Talib (may Allah be pleased with him) about wiping over the socks. He said: The Messenger of Allah (peace and blessings of Allah be upon him) stipulated (the upper limit for this) as three days and three nights for a traveller and one day and one night for the resident. (*Muslim*)

٥١٨ ـ وَعَنِ الْمُغِيْرَةِ بْنِ شُعْبَةَ : أَنَّهُ غَزَا مَعَ رَسُولِ اللهِ ﷺ غَزْوَةَ تَبُوْكَ .
قَالَ الْمُغِيْرَةُ : فَتَبَرَّزَ رَسُولُ اللهِ ﷺ قِبَلَ الْغَائِطِ ، فَحَمَلْتُ مَعَهُ إِدَاوَةً
قَبْلَ الْفَجْرِ ، فَلَمَّا رَجَعَ أَخَذْتُ أُهْرِيقُ عَلَى يَدَيْهِ مِنَ الْإِدَاوَةِ ، فَغَسَلَ
يَدَيْهِ وَوَجْهَهُ ، وَعَلَيْهِ جُبَّةٌ مِنْ صُوْفٍ ، ذَهَبَ يَحْسِرُعَنْ ذِرَاعَيْهِ
فَضَاقَ كُمُّ الْجُبَّةِ ، فَأَخْرَجَ يَدَيْهِ مِنْ تَحْتِ الْجُبَّةِ ، وَأَلْقَى الْجُبَّةَ عَلَى
مَنْكِبَيْهِ ، وَغَسَلَ ذِرَاعَيْهِ ، ثُمَّ مَسَحَ بِنَاصِيَتِهِ وَعَلَى الْعِمَامَةِ ، ثُمَّ
أَهْوَيْتُ لِأَنْزِعَ خُفَّيْهِ ، فَقَالَ : "دَعْهُمَا فَإِنِّى أَدْخَلْتُهُمَا طَاهِرَتَيْنِ" فَمَسَحَ
عَلَيْهِمَا ، ثُمَّ رَكِبَ وَرَكِبْتُ ، فَانْتَهَيْنَا إِلَى الْقَوْمِ ، وَقَدْ قَامُوا إِلَى الصَّلَاةِ
وَيُصَلِّى بِهِمْ عَبْدُ الرَّحْمٰنِ بْنُ عَوْفٍ ، وَقَدْ رَكَعَ بِهِمْ رَكْعَةً ، فَلَمَّا أَحَسَّ
بِالنَّبِىِّ ﷺ ذَهَبَ يَتَأَخَّرُ ، فَأَوْمَأَ إِلَيْهِ ، فَأَدْرَكَ النَّبِىُّ ﷺ إِحْدَى
الرَّكْعَتَيْنِ مَعَهُ ، فَلَمَّا سَلَّمَ ، قَامَ النَّبِىُّ ﷺ وَقُمْتُ مَعَهُ ، فَرَكَعْنَا الرَّكْعَةَ
الَّتِى سَبَقَتْنَا . رَوَاهُ مُسْلِمٌ .

518 Mughira b. Shu'ba reported that he went along with Allah's Messenger (peace and blessings of Allah be upon him) on an expedition to Tabuk. Mughira further reported : Allah's Messenger (peace and blessings of Allah be upon him) went out in the field for relieving himself before the dawn prayer and I took hold of a jar of water (and went on) along with him. As he came back I began to pour water over his hands from that jar. He washed his hands and his nose and there was a woollen cloak over him. He tried to get his forearms out, but the sleeves of the gown were very tight, so he brought his hands out from under the gown and put the gown on his shoulders and washed his forearms. He then wiped his forelock and his turban. I then bent down to take off his socks but he said: Leave them for my feet were clean (with an ablution) when I put them in and he (the Holy Prophet) only wiped over them. He mounted over the ride and I also mounted over the ride till we came to the people and they had been standing in prayer and 'Abdur Rahman b. 'Auf had been leading the prayer. He ('Abdur Rahman) observed one Raka' along with them and when he ('Abdur Radman b. 'Auf) perceived (of the presence) of Allah's Apostle (peace and blessings of Allah be upon him) he tried to come behind but he (the Holy Prophet) made a gesture and Allah's Apostle (peace and blessings of Allah be upon him) observed one of the two Raka's along with him and when he concluded the prayer by saying Assalam-o-'Alaikum, Allah's Apostle (peace and blessings of Allah be upon him) stood up. I stood along with and we observed prayer that had been observed before (we came). (*Muslim*)

Section II الْفَصْلُ الثَّانِي

٥١٩ - عَنْ أَبِي بَكْرَةَ، عَنِ النَّبِيِّ ﷺ : أَنَّهُ رَخَّصَ لِلْمُسَافِرِ ثَلَاثَةَ أَيَّامٍ وَلَيَالِيَهِنَّ، وَلِلْمُقِيمِ يَوْمًا وَلَيْلَةً، إِذَا تَطَهَّرَ فَلِبِسَ خُفَّيْهِ أَنْ يَمْسَحَ عَلَيْهِمَا، رَوَاهُ الْأَثْرَمُ فِي "سُنَنِهِ"، وَابْنُ خُزَيْمَةَ، وَالدَّارُ قُطْنِيٌّ. وَقَالَ الْخَطَّابِيُّ : هُوَ صَحِيحُ الْإِسْنَادِ، هَكَذَا فِي "الْمُنْتَقَى":

519 **Abu Bakra** reported that Allah's Apostle (peace and blessings of Allah be upon him) granted concession for the traveller for three days and three nights and for the resident one day and one night for wiping over them after he had washed (his feet) and then put on socks. (*Al-Athram transmitted it in his Sunan, Ibn Khuzaima and Daraqutni also transmitted it, Al-Khattabi said : The chain of transmission is sound and the same is said in Al-Muntaqa*)

٥٢٠ ـ وَعَنْ صَفْوَانَ بْنِ عَسَّالٍ، قَالَ، كَانَ رَسُوْلُ اللهِ ﷺ يَأْمُرُنَا إِذَا

كُنَّا سَفَرًا أَنْ لَا نَنْزِعَ خِفَافَنَا ثَلَاثَةَ أَيَّامٍ وَلَيَالِيهِنَّ إِلَّا مِّنْ جَنَابَةٍ،

وَلٰكِنْ مِنْ غَائِطٍ وَبَوْلٍ وَنَوْمٍ. رَوَاهُ التِّرْمِذِيُّ، وَالنَّسَائِيُّ

520 **Safwan b. 'Assal** reported: Allah's Messenger (peace and blessings of Allah be upon him) commanded us that when we were travelling we should not take off shoes for three days and three nights except in case of seminal emission and not to do so because of easing ourselves, urinating or sleeping.

٥٢١ ـ وَعَنِ الْمُغِيْرَةِ بْنِ شُعْبَةَ، قَالَ : وَضَّأْتُ النَّبِيَّ ﷺ فِيْ غَزْوَةِ تَبُوْكَ،

فَمَسَحَ أَعْلَى الْخُفِّ وَأَسْفَلَهُ. رَوَاهُ أَبُوْدَاوُدَ، وَ التِّرْمِذِيُّ، وَابْنُ

مَاجَةَ. وَقَالَ التِّرْمِذِيُّ : هٰذَا حَدِيْثٌ مَعْلُوْلٌ وَسَأَلْتُ أَبَا زُرْعَةَ وَ

مُحَمَّدًا ـ يَعْنِي الْبُخَارِيَّ ـ عَنْ هٰذَا الْحَدِيْثِ، فَقَالَا : لَيْسَ بِصَحِيْحٍ .

وَكَذَا ضَعَّفَهُ أَبُوْ دَاوُدَ .

521 **Mughira b. Shu'ba** reported: I helped Allah's Apostle (peace and blessings of Allah be upon him) in performing ablution during the expedition of Tabuk and he wiped on the upper side of socks and on the lower side. (*Transmitted by Abu Dawud, Tirmidhi, Ibn Majah. Tirmidhi said: There is some weakness in this tradition. I asked Abu Zur'a and Muhammad i.e. Bukhari, about this hadith and they said it is not sound and Abu Dawud has also declared it to be weak*).

٥٢٢ ـ وَعَنْهُ، أَنَّهُ قَالَ : رَأَيْتُ النَّبِيَّ ﷺ يَمْسَحُ عَلَى الْخُفَّيْنِ عَلَى ظَاهِرِهِمَا،

رَوَاهُ التِّرْمِذِيُّ، وَأَبُوْ دَاوُدَ .

522 It is reported on the same authority: I saw Allah's Apostle (peace and blessings of Allah be upon him) wiping over his socks or their upper side. (*Tirmidhi and Abu Dawud*)

٥٢٣ - وَعَنْهُ، قَالَ : تَوَضَّأَ النَّبِيُّ ﷺ . وَمَسَحَ عَلَى الْجَوْرَبَيْنِ وَ النَّعْلَيْنِ .
رَوَاهُ أَحْمَدُ، وَ التِّرْمِذِيُّ، وَ أَبُوْ دَاوُدَ، وَ ابْنُ مَاجَهْ

523 It is reported on the same authority that Allah's Apostle (peace and blessings of Allah be upon him) performed ablution and wiped over his stockings and his sandals.[1] (*Ahmad, Tirmidhi, Abu Dawud and Ibn Majah*)

> 1. It is permissible to wipe over the stockings provided these are quite thick or have a leather covering beneath or over them. So far as the wiping over the sandals is concerned it is in fact wiping over the socks with sandals beneath them. It may also mean the socks which have a leather covering over them.

٥٢٤ - عَنِ الْمُغِيْرَةِ، قَالَ مَسَحَ رَسُوْلُ اللهِ ﷺ عَلَى الْخُفَّيْنِ . فَقُلْتُ : يَا رَسُوْلَ اللهِ ! نَسِيْتَ ؟ قَالَ : "بَلْ أَنْتَ نَسِيْتَ ؛ بِهٰذَا أَمَرَنِيْ رَبِّيْ عَزَّ وَجَلَّ " رَوَاهُ أَحْمَدُ، وَ أَبُوْ دَاوُدَ .

524 **Mughira** reported that Allah's Messenger (peace and blessings of Allah be upon him) wiped over the socks. I said: Allah's Messenger, you have forgotten; whereupon he said: But you have forgotten; *i.e.*, the command of my Lord, the Exalted and Glorious. (*Ahmad and Abu Dawud*)

٥٢٥ - وَعَنْ عَلِيٍّ رَضِيَ اللهُ عَنْهُ، أَنَّهُ قَالَ : لَوْ كَانَ الدِّيْنُ بِالرَّأْيِ لَكَانَ أَسْفَلُ الْخُفِّ أَوْلَى بِالْمَسْحِ مِنْ أَعْلَاهُ، وَقَدْ رَأَيْتُ رَسُوْلَ اللهِ ﷺ يَمْسَحُ عَلَى ظَاهِرِ خُفَّيْهِ . رَوَاهُ أَبُوْ دَاوُدَ، وَ لِلدَّارِمِيِّ مَعْنَاهُ .

525 'Ali (may Allah be pleased with him) reported: If the religion were based on the discretion (of individual) then it would have been more important to wipe the lower side of the socks as compared with its upper side but I saw Allah's Messenger (peace and blessings of Allah be upon him) wiping the upper part of his socks. (*Abu Dawud and Darimi transmitted something like it.*)

CHAPTER 18

TAYAMMUM[1]

Section I اَلْفَصْلُ الْأَوَّلُ

1. The word 'Tayammum' is derived from 'amma' : 'he repaired a thing' and 'Tayammum', therefore, means, originally, betaking oneself to a thing and, since the word is used here in connection with betaking oneself to pure earth, 'Tayammum' has come technically to mean this particular practice of touching the earth and then wiping over the face and hands.

Tayammum is a practice of special significance in Islam. The main purpose behind ablution and bath is religious one and the hygienic one is a matter of secondary importance. These practices have been enjoined upon us as religious duties in order to prepare ourselves physically and mentally for the performance of the main duty (prayer). Allah has directed to perform Tayammum in case water is not available or we are handicapped to make use of that. This practice is meant to retain the spiritual value of ablution as a means of distracting us from the mundane activities of life and directing us to the presence of Lord.

The Qur'ān says: And if you are sick or on a journey or one of you comes from the privy, or you have touched the women, and you cannot find water, then betake yourself to clean earth and wipe your faces and hands therewith" (v: 6)

The question may be asked as to why earth has been recommended for purification. The answer is that next to water the most easily available thing in the world is earth. Secondly, its use reminds a man of his origin and his abode in the grave. Moreover, its wiping over the face and hands strikes at the very root of man's vanity and pride and inculcates in him a spirit of humility (Shah Waliullah, *Hujjat Allah il-Baligha*, p. 180).

٥٢٦ - عَنْ حُذَيْفَةَ ، قَالَ قَالَ رَسُولُ اللهِ ﷺ فُضِّلْنَا عَلَى النَّاسِ بِثَلَاثٍ: جُعِلَتْ صُفُوفُنَا كَصُفُوفِ الْمَلَائِكَةِ ، وَجُعِلَتْ لَنَا الْأَرْضُ كُلُّهَا مَسْجِدًا، وَجُعِلَتْ تُرْبَتُهَا لَنَا طَهُورًا إِذَا لَمْ نَجِدِ الْمَاءَ : رَوَاهُ مُسْلِمٌ.

526 Hudhaifa reported: The Messenger of Allah (peace and blessings of Allah be upon him) said: We have been made to excel (other) people in three (things): Our rows have been made like the rows of angels[2] and, the whole earth has been made a mosque for us, and its dust has been made a purifier for us in case water is not available. (*Muslim*)

2. Just as angels keep their ranks and do whatever service is assigned to them and do not question God's plan, similarly the Muslims believe in willing submissinon to the Creator. This hadith has a reference to the following verse of the Holy Qur'ān:

And we are verily ranged in ranks (for service). And we are verily those who declare God's Glory. (37: 165, 166).

٥٢٧ - وَعَنْ عِمْرَانَ، قَالَ: كُنَّا فِي سَفَرٍ مَعَ النَّبِيِّ ﷺ، فَصَلَّى بِالنَّاسِ، فَلَمَّا انْفَتَلَ مِنْ صَلَاتِهِ، إِذَا هُوَ بِرَجُلٍ مُعْتَزِلٍ لَمْ يُصَلِّ مَعَ الْقَوْمِ فَقَالَ: مَا مَنَعَكَ يَا فُلَانُ! أَنْ تُصَلِّيَ مَعَ الْقَوْمِ؟ قَالَ: أَصَابَتْنِي جَنَابَةٌ وَلَا مَاءَ. قَالَ: عَلَيْكَ بِالصَّعِيدِ، فَإِنَّهُ يَكْفِيكَ. مُتَّفَقٌ عَلَيْهِ.

527 'Imran reported Allah's Messenger (peace and blessings of Allah be upon him) as saying: We were along with Allah's Messenger (peace and blessings of Allah be upon him) in a journey. He led the people in prayer and when the prayer was over (he found a person) away from prayer (who) did not say prayer with (other) people. He said: O so and so what detained you that you did not observe prayer along with the people. He said: I became *junubi* and there was no water. He said: You must have made use of the earth and that would have suffced you. (*Agreed upon*)

٥٢٨ - وَعَنْ عَمَّارٍ، قَالَ: جَاءَ رَجُلٌ إِلَى عُمَرَ بْنِ الْخَطَّابِ رَضِيَ اللهُ عَنْهُ، فَقَالَ: إِنِّي أَجْنَبْتُ فَلَمْ أُصِبِ الْمَاءَ. قَالَ عَمَّارٌ لِعُمَرَ: أَمَا تَذْكُرُ إِنَّا كُنَّا فِي سَفَرٍ أَنَا وَأَنْتَ؟ فَأَمَّا أَنْتَ فَلَمْ تُصَلِّ، وَأَمَّا أَنَا فَتَمَعَّكْتُ فَصَلَّيْتُ، فَذَكَرْتُ ذَلِكَ لِلنَّبِيِّ ﷺ. فَقَالَ: إِنَّمَا كَانَ يَكْفِيكَ هَكَذَا فَضَرَبَ النَّبِيُّ ﷺ بِكَفَّيْهِ الْأَرْضَ وَنَفَخَ فِيهِمَا، ثُمَّ مَسَحَ بِهِمَا وَجْهَهُ وَكَفَّيْهِ. رَوَاهُ الْبُخَارِيُّ. وَلِمُسْلِمٍ نَحْوُهُ، وَفِيهِ: قَالَ: إِنَّمَا يَكْفِيكَ أَنْ تَضْرِبَ بِيَدَيْكَ الْأَرْضَ، ثُمَّ تَنْفُخَ، ثُمَّ تَمْسَحَ بِهِمَا وَجْهَكَ وَكَفَّيْكَ.

528 'Ammar reported that a person came to 'Umar b. Khattab (may Allah be pleased with him) and said: I am affected by seminal emission but find no water. 'Ammar said to 'Umar: Do you remember when I and you were in a journey (and I and you had a seminal emission) and you did not observe prayer whereas I rolled in dust and observed prayer and I made a mention of that to Allah's Apostle (peace and blessings of Allah be upon him) and he said: This much had been enough for you. And Allah's Apostle (peace and blessings of Allah be upon him) struck his palms upon the earth and then blew (the dust) from them (his hands). He then wiped his face and his palms also. (*Transmitted by Bukhari and transmitted by Muslim like this: It would have been sufficient for you that you struck the hand upon the earth and then blew (the dust from them) and then wiped your face and palms with them.*)

٥٢٩ - وَعَنْ أَبِى الْجُهَيْمِ بْنِ الْحَارِثِ بْنِ الصِّمَّةِ. قَالَ: مَرَرْتُ عَلَى النَّبِيِّ ﷺ وَ هُوَ يَبُولُ، فَسَلَّمْتُ عَلَيْهِ، فَلَمْ يَرُدَّ عَلَىَّ حَتَّى قَامَ إِلَى جِدَارٍ، فَحَتَّهُ بِعَصًى كَانَتْ مَعَهُ، ثُمَّ وَضَعَ يَدَيْهِ عَلَى الْجِدَارِ، فَمَسَحَ وَجْهَهُ وَ ذِرَاعَيْهِ، ثُمَّ رَدَّ عَلَىَّ. وَ لَمْ أَجِدْ هٰذِهِ الرِّوَايَةَ فِي "الصَّحِيحَيْنِ"، وَلَا فِي "كِتَابِ الْحُمَيْدِيِّ"، وَلٰكِنْ ذَكَرَهُ فِي "شَرْحِ السُّنَّةِ" وَقَالَ: هٰذَا حَدِيثٌ حَسَنٌ.

529 Abu Juhaim b. Harith b. al-Simmah reported: I happened to pass by Allah's Apostle (peace and blessings of Allah be upon him) as he was passing water. I greeted him but he did not return my greetings till he went towards the wall and after scraping it with a stick which was with him, he put his hands on the wall and wiped his face and his fore-arms and then responded to my greetings. I have not found this version in two *Sahihs* or in *Al-Humaidi's* book but *Baghawi* mentioned it in *Sharh-al-Sunnah* saying that this is a *hasan* tradition.

Section II أَلْفَصْلُ الثَّانِى

٥٣٠ - عَنْ أَبِى ذَرٍّ، قَالَ: قَالَ رَسُولُ اللهِ ﷺ: إِنَّ الصَّعِيدَ الطَّيِّبَ وَضُوءُ الْمُسْلِمِ، وَإِنْ لَمْ يَجِدِ الْمَاءَ عَشْرَ سِنِينَ، فَإِذَا وَجَدَ الْمَاءَ فَلْيُمِسَّهُ بَشَرَهُ، فَإِنَّ ذَلِكَ خَيْرٌ. رَوَاهُ أَحْمَدُ، وَ التِّرْمِذِىُّ، وَ أَبُو دَاوُدَ.

وَ رَوَى النَّسَائِىُّ نَحْوَهُ إِلَى قَوْلِهِ "عَشْرَ سِنِينَ"

530 Abu Dharr reported that Allah's Messenger (peace be upon him) said: Verily clean earth (is fit) for ablution for a Muslim, even if he does not find water for ten years[1] and when he finds water he should touch his skin[2] as that is better. (*Ahmad, Tirmidhi, Abu Dawud*)

(*And Nasa'i has transmitted something similar to it upto the saying: Ten years*)

1. "Ten years" do not actually mean the duration of full ten years, but it implies long duration.
2. Here it means that when water is available, he should then use that and stop performing Tayammum.

٥٣١ - وَعَنْ جَابِرٍ، قَالَ: خَرَجْنَا فِى سَفَرٍ، فَأَصَابَ رَجُلاً مِنَّا حَجَرٌ فَشَجَّهُ فِى رَأْسِهِ، فَاحْتَلَمَ، فَسَأَلَ أَصْحَابَهُ: هَلْ تَجِدُونَ لِى رُخْصَةً فِى التَّيَمُّمِ؟ قَالُوا: مَا نَجِدُ لَكَ رُخْصَةً وَ أَنْتَ تَقْدِرُ عَلَى الْمَاءِ. فَاغْتَسَلَ فَمَاتَ. فَلَمَّا قَدِمْنَا عَلَى النَّبِىِّ ﷺ أُخْبِرَ بِذَلِكَ. قَالَ "قَتَلُوهُ، قَتَلَهُمُ اللهُ: أَلاَ سَأَلُوا إِذَا لَمْ يَعْلَمُوا، فَإِنَّمَا شِفَاءُ الْعِىِّ السُّؤَالُ، إِنَّمَا كَانَ يَكْفِيهِ أَنْ يَتَيَمَّمَ، وَ يَعْصِبَ عَلَى جُرْحِهِ خِرْقَةً، ثُمَّ يَمْسَحَ عَلَيْهَا، وَ يَغْسِلَ سَائِرَ جَسَدِهِ" رَوَاهُ أَبُو دَاوُدَ.

531 Jabir reported: We set out on a journey that a person amongst us was hit with stone upon his head and he also saw a wet dream. He asked his companions: Do you find any relaxation for me that I may perform Tayammum. They said: We do not find any relaxation for you, for water is available to you. So he took a bath and died. When we came back to Allah's Apostle (peace be upon him) he was informed of it and he said: They have killed him, may Allah kill them.[1] Why did not they ask, when they did not know (about a religious verdict). Verily the remedy of the lack of knowledge is to make an enquiry. It would have been sufficient for him to perform Tayammum and bandage his wound with a piece of cloth, and then wipe over it and wash the whole body (except head). (*Abu Dawud*)

1. It is not a curse, but an expression of disapproval-*cum*-annoyance.

٥٣٢ - وَرَوَاهُ ابْنُ مَاجَةَ، عَنْ عَطَاءِ بْنِ أَبِي رَبَاحٍ، عَنِ ابْنِ عَبَّاسٍ .

532 This hadith has been transmitted by **Ibn Majah** on the authority of 'Ata b. Abi Rabah, from Ibn 'Abbas.

٥٣٣ - وَعَنْ أَبِي سَعِيدٍ الْخُدْرِيِّ، قَالَ : خَرَجَ رَجُلَانِ فِي سَفَرٍ، فَحَضَرَتِ الصَّلَاةُ وَلَيْسَ مَعَهُمَا مَاءٌ، فَتَيَمَّمَا صَعِيدًا طَيِّبًا، فَصَلَّيَا، ثُمَّ وَجَدَا الْمَاءَ فِي الْوَقْتِ، فَأَعَادَ أَحَدُهُمَا الصَّلَاةَ بِوُضُوءٍ، وَلَمْ يُعِدِ الْآخَرُ. ثُمَّ أَتَيَا رَسُولَ اللهِ ﷺ فَذَكَرَا ذَلِكَ . فَقَالَ لِلَّذِي لَمْ يُعِدْ : "أَصَبْتَ السُّنَّةَ . وَأَجْزَأَتْكَ صَلَاتُكَ" وَقَالَ لِلَّذِي تَوَضَّأَ وَأَعَادَ : "لَكَ الْأَجْرُ مَرَّتَيْنِ" رَوَاهُ أَبُو دَاوُدَ، وَالدَّارِمِيُّ، وَرَوَى النَّسَائِيُّ نَحْوَهُ .

533 **Abu Sa'id al-Khudri** reported: Two persons set out on a journey and there came the time for prayer, but there was no water available for them. So they both performed Tayammum with the help of clean earth and both of them observed prayer. Then both of them found water at that time. One of them repeated prayer with ablution, but the other one did not repeat that. Then both of them came to Allah's Messenger (peace be upon him) and made a mention of that to him. He (the Holy Prophet) said to one who had not repeated (the prayer): You have observed Sunnah and sufficient is your prayer. And he said to one who had performed ablution and repeated the prayer: For you is the double reward. (*Abu Dawud, Darimi and Nasa'i transmitted something similar*).

٥٣٤ ـ وَقَدْ رَوَى هُوَ وَأَبُوْ دَاوُدَ أَيْضًا عَنْ عَطَاءِ بْنِ يَسَارٍ مُرْسَلاً .

534 He (**Nasa'i**) and **Abu Dawud** transmitted it from 'Ata b. Yasar in *Mursal* form.

Section III ٱلْفَصْلُ الثَّالِثُ

٥٣٥ ـ عَنْ أَبِي الْجُهَيْمِ بْنِ حَارِثِ بْنِ الصِّمَّةِ ، قَالَ : أَقْبَلَ النَّبِيُّ ﷺ مِنْ نَحْوِ بِئْرِ جَمَلٍ ، فَلَقِيَهُ رَجُلٌ فَسَلَّمَ عَلَيْهِ ، فَلَمْ يَرُدَّ النَّبِيُّ ﷺ حَتَّى أَقْبَلَ عَلَى الْجِدَارِ ، فَمَسَحَ بِوَجْهِهِ وَ يَدَيْهِ ، ثُمَّ رَدَّ عَلَيْهِ السَّلَامَ . مُتَّفَقٌ عَلَيْهِ .

535 **Abu Jahaim b. al-Harith b. Simmat** said that Allah's Apostle (peace be upon him) came from the direction of Bi'r Jamal, that a person met him and greeted him, but Allah's Apostle (peace be upon him) made no response, till he came to the wall (and after touching it), wiped his face and hands and then responded to his greetings. (*Agreed upon*)

٥٣٦ ـ وَعَنْ عَمَّارِ بْنِ يَاسِرٍ أَنَّهُ كَانَ يُحَدِّثُ : أَنَّهُمْ تَمَسَّحُوا وَهُمْ مَعَ رَسُوْلِ اللهِ ﷺ بِالصَّعِيْدِ لِصَلَاةِ الْفَجْرِ ، فَضَرَبُوْا بِأَكُفِّهِمُ الصَّعِيْدَ ، ثُمَّ مَسَحُوا بِوُجُوْهِهِمْ مَسْحَةً وَّاحِدَةً ، ثُمَّ عَادُوْا ، فَضَرَبُوْا بِأَكُفِّهِمُ الصَّعِيْدَ مَرَّةً أُخْرَى ، فَمَسَحُوا بِأَيْدِيِهِمْ كُلِّهَا إِلَى الْمَنَاكِبِ وَ الْأَبَاطِ مِنْ بُطُوْنِ أَيْدِيِهِمْ . رَوَاهُ أَبُوْ دَاوُدَ .

536 **'Ammar b. Yasir** used to narrate that while they were in the company of Allah's Messenger (peace be upon him) they wiped themselves (they performed Tayammum) with the help of (clean) earth for the Dawn prayer. They struck their palms upon the earth, and then wiped their faces once and then repeated and struck their palms upon the earth for the second time, and then wiped their hands each upto the shoulders[1] and upto the armpits, and then[2] from inside of their arms. (*Abu Dawud*)

1. It is the largest conceivable extent, but the common rule is to wipe hands upto the elbows as is done in case of ablution.

   (*Mirqat*, Vol. II, p. 91)

2. That is the part of the body from where the wiping of the hand is to be started. (*Mirqat*, Vol. II, p. 91).

CHAPTER 19
BATH ENJOINED AS SUNNAH

Section I أَلْفَصْلُ الْأَوَّلُ

٥٣٧ - عَنِ ابْنِ عُمَرَ رَضِيَ اللهُ عَنْهُمَا، قَالَ: قَالَ رَسُولُ اللهِ ﷺ
إِذَا جَاءَ أَحَدُكُمُ الْجُمُعَةَ فَلْيَغْتَسِلْ " مُتَّفَقٌ عَلَيْهِ .

537 Ibn 'Umar (may Allah be pleased with him) reported Allah's Messenger (peace be upon him) as saying: When anyone of you (intends) to go for Jumu'a prayer, he should take a bath. (*Agreed upon*)

٥٣٨ - وَعَنْ أَبِي سَعِيدٍ الْخُدْرِيِّ، قَالَ: قَالَ رَسُولُ اللهِ ﷺ: "غُسْلُ يَوْمِ
الْجُمُعَةِ وَاجِبٌ عَلَى كُلِّ مُحْتَلِمٍ . مُتَّفَقٌ عَلَيْهِ .

538 Abu Sa'id al-Khudri reported Allah's Messenger (may peace be upon him) as saying: Taking a bath on Friday is essential[1] for every adult person. (*Agreed upon*)

  1. Bath on Friday is essential and merits great reward, but it is not obligatory (فرض).

٥٣٩ - وَعَنْ أَبِي هُرَيْرَةَ، قَالَ: قَالَ رَسُولُ اللهِ ﷺ: "حَقٌّ عَلَى كُلِّ
مُسْلِمٍ أَنْ يَغْتَسِلَ فِي كُلِّ سَبْعَةِ أَيَّامٍ يَوْمًا، يَغْسِلُ فِيهِ رَأْسَهُ
وَجَسَدَهُ " مُتَّفَقٌ عَلَيْهِ .

539 Abu Huraira reported Allah's Messenger (peace be upon him) as saying: It is the duty of every Muslim to take a bath on a day (at least) amongst the seven days (of the week). He should wash his head and his body. (*Agreed upon*)

Section II أَلْفَصْلُ الثَّانِي

٥٤٠ - عَنْ سَمُرَةَ بْنِ جُنْدُبٍ، قَالَ: قَالَ رَسُولُ اللهِ ﷺ "مَنْ تَوَضَّأَ يَوْمَ
الْجُمُعَةِ فَبِهَا وَنِعْمَتْ، وَمَنِ اغْتَسَلَ فَالْغُسْلُ أَفْضَلُ " رَوَاهُ أَحْمَدُ،
وَأَبُودَاوُدَ، وَالتِّرْمِذِيُّ، وَالنَّسَائِيُّ، وَالدَّارِمِيُّ

540 Samura b. Jundub reported Allah's Messenger (peace be upon him) as saying: He who performs ablution on Friday, it is well and good, but he who takes a bath, it is more excellent. (*Ahmad, Abu Dawud, Tirmidhi, Nasa'i and Darimi*)

٥٤١ - وَعَنْ أَبِي هُرَيْرَةَ ، قَالَ : قَالَ رَسُولُ اللهِ ﷺ : "مَنْ غَسَّلَ مَيْتًا فَلْيَغْتَسِلْ" رَوَاهُ ابْنُ مَاجَهْ

وَزَادَ أَحْمَدُ وَ التِّرْمِذِيُّ وَ أَبُو دَاوُدَ : "وَ مَنْ حَمَلَهُ فَلْيَتَوَضَّأْ" :

541 Abu Huraira reported Allah's Messenger (peace be upon him) as saying: He who washed the dead body, he should take a bath. (*Ibn Majah*).

(*And Ahmad, Tirmidhi and Abu Dawud made this addition; He who carried that (the dead body) he should perform ablution*).

٥٤٢ - وَعَنْ عَائِشَةَ ، رَضِيَ اللهُ عَنْهَا، أَنَّ النَّبِيَّ ﷺ كَانَ يَغْتَسِلُ مِنْ أَرْبَعٍ : مِنَ الْجَنَابَةِ، وَ يَوْمِ الْجُمُعَةِ، وَ مِنَ الْحِجَامَةِ، وَمِنْ غُسْلِ الْمَيِّتِ . رَوَاهُ أَبُو دَاوُدَ .

542 'A'isha (may Allah be pleased with her) reported that Allah's Apostle (peace be upon him) used to take a bath on four occasions: Al-Janabah (seminal emission), on Friday, (after) applying suction with cupping-glass,[1] and (after) washing the dead body.[2] (*Abu Dawud*)

1. It is not an obligatory act, but just a practical step for removing impurities from the different parts of the body.
2. It is not obligatory as the dead body is not impure, the bath is only desirable, and if one does not take it after washing the lifeless body, there is no harm in it. Imam Shawkani, *Nail-ul-Awtar*, Vol. I, pp. 259 260).

٥٤٣ - وَعَنْ قَيْسِ بْنِ عَاصِمٍ : أَنَّهُ أَسْلَمَ ، فَأَمَرَهُ النَّبِيُّ ﷺ أَنْ يَغْتَسِلَ بِمَاءٍ وَ سِدْرٍ . رَوَاهُ التِّرْمِذِيُّ ، وَ أَبُو دَاوُدَ ، وَ النَّسَائِيُّ .

543 Qais b. 'Asim reported that he embraced Islam and Allah's Apostle (peace be upon him) commanded him to take a bath with the leaves of the Lote tree mixed into water.

(*Tirmidi, Abu Dawud and Nasa'i*)

Section III اَلْفَصْلُ الثَّالِثُ

٥٤٤ - عَنْ عِكْرِمَةَ، قَالَ: إِنَّ نَاسًا مِنْ أَهْلِ الْعِرَاقِ جَاءُوا فَقَالُوا:
يَا ابْنَ عَبَّاسٍ! أَتَرَى الْغُسْلَ يَوْمَ الْجُمُعَةِ وَاجِبًا؟ قَالَ: لَا، وَلٰكِنَّهُ
أَطْهَرُ وَخَيْرٌ لِمَنِ اغْتَسَلَ، وَمَنْ لَمْ يَغْتَسِلْ فَلَيْسَ عَلَيْهِ بِوَاجِبٍ. وَ
سَأُخْبِرُكُمْ كَيْفَ بَدْءُ الْغُسْلِ: كَانَ النَّاسُ مَجْهُودِينَ يَلْبَسُونَ
الصُّوفَ، وَيَعْمَلُونَ عَلَى ظُهُورِهِمْ، وَكَانَ مَسْجِدُهُمْ ضَيِّقًا مُقَارِبَ
السَّقْفِ، إِنَّمَا هُوَ عَرِيشٌ، فَخَرَجَ رَسُولُ اللّٰهِ ﷺ فِي يَوْمٍ حَارٍّ،
وَعَرِقَ النَّاسُ فِي ذٰلِكَ الصُّوفِ، حَتَّى ثَارَتْ مِنْهُمْ رِيَاحٌ اذَى
بِذٰلِكَ بَعْضُهُمْ بَعْضًا. فَلَمَّا وَجَدَ رَسُولُ اللّٰهِ ﷺ تِلْكَ الرِّيَاحَ، قَالَ
أَيُّهَا النَّاسُ! إِذَا كَانَ هٰذَا الْيَوْمُ؛ فَاغْتَسِلُوا، وَلْيَمَسَّ أَحَدُكُمْ
أَفْضَلَ مَا يَجِدُ مِنْ دُهْنِهِ وَطِيبِهِ" قَالَ ابْنُ عَبَّاسٍ: ثُمَّ جَاءَ اللّٰهُ
بِالْخَيْرِ، وَلِبَسُوا غَيْرَ الصُّوفِ، وَكُفُوا الْعَمَلَ، وَوُسِّعَ مَسْجِدُهُمْ
وَذَهَبَ بَعْضُ الَّذِي كَانَ يُؤْذِى بَعْضُهُمْ بَعْضًا مِنَ الْعَرَقِ. رَوَاهُ
أَبُو دَاوُدَ.

544 'Ikrima reported: Some persons from Iraq came and said:
Ibn 'Abbas, do you look upon the bath on Friday as an
obligatory one. He said: No, but it is of course, an act of
more cleanliness and is excellent for one who takes a bath,
but he who does not take a bath, it is not obligatory for
him. Nay, I tell you how (this practice of Friday) bath
started. The people were (commonly) poor, and they put
on woollen clothes and carried the (load) on their backs,
whereas the mosque of theirs was not spacious and its ceiling
was low. It was in fact a thatched roof. It was on a hot
day that Allah's Messenger (peace be upon him) came

out (and he found people) perspiring in the woollen (clothes) and a repugnant smell was emitting giving trouble to one another. When Allah's Messenger (peace be upon him) found such a repugnant smell, he said: O people, when this day (comes) take a bath, and every one of you should apply the best oil, and perfume, available to him. Ibn 'Abbas said: Then Allah brought good (to the Muslim society and the extreme poverty of the people was changed to good financial condition) and they began to put on clothes other than those made of wool, and there was some relief in manual labour and the mosque was expanded and the perspiration that caused trouble to one another was no more. (*Abu Dawud*)

CHAPTER 20

Section I الفصل الأول

٥٤٥ - عَنْ أَنَسِ بْنِ مَالِكٍ، قَالَ : إِنَّ الْيَهُودَ كَانُوا إِذَا حَاضَتِ الْمَرْأَةُ
فِيهِمْ لَمْ يُؤَاكِلُوهَا، وَلَمْ يُجَامِعُوهُنَّ فِي الْبُيُوتِ، فَسَأَلَ أَصْحَبُ النَّبِيِّ ﷺ
النَّبِيَّ ﷺ، فَأَنْزَلَ اللهُ تَعَالَى : ﴿ وَيَسْتَلُونَكَ عَنِ الْمَحِيضِ ﴾ ، الآيَةَ .
فَقَالَ رَسُولُ اللهِ ﷺ : ﴿ اصْنَعُوا كُلَّ شَيْءٍ إِلَّا النِّكَاحَ ﴾ . فَبَلَغَ ذَلِكَ
الْيَهُودَ . فَقَالُوا : مَا يُرِيدُ هَذَا الرَّجُلُ أَنْ يَدَعَ مِنْ أَمْرِنَا شَيْئًا إِلَّا
خَالَفَنَا فِيهِ . فَجَاءَ أُسَيْدُ بْنُ حُضَيْرٍ وَعَبَّادُ بْنُ بِشْرٍ ، فَقَالَا : يَا رَسُولَ
اللهِ ! إِنَّ الْيَهُودَ تَقُولُ كَذَا وَكَذَا . أَفَلَا نُجَامِعُهُنَّ ؟ فَتَغَيَّرَ وَجْهُ رَسُولِ
اللهِ ﷺ حَتَّى ظَنَنَّا أَنْ قَدْ وَجَدَ عَلَيْهِمَا . فَخَرَجَا ، فَاسْتَقْبَلَتْهُمَا هَدِيَّةٌ
مِنْ لَبَنٍ إِلَى النَّبِيِّ ﷺ ، فَأَرْسَلَ فِي آثَارِهِمَا فَسَقَاهُمَا ، فَعَرَفْنَا أَنَّهُ
لَمْ يَجِدْ عَلَيْهِمَا ، رَوَاهُ مُسْلِمٌ .

545 Anas b. Malik reported : Amongst the Jews, when a woman
menstruated, they did not dine with her, nor did they live
with them in their houses; so the Companions of the Apostle
(peace and blessings of Allah be upon him) asked the Apostle
(peace and blessings of Allah be upon him), and Allah, the
Exalted and Glorious revealed : "And they ask you about
menstruation ; say it is a pollution, so keep away from woman
during menstruation"[1] to the end (Qur'an, ii: 222). The
Messenger of Allah (peace and blessings of Allah be upon
him) said : Do every thing except intercourse.[2] The Jews
heard of that and said : This man does not want to leave
anything we do without opposing us in it. Usaid b. Hudair
and 'Abbad b. Bishr came and said : Messenger of Allah, the
Jews say such and such thing.[3] Should we not have,
therefore, sexual intercourse with them ? The face of the
Messenger of Allah (peace and blessings of Allah be
upon him) underwent such a change that we thought he

was angry with them, but when they went out, they
happened to receive a gift of milk which was sent to the
Apostle of Allah (peace and blessings of Allah be upon him).
He (the Holy Prophet) called for them and gave them drink,
whereby they knew that he was not angry with them. (*Muslim*)

1. Mahid (محيض) menstruation which has been described in the Qur'ān
   as اذى (pollution), is a noun of place (momina loci). It is, therefore,
   the female organ which secretes the bloods of menstruation that is
   polluted and not the whole of woman's body. If women are not
   permitted to enter the mosque during this period, it is not because they
   are defiled or polluted but due to the reason that the drops of blood
   may fall on the sacred place.

2. The prohibition of sexual intercourse with a menstruating woman is
   justified on medical and hygienic grounds. According to a well-
   known authority, severe menorrhagia, perimetritic irrigation and
   parametritic inflammations have been observed to follow such indis-
   cretion (Coition) (Kisch, *Sexual Life of Women*, p. 173).

3. Compare the attitude of Islam towards the menstruating woman
   with that of Biblical regulations: "....She shall be put apart seven
   days : and whosoever toucheth her shall be unclean until the even.
   And every thing that she lieth upon in her separation shall be unclean:
   every thing also that she sitteth upon shall be unclean. And whosoever
   toucheth her shall wash his clothes, and bath himself in water, and be
   unclean until the even......And if any man lieth with her at all,
   and her flowers be upon him, he shall be unclean seven days, and all
   the bed whereon he lieth shall be unclean" (Leviticus 15, 19-24).

More onerous still are the laws prescribed by the Jewish doctors.
"According to them woman must reckon seven days after the ter-
mination of the period. If then, this lasts seven days she cannot
become pure until the fifteenth day. Purification, furthermore, can
be gained only by a ritual bath: and until the woman has taken this,
she remains unclean. In addition to all this, a woman who does not
menstruate regularly is unclean for a certain time before she becomes
aware that the period has begun and objects which she touches are
defiled" (*The Jewish Encyclopaedia*, Vol. IX, p. 301).

٥٢٧ ـ وَعَنْ عَائِشَةَ، قَالَتْ: كُنْتُ أَغْتَسِلُ أَنَا وَالنَّبِيُّ ﷺ مِنْ إِنَاءٍ
وَاحِدٍ، وَكِلَانَا جُنُبٌ، وَكَانَ يَأْمُرُنِي، فَأَتَّزِرُ، فَيُبَاشِرُنِي وَأَنَا
حَائِضٌ. وَكَانَ يُخْرِجُ رَأْسَهُ إِلَيَّ وَهُوَ مُعْتَكِفٌ، فَأَغْسِلُهُ، وَأَنَا
حَائِضٌ. مُتَّفَقٌ عَلَيْهِ.

546 'A'isha reported: I and Allah's Apostle (peace and blessings of Allah be upon him) took a bath from one vessel because of *janaba* and he commanded me to tie waist-wrapper and he then embraced me as I was menstruating and he put out his head towards me while he himself was in the mosque in I'tikaf and I washed his hair (even) in my state of menstruation. (*Agreed upon*)

٥٤٧ ـ وَعَنْهَا، قَالَتْ : كُنْتُ أَشْرَبُ وَأَنَا حَائِضٌ ، ثُمَّ أُنَاوِلُهُ النَّبِيَّ ﷺ ، فَيَضَعُ فَاهُ عَلَى مَوْضِعٍ فِيَّ فَيَشْرَبُ ؛ وَأَتَعَرَّقُ الْعَرْقَ ، وَأَنَا حَائِضٌ ، ثُمَّ أُنَاوِلُهُ النَّبِيَّ ﷺ ؛ فَيَضَعُ فَاهُ عَلَى مَوْضِعٍ فِيَّ . رَوَاهُ مُسْلِمٌ

547 It is reported on the same authority: I would drink when I was menstruating then I would hand over the vessel to the Apostle (peace and blessings of Allah be upon him) and he would put his mouth where mine had been and he would drink and I would eat flesh from a bone while I was menstruating and then handed it over to Allah's Apostle (peace and blessings of Allah be upon him) and he would put his mouth where mine had been. (*Muslim*)

٥٤٨ ـ وَعَنْهَا، قَالَتْ : كَانَ النَّبِيُّ ﷺ يَتَّكِئُ فِي حِجْرِي وَأَنَا حَائِضٌ ، ثُمَّ يَقْرَأُ الْقُرْآنَ . مُتَّفَقٌ عَلَيْهِ

548 It is reported on the same authority that she ('A'isha) said: Allah's Apostle (peace and blessings of Allah be upon him) reclined (his head) in my lap, whereas I was in the state of menstruation.

٥٤٩ ـ وَعَنْهَا، قَالَتْ : قَالَ لِيَ النَّبِيُّ ﷺ " نَاوِلِينِي الْخُمْرَةَ مِنَ الْمَسْجِدِ " فَقُلْتُ : إِنِّي حَائِضٌ . فَقَالَ : إِنَّ حَيْضَتَكِ لَيْسَتْ فِي يَدِكِ " . رَوَاهُ مُسْلِمٌ .

549 It is reported on the same authority that the Apostle of Allah (peace and blessings of Allah be upon him) said: Get me the mat from the mosque. I said: I am menstruating. Upon this he remarked: Your menstruation is not in your hand.[1] (*Muslim*)

1. You are permitted to take hold of the mat, while standing outside the mosque.

٥٥٠ ـ وَعَنْ مَيْمُونَةَ، رَضِيَ اللهُ عَنْهَا، قَالَتْ : كَانَ رَسُولُ اللهِ ﷺ

يُصَلِّي فِي مِرْطٍ، بَعْضُهُ عَلَيَّ وَبَعْضُهُ عَلَيْهِ، وَأَنَا حَائِضٌ. مُتَّفَقٌ عَلَيْهِ.

550 Maimuna reported: Allah's Messenger (peace and blessings of Allah be upon him) used to pray in woollen garment which was partly over him and partly over me while I was menstruating. (*Agreed upon*)

Section II   اَلْفَصْلُ الثَّانِي

٥٥١ ـ عَنْ أَبِي هُرَيْرَةَ، قَالَ : قَالَ رَسُولُ اللهِ ﷺ : "مَنْ أَتَى حَائِضاً، أَوِ

امْرَأَةً فِي دُبُرِهَا، أَوْ كَاهِناً، فَقَدْ كَفَرَ بِمَا أُنْزِلَ عَلَى مُحَمَّدٍ" رَوَاهُ

التِّرْمِذِيُّ. وَابْنُ مَاجَهْ، وَالدَّارِمِيُّ وَفِي رِوَايَتِهِمَا : "فَصَدَّقَهُ بِمَا

يَقُولُ، فَقَدْ كَفَرَ"

وَقَالَ التِّرْمِذِيُّ : لَا نَعْرِفُ هٰذَا الْحَدِيثَ إِلَّا مِنْ (حَدِيثِ) حَكِيمٍ

الْأَثْرَمِ، عَنْ أَبِي تَمِيمَةَ، عَنْ أَبِي هُرَيْرَةَ.

551 Abu Huraira reported Allah's Messenger (peace be upon him) as saying: He who comes to the menstruating woman, or to a woman from her back (for sexual intercourse), or to a *kahin* (soothsayer), he belied that what was revealed to Muhammad (*Tirmidhi*)

And in the narration of *Ibn Majah* and *Darimi* (the words are): He testified him in what he (*kahin*) said, he in fact committed infidelity.

Tirmidhi said: We do not know this hadith but from the hadith transmitted by Hakim al-Athram, from Abi Tamima, from Abu Huraira.

٥٥٢ ـ وَعَنْ مُعَاذِ بْنِ جَبَلٍ، قَالَ : قُلْتُ : يَا رَسُولَ اللهِ! مَا يَحِلُّ لِي مِنِ

امْرَأَتِي وَهِيَ حَائِضٌ؟ قَالَ : "مَا فَوْقَ الْإِزَارِ، وَالتَّعَفُّفُ عَنْ ذٰلِكَ

أَفْضَلُ" رَوَاهُ رَزِينٌ. وَقَالَ مُحْيِ السُّنَّةِ : إِسْنَادُهُ لَيْسَ بِقَوِيٍّ.

552 Mu'adh b. Jabal reported: I said: Allah's Messenger, what is lawful for me in regard to my wife in her state of menses. He said: What is above the lower garment and if you restrain from that even, it is more excellent. (*Razin*). *Muhyi al-Sunnah* said: Its chain of transmission is not sound.

٥٥٣ - وَعَنِ ابْنِ عَبَّاسٍ، قَالَ: قَالَ رَسُولُ اللهِ ﷺ: "إِذَا وَقَعَ الرَّجُلُ بِأَهْلِهِ، وَهِيَ حَائِضٌ، فَلْيَتَصَدَّقْ بِنِصْفِ دِينَارٍ" رَوَاهُ التِّرْمِذِيُّ، وَأَبُو دَاوُدَ، وَالنَّسَائِيُّ، وَالدَّارِمِيُّ، وَابْنُ مَاجَهَ.

553 Ibn 'Abbas reported that Allah's Messenger (peace be upon him) said: When a person has sexual intercourse with his wife as she is menstruating, he should give half dinar as a charity (for this act of transgression). (*Tirmidhi, Abu Dawud, Nasa'i, Darimi and Ibn Majah*)

٥٥٤ - وَعَنْهُ، عَنِ النَّبِيِّ ﷺ، قَالَ: "إِذَا كَانَ دَمًا أَحْمَرَ، فَدِينَارٌ، وَإِذَا كَانَ دَمًا أَصْفَرَ، فَنِصْفُ دِينَارٍ" رَوَاهُ التِّرْمِذِيُّ.

554 It is reported on the same authority that Allah's Apostle (peace be upon him) said: (This compulsory charity) is one dinar if the blood is completely red and half a dinar, when the blood is (somewhat) yellow. (*Tirmidhi*)

Section III   اَلْفَصْلُ الثَّالِثُ

٥٥٥ - عَنْ زَيْدِ بْنِ أَسْلَمَ، قَالَ: إِنَّ رَجُلًا سَأَلَ رَسُولَ اللهِ ﷺ، فَقَالَ مَا يَحِلُّ لِي مِنِ امْرَأَتِي وَهِيَ حَائِضٌ؟ فَقَالَ رَسُولُ اللهِ ﷺ: تَشُدُّ عَلَيْهَا إِزَارَهَا، ثُمَّ شَأْنُكَ بِأَعْلَاهَا؟ رَوَاهُ مَالِكٌ، وَالدَّارِمِيُّ مُرْسَلًا.

555 Zaid b. Aslam reported that a person asked Allah's Messenger (peace be upon him): What is lawful for me in my wife as she is menstruating. Allah's Messenger (peace be upon him) said: Wrap her lower garment (tightly over her private part), then do as you like above that. (*Malik and Darimi as Mursal*)

٥٥٧ ـ وَعَنْ عَائِشَةَ، قَالَتْ : كُنْتُ إِذَا حِضْتُ نَزَلْتُ عَنِ الْمِثَالِ عَلَى
الْحَصِيرِ، فَلَمْ نَقْرَبْ رَسُولَ اللهِ ﷺ ، وَ لَمْ نَدْنُ مِنْهُ حَتَّى
نَطْهُرَ . رَوَاهُ أَبُو دَاوُدَ .

556 'Ā'isha reported: When I was in the state of menses I came
down from the bed to the mat and we (the wives of the
Holy Prophet) did not go near Allah's Messenger (peace be
upon him) or go close to him, till we were pure.[1]

(Abu Dawud)

1. There is a difference of opinion amongst the scholars about the meaning
   of this hadith. Some of the scholars are of the opinion that it should
   be taken in its literal sense and one should keep one's wife at a distance,
   during her menses. This meaning conflicts with other traditions in
   which we have been told that it is permissible to touch the wife, embrace
   and kiss her even during the days of her menses and that it is only
   sexual intercourse which is prohibited. So in the light of these facts
   the correct implication of going near one's wife or going close to her
   is sexual intercourse.

CHAPTER 21

PERTAINING TO *MUSTAHADA*[1]

(The woman who has a prolonged flow of blood)

1. The woman who bleeds not because of menses or after child birth is known as *Mustahada* Prayer and fasting are binding on her like other women and sexual intercourse is permitted with her. There is, however, one condition for prayer which has been pointed out in the forthcoming ahadith.

Section I   اَلْفَصْلُ الْأَوَّلُ

٥٥٧ - عَنْ عَائِشَةَ، رَضِيَ اللهُ عَنْهَا، قَالَتْ: جَاءَتْ فَاطِمَةُ بِنْتُ أَبِى حُبَيْشٍ إِلَى النَّبِيِّ ﷺ، فَقَالَتْ: يَا رَسُولَ اللهِ! إِنِّى امْرَأَةٌ أُسْتَحَاضُ، فَلَا أَطْهُرُ؛ أَفَأَدَعُ الصَّلَاةَ؟ فَقَالَ: "لَا، إِنَّمَا ذَلِكِ عِرْقٌ وَلَيْسَ بِحَيْضٍ، فَإِذَا أَقْبَلَتْ حَيْضَتُكِ فَدَعِى الصَّلَاةَ، وَإِذَا أَدْبَرَتْ فَاغْسِلِى عَنْكِ الدَّمَ ثُمَّ صَلِّى؛ مُتَّفَقٌ عَلَيْهِ.

557 'Ā'isha (may Allah be pleased with her) reported that Fatimah bint Abu Hubaish came to Allah's Apostle (peace be upon him) and said: Allah's Messenger, I am a woman whose blood flows (even after the period of menstruation) and thus I am not purified; should I, therefore, abandon prayer. Thereupon he (the Holy Prophet) said: No, for that is only a vein,[2] and is not menstruation. So when you enter (the period of) menses, abandon the prayer and when it is over, then wash the blood from yourself and observe prayer.

(*Agreed upon*)

2. The blood during menstrual period oozes out from endometrium of uterus along with secretions of ovary (with the drops of semen). This period extends normally from five to ten days at the most. But due to some abnormalities in the normal process of menstruation blood continues to flow beyond the menses period. It may be due to haemorrhage in the vein or any other harmonic trouble. This blood is free from female sex cells and comes from the ovary.

٥٥٨ - عَنْ عُرْوَةَ بْنِ الزُّبَيْرِ، عَنْ فَاطِمَةَ بِنْتِ أَبِى حُبَيْشٍ، أَنَّهَا كَانَتْ
تُسْتَحَاضُ، فَقَالَ لَهَا النَّبِىُّ ﷺ: "إِذَا كَانَ دَمُ الْحَيْضِ فَإِنَّهُ دَمٌ
أَسْوَدُ يُعْرَفُ، فَإِذَا كَانَ ذَلِكِ، فَأَمْسِكِى عَنِ الصَّلَاةِ؛ فَإِذَا كَانَ
الْآخَرُ، فَتَوَضَّئِى وَصَلِّى، فَإِنَّمَا هُوَ عِرْقٌ" رَوَاهُ أَبُو دَاوُدَ، وَالنَّسَائِىُّ.

558 'Urwa b. Zubair reported that Fatimah bint Abu Hubaish
had a prolonged flow of blood (after menses) and Allah's
Apostle (peace be upon him) said to her : When there
is a blood of menses, its colour is dark, which can be
recognized and when that is the case, then avoid prayer, and
when otherwise is the case (when the colour of the blood
ceases to be dark), then perform ablution[1] and observe prayer
for that is a vein (secretion). (*Abu Dawud, and Nasa'i*)

   1. This means to perform ablution after taking a bath which is essential
   at the end of menstrual period. (*Aun-ul-Ma'bud*, Vol. I, p. 115).

٥٥٩ - وَعَنْ أُمِّ سَلَمَةَ، قَالَتْ: إِنَّ امْرَأَةً كَانَتْ تُهَرَاقُ الدَّمَ مَرَّ عَلَى
عَهْدِ رَسُولِ اللهِ ﷺ فَاسْتَفْتَتْ لَهَا أُمُّ سَلَمَةَ النَّبِىَّ ﷺ. فَقَالَ:
لِتَنْظُرْ عَدَدَ اللَّيَالِى وَالْأَيَّامِ الَّتِى كَانَتْ تَحِيضُهُنَّ مِنَ الشَّهْرِ قَبْلَ أَنْ
يُصِيبَهَا الَّذِى أَصَابَهَا، فَلْتَتْرُكِ الصَّلَاةَ قَدَرَ ذَلِكَ مِنَ الشَّهْرِ،
فَإِذَا خَلَّفَتْ ذَلِكِ، فَلْتَغْتَسِلْ، ثُمَّ لِتَسْتَثْفِرْ بِثَوْبٍ، ثُمَّ لِتُصَلِّ:
رَوَاهُ مَالِكٌ، وَأَبُو دَاوُدَ وَالدَّارِمِىُّ. وَرَوَى النَّسَائِىُّ مَعْنَاهُ.

559 Umm Salamah reported that a woman had a prolonged flow
of blood during the lifetime of Allah's Messenger (peace be
upon him). Umm Salamah asked for religious verdict for her
from Allah's Apostle (peace be upon him). So he (the
Holy Prophet) said: She should count the number of nights
and days for which she (normally) had menses during the
month prior to this trouble from which she had suffered. She
should abandon the prayer for this much time (for which she
had normally menses) during the month and when that (time)
is over she should take a bath and tie a piece of cloth (over

her private parts) and then observe prayer. (*Malik, Abu Dawud, Darimi and Nasa'i transmitted to the same effect*)

٥٦٠ - وَعَنْ عَدِيِّ بْنِ ثَابِتٍ ، عَنْ أَبِيهِ ، عَنْ جَدِّهِ - قَالَ يَحْىَ بْنُ
مَعِينٍ : جَدُّ عَدِيٍّ بِاسْمِهِ دِينَارٌ - عَنِ النَّبِيِّ ﷺ ، أَنَّهُ قَالَ فِي
الْمُسْتَحَاضَةِ : تَدَعُ الصَّلَاةَ أَيَّامَ أَقْرَائِهَا الَّتِي كَانَتْ تَحِيضُ فِيهَا ،
ثُمَّ تَغْتَسِلُ ، وَ تَتَوَضَّأُ عِنْدَ كُلِّ صَلَاةٍ ، وَ تَصُومُ ، وَ تُصَلِّي . رَوَاهُ
التِّرْمِذِيُّ ، وَأَبُو دَاوُدَ .

560 **'Adi b. Thabit** reported on the authority of his father who reported on the authority of his father, whose name (the name of Adi's grandfather) is given by Yahya b. Ma'in, as Dinar that Allah's Apostle (peace be upon him) said in regard to a *Mustahada*: Abandon prayer during the days that she (normally) had her monthly courses, then take a bath, and perform ablution for every prayer and observe fast, and say prayer. (*Tirmidhi and Abu Dawud*)

أَلْفَصْلُ الثَّانِي Section II'

٥٦١ - وَعَنْ حَمْنَةَ بِنْتِ جَحْشٍ ، قَالَتْ ، كُنْتُ أُسْتَحَاضُ حَيْضَةً كَثِيرَةً
شَدِيدَةً ، فَأَتَيْتُ النَّبِيَّ ﷺ أُسْتَفْتِيهِ وَ أُخْبِرُهُ ، فَوَجَدْتُهُ فِي بَيْتِ
أُخْتِي زَيْنَبَ بِنْتِ جَحْشٍ ، فَقُلْتُ : يَا رَسُولَ اللهِ ! إِنِّي أُسْتَحَاضُ
حَيْضَةً كَثِيرَةً شَدِيدَةً ، فَمَا تَأْمُرُنِي فِيهَا ؛ قَدْ مَنَعَتْنِي الصَّلَاةَ وَ
الصِّيَامَ . قَالَ : " أَنْعَتُ لَكِ الْكُرْسُفَ ، فَإِنَّهُ يُذْهِبُ الدَّمَ " قَالَتْ :
هُوَ أَكْثَرُ مِنْ ذَلِكَ . قَالَ : " فَتَلَجَّمِي " قَالَتْ : هُوَ أَكْثَرُ مِنْ ذَلِكَ .
قَالَ : " فَاتَّخِذِي ثَوْبًا " قَالَتْ : هُوَ أَكْثَرُ مِنْ ذَلِكَ ، إِنَّمَا أَثُجُّ ثَجًّا .
فَقَالَ النَّبِيُّ ﷺ " سَآمُرُكِ بِأَمْرَيْنِ ، أَيَّهُمَا صَنَعْتِ أَجْزَأَ عَنْكِ مِنْ

لِلْآخَرِ، وَإِنْ قَوِيتِ عَلَيْهِمَا فَأَنْتِ أَعْلَمُ" قَالَ لَهَا "إِنَّمَا هٰذِهِ رَكْضَةٌ
مِنْ رَكَضَاتِ الشَّيْطَانِ، فَتَحَيَّضِي سِتَّةَ أَيَّامٍ أَوْ سَبْعَةَ أَيَّامٍ فِي عِلْمِ
اللهِ، ثُمَّ اغْتَسِلِي، حَتَّى إِذَا رَأَيْتِ أَنَّكِ قَدْ طَهُرْتِ وَاسْتَنْقَأْتِ، فَصَلِّي
ثَلَاثًا وَعِشْرِينَ لَيْلَةً، أَوْ أَرْبَعًا وَعِشْرِينَ لَيْلَةً، وَأَيَّامَهَا وَصُومِي؛
فَإِنَّ ذٰلِكِ يُجْزِئُكِ. وَكَذٰلِكِ فَافْعَلِي كُلَّ شَهْرٍ كَمَا تَحِيضُ النِّسَاءُ وَكَمَا
يَطْهُرْنَ، مِيقَاتَ حَيْضِهِنَّ وَطُهْرِهِنَّ. وَإِنْ قَوِيتِ عَلَى أَنْ تُؤَخِّرِينَ
الظُّهْرَ وَتُعَجِّلِينَ الْعَصْرَ، فَتَغْتَسِلِينَ وَتَجْمَعِينَ بَيْنَ الصَّلَاتَيْنِ
الظُّهْرِ وَالْعَصْرِ، وَتُؤَخِّرِينَ الْمَغْرِبَ وَتُعَجِّلِينَ الْعِشَاءَ، ثُمَّ تَغْتَسِلِينَ
وَتَجْمَعِينَ بَيْنَ الصَّلَاتَيْنِ، فَافْعَلِي وَتَغْتَسِلِينَ مَعَ الْفَجْرِ فَافْعَلِي؛ وَ
صُومِي إِنْ قَدَرْتِ عَلَى ذٰلِكِ" قَالَ رَسُولُ اللهِ ﷺ "وَهٰذَا أَعْجَبُ الْأَمْرَيْنِ
إِلَيَّ" رَوَاهُ أَحْمَدُ، وَأَبُو دَاوُدَ؛ وَالتِّرْمِذِيُّ.

561 Hamna, the daughter of Jahsh said: I bled profusely in my menses. I came to Allah's Apostle (peace and blessings of Allah be upon him) in order to seek for religious verdict and told him about this. I found him in the house of my sister, Zainab bint Jahsh. I said: Allah's Messenger, I am a woman who bleeds profusely in her menses, what do you command me to do? It has prevented me from prayer and fasting. He said: I advise you to use a piece of cotton for it removes the blood. She said: It is more than that which can be (controlled) with the help of it. Whereupon he said: Then use a tight rag. She said: It is more than that. Whereupon he said: Then use cloth (for controlling it). She said: It is more than that for it flows profusely. Thereupon Allah's Apostle (peace and blessings of Allah be upon him) said: I give you two directions which of them you do that would suffice the other one also. If you have a power enough to do the both, it is you who have the best knowledge of it and he said to her: It is a stroke from the strokes of Satan.[1] So observe your menses for six or seven days. God alone knows about it, then take a bath and when you see that you are purified and you are cleaned then observe prayer for twenty-three nights or twenty-four nights or days and observe the fast for that would suffice you and this is how you should do during every month just as the women menstruate and purify at the time (of conclusion of their menstrual periods) and are purified and if you can manage to defer the noon prayer and offer early the afternoon prayer then take a bath and combine the two prayers (the noon and the afternoon prayer) and defer the sunset prayer and observe early the night prayer then take a bath and combine two prayers and then do this and take a bath along with the dawn prayer and then do that and observe fast if it lies in your power. Allah's Apostle (peace and blessings of Allah be upon him) said: This is one which is liked by me more out of the two methods.

(*Ahmad, Abu Dawud and Tirmidhi*)

1. The period of menstruation extends normally from five to ten days every month, but due to some injury or other trouble in the ovary the normal process of menstruation blood continues to flow beyond the period of menses. As this is not the menstrual blood a Muslim woman is, therefore, ordained to observe prayer and fast during this period of prolonged flow of blood. So far as the sentence: 'It is a stroke from the strokes of Satan', is concerned two interpretations seem to be quite valid: The one is that since it is a disease, it has been, therefore, called metaphorically the stroke of the Satan as it has put the woman to unnecessary trouble. The second interpretation is that since prolonged flow of blood causes confusion to the woman who suffers from this disease; at times it becomes difficult for her to demarcate between the normal period of menstruation and the period in which it flows because of abnormality and this affects her prayer and fasting. The confusion is an act of Satan, the Holy Prophet, therefore, called it as the stroke of Satan.

Section III ٱلْفَصْلُ ٱلثَّالِثُ

٥٧٢ ـ عَنْ أَسْمَاءَ بِنْتِ عُمَيْسٍ، قَالَتْ : قُلْتُ : يَا رَسُوْلَ اللهِ ! إِنَّ فَاطِمَةَ

بِنْتَ أَبِيْ حُبَيْشٍ بِاسْتُحِيْضَتْ مُنْذُ كَذَا وَكَذَا فَلَمْ تُصَلِّ. فَقَالَ رَسُوْلُ اللهِ

ﷺ : "سُبْحَانَ اللهِ! إِنَّ هٰذَا مِنَ الشَّيْطَانِ . لِتَجْلِسْ فِي مِرْكَنٍ ، فَإِذَا

رَأَتْ صُفَارَةً فَوْقَ الْمَاءِ ، فَلْتَغْتَسِلْ لِلظُّهْرِ وَ الْعَصْرِ غُسْلًا وَاحِدًا.

وَ تَغْتَسِلْ لِلْمَغْرِبِ وَ الْعِشَاءِ غُسْلًا وَاحِدًا. وَ تَغْتَسِلْ لِلْفَجْرِ غُسْلًا

وَاحِدًا . وَ تَوَضَّأْ فِيمَا بَيْنَ ذٰلِكَ " رَوَاهُ أَبُو دَاوُدَ ، وَ قَالَ :

562 Asma bint Umais reported that she said: Allah's Messenger,
Fatimah bint Abi Hubaish had the menses for such period
and she had not observed prayer. Whereupon Allah's Messenger (peace and blessings of Allah be upon him) said:
Hallowed be Allah, this is from the Satan. She should sit in
a tub and when she sees yellowness visible on the surface (of
water) she should take one bath for noon and afternoon
prayer then take one bath for evening and night prayer and
take a bath for dawn prayer and only perform ablution
between them. (*Abu Dawud*)

٥٦٣ - رَوَىٰ مُجَاهِدٌ عَنِ ابْنِ عَبَّاسٍ : لَمَّا اشْتَدَّ عَلَيْهَا الْغُسْلُ ، أَمَرَهَا

أَنْ تَجْمَعَ بَيْنَ الصَّلَاتَيْنِ .

563 Mujahid reported on the authority of Ibn 'Abbas: When
taking of bath became burdensome for her, he commanded her
to combine the two prayers.[1]

   1. For the *Mustahada* the general rule is that if she can afford to take a
    bath before every prayer, she should do so, but the most desirable
    act is that she should take bath for observing two prayers, combining
    them together. But if her health does not permit her to stand this
    rigour, she is allowed to observe prayer only with ablution, but she
    is required to perform ablution at the time of every prayer. (See Imam
    Shawkhani, *Nail-ul-Awtar*, Vol. I, pp. 241-243).

GENERAL INDEX

(PROPER NAMES, PEOPLES, BOOKS, PLACES ETC.)

ISNAD INDEX

A

'Abdallah b. 'Abbas, 172, 205, 210, 249

'Abdallah b. Abi Bakr b. Muhammad b. 'Amr b. Hazm, 232

'Abdallah b. 'Amr, 7, 34, 36, 54, 62, 66, 68, 101, 110, 111, 125, 129, 141, 147, 206

'Abdallah b. 'Amr b. al-'As, 215

'Abdallah b. Mas'ud, 33, 42, 45, 56, 72, 103, 109, 119, 120, 126, 132, 138, 139, 141, 150, 153, 156, 180, 186, 195, 242, 254

'Abdallah b. Mughaffal, 212

'Abdallah b. Sarjis, 188, 237

'Abdullah as-Sunabihi, 166

'Abdallah b. 'Ukaim, 252

'Abdallah b. 'Umar, 6, 9, 37, 55, 70, 84, 91, 112, 121, 137, 165, 169, 180, 181, 199, 216, 226, 228, 231, 239, 254, 256

'Abdallah b. Zaid, 205, 210, 214

'Abd Khair, 209

'Abdur Rahman b. Hasana, 194

'Ali b. Talq, 174

Abu Bakra, 257

Abu al-Darda, 72, 76, 80, 143, 148, 152, 168

Abu Dharr, 18, 22, 117, 262

Abu Hayya, 209

Abu Hudhaifa, 40, 154, 196

Abu Huraira, 5, 6, 8, 10, 15, 16, 22, 25, 30, 34, 35, 36, 39, 41, 42, 43, 45, 55, 59, 61, 62, 63, 67, 76, 86, 93, 95, 99, 102, 104, 113, 114, 115, 126, 135, 136, 137, 138, 140, 142, 143, 146, 153, 154, 156, 160, 161, 164, 167, 169, 170, 172, 173, 176, 183, 187, 190, 192, 196, 202, 206, 216, 217, 223, 227, 238

Abu Juhaim b. Harith b. al-Simmah, 261, 264

Abu Malih b. Usama, 251, 252

Abu Malik al-Ash'ari, 159

Abu Mas'ud al-Ansari, 130

Abu Musa al-Ash'ari, 8, 16, 62, 68, 69, 99, 100, 185, 194

Abu Nadra, 77

Abu Qatada, 183

Abu Rafi', 106, 178, 216, 235

Abu Sa'id, 90, 174, 189

Abu Sa'id Khudri, 14, 114, 135, 137, 207, 229, 239, 245, 263, 266

Abu Salama, 200

Abu Umama, 22, 30, 115, 199, 211

Abu Umama al-Bahili, 134

Abu Zaid, 241

'Aisha (wife of the Prophet), 57, 71, 73, 84, 94, 97, 101, 147, 177, 185, 189, 191, 192, 197, 198, 200, 206, 213, 219, 221, 222, 223, 224, 229, 231, 252, 267, 272, 275, 276

'Adi b. Thabit, 278

Al-Ahwas b. Hakim, 151

Al-A'mash, 151

'Ali, 58, 69, 74, 145, 154, 169, 173, 174, 189, 224, 225, 231, 232, 258

'Ali b. Talq, 174

'Alqama, 242, 248

'Ammar, 261

'Ammar b. Yasir, 232, 264

'Amr b. 'Abasa, 31

'Amr b. al-'As, 20

'Amr b. al-Ahwas, 45

'Amr b. 'Auf, 111

'Amr b. Shu'aib, 67, 141, 211

Anas b. Malik (Prophet's servant), 7, 10, 17, 23, 34, 38, 42, 46, 68, 83, 97, 113, 115, 130, 136, 148, 175, 179, 182, 184, 185, 193, 199, 208, 214, 221, 229, 247, 270

Asma' (daughter of Abu Bakr), 91, 247

Asma bint Umais, 281

As-Sa'ib b. Yazid, 239

Aswad, 248

'Ata b. Yasar, 264

'Auf b. Malik al-Ashja'i, 141

'Aun, 149

B

Baihaqi, 23, 119, 151

Bara b. 'Azib, 82, 88, 254

Bilal b. Harith al-Muzani, 110

Buraida, 172

Busra, 175